Ultra Maniac

Story and Art by

Vol. 4

Wataru Yoshizumi

Contents

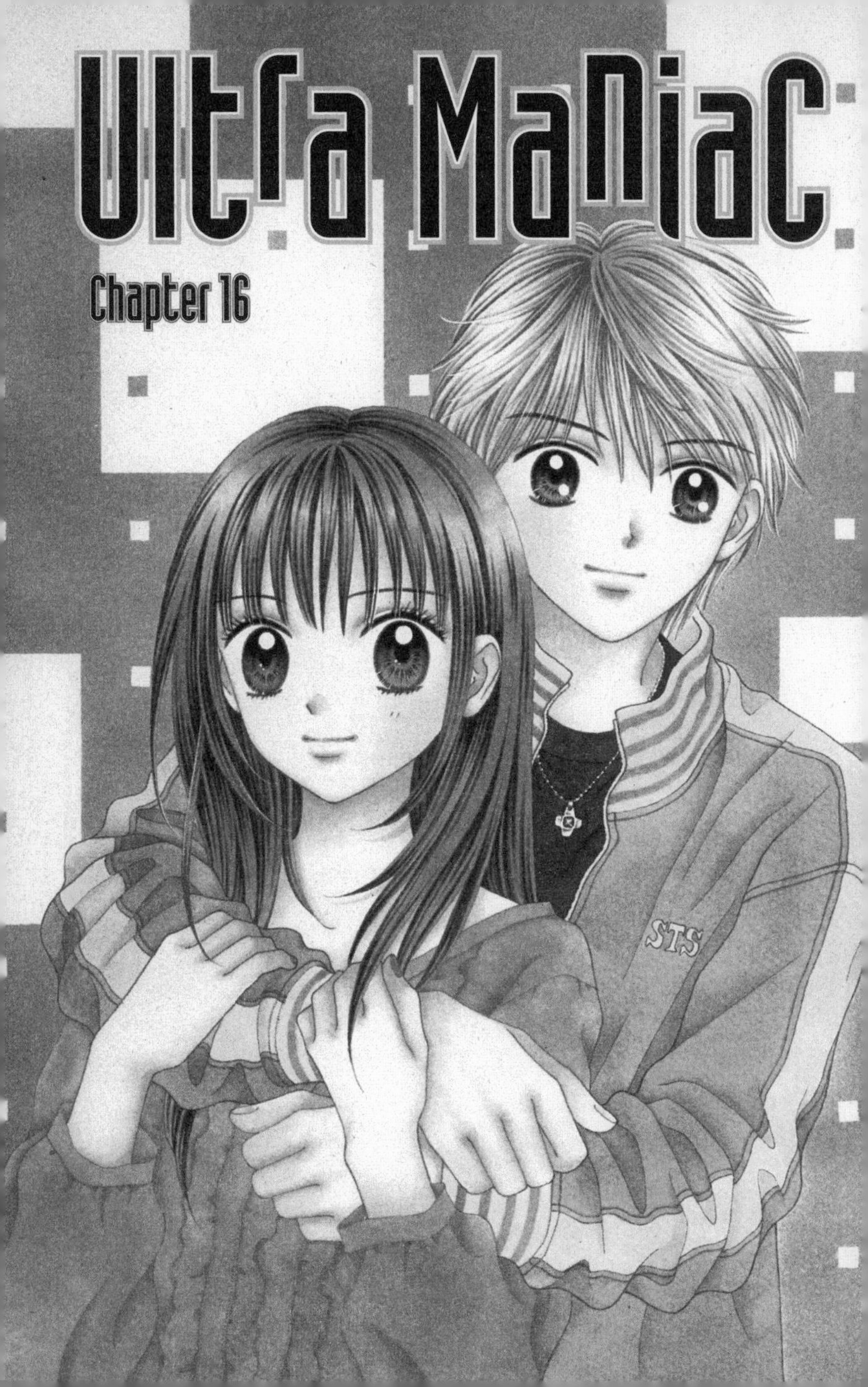
Ultra Maniac
Chapter 16
STS

Characters

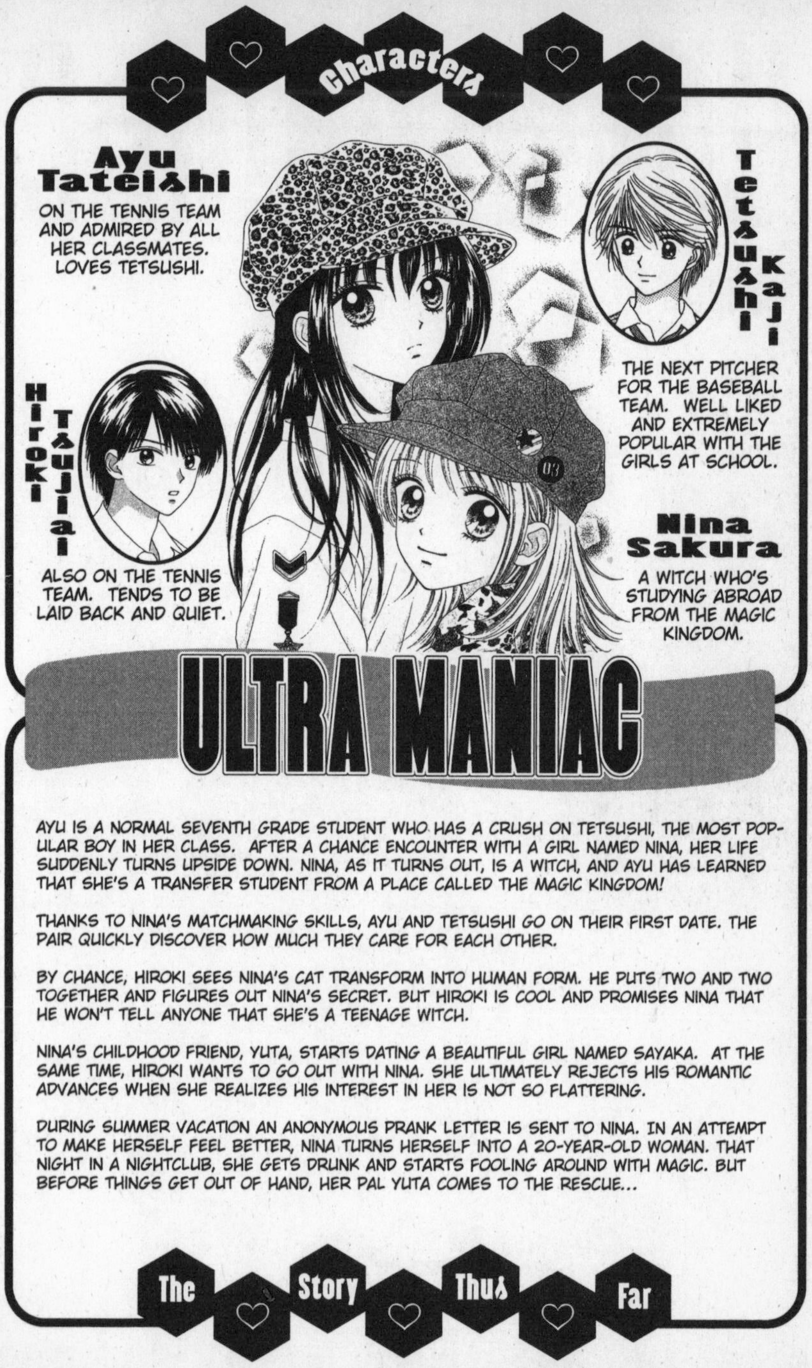

Ayu Tateishi

ON THE TENNIS TEAM AND ADMIRED BY ALL HER CLASSMATES. LOVES TETSUSHI.

Tetsushi Kaji

THE NEXT PITCHER FOR THE BASEBALL TEAM. WELL LIKED AND EXTREMELY POPULAR WITH THE GIRLS AT SCHOOL.

Hiroki Tsujiai

ALSO ON THE TENNIS TEAM. TENDS TO BE LAID BACK AND QUIET.

Nina Sakura

A WITCH WHO'S STUDYING ABROAD FROM THE MAGIC KINGDOM.

ULTRA MANIAC

AYU IS A NORMAL SEVENTH GRADE STUDENT WHO HAS A CRUSH ON TETSUSHI, THE MOST POPULAR BOY IN HER CLASS. AFTER A CHANCE ENCOUNTER WITH A GIRL NAMED NINA, HER LIFE SUDDENLY TURNS UPSIDE DOWN. NINA, AS IT TURNS OUT, IS A WITCH, AND AYU HAS LEARNED THAT SHE'S A TRANSFER STUDENT FROM A PLACE CALLED THE MAGIC KINGDOM!

THANKS TO NINA'S MATCHMAKING SKILLS, AYU AND TETSUSHI GO ON THEIR FIRST DATE. THE PAIR QUICKLY DISCOVER HOW MUCH THEY CARE FOR EACH OTHER.

BY CHANCE, HIROKI SEES NINA'S CAT TRANSFORM INTO HUMAN FORM. HE PUTS TWO AND TWO TOGETHER AND FIGURES OUT NINA'S SECRET. BUT HIROKI IS COOL AND PROMISES NINA THAT HE WON'T TELL ANYONE THAT SHE'S A TEENAGE WITCH.

NINA'S CHILDHOOD FRIEND, YUTA, STARTS DATING A BEAUTIFUL GIRL NAMED SAYAKA. AT THE SAME TIME, HIROKI WANTS TO GO OUT WITH NINA. SHE ULTIMATELY REJECTS HIS ROMANTIC ADVANCES WHEN SHE REALIZES HIS INTEREST IN HER IS NOT SO FLATTERING.

DURING SUMMER VACATION AN ANONYMOUS PRANK LETTER IS SENT TO NINA. IN AN ATTEMPT TO MAKE HERSELF FEEL BETTER, NINA TURNS HERSELF INTO A 20-YEAR-OLD WOMAN. THAT NIGHT IN A NIGHTCLUB, SHE GETS DRUNK AND STARTS FOOLING AROUND WITH MAGIC. BUT BEFORE THINGS GET OUT OF HAND, HER PAL YUTA COMES TO THE RESCUE...

The Story Thus Far

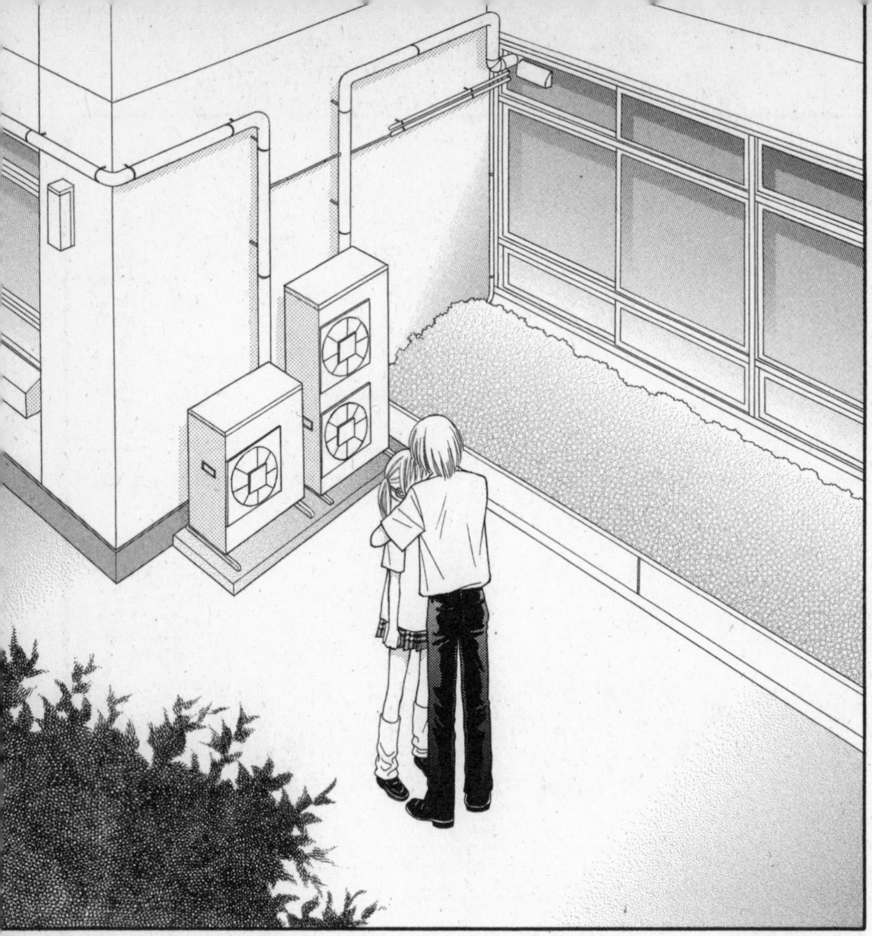
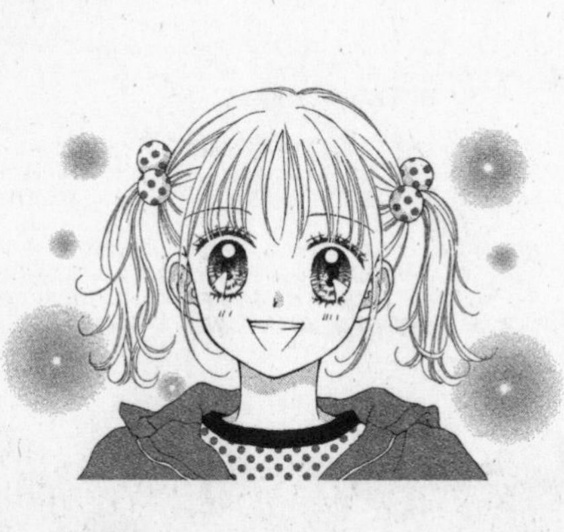

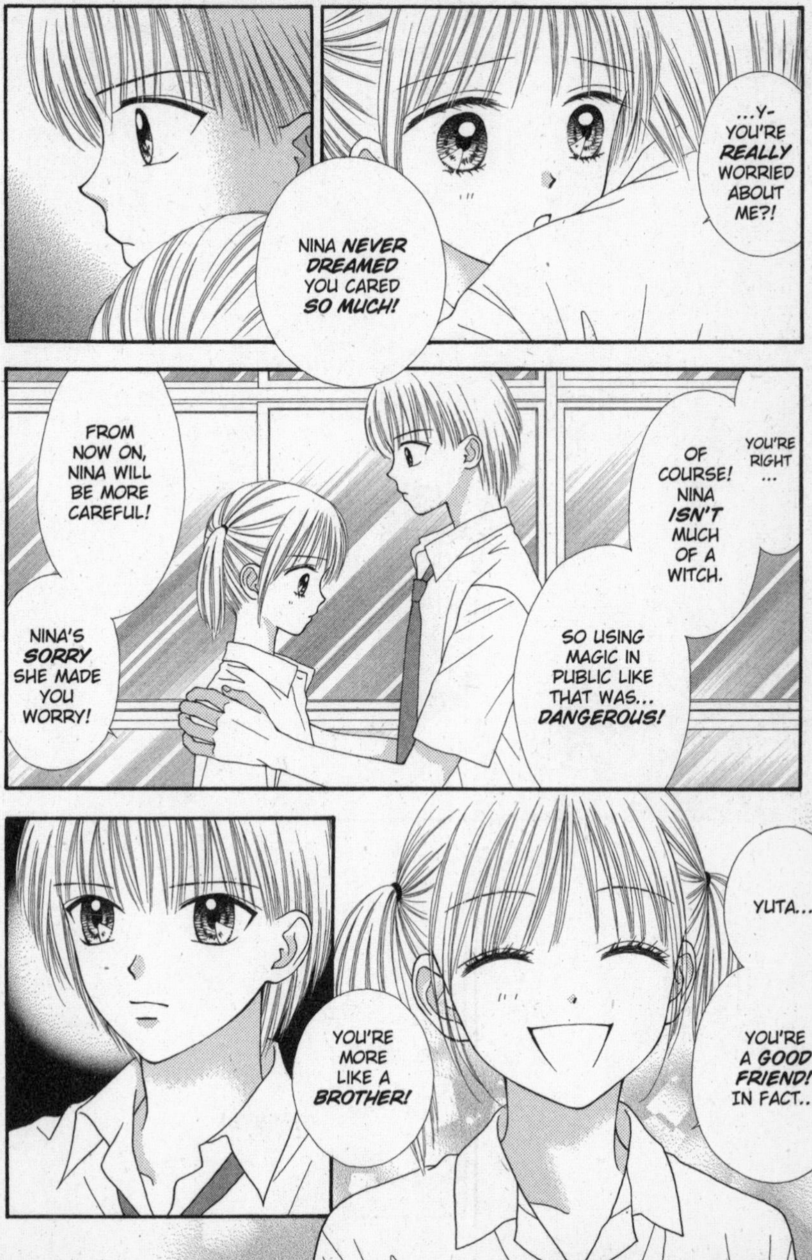
...Y- YOU'RE **REALLY** WORRIED ABOUT ME?!
NINA **NEVER DREAMED** YOU CARED **SO MUCH!**
YOU'RE RIGHT ...
OF COURSE! NINA **ISN'T** MUCH OF A WITCH.
SO USING MAGIC IN PUBLIC LIKE THAT WAS... **DANGEROUS!**
FROM NOW ON, NINA WILL BE MORE CAREFUL!
NINA'S **SORRY** SHE MADE YOU WORRY!
YUTA...
YOU'RE A **GOOD FRIEND!** IN FACT...
YOU'RE MORE LIKE A **BROTHER!**

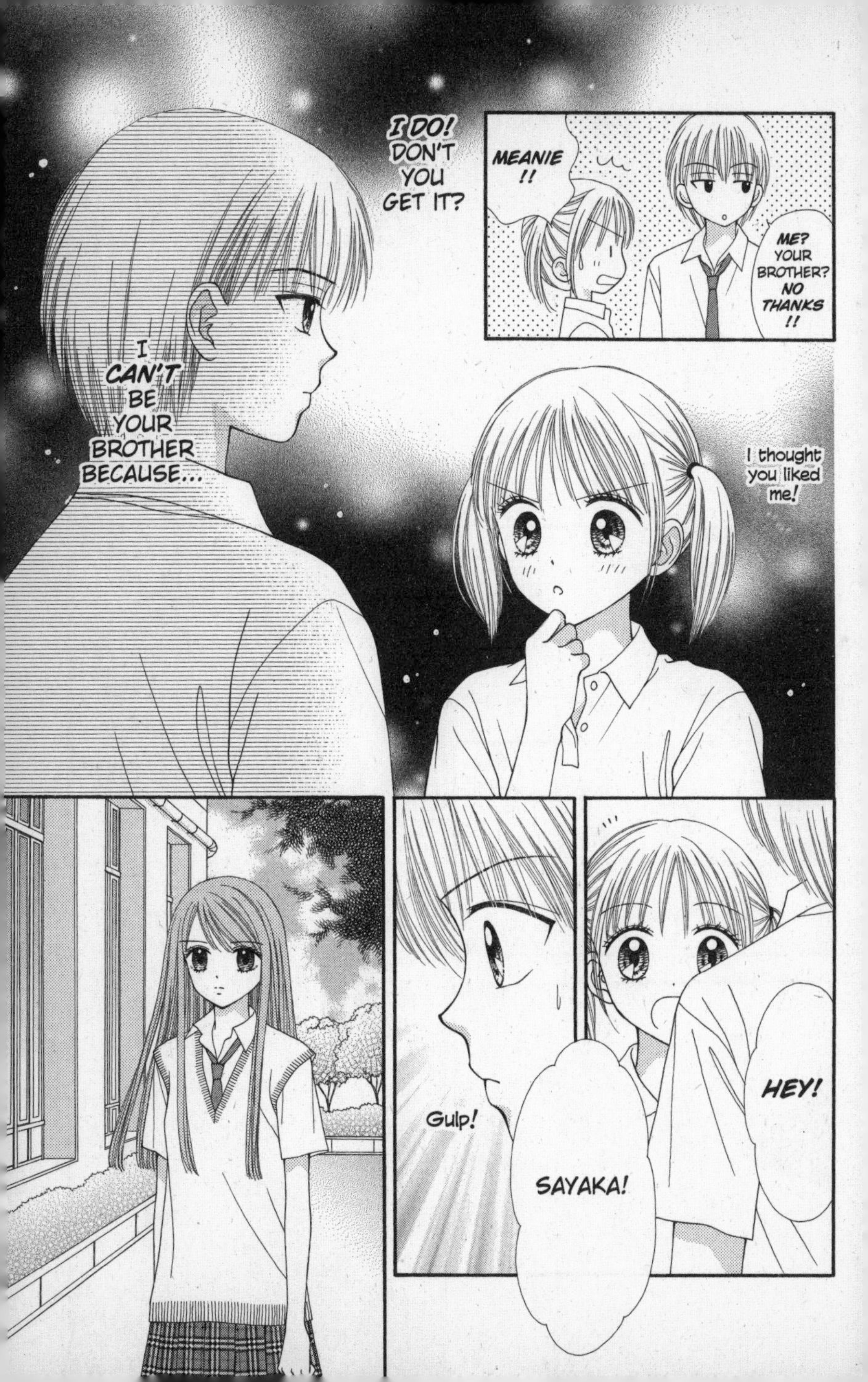
ME? YOUR BROTHER? NO THANKS!!
MEANIE!!
I thought you liked me!
I DO! DON'T YOU GET IT?
I CAN'T BE YOUR BROTHER BECAUSE...
HEY!
SAYAKA!
Gulp!

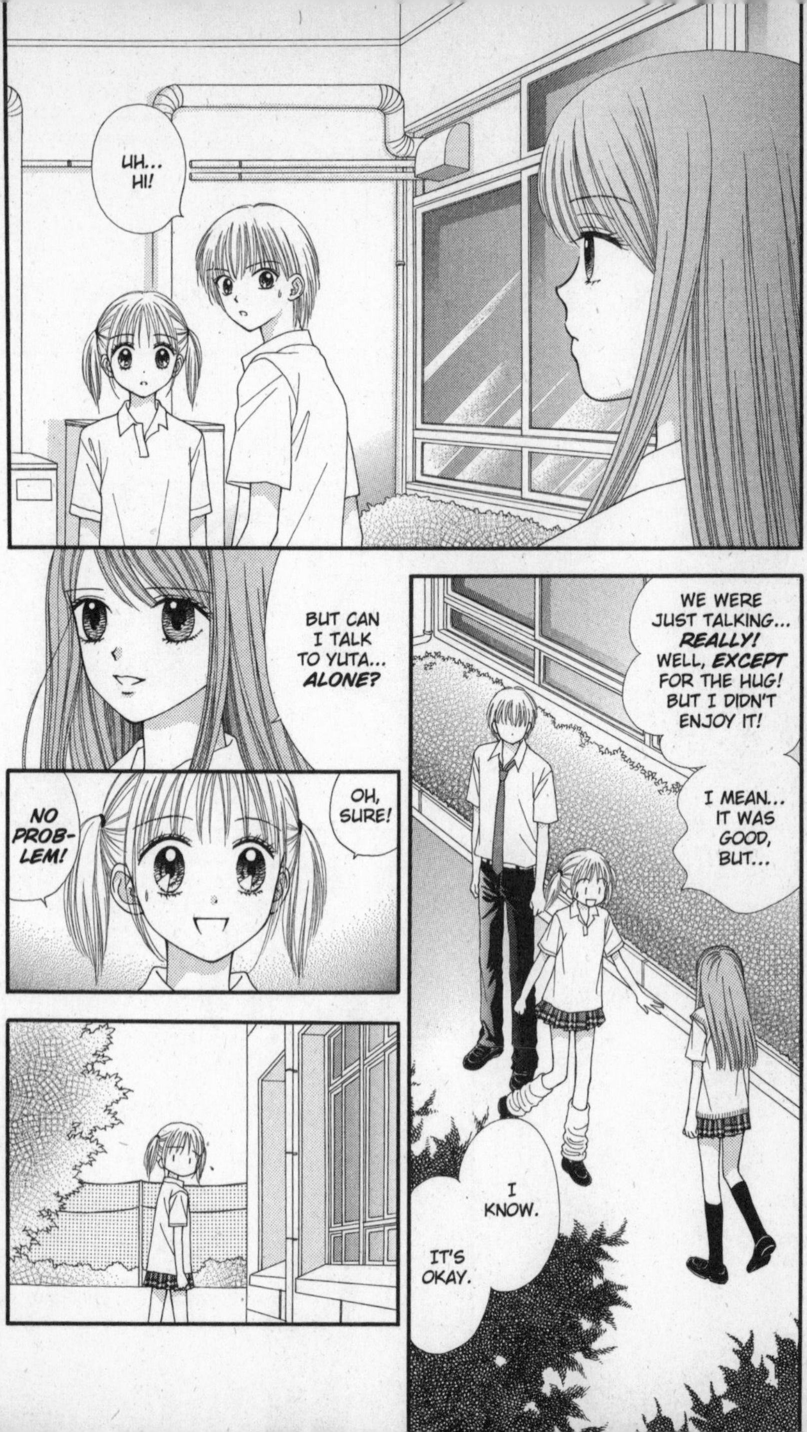
UH... HI!
WE WERE JUST TALKING... *REALLY!* WELL, *EXCEPT* FOR THE HUG! BUT I DIDN'T ENJOY IT!
I MEAN... IT WAS GOOD, BUT...
I KNOW.
IT'S OKAY.
BUT CAN I TALK TO YUTA... *ALONE?*
OH, SURE!
NO PROBLEM!

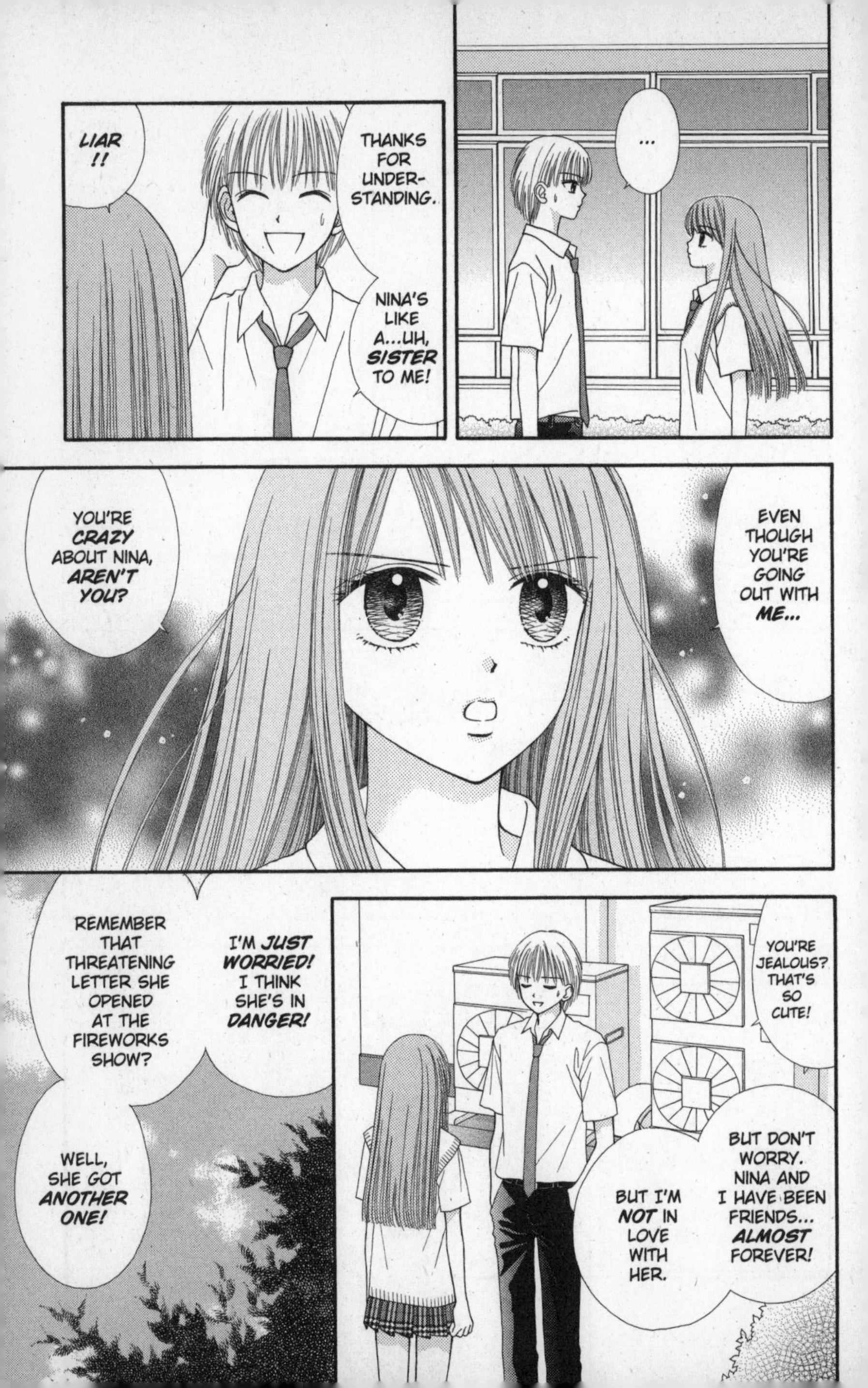
...
THANKS FOR UNDER-STANDING.
NINA'S LIKE A...UH, SISTER TO ME!
LIAR!!
EVEN THOUGH YOU'RE GOING OUT WITH ME...
YOU'RE CRAZY ABOUT NINA, AREN'T YOU?
YOU'RE JEALOUS? THAT'S SO CUTE!
BUT DON'T WORRY. NINA AND I HAVE BEEN FRIENDS... ALMOST FOREVER!
BUT I'M NOT IN LOVE WITH HER.
I'M JUST WORRIED! I THINK SHE'S IN DANGER!
REMEMBER THAT THREATENING LETTER SHE OPENED AT THE FIREWORKS SHOW?
WELL, SHE GOT ANOTHER ONE!

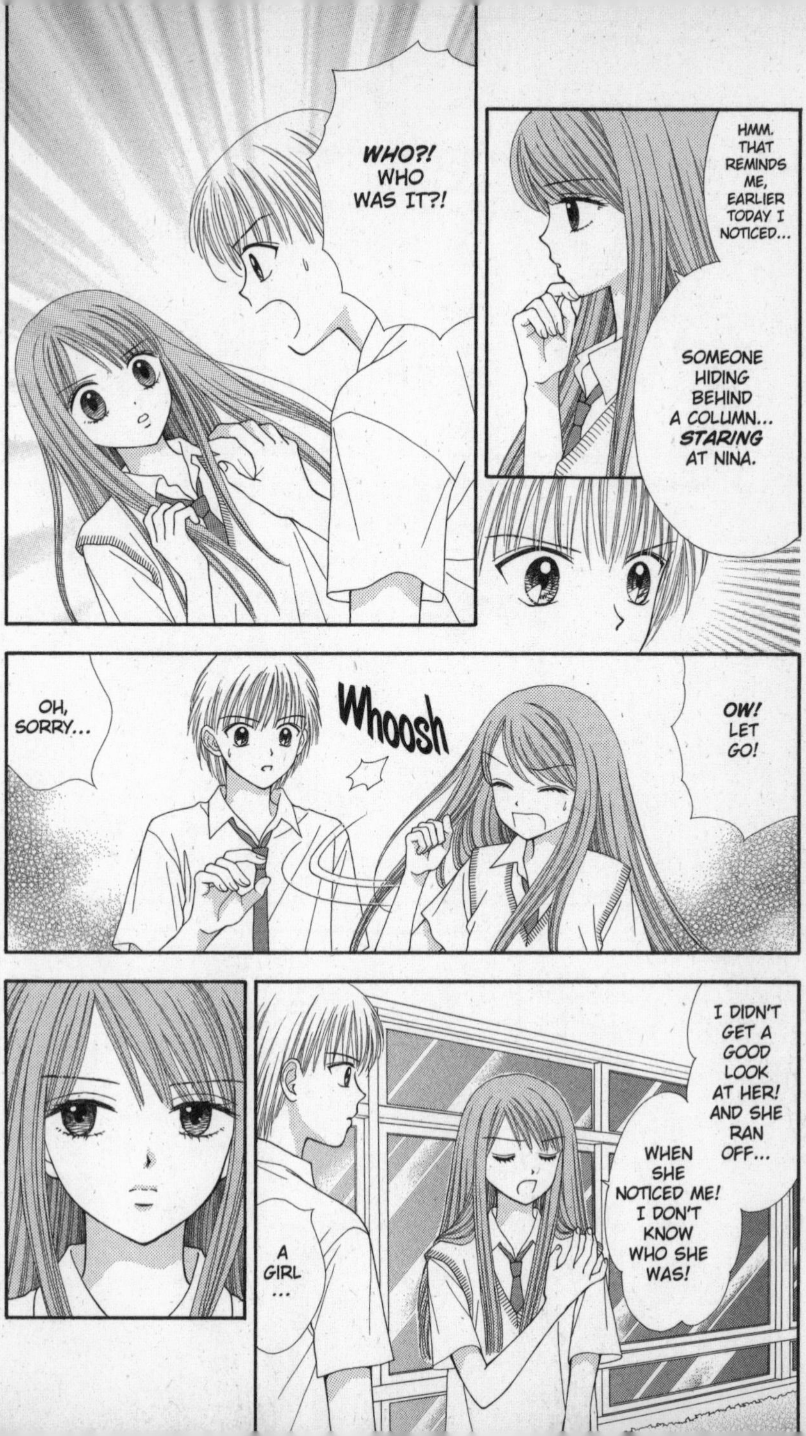
HMM. THAT REMINDS ME, EARLIER TODAY I NOTICED...
SOMEONE HIDING BEHIND A COLUMN... STARING AT NINA.
WHO?! WHO WAS IT?!
OW! LET GO!
Whoosh
OH, SORRY...
I DIDN'T GET A GOOD LOOK AT HER! AND SHE RAN OFF...
WHEN SHE NOTICED ME! I DON'T KNOW WHO SHE WAS!
A GIRL...

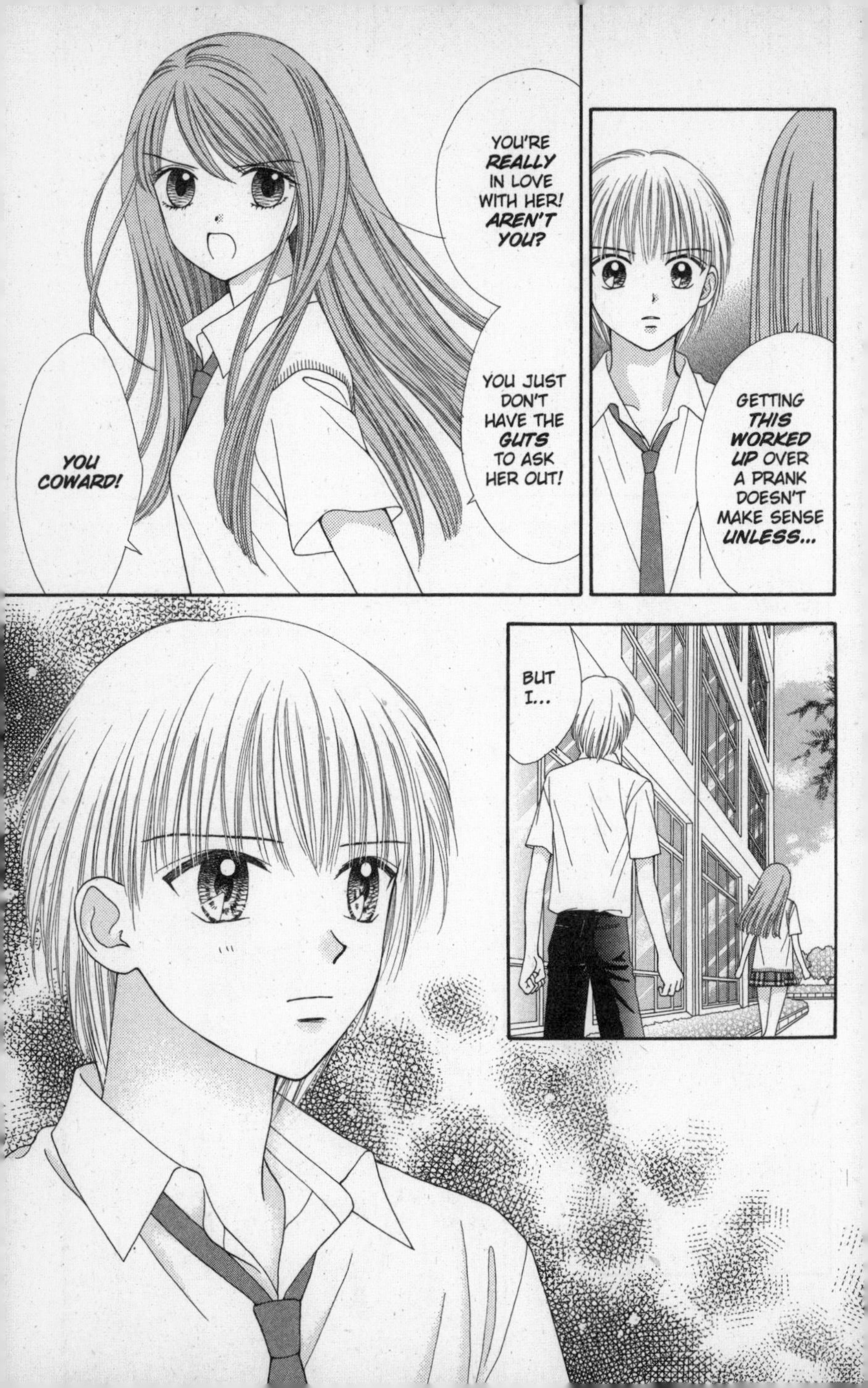
GETTING THIS WORKED UP OVER A PRANK DOESN'T MAKE SENSE UNLESS...
YOU'RE REALLY IN LOVE WITH HER! AREN'T YOU?
YOU JUST DON'T HAVE THE GUTS TO ASK HER OUT!
YOU COWARD!
BUT I...

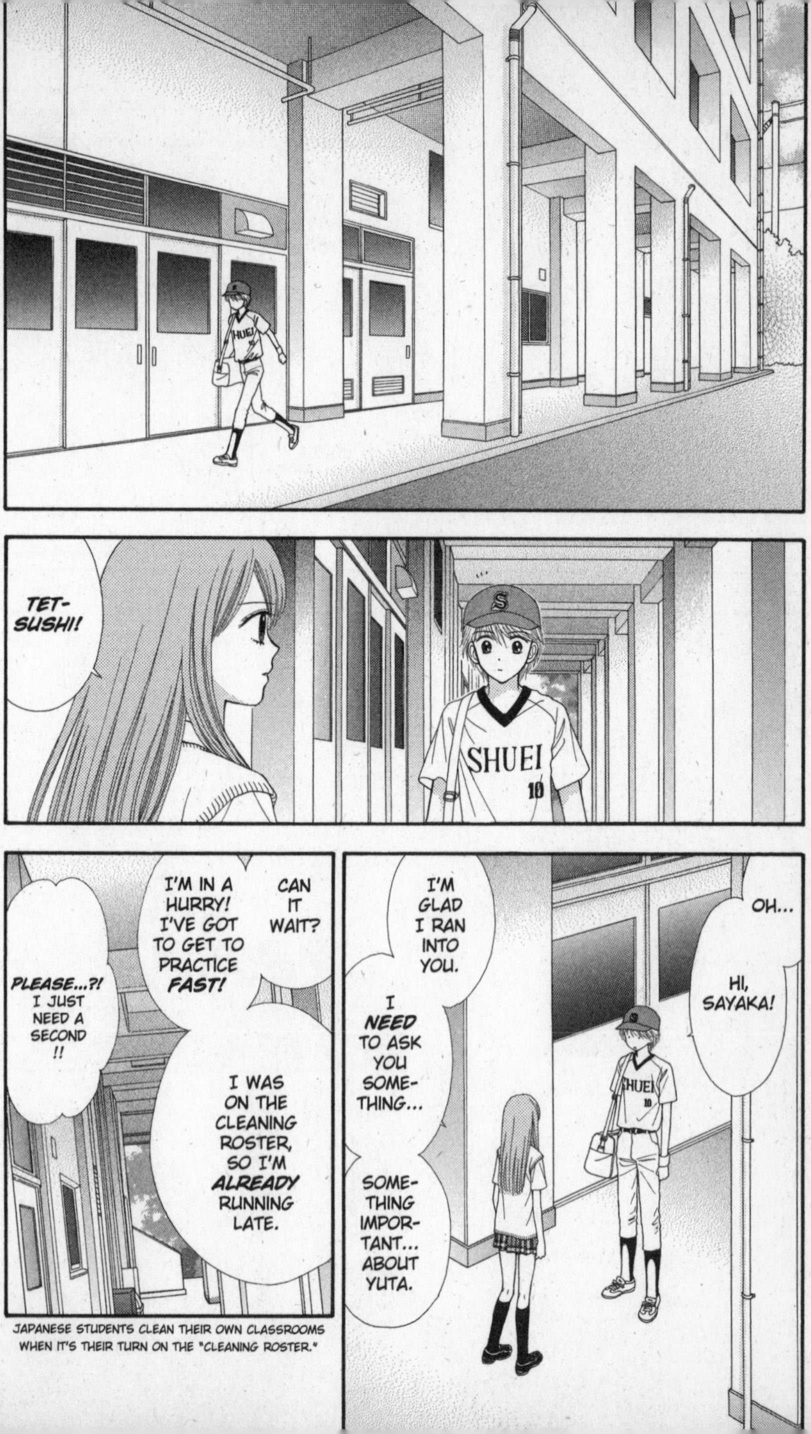
SHUEI
TET-SUSHI!
SHUEI 10
OH...
HI, SAYAKA!
I'M GLAD I RAN INTO YOU.
I NEED TO ASK YOU SOME-THING...
SOME-THING IMPOR-TANT... ABOUT YUTA.
CAN IT WAIT?
I'M IN A HURRY! I'VE GOT TO GET TO PRACTICE FAST!
PLEASE...?! I JUST NEED A SECOND !!
I WAS ON THE CLEANING ROSTER, SO I'M ALREADY RUNNING LATE.
JAPANESE STUDENTS CLEAN THEIR OWN CLASSROOMS WHEN IT'S THEIR TURN ON THE "CLEANING ROSTER."

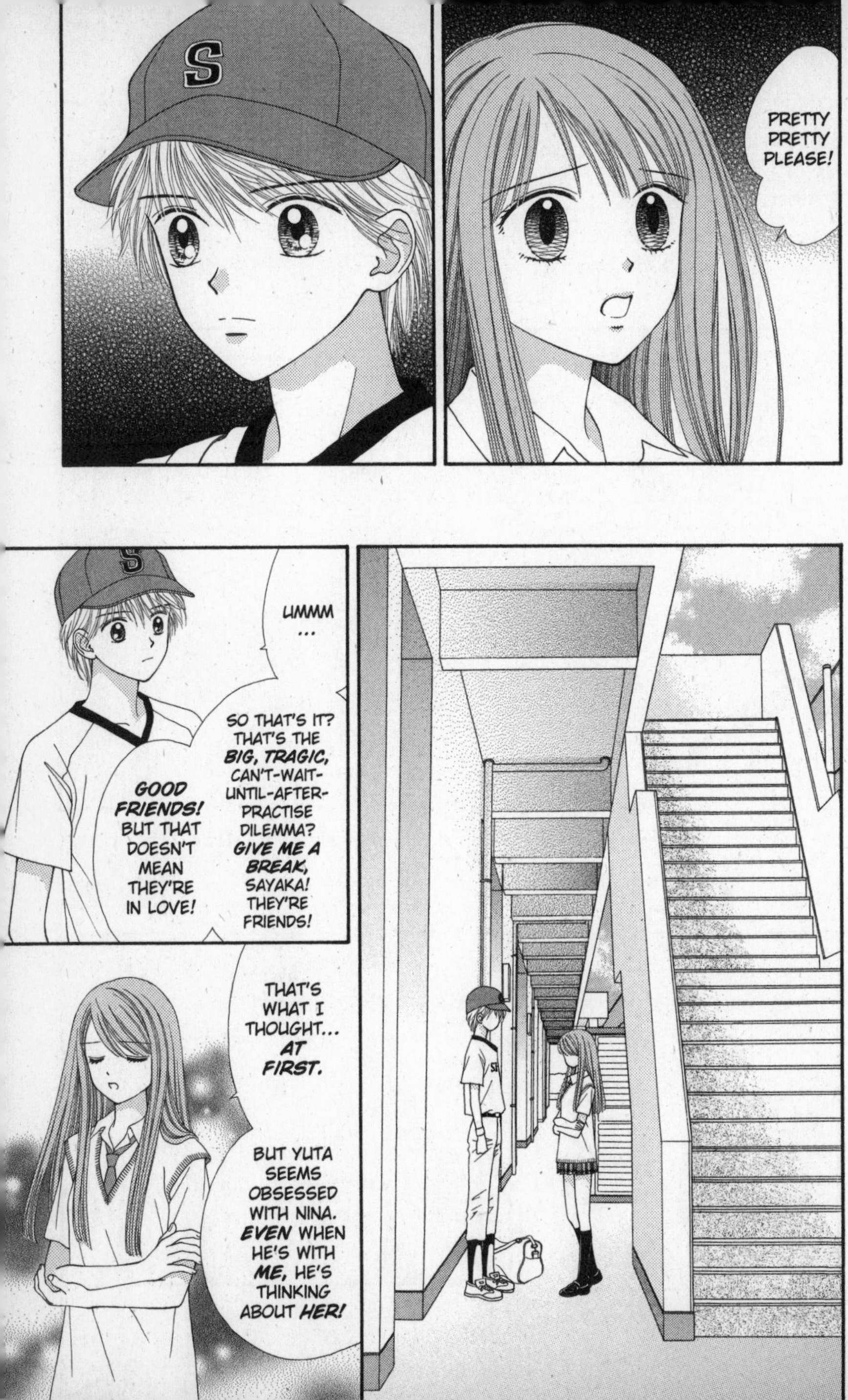

PRETTY PRETTY PLEASE!
UMMM...
SO THAT'S IT? THAT'S THE BIG, TRAGIC, CAN'T-WAIT-UNTIL-AFTER-PRACTISE DILEMMA? GIVE ME A BREAK, SAYAKA! THEY'RE FRIENDS!
GOOD FRIENDS! BUT THAT DOESN'T MEAN THEY'RE IN LOVE!
THAT'S WHAT I THOUGHT... AT FIRST.
BUT YUTA SEEMS OBSESSED WITH NINA. EVEN WHEN HE'S WITH ME, HE'S THINKING ABOUT HER!

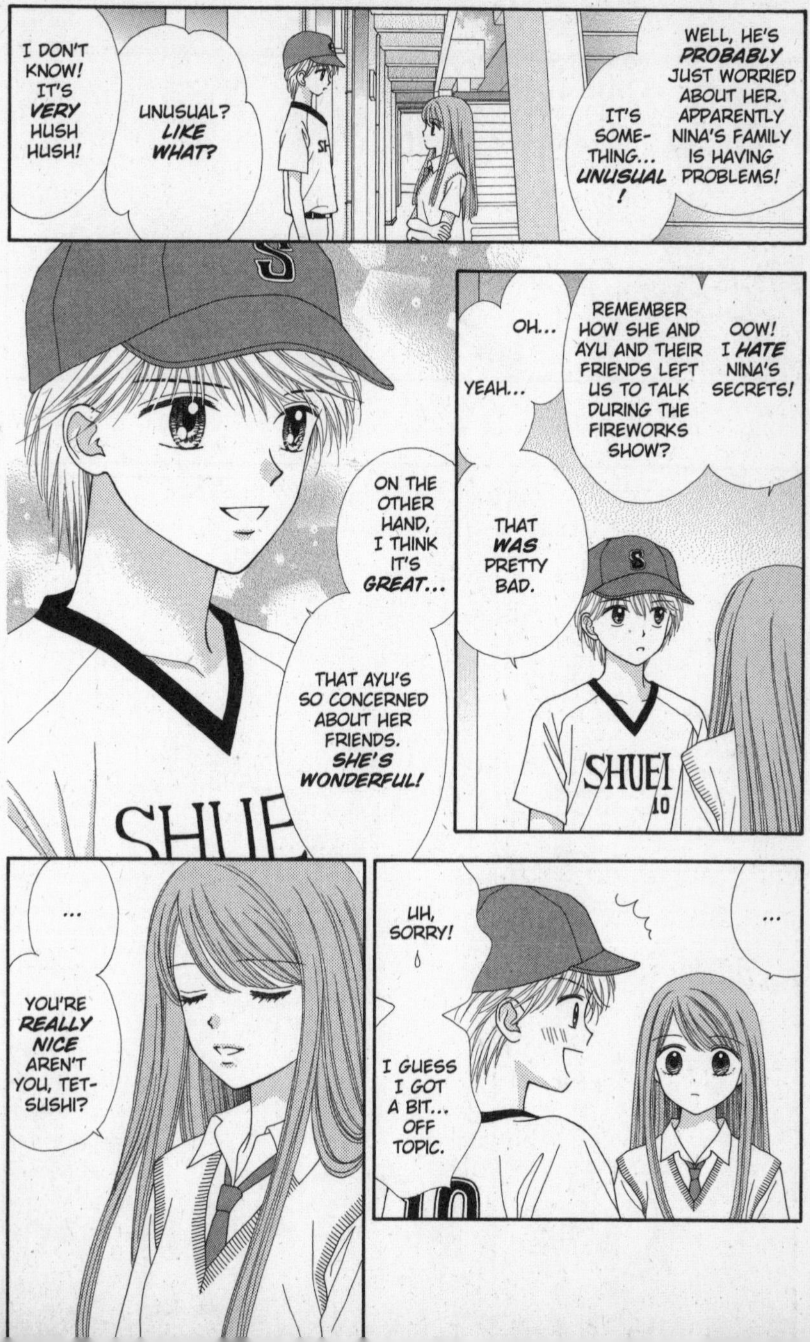
WELL, HE'S PROBABLY JUST WORRIED ABOUT HER. APPARENTLY NINA'S FAMILY IS HAVING PROBLEMS!
IT'S SOMETHING... UNUSUAL!
UNUSUAL? LIKE WHAT?
I DON'T KNOW! IT'S VERY HUSH HUSH!
OOW! I HATE NINA'S SECRETS!
REMEMBER HOW SHE AND AYU AND THEIR FRIENDS LEFT US TO TALK DURING THE FIREWORKS SHOW?
OH... YEAH...
THAT WAS PRETTY BAD.
ON THE OTHER HAND, I THINK IT'S GREAT...
THAT AYU'S SO CONCERNED ABOUT HER FRIENDS. SHE'S WONDERFUL!
...
UH, SORRY!
I GUESS I GOT A BIT... OFF TOPIC.
...
YOU'RE REALLY NICE AREN'T YOU, TETSUSHI?

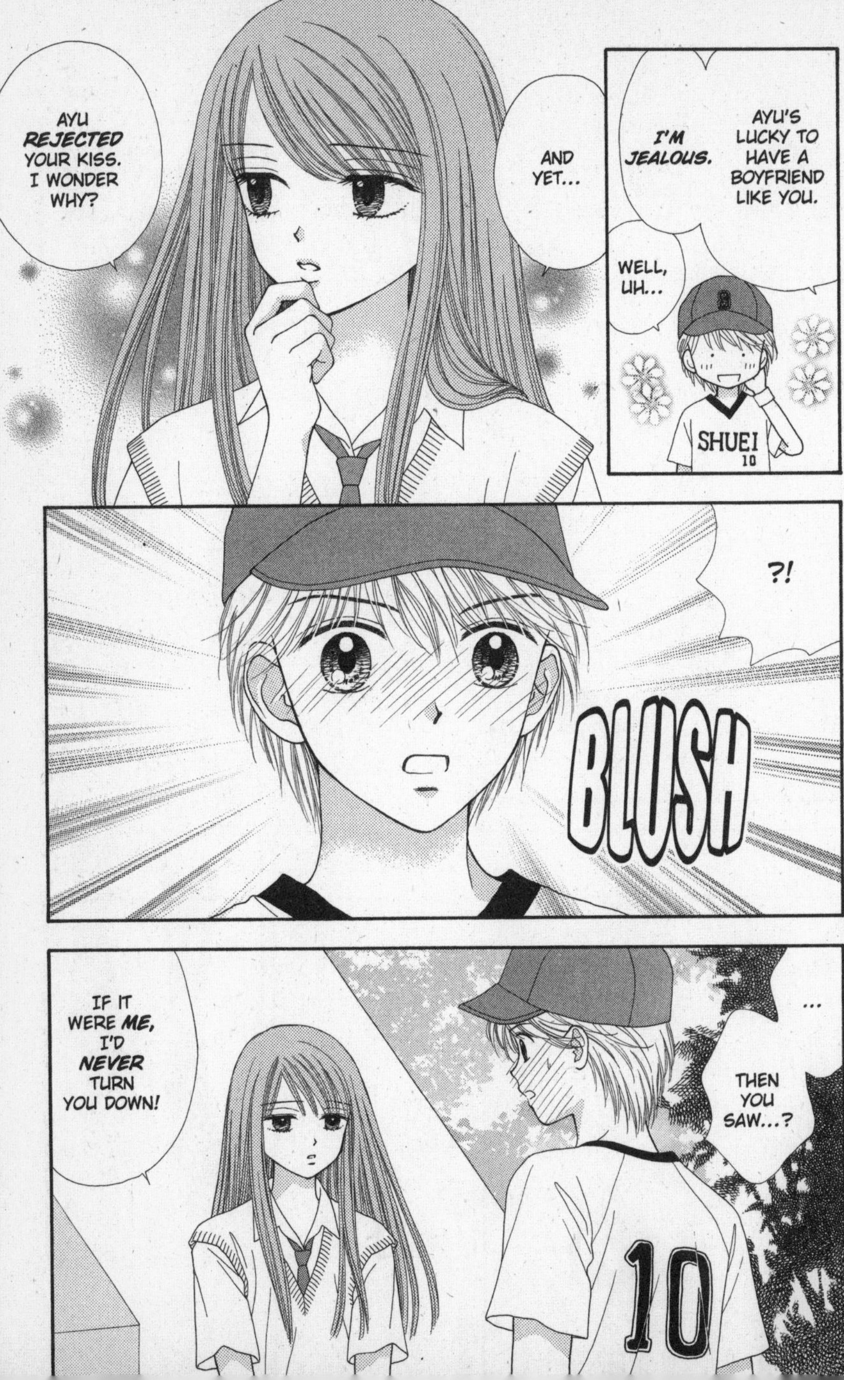
AYU'S LUCKY TO HAVE A BOYFRIEND LIKE YOU.
I'M JEALOUS.
WELL, UH...
SHUEI 10
AND YET...
AYU ***REJECTED*** YOUR KISS. I WONDER WHY?
?!
BLUSH
...
IF IT WERE ***ME,*** I'D ***NEVER*** TURN YOU DOWN!
THEN YOU SAW...?
10

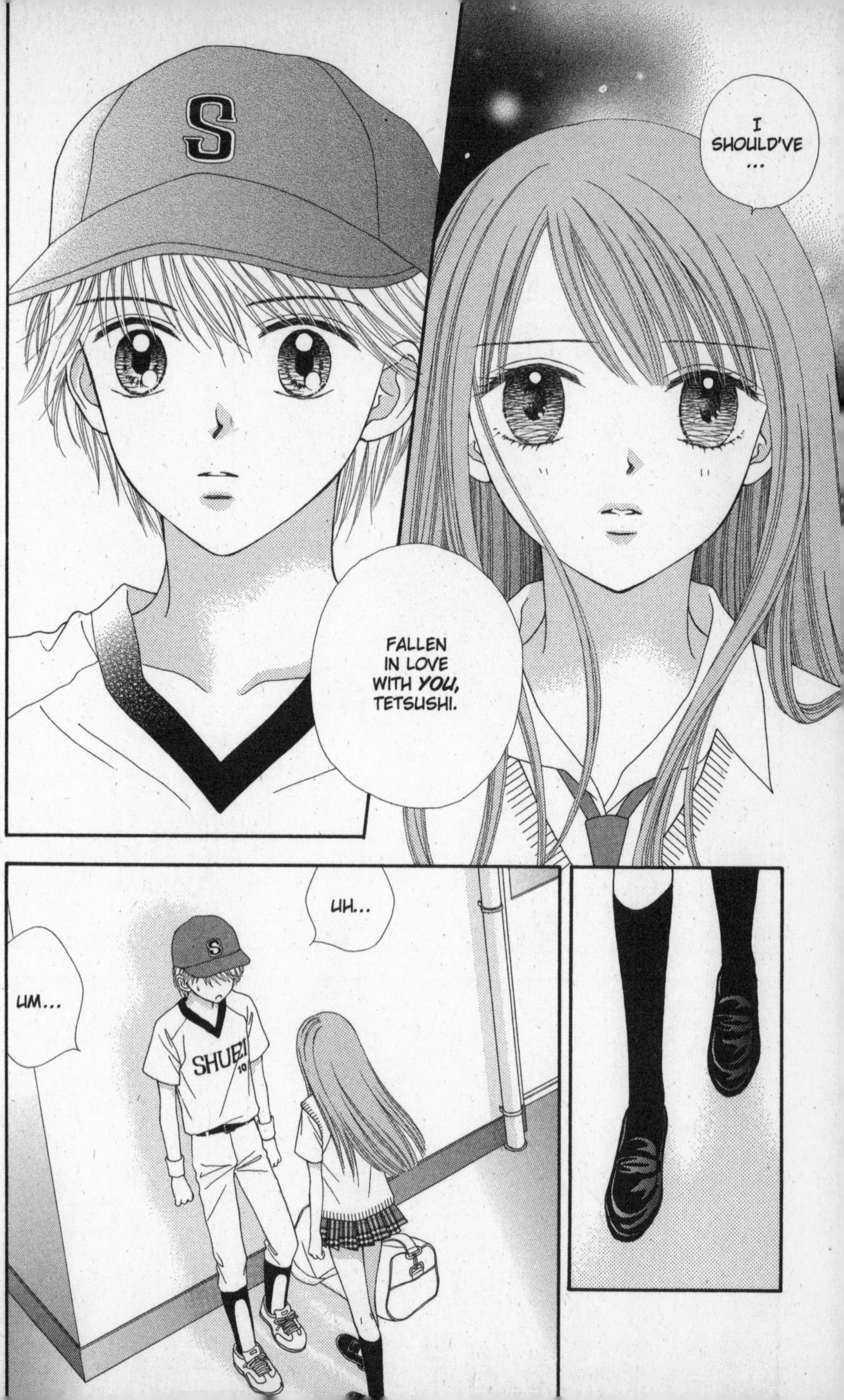
I SHOULD'VE ...
FALLEN IN LOVE WITH *YOU*, TETSUSHI.
UH...
UM...

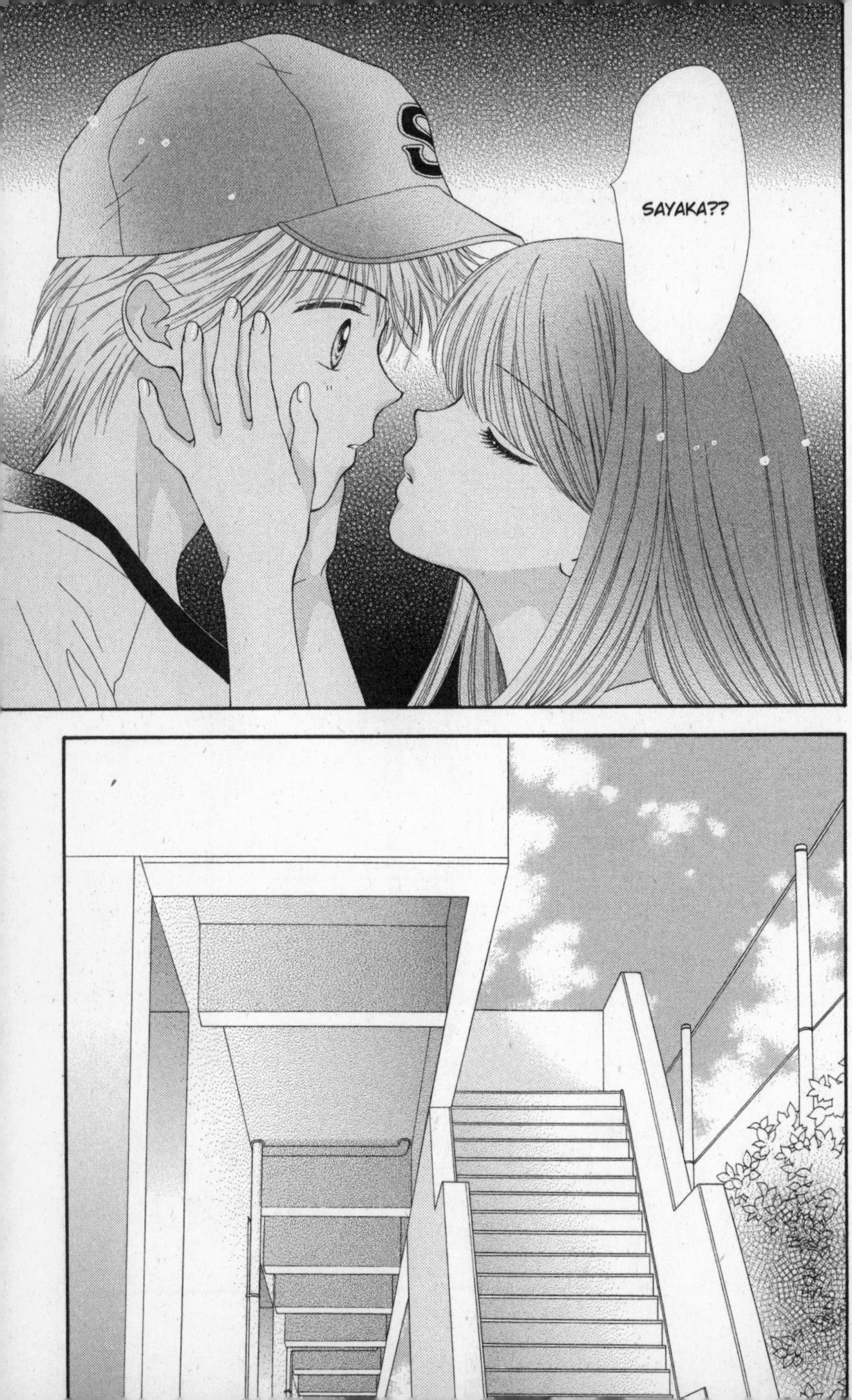
SAYAKA??

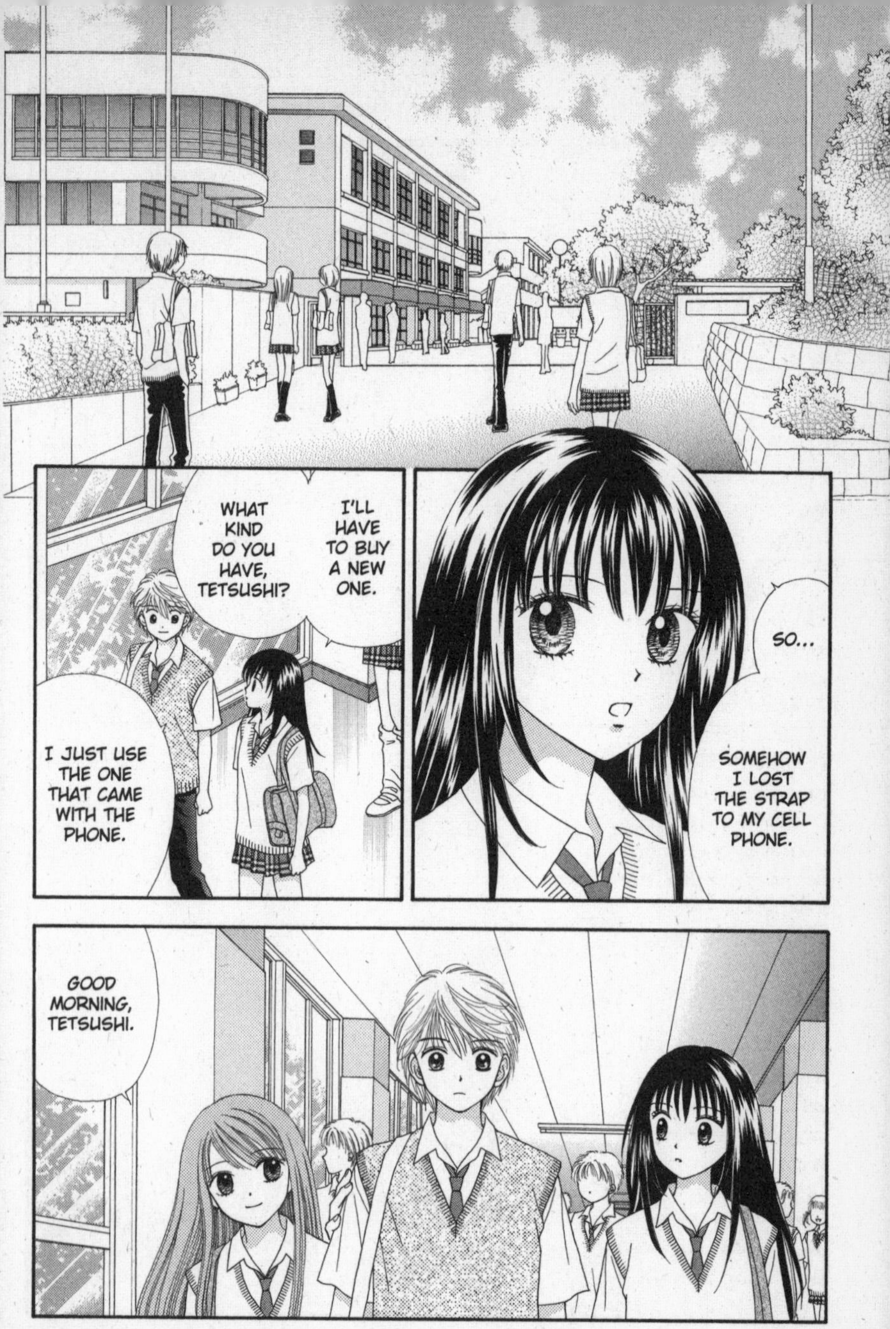
SO...
SOMEHOW I LOST THE STRAP TO MY CELL PHONE.
I'LL HAVE TO BUY A NEW ONE.
WHAT KIND DO YOU HAVE, TETSUSHI?
I JUST USE THE ONE THAT CAME WITH THE PHONE.
GOOD MORNING, TETSUSHI.

FREE TALK 1

Hello, it's Wataru again.

It's late November as I write this. I've already finished writing the final chapter of *Ultra Maniac* for the January 2004 issue. Actually, this Free Talk was supposed to have been completed before now, but I ran out of time working on the cover art. So I begged to have the deadline stretched.

Ultra Maniac's 24 chapters were serialized over a period of two years. Frankly, this is the longest I've ever been continuously published without taking a break. I've had several series that were published longer than *Ultra Maniac*, but I managed to get a break part way through all of them. (I think the longest I've gone—until now—was about a year and a half.)

Near the end, I was exhausted. I had headaches and my shoulders were stiff from working continuously for so many days. (It was really bad!) But I managed to complete the series and I think things turned out well. So I'm glad.

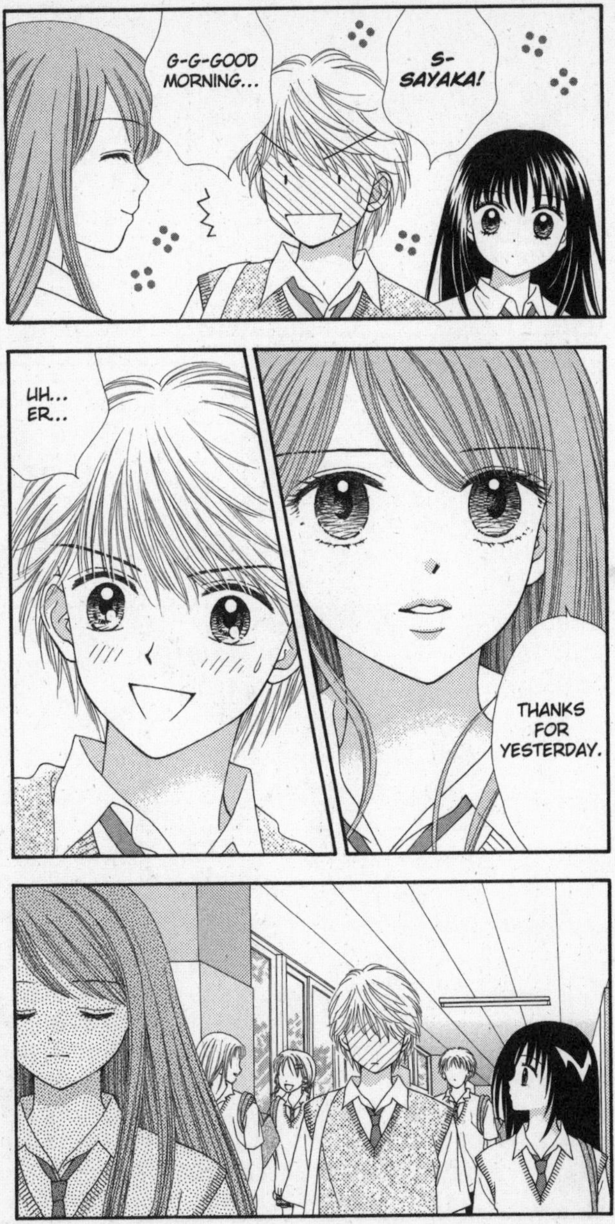
S- SAYAKA!
G-G-GOOD MORNING...
THANKS FOR YESTERDAY.
UH... ER...

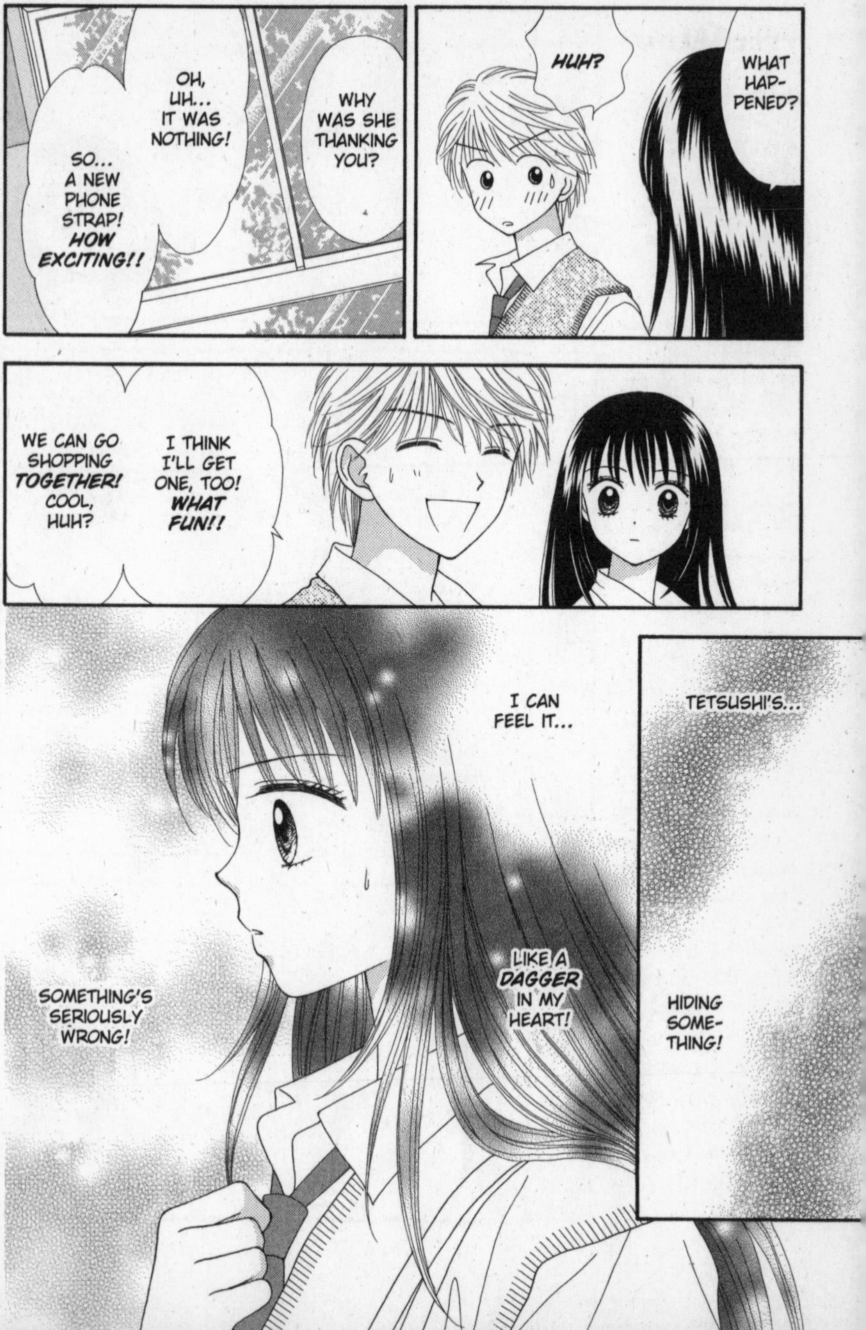
WHAT HAP-PENED?
HUH?
WHY WAS SHE THANKING YOU?
OH, UH... IT WAS NOTHING!
SO... A NEW PHONE STRAP! HOW EXCITING!!
I THINK I'LL GET ONE, TOO! WHAT FUN!!
WE CAN GO SHOPPING TOGETHER! COOL, HUH?
TETSUSHI'S...
HIDING SOME-THING!
I CAN FEEL IT...
LIKE A DAGGER IN MY HEART!
SOMETHING'S SERIOUSLY WRONG!

FREE TALK 2

Actually, I thought I was done with Ultra Maniac before this. But I wasn't. I still had to do an extra story for the March 2004 issue!

You see, Ultra Maniac was supposed to end in the January issue. But it turned out that Volume 5 of the collected series was too short. So I was going to create a new short story—something without the Ultra Maniac characters—to fill out the book. That was kind of exciting because it felt like it'd been "forever" since I'd gotten to do a stand-alone short story.

But then I was asked to have it ready for the March issue. So I didn't have enough time to develop new characters for the short story. So I ended up doing an Ultra Maniac side story instead.

I originally wanted to write a story that had ice hockey in it. But that'll have to wait for another time.

I hadn't planned to do a side story, but I thought it would be fun to write about what happened to Ayu and company after the regular series ended. So I'm working on that. Once that's done, I am going to take a quick vacation and refresh my body and spirit.

By the way, I want to thank everyone who watched the Ultra Maniac anime series. Apparently the ratings were pretty good when it was on TV in Japan. By the time you read this, it'll also be available on DVD for Japan. (And in America!)

SAYAKA!
AYU...
WHAT'S UP?
UH...
WELL...

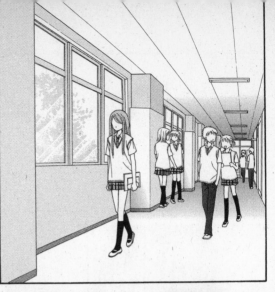

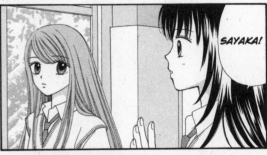

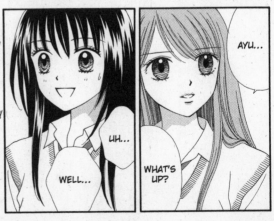

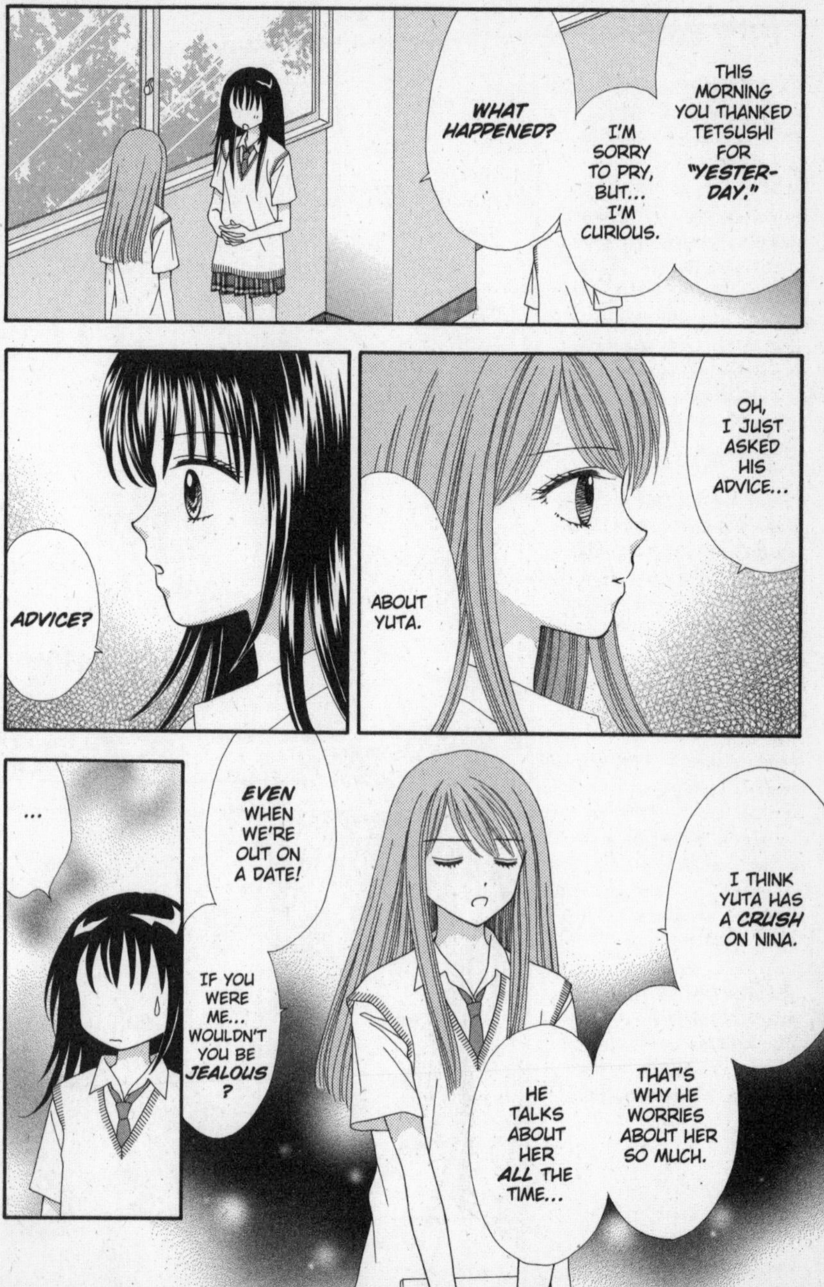
THIS MORNING YOU THANKED TETSUSHI FOR "YESTER-DAY."
I'M SORRY TO PRY, BUT... I'M CURIOUS.
WHAT HAPPENED?
OH, I JUST ASKED HIS ADVICE...
ABOUT YUTA.
ADVICE?
I THINK YUTA HAS A CRUSH ON NINA.
THAT'S WHY HE WORRIES ABOUT HER SO MUCH.
HE TALKS ABOUT HER ALL THE TIME...
EVEN WHEN WE'RE OUT ON A DATE!
IF YOU WERE ME... WOULDN'T YOU BE JEALOUS?
...

FREE TALK 3

The DVD box sets (released in Japan) are labeled "Magic I, II and III" and have a really cute package design. Episodes three and 13 had their art retouched from the televised version, so they're even better. People who've seen the TV program will probably have fun comparing the versions. (Episode 22 is to be retouched too from what I hear.)

A CD will also be released. The album "Magical Songs" will have background music from the series plus seven character songs.

Nina's and Hiroki's songs are supposed be about "the importance of friends." But Ayu's and Tetsushi's are love songs. Tetsushi's song "Boy, you love Ayu that much don't you?" is a particularly emotional song sung by Tetsushi's voice actor, Katsushi Kamiya. I highly recommend it for those of you who are Ayu-Tetsushi fans.

Ayu is played by Yui Horie. I knew she was a really popular singer and voice actress, but this CD is the first time I've actually heard her sing. I've become a huge fan of hers.

I guess you'd say her voice has "clarity." It's incredibly pleasant.

Ms. Horie teamed up with Akemi Kanda (who played the part of Nina) for a single that was released separately called "Love, Dream and Kiss" (koi shite, yume mite, KISS shite...) It's a cute song!

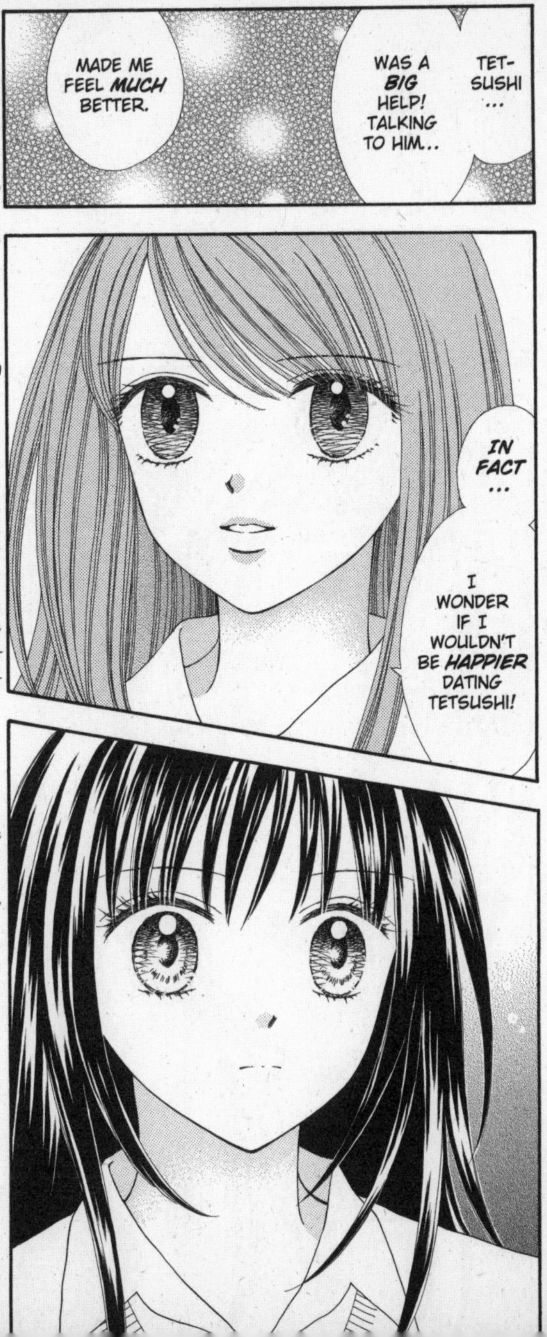
TET-SUSHI ...
WAS A BIG HELP! TALKING TO HIM...
MADE ME FEEL MUCH BETTER.
IN FACT ...
I WONDER IF I WOULDN'T BE HAPPIER DATING TETSUSHI!

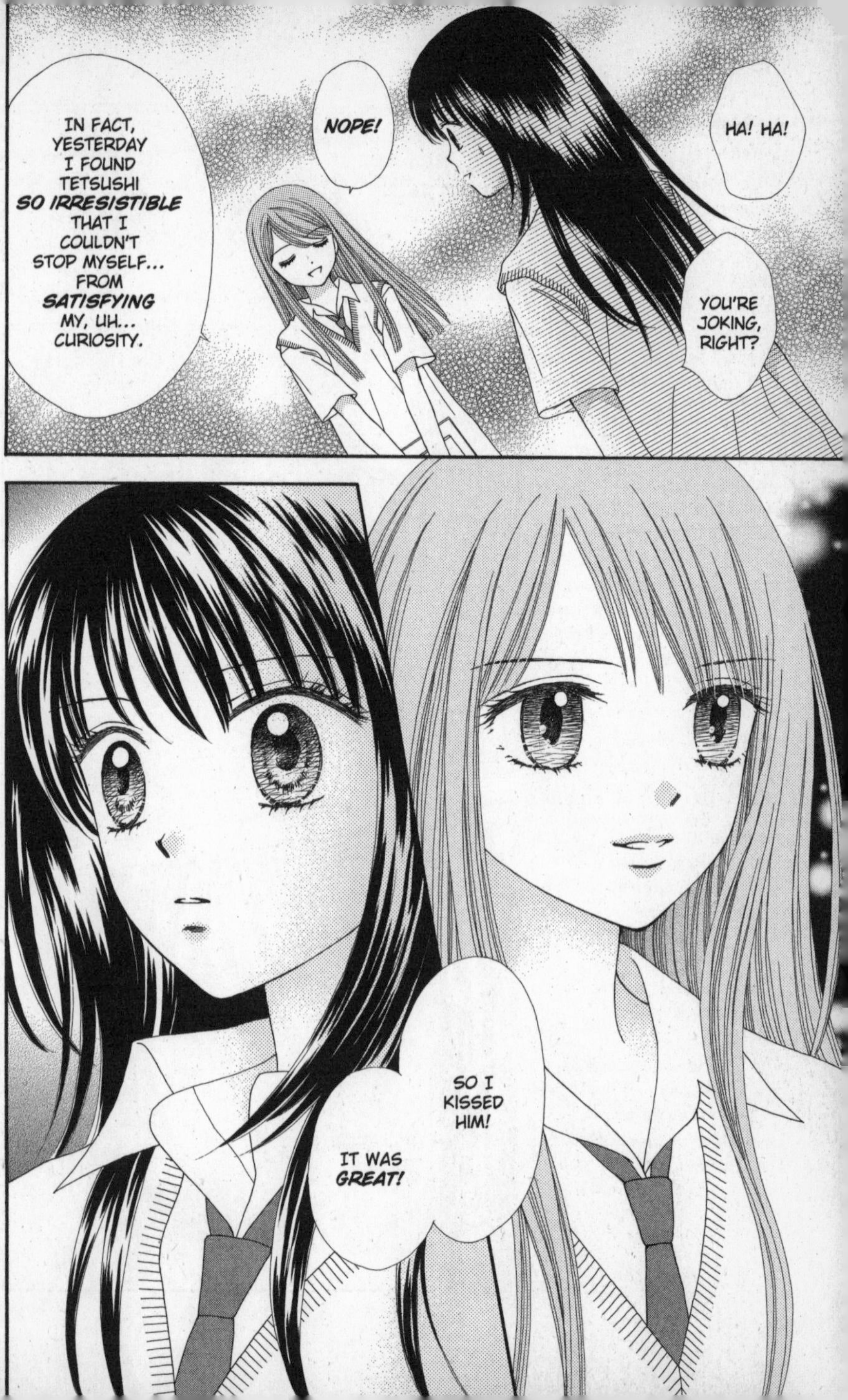
HA! HA!
YOU'RE JOKING, RIGHT?
NOPE!
IN FACT, YESTERDAY I FOUND TETSUSHI SO IRRESISTIBLE THAT I COULDN'T STOP MYSELF... FROM SATISFYING MY, UH... CURIOSITY.
SO I KISSED HIM!
IT WAS GREAT!

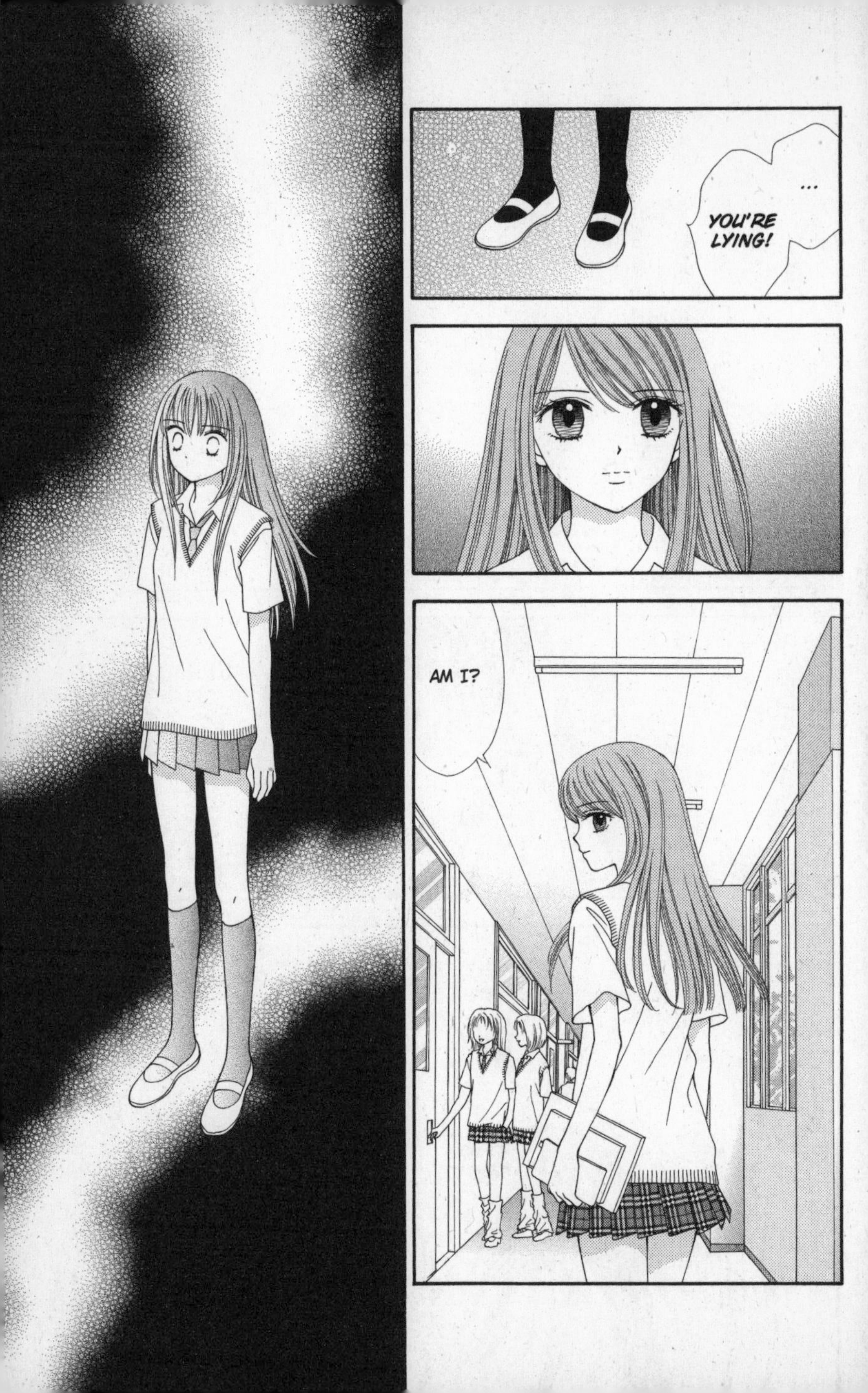
...
YOU'RE LYING!
AM I?

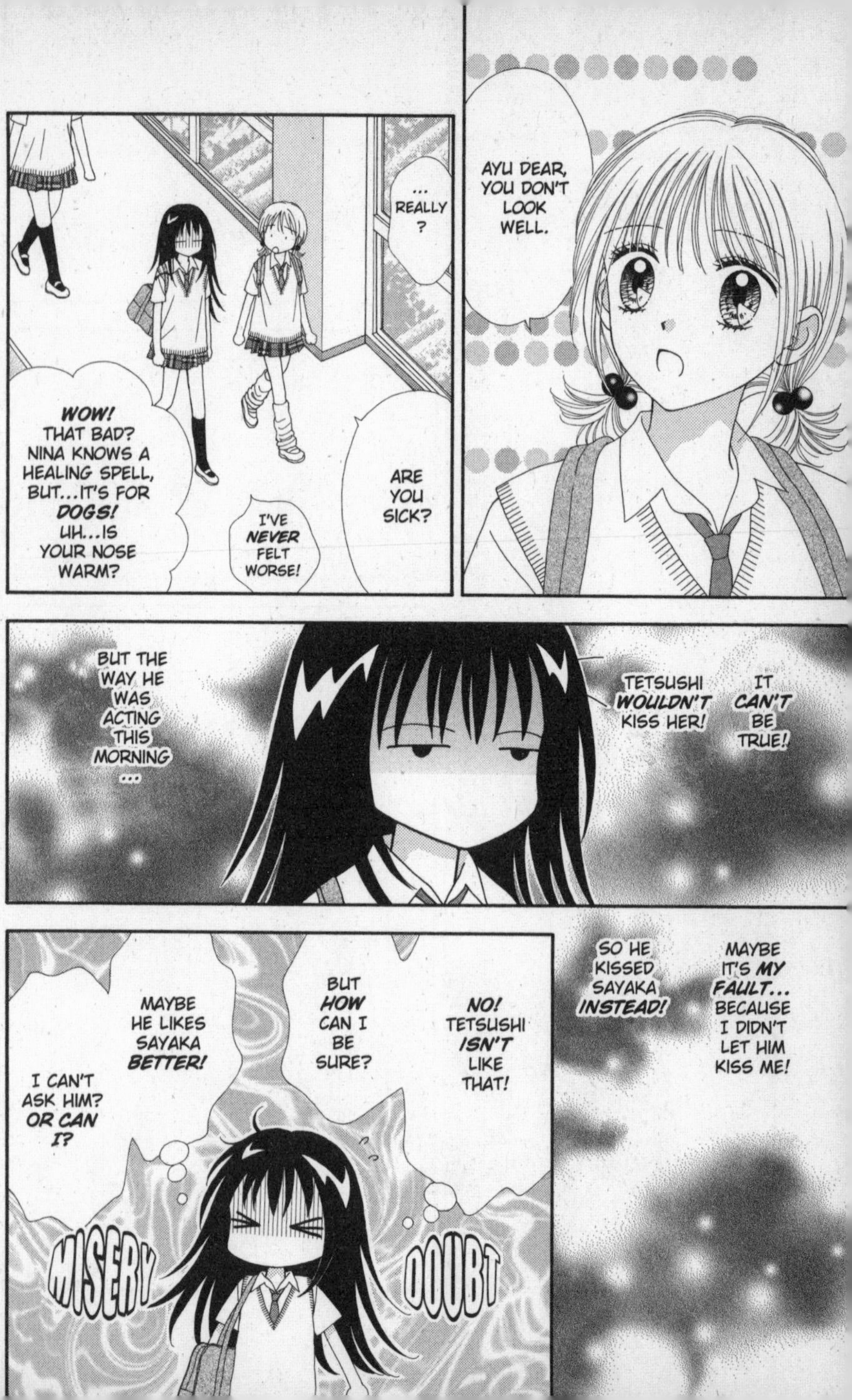
AYU DEAR, YOU DON'T LOOK WELL.
...REALLY?
ARE YOU SICK?
I'VE NEVER FELT WORSE!
WOW! THAT BAD? NINA KNOWS A HEALING SPELL, BUT...IT'S FOR DOGS! UH...IS YOUR NOSE WARM?
IT CAN'T BE TRUE!
TETSUSHI WOULDN'T KISS HER!
BUT THE WAY HE WAS ACTING THIS MORNING...
MAYBE IT'S MY FAULT... BECAUSE I DIDN'T LET HIM KISS ME!
SO HE KISSED SAYAKA INSTEAD!
NO! TETSUSHI ISN'T LIKE THAT!
BUT HOW CAN I BE SURE?
MAYBE HE LIKES SAYAKA BETTER!
I CAN'T ASK HIM? OR CAN I?
DOUBT
MISERY

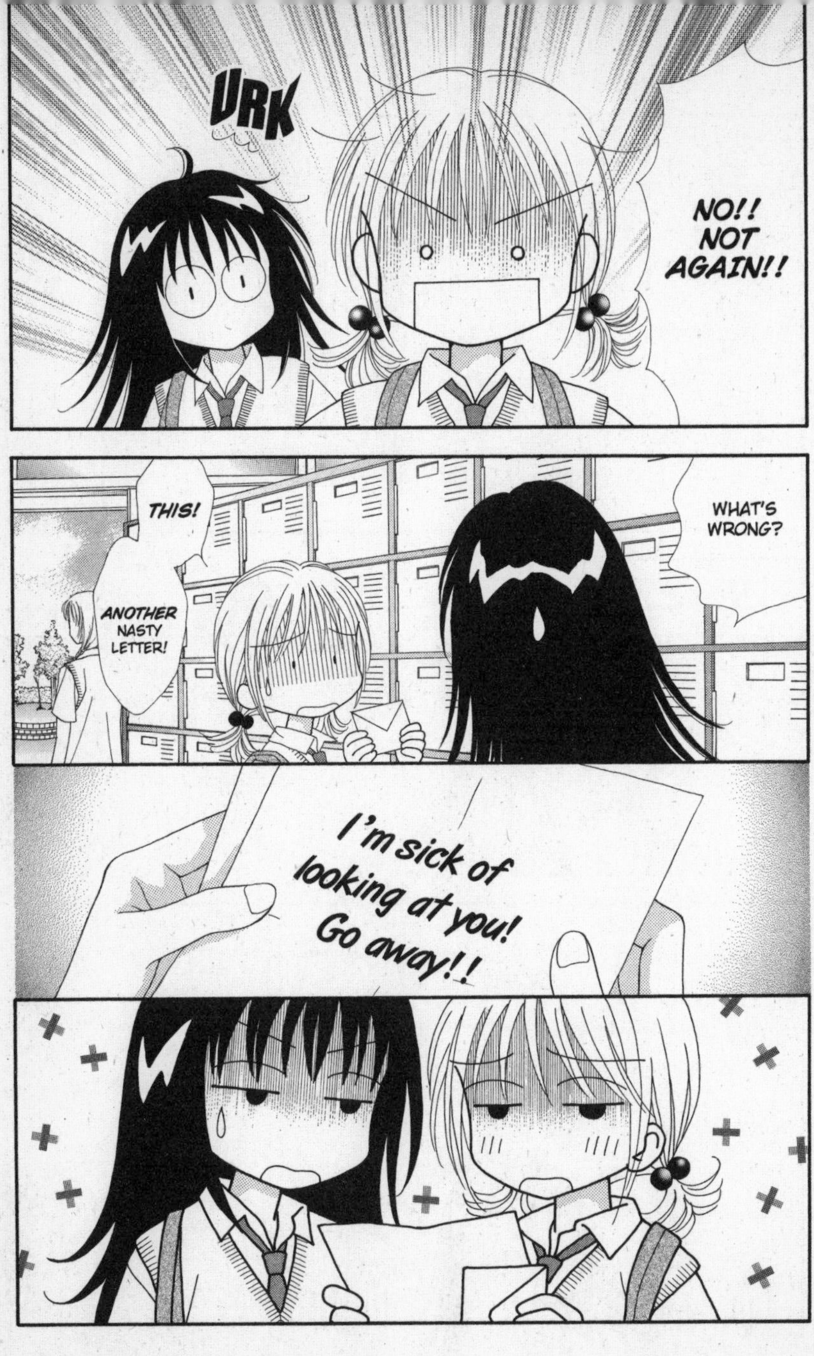
NO!! NOT AGAIN!!
URK
WHAT'S WRONG?
THIS!
ANOTHER NASTY LETTER!
I'm sick of looking at you! Go away!!

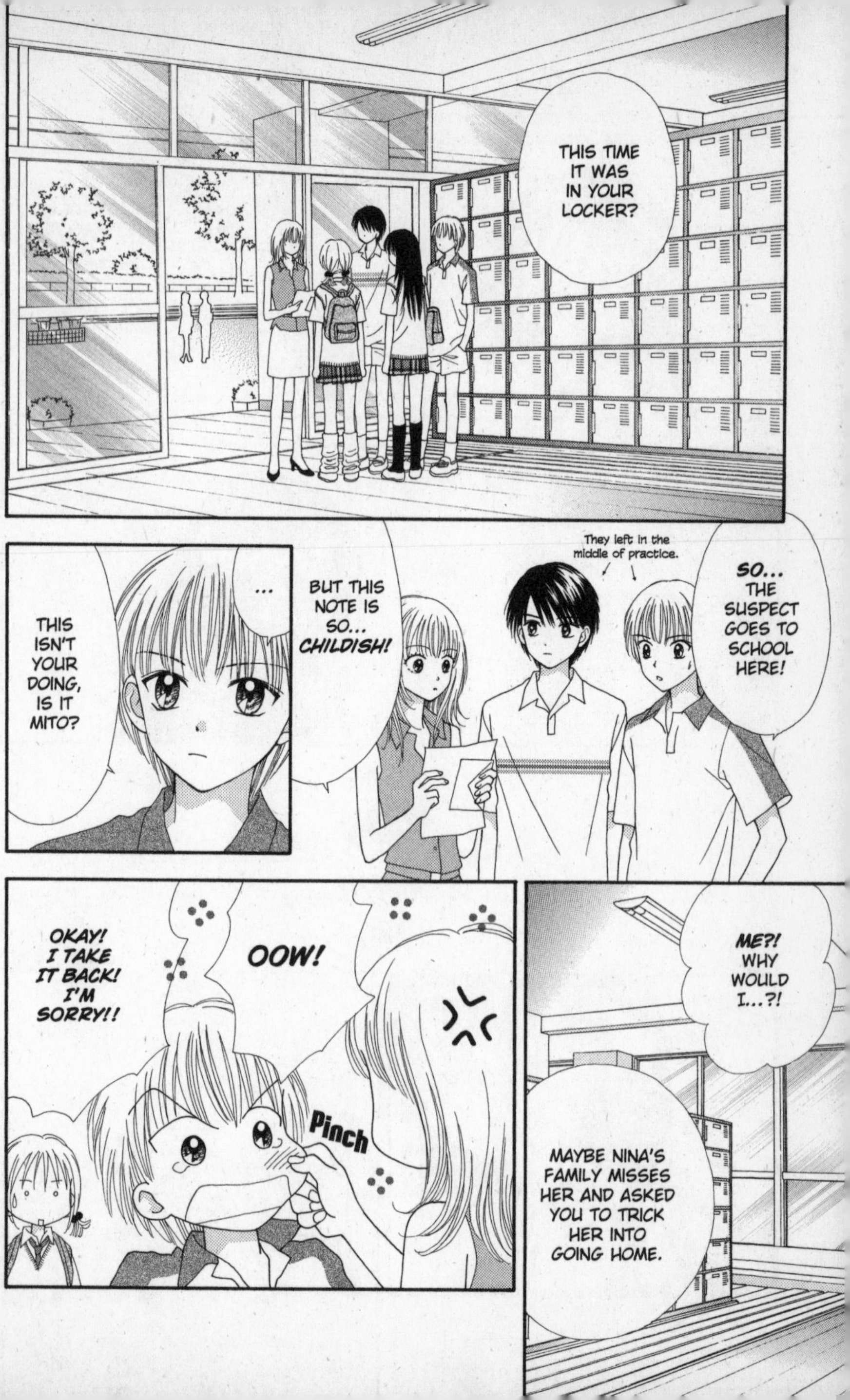
THIS TIME IT WAS IN YOUR LOCKER?
SO... THE SUSPECT GOES TO SCHOOL HERE!
They left in the middle of practice.
BUT THIS NOTE IS SO... CHILDISH!
...
THIS ISN'T YOUR DOING, IS IT MITO?
ME?! WHY WOULD I...?!
MAYBE NINA'S FAMILY MISSES HER AND ASKED YOU TO TRICK HER INTO GOING HOME.
OOW!
OKAY! I TAKE IT BACK! I'M SORRY!!
Pinch

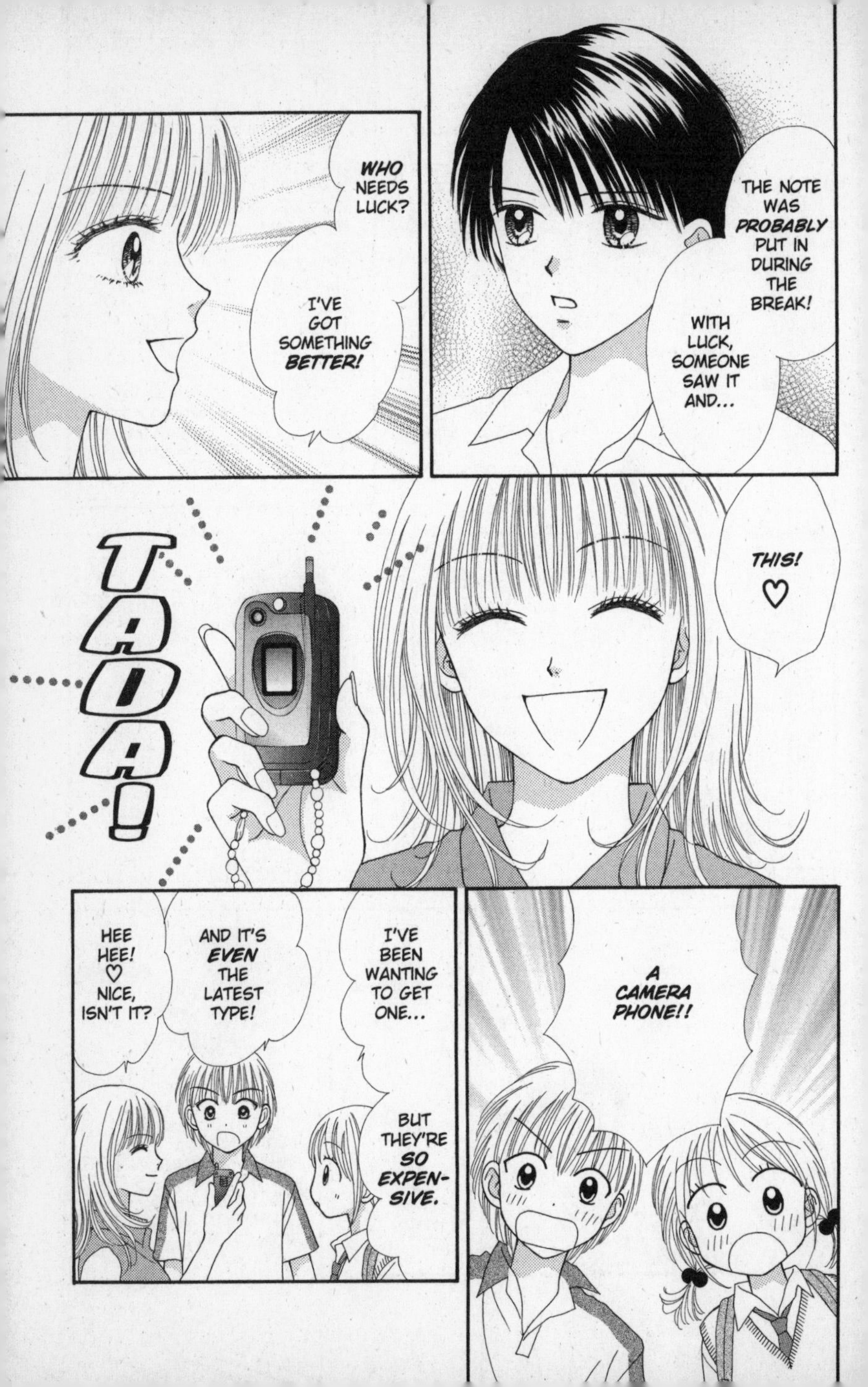
THE NOTE WAS PROBABLY PUT IN DURING THE BREAK!
WITH LUCK, SOMEONE SAW IT AND...
WHO NEEDS LUCK?
I'VE GOT SOMETHING BETTER!
THIS! ♡
TADA!
A CAMERA PHONE!!
I'VE BEEN WANTING TO GET ONE...
BUT THEY'RE SO EXPEN-SIVE.
AND IT'S EVEN THE LATEST TYPE!
HEE HEE! ♡ NICE, ISN'T IT?

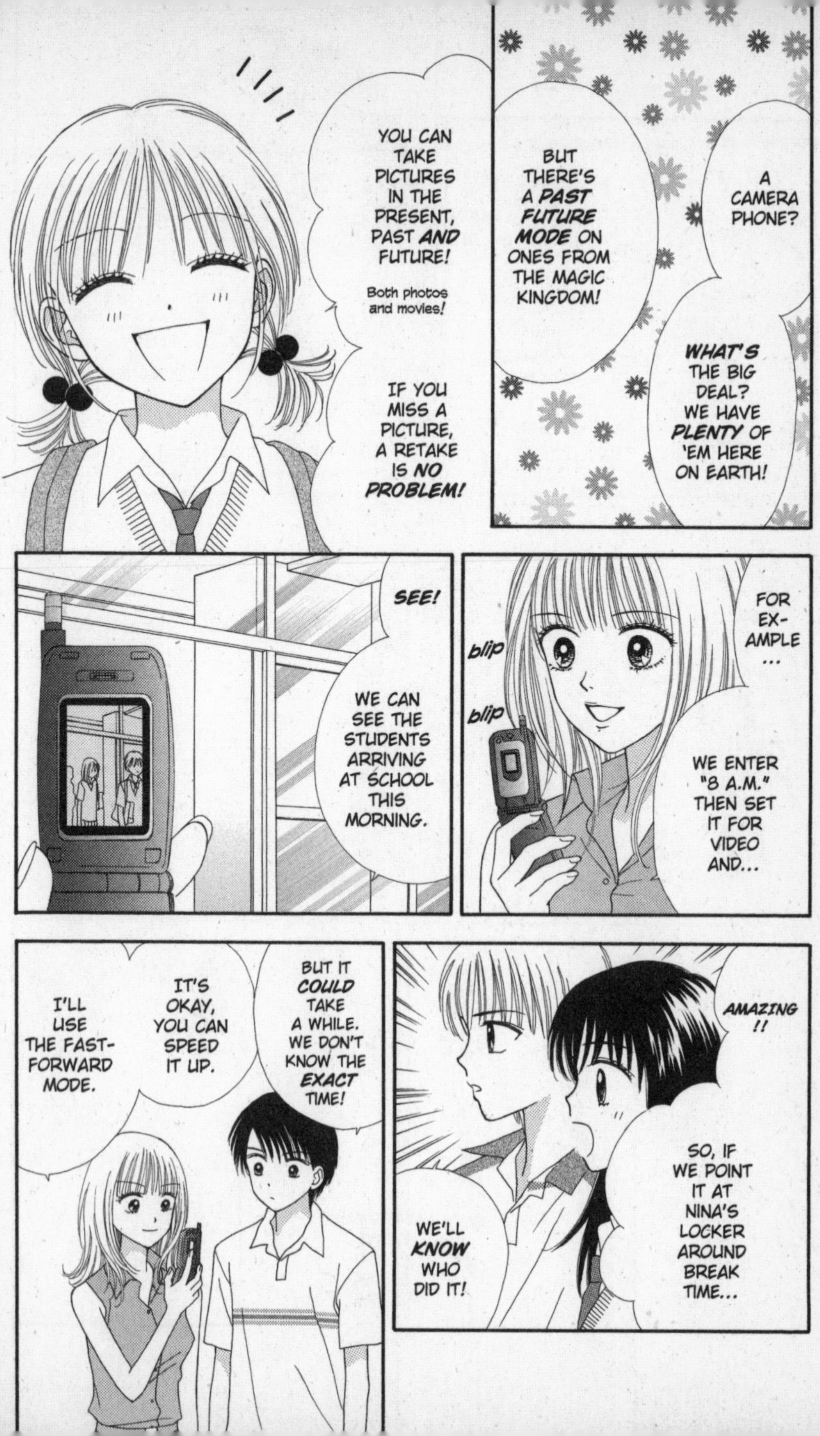
A CAMERA PHONE?
WHAT'S THE BIG DEAL? WE HAVE PLENTY OF 'EM HERE ON EARTH!
BUT THERE'S A PAST FUTURE MODE ON ONES FROM THE MAGIC KINGDOM!
YOU CAN TAKE PICTURES IN THE PRESENT, PAST AND FUTURE!
Both photos and movies!
IF YOU MISS A PICTURE, A RETAKE IS NO PROBLEM!
FOR EX-AMPLE ...
blip
blip
WE ENTER "8 A.M." THEN SET IT FOR VIDEO AND...
SEE!
WE CAN SEE THE STUDENTS ARRIVING AT SCHOOL THIS MORNING.
AMAZING !!
SO, IF WE POINT IT AT NINA'S LOCKER AROUND BREAK TIME...
WE'LL KNOW WHO DID IT!
BUT IT COULD TAKE A WHILE. WE DON'T KNOW THE EXACT TIME!
IT'S OKAY, YOU CAN SPEED IT UP.
I'LL USE THE FAST-FORWARD MODE.

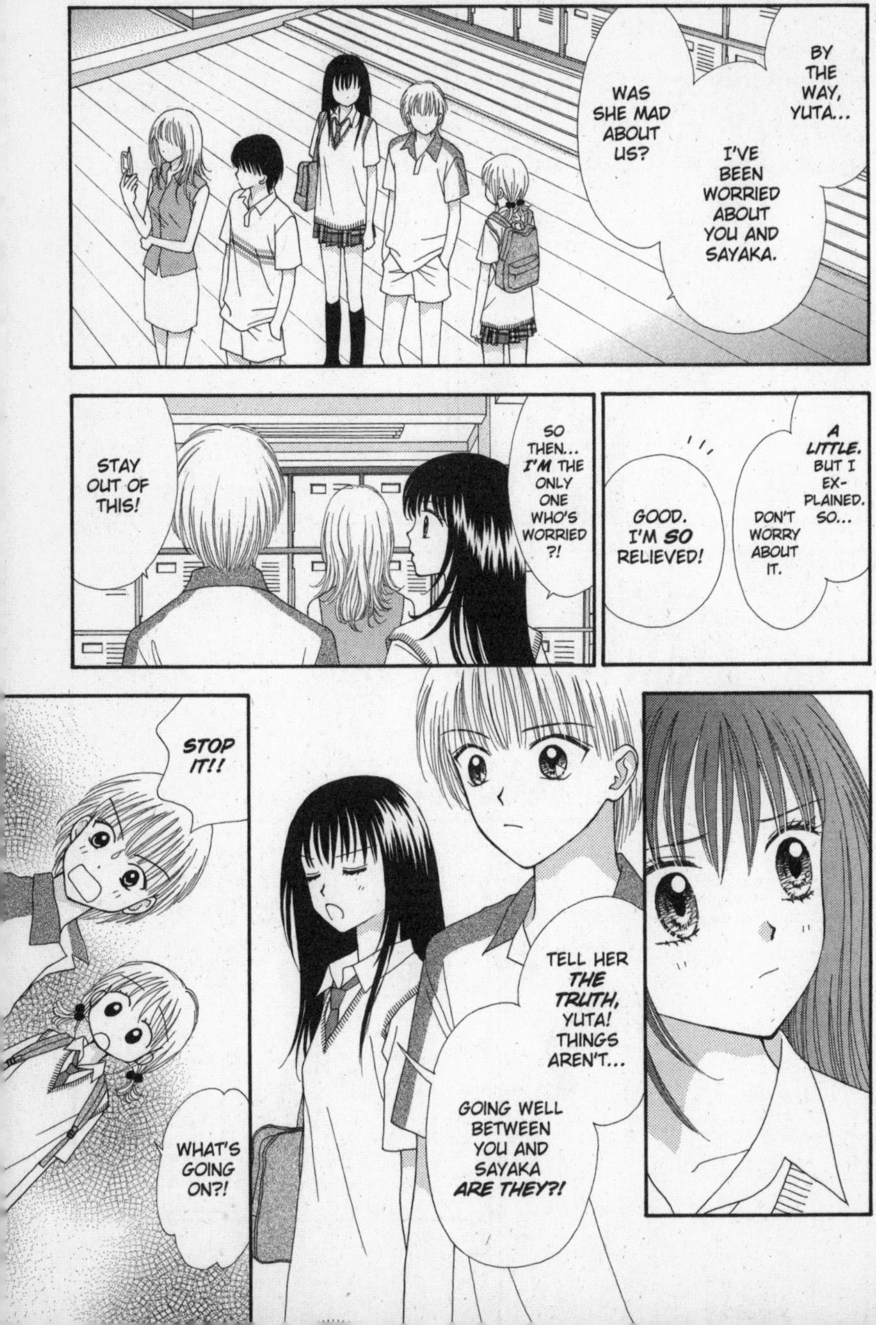
BY THE WAY, YUTA...
I'VE BEEN WORRIED ABOUT YOU AND SAYAKA.
WAS SHE MAD ABOUT US?
A *LITTLE.* BUT I EX-PLAINED. SO...
DON'T WORRY ABOUT IT.
GOOD. I'M *SO* RELIEVED!
SO THEN... *I'M* THE ONLY ONE WHO'S WORRIED ?!
STAY OUT OF THIS!
TELL HER *THE TRUTH,* YUTA! THINGS AREN'T...
GOING WELL BETWEEN YOU AND SAYAKA *ARE THEY?!*
STOP IT!!
WHAT'S GOING ON?!

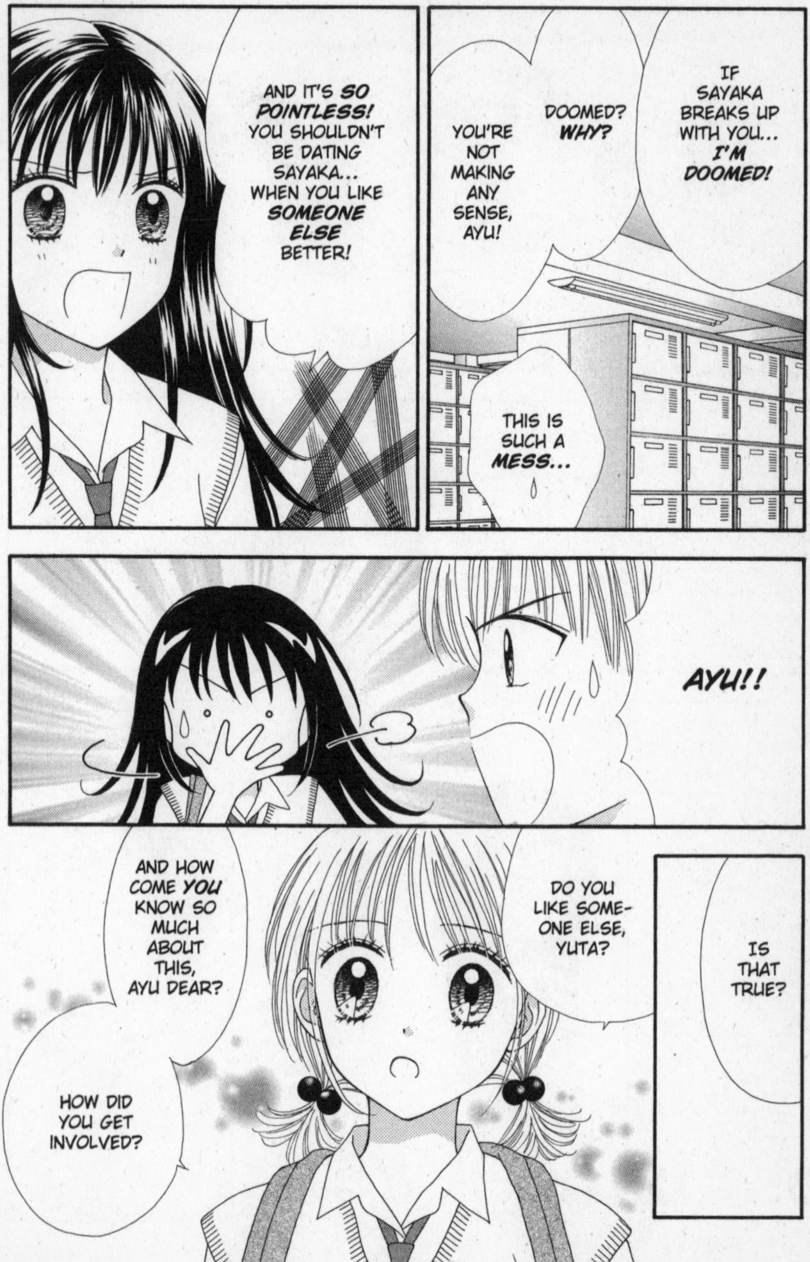
IF SAYAKA BREAKS UP WITH YOU... I'M DOOMED!
DOOMED? WHY?
YOU'RE NOT MAKING ANY SENSE, AYU!
THIS IS SUCH A MESS...
AND IT'S SO POINTLESS! YOU SHOULDN'T BE DATING SAYAKA... WHEN YOU LIKE SOMEONE ELSE BETTER!
AYU!!
IS THAT TRUE?
DO YOU LIKE SOME-ONE ELSE, YUTA?
AND HOW COME YOU KNOW SO MUCH ABOUT THIS, AYU DEAR?
HOW DID YOU GET INVOLVED?

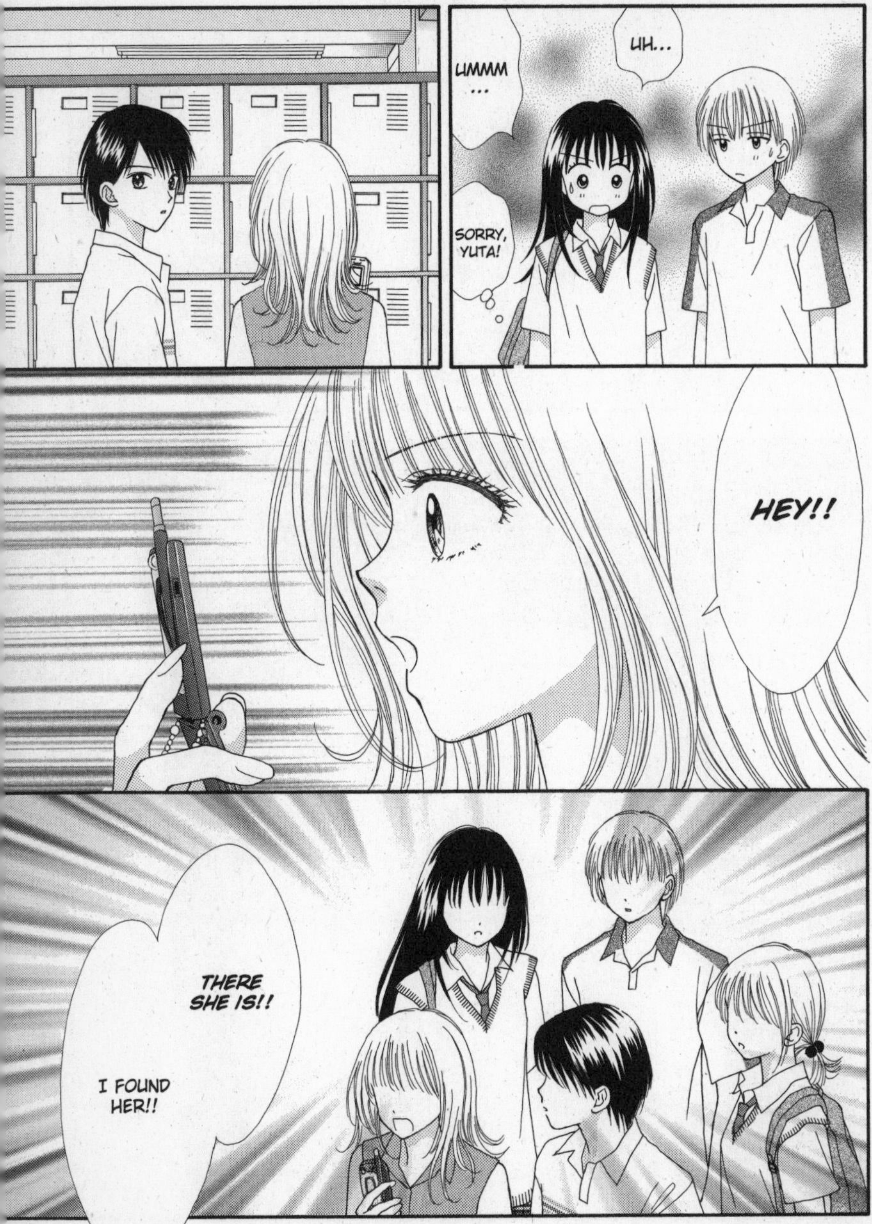
UH...
UMMM ...
SORRY, YUTA!
HEY!!
THERE SHE IS!!
I FOUND HER!!

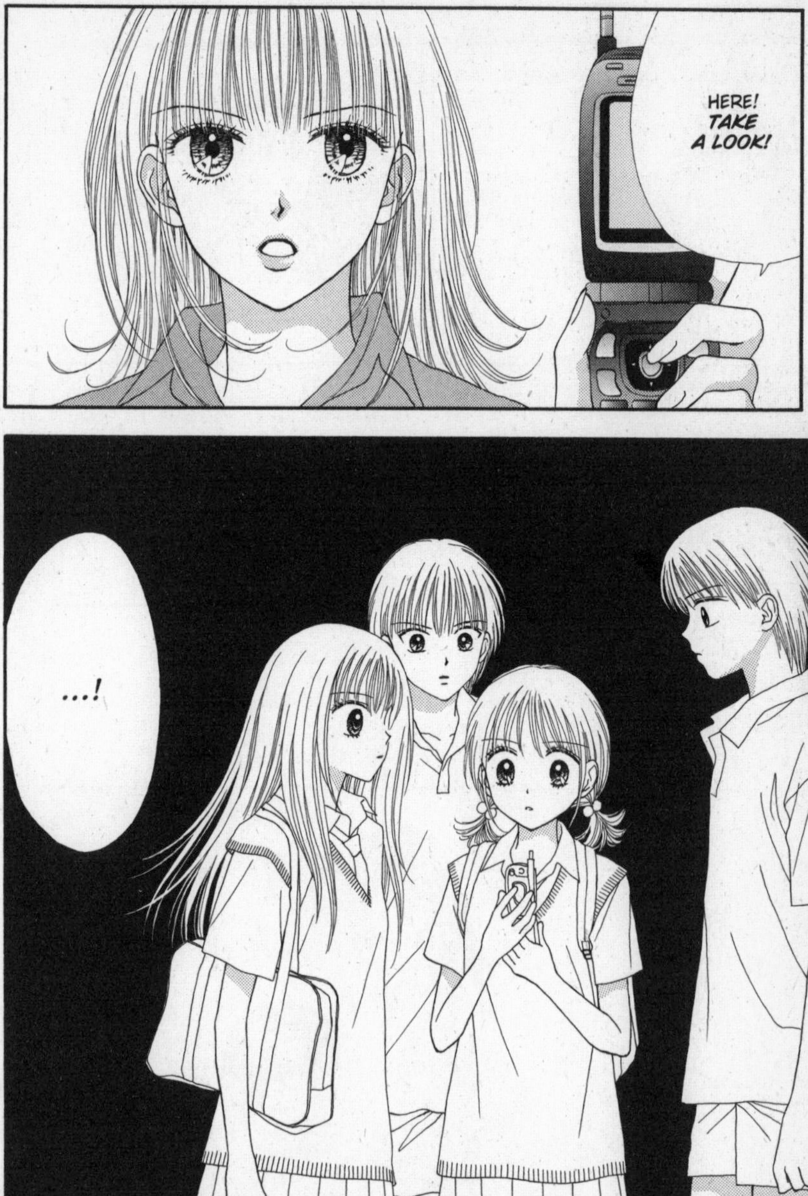
HERE! TAKE A LOOK!
...!

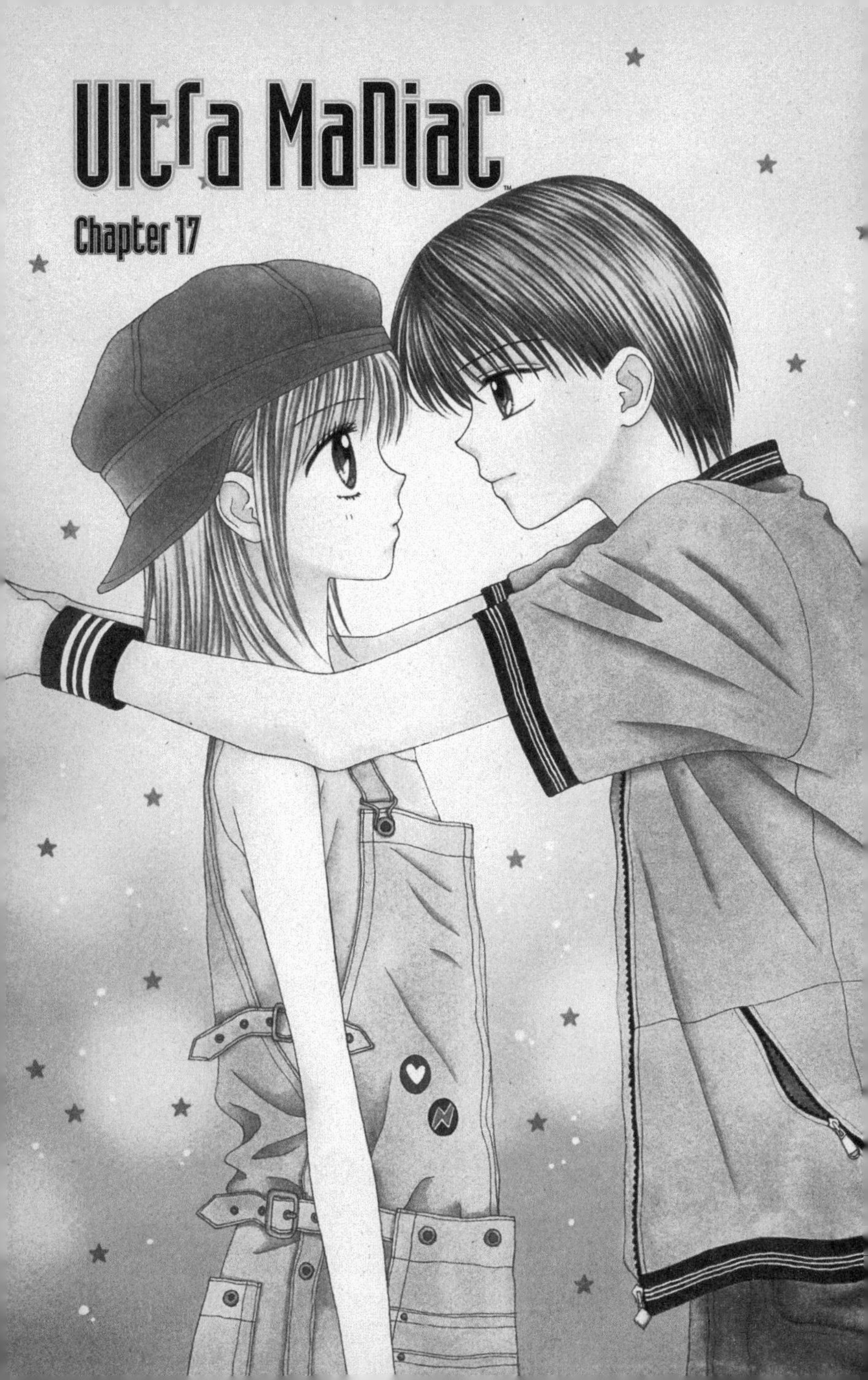
Ultra Maniac
Chapter 17

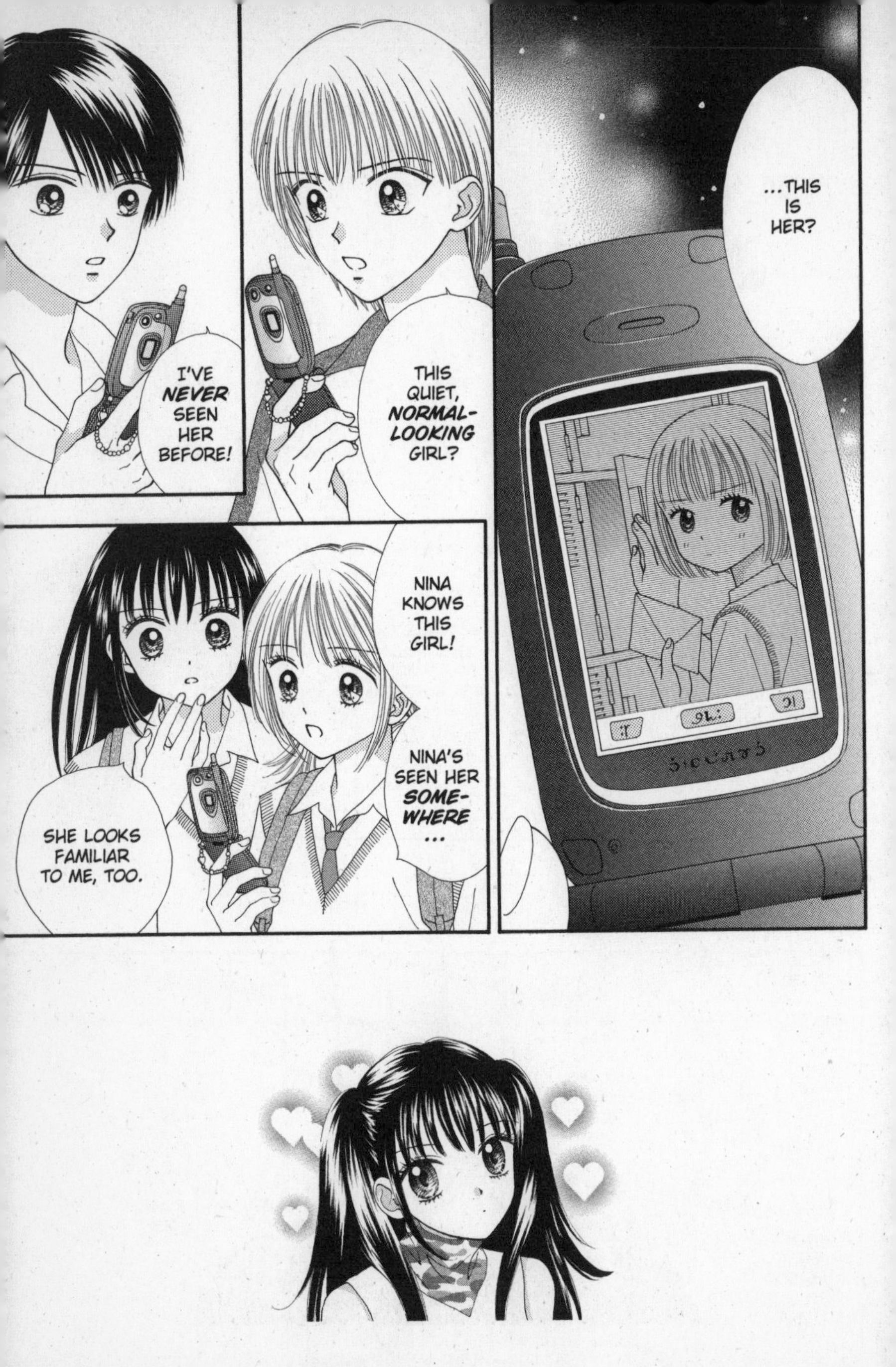
...THIS IS HER?
THIS QUIET, NORMAL-LOOKING GIRL?
I'VE NEVER SEEN HER BEFORE!
NINA KNOWS THIS GIRL!
NINA'S SEEN HER SOMEWHERE...
SHE LOOKS FAMILIAR TO ME, TOO.

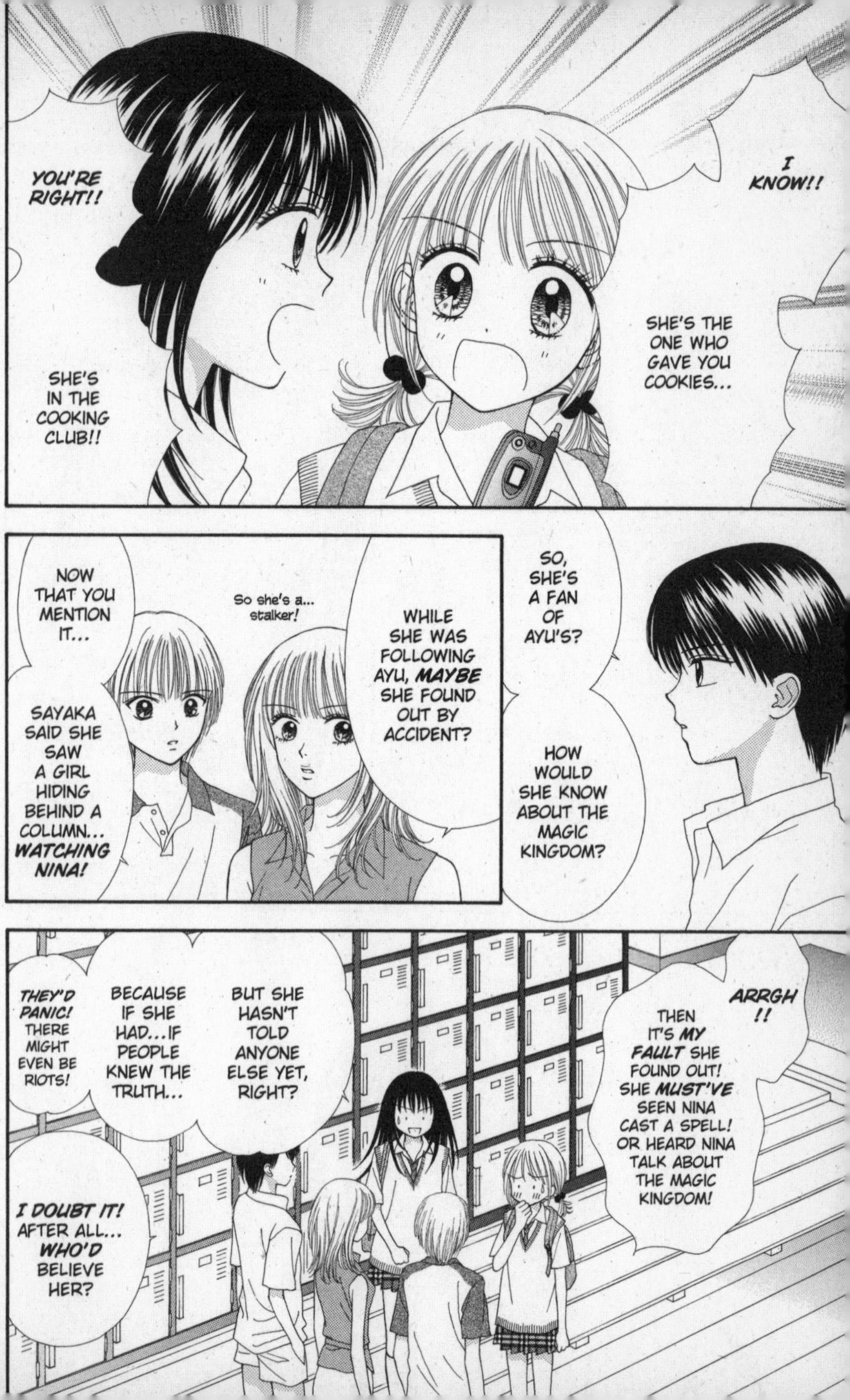

I KNOW!!
SHE'S THE ONE WHO GAVE YOU COOKIES...
YOU'RE RIGHT!!
SHE'S IN THE COOKING CLUB!!
SO, SHE'S A FAN OF AYU'S?
HOW WOULD SHE KNOW ABOUT THE MAGIC KINGDOM?
WHILE SHE WAS FOLLOWING AYU, MAYBE SHE FOUND OUT BY ACCIDENT?
So she's a... stalker!
NOW THAT YOU MENTION IT...
SAYAKA SAID SHE SAW A GIRL HIDING BEHIND A COLUMN... WATCHING NINA!
ARRGH!!
THEN IT'S MY FAULT SHE FOUND OUT! SHE MUST'VE SEEN NINA CAST A SPELL! OR HEARD NINA TALK ABOUT THE MAGIC KINGDOM!
BUT SHE HASN'T TOLD ANYONE ELSE YET, RIGHT?
BECAUSE IF SHE HAD...IF PEOPLE KNEW THE TRUTH...
THEY'D PANIC! THERE MIGHT EVEN BE RIOTS!
I DOUBT IT! AFTER ALL... WHO'D BELIEVE HER?

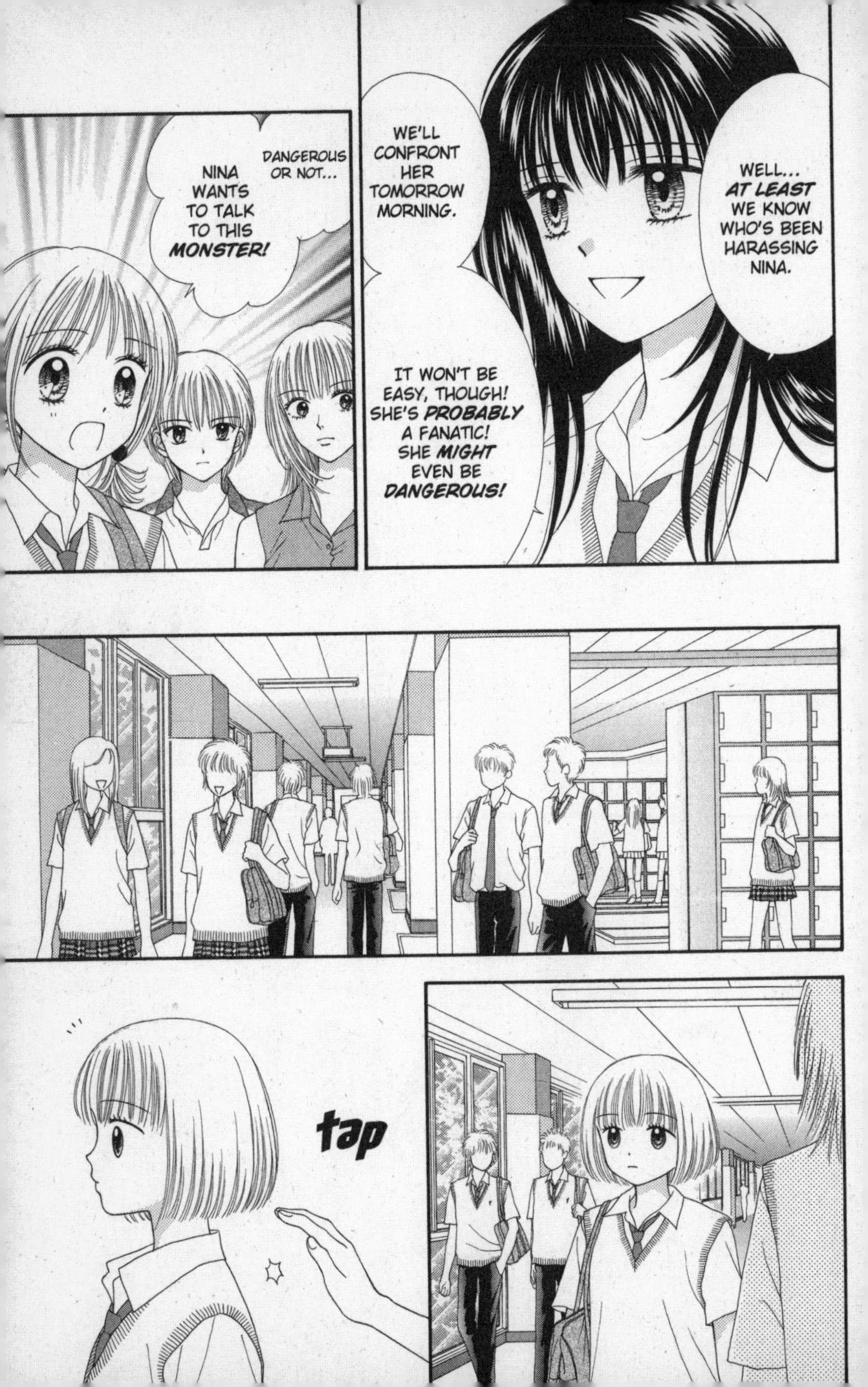
WELL... AT LEAST WE KNOW WHO'S BEEN HARASSING NINA.
WE'LL CONFRONT HER TOMORROW MORNING.
IT WON'T BE EASY, THOUGH! SHE'S PROBABLY A FANATIC! SHE MIGHT EVEN BE DANGEROUS!
DANGEROUS OR NOT...
NINA WANTS TO TALK TO THIS MONSTER!
tap

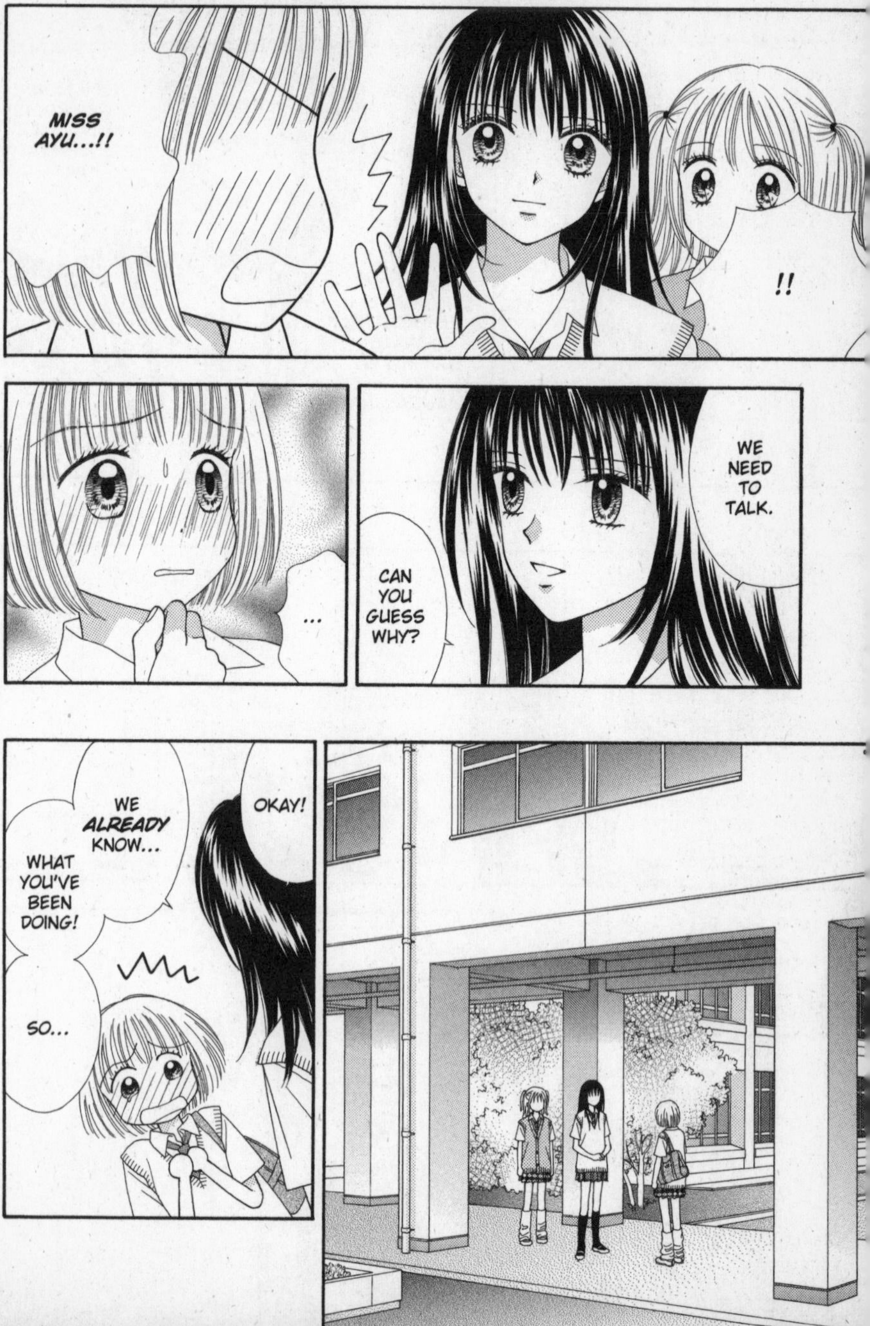
!!
MISS AYU...!!
WE NEED TO TALK.
CAN YOU GUESS WHY?
...
OKAY!
WE ALREADY KNOW...
WHAT YOU'VE BEEN DOING!
SO...

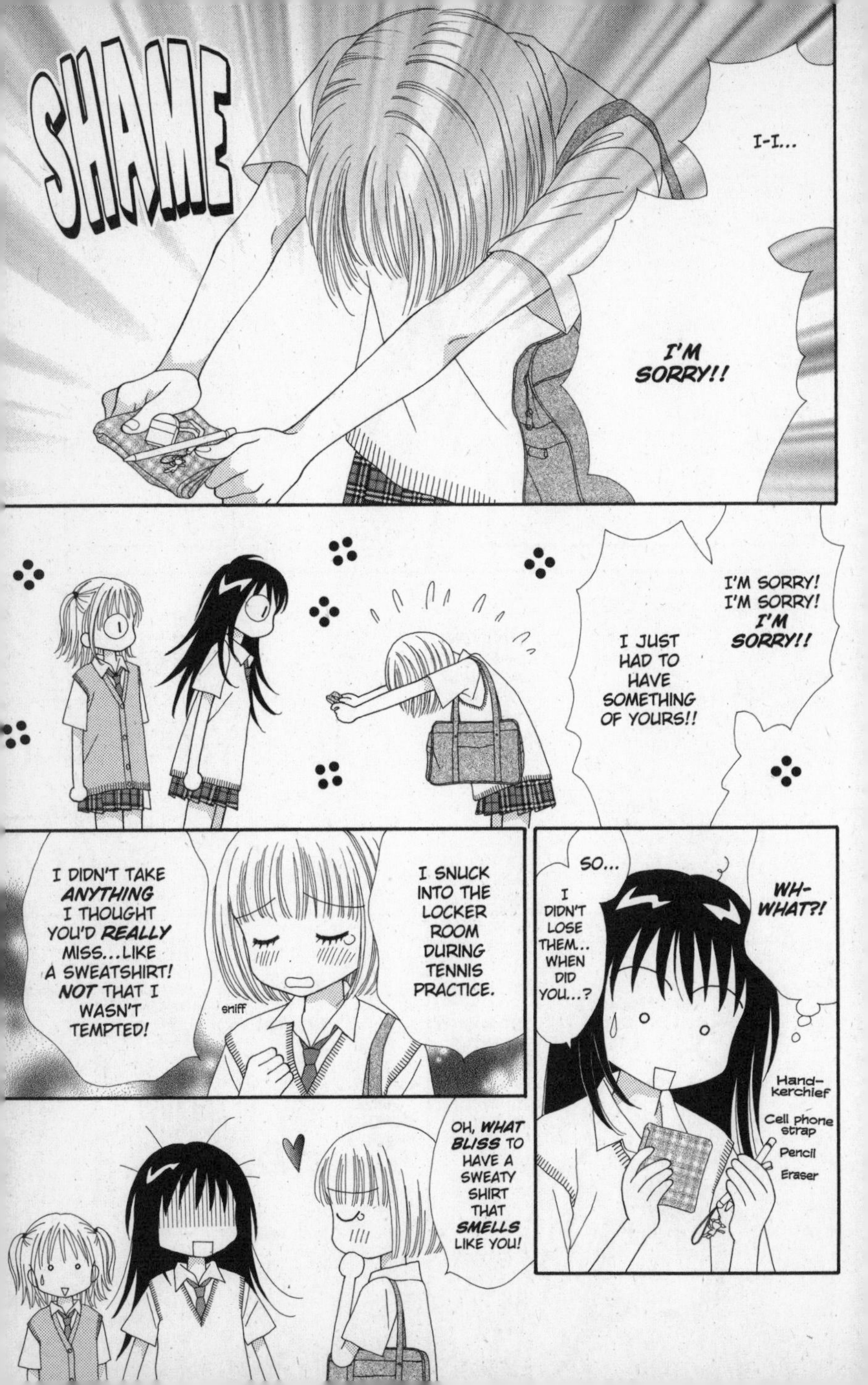
I-I...
SHAME
I'M SORRY!!
I'M SORRY! I'M SORRY! I'M SORRY!!
I JUST HAD TO HAVE SOMETHING OF YOURS!!
WH-WHAT?!
SO...
I DIDN'T LOSE THEM... WHEN DID YOU...?
Hand-kerchief
Cell phone strap
Pencil
Eraser
I SNUCK INTO THE LOCKER ROOM DURING TENNIS PRACTICE.
sniff
I DIDN'T TAKE ANYTHING I THOUGHT YOU'D REALLY MISS...LIKE A SWEATSHIRT! NOT THAT I WASN'T TEMPTED!
OH, WHAT BLISS TO HAVE A SWEATY SHIRT THAT SMELLS LIKE YOU!

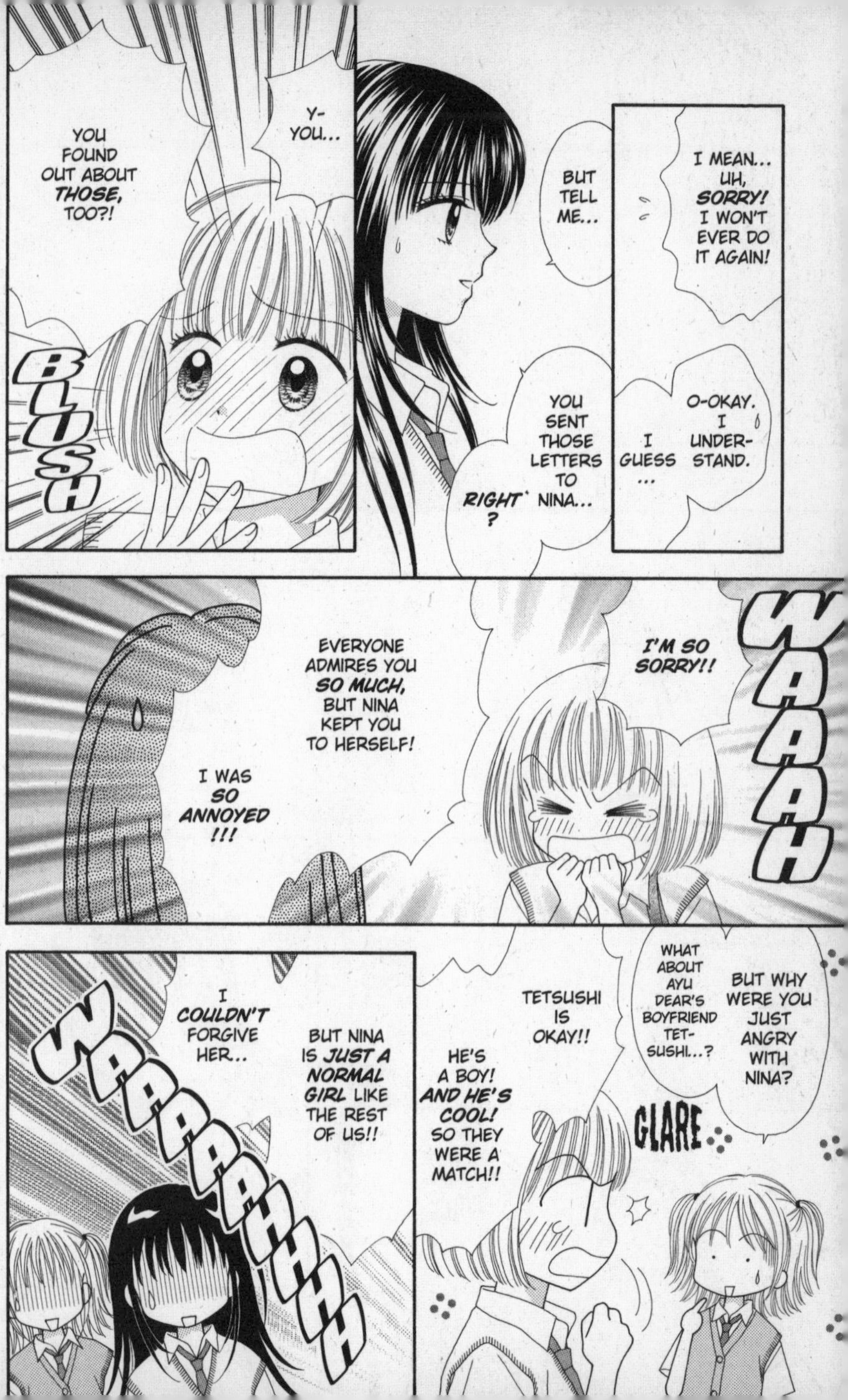
I MEAN... UH, SORRY! I WON'T EVER DO IT AGAIN!
O-OKAY. I UNDERSTAND.
I GUESS...
BUT TELL ME...
YOU SENT THOSE LETTERS TO NINA...
RIGHT?
Y-YOU...
YOU FOUND OUT ABOUT THOSE, TOO?!
BLUSH
WAAAAH
I'M SO SORRY!!
EVERYONE ADMIRES YOU SO MUCH, BUT NINA KEPT YOU TO HERSELF!
I WAS SO ANNOYED!!!
BUT WHY WERE YOU JUST ANGRY WITH NINA?
WHAT ABOUT AYU DEAR'S BOYFRIEND TET-SUSHI...?
GLARE
TETSUSHI IS OKAY!!
HE'S A BOY! AND HE'S COOL! SO THEY WERE A MATCH!!
BUT NINA IS JUST A NORMAL GIRL LIKE THE REST OF US!!
I COULDN'T FORGIVE HER...
WAAAAAHHHH

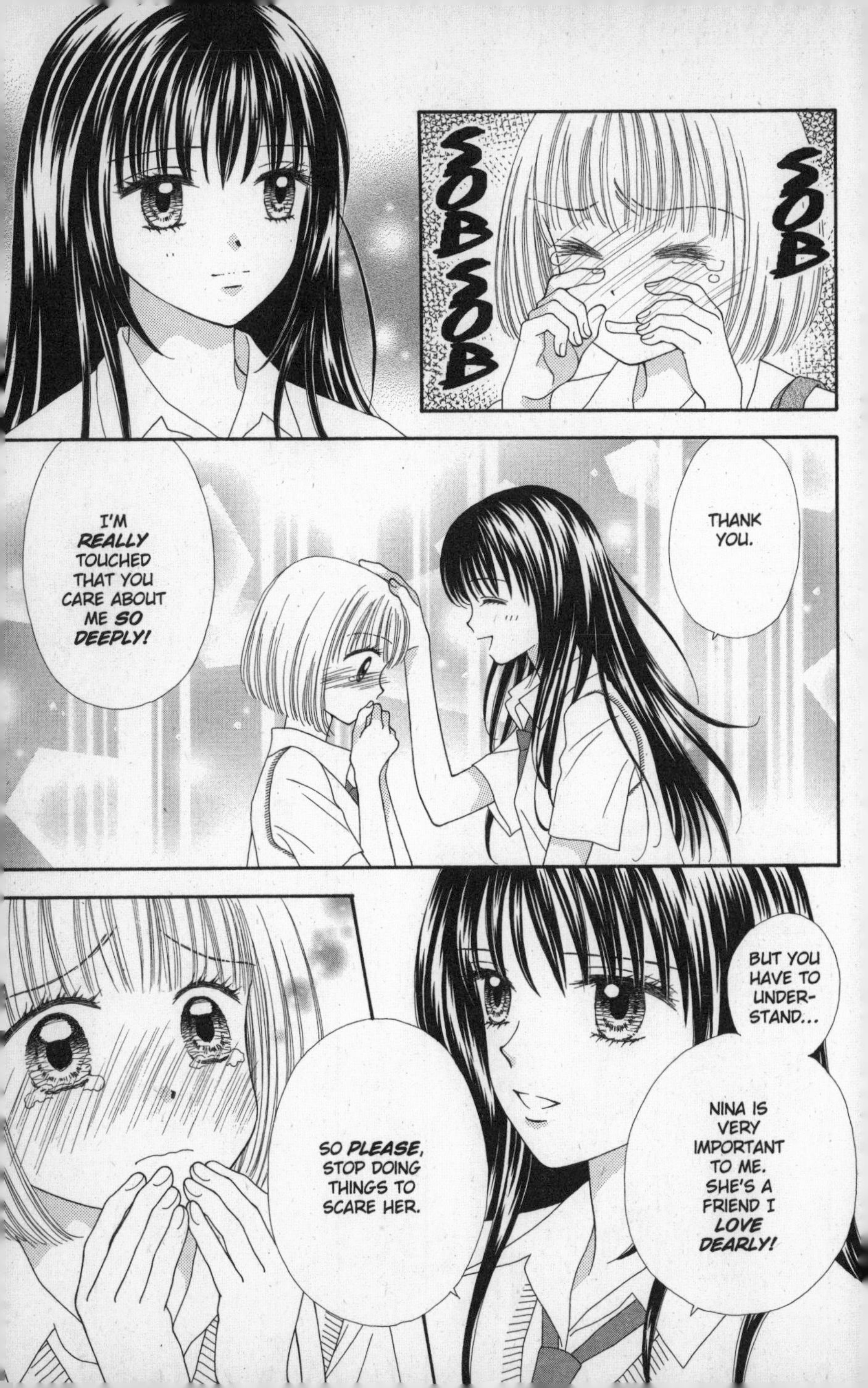
SOB
SOB SOB SOB
THANK YOU.
I'M *REALLY* TOUCHED THAT YOU CARE ABOUT ME *SO DEEPLY!*
BUT YOU HAVE TO UNDER-STAND...
NINA IS VERY IMPORTANT TO ME. SHE'S A FRIEND I *LOVE DEARLY!*
SO *PLEASE*, STOP DOING THINGS TO SCARE HER.

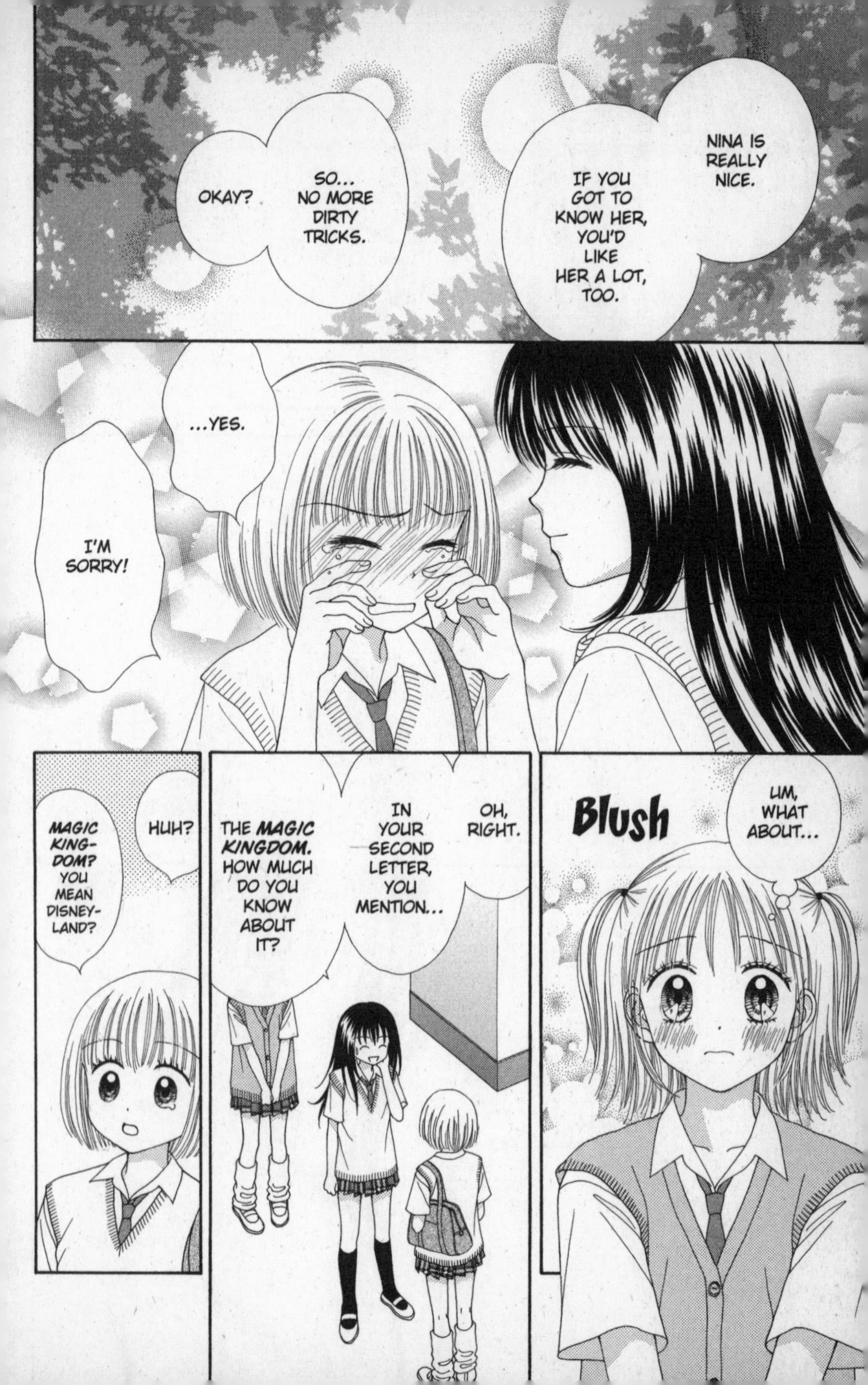
NINA IS REALLY NICE.
IF YOU GOT TO KNOW HER, YOU'D LIKE HER A LOT, TOO.
SO... NO MORE DIRTY TRICKS.
OKAY?
...YES.
I'M SORRY!
UM, WHAT ABOUT...
Blush
OH, RIGHT.
IN YOUR SECOND LETTER, YOU MENTION...
THE *MAGIC KINGDOM.* HOW MUCH DO YOU KNOW ABOUT IT?
HUH?
MAGIC KINGDOM? YOU MEAN DISNEYLAND?

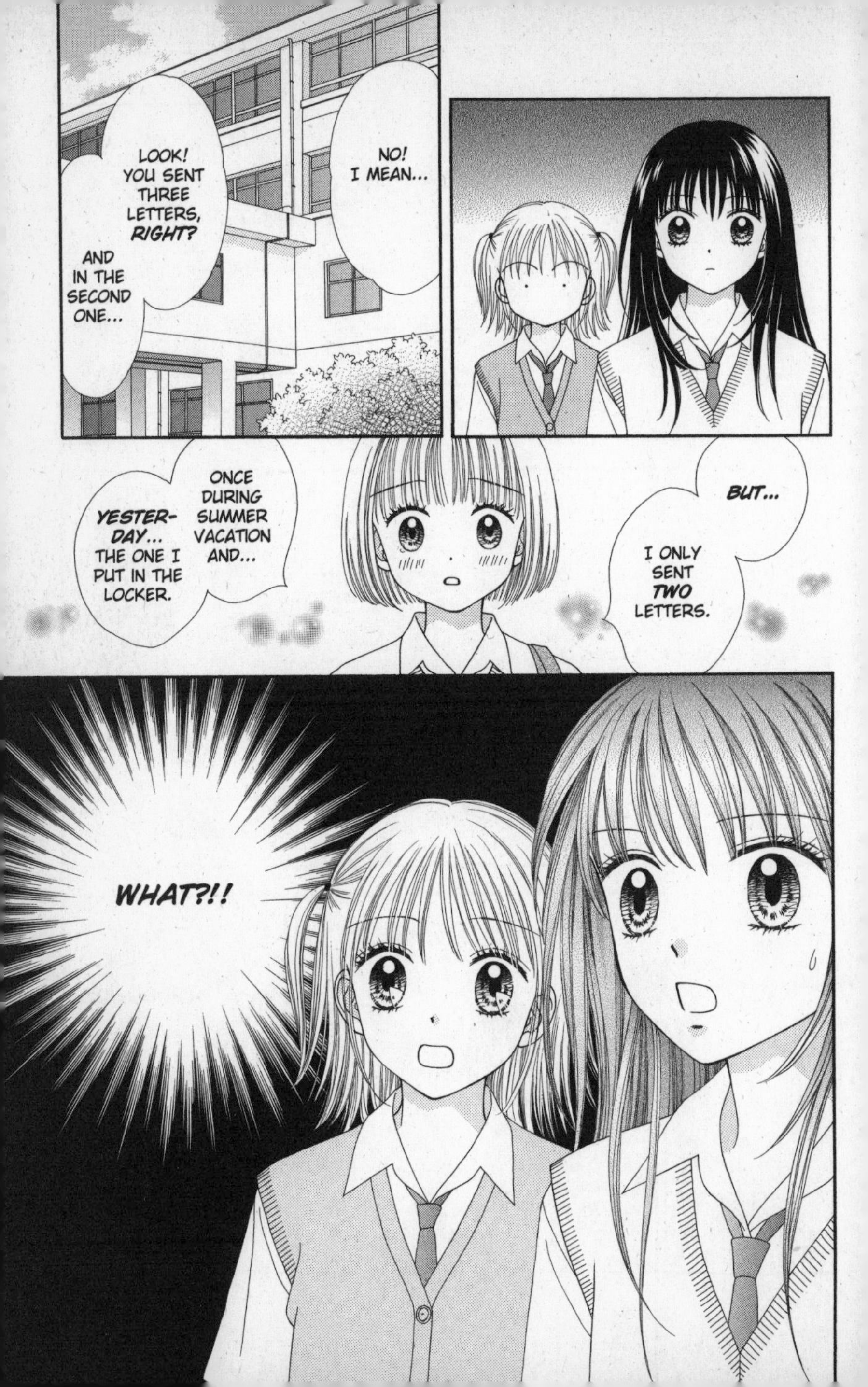
NO! I MEAN...
LOOK! YOU SENT THREE LETTERS, *RIGHT?*
AND IN THE SECOND ONE...
BUT...
I ONLY SENT *TWO* LETTERS.
ONCE DURING SUMMER VACATION AND...
YESTER-DAY... THE ONE I PUT IN THE LOCKER.
WHAT?!!

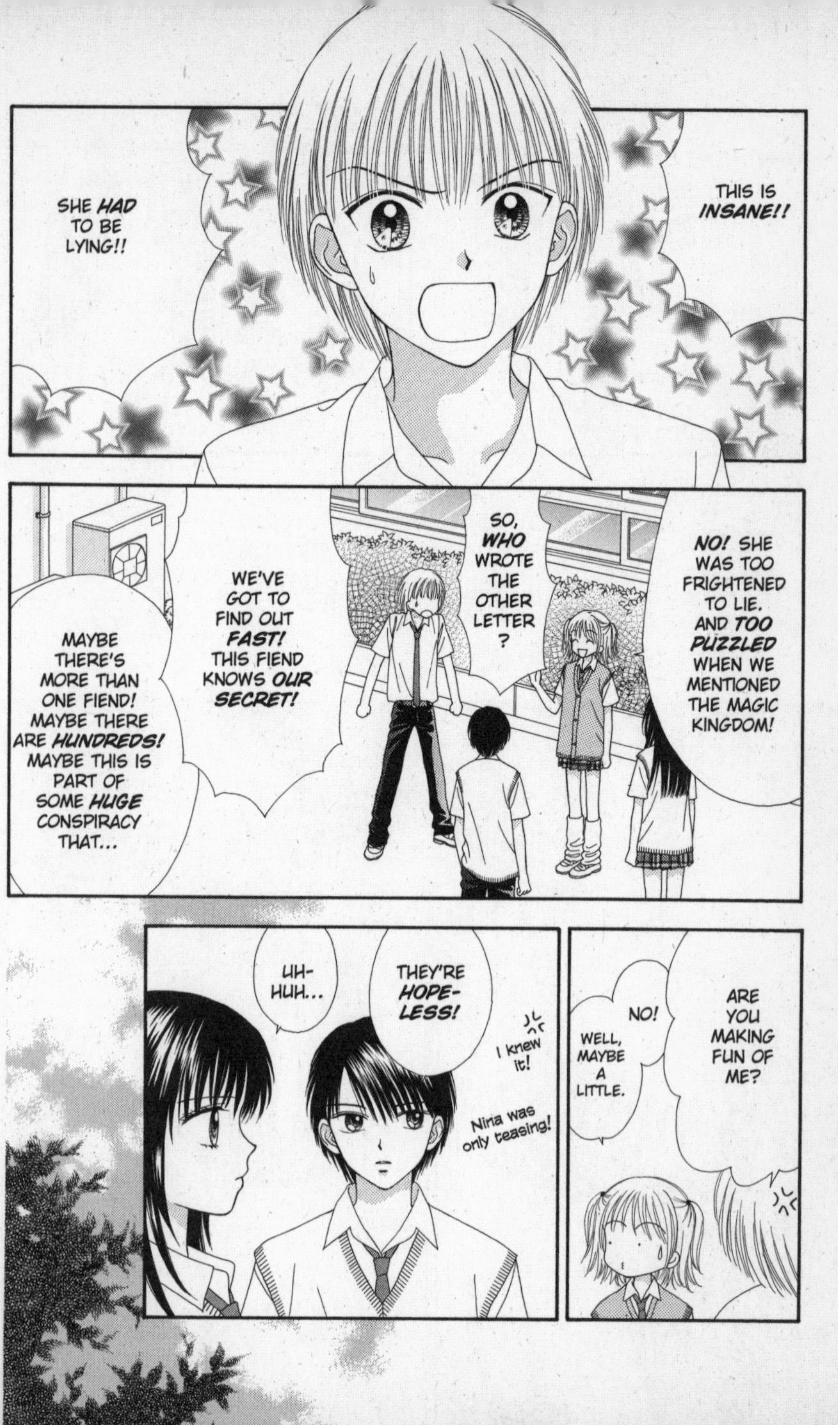
THIS IS INSANE!!
SHE HAD TO BE LYING!!
NO! SHE WAS TOO FRIGHTENED TO LIE. AND TOO PUZZLED WHEN WE MENTIONED THE MAGIC KINGDOM!
SO, WHO WROTE THE OTHER LETTER?
WE'VE GOT TO FIND OUT FAST! THIS FIEND KNOWS OUR SECRET!
MAYBE THERE'S MORE THAN ONE FIEND! MAYBE THERE ARE HUNDREDS! MAYBE THIS IS PART OF SOME HUGE CONSPIRACY THAT...
ARE YOU MAKING FUN OF ME?
NO!
WELL, MAYBE A LITTLE.
THEY'RE HOPELESS!
UH-HUH...
I knew it!
Nina was only teasing!

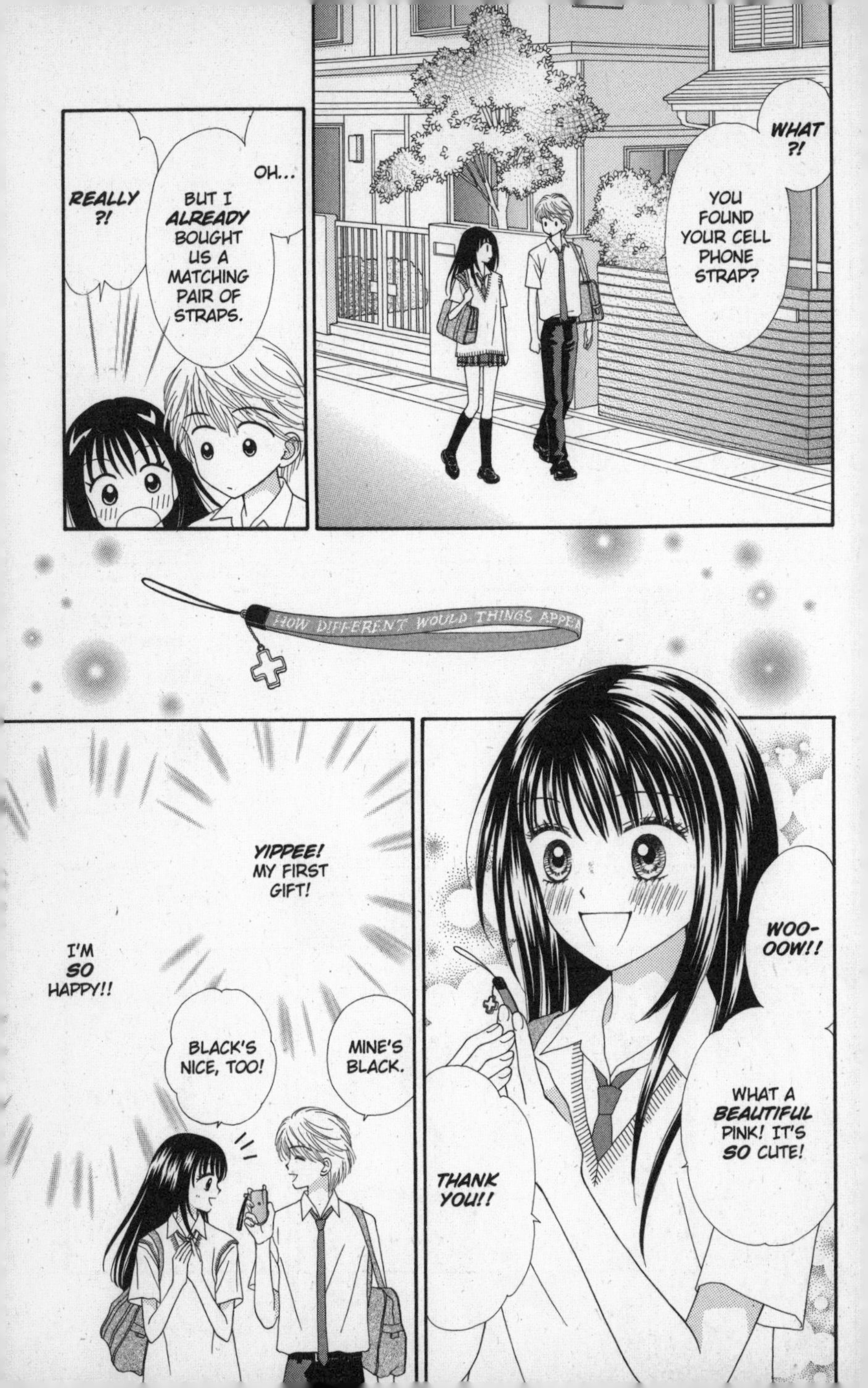
WHAT ?!
YOU FOUND YOUR CELL PHONE STRAP?
OH...
BUT I ALREADY BOUGHT US A MATCHING PAIR OF STRAPS.
REALLY ?!
HOW DIFFERENT WOULD THINGS APPEA
WOO-OOW!!
WHAT A BEAUTIFUL PINK! IT'S SO CUTE!
THANK YOU!!
YIPPEE! MY FIRST GIFT!
I'M SO HAPPY!!
MINE'S BLACK.
BLACK'S NICE, TOO!

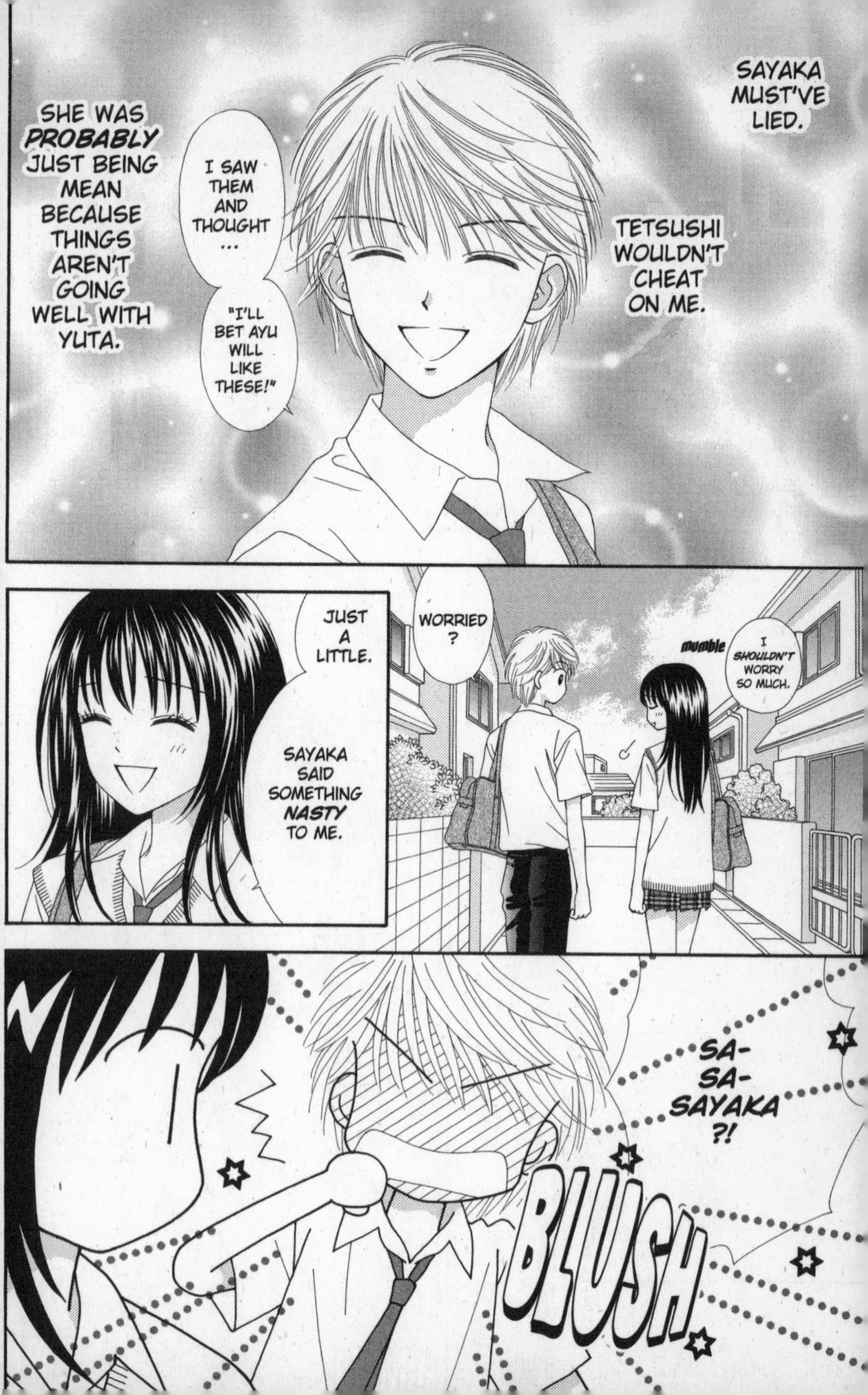
SAYAKA MUST'VE LIED.
TETSUSHI WOULDN'T CHEAT ON ME.
I SAW THEM AND THOUGHT...
"I'LL BET AYU WILL LIKE THESE!"
SHE WAS PROBABLY JUST BEING MEAN BECAUSE THINGS AREN'T GOING WELL WITH YUTA.
mumble
I SHOULDN'T WORRY SO MUCH.
WORRIED?
JUST A LITTLE.
SAYAKA SAID SOMETHING NASTY TO ME.
SA-SA-SAYAKA?!
BLUSH

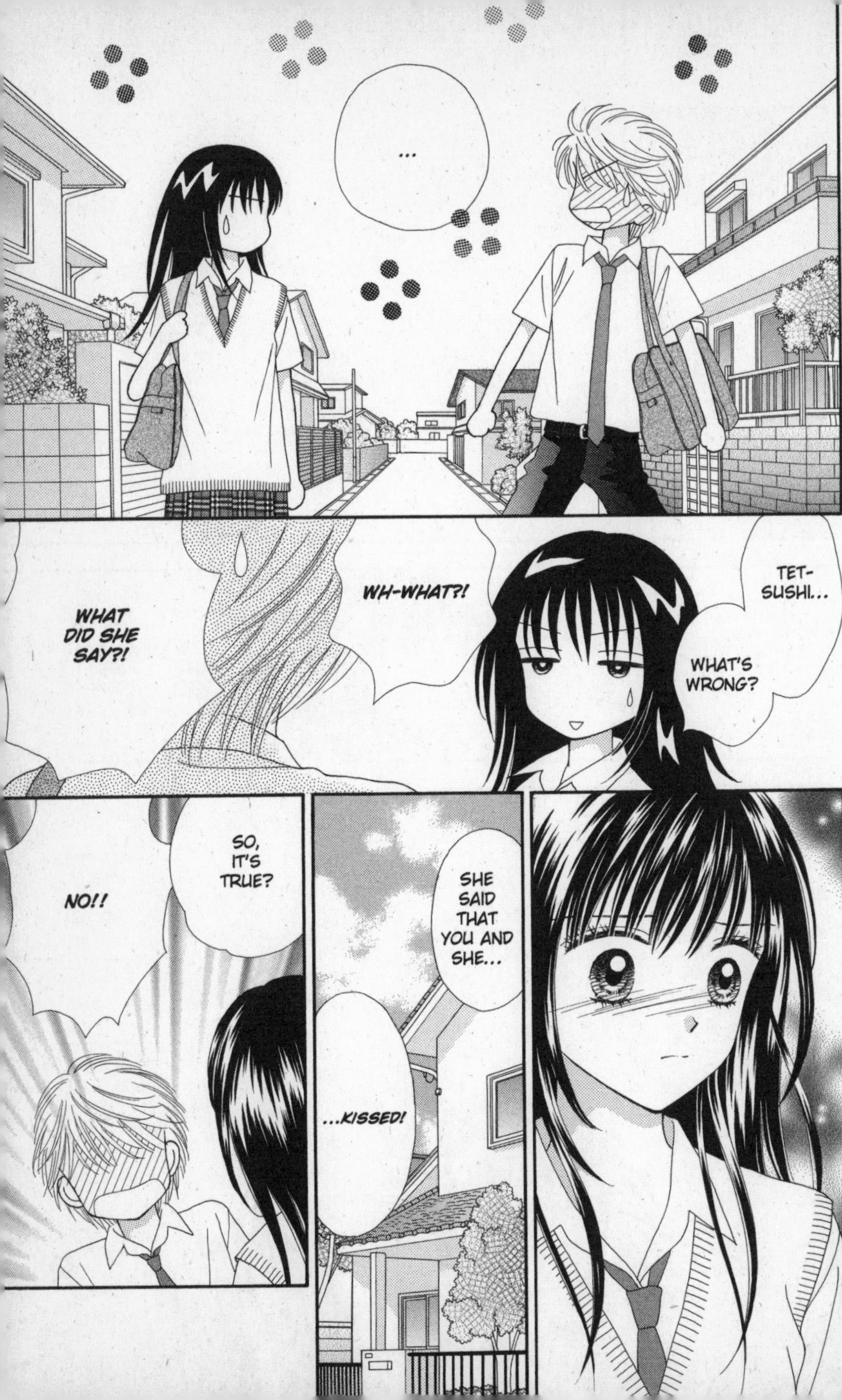
...
TET-SUSHI...
WHAT'S WRONG?
WH-WHAT?!
WHAT DID SHE SAY?!
SHE SAID THAT YOU AND SHE...
...KISSED!
SO, IT'S TRUE?
NO!!

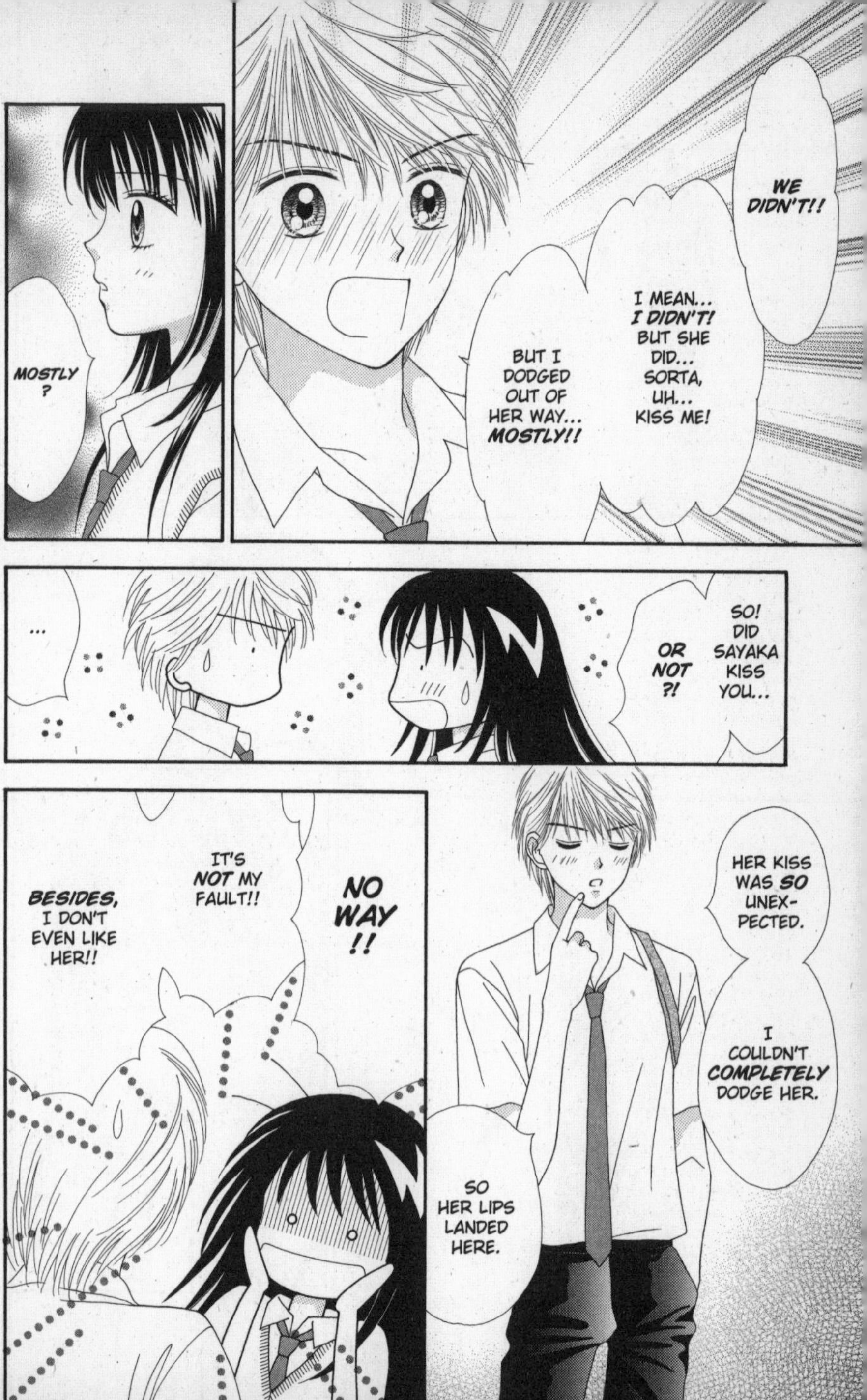
WE DIDN'T!!
I MEAN... I DIDN'T! BUT SHE DID... SORTA, UH... KISS ME!
BUT I DODGED OUT OF HER WAY... MOSTLY!!
MOSTLY?
SO! DID SAYAKA KISS YOU...
OR NOT?!
...
HER KISS WAS SO UNEXPECTED.
I COULDN'T COMPLETELY DODGE HER.
SO HER LIPS LANDED HERE.
NO WAY!!
IT'S NOT MY FAULT!!
BESIDES, I DON'T EVEN LIKE HER!!

FREE TALK 4

Near the end of September, I went to watch the "afureco" taping of Episode 23 from the *Ultra Maniac* anime.

("Afureco" is an audio version of an anime that's sometimes created to promote a series. The producers often place parts of an episode interspersed with music onto a CD. Or they create extra scenes that add depth to the episode.)

It was **really** interesting. It started out with a scene involving the four main characters—Ayu, Nina, Tetsushi and Hiroki having a discussion. The voice actors for Ayu, Nina and Hiroki were all taped together. And then the actor playing Tetsushi was taped separately. I asked the director why they did that. He said that the other characters were talking at a distance from Tetsushi. So, to create the impression of the distance, they recorded them separately, and then combined the voices in post-recording!

Something else that surprised me was how quickly the voice actors were able to adjust their performances when needed. The audio director would tell them what he wanted done differently and they'd **immediately** modify their acting and voices perfectly.

I'd understand if they were being given simple commands like "act more surprised" or "act like you're teasing." But they were being told things like, "Don't act like you're done talking. Make it sound as if there's something more that needs to be said."

Even with direction like that, the actors would say "Okay, I understand" and, **amazingly**, fix it in one take. There were even voice actors and actresses there who got everything right on the first take. . .so the director didn't ask them to change anything. I guess that's **even more** amazing.

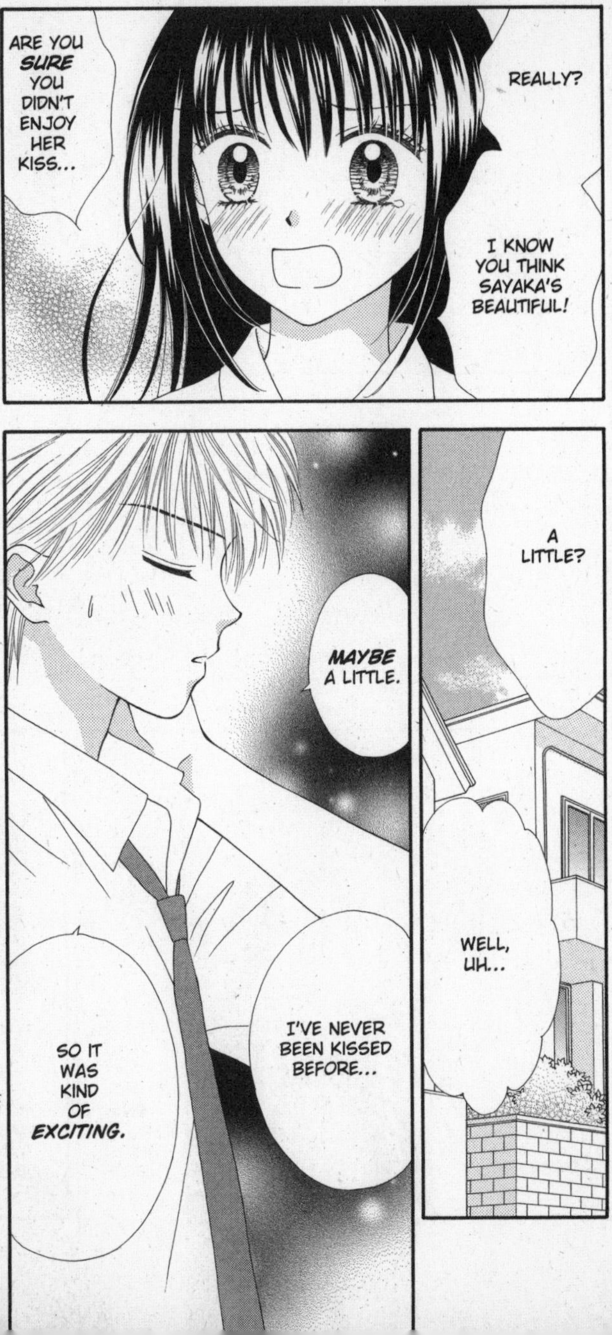
ARE YOU ***SURE*** YOU DIDN'T ENJOY HER KISS...
REALLY?
I KNOW YOU THINK SAYAKA'S BEAUTIFUL!
A LITTLE?
WELL, UH...
MAYBE A LITTLE.
I'VE NEVER BEEN KISSED BEFORE...
SO IT WAS KIND OF ***EXCITING.***

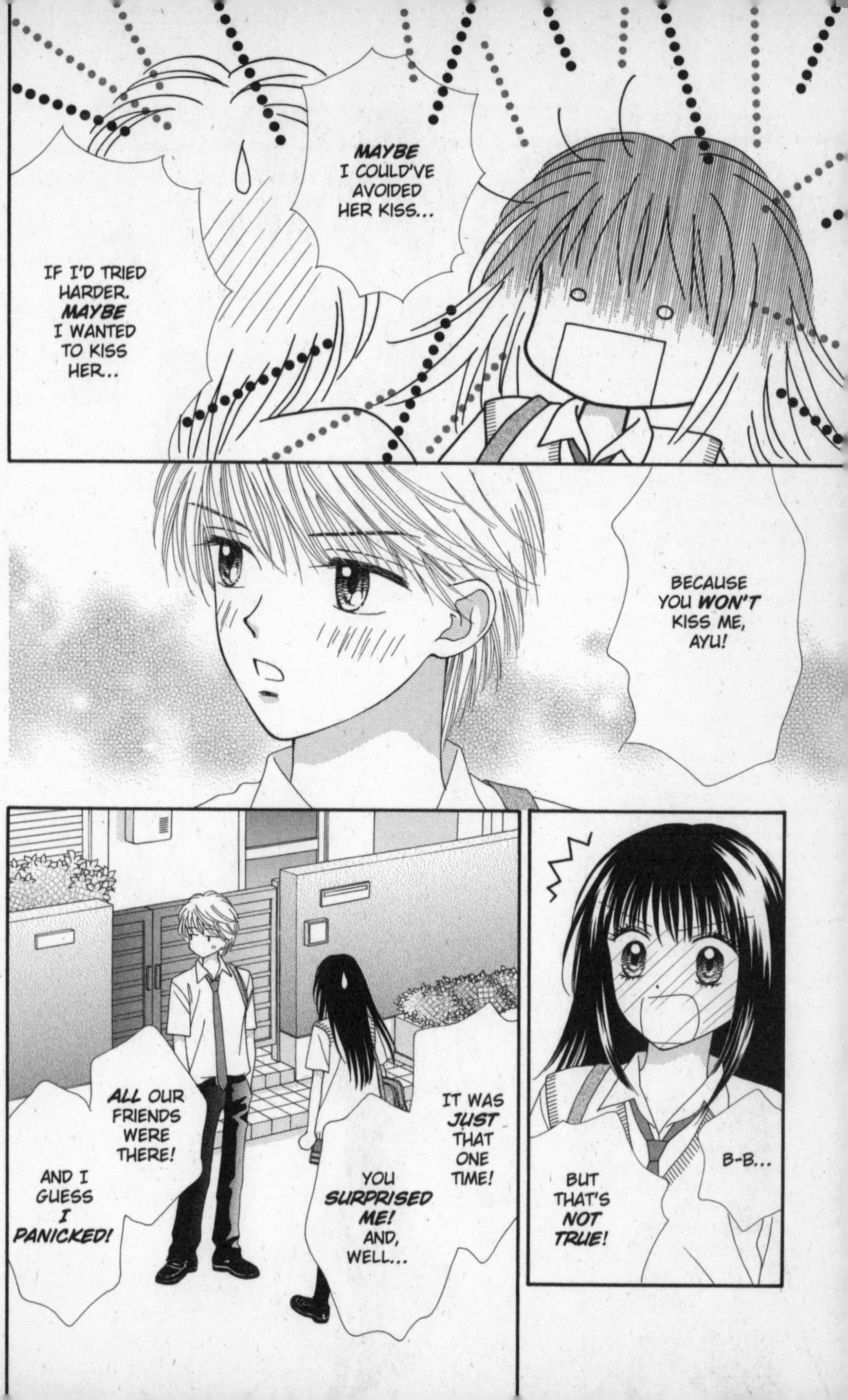
MAYBE I COULD'VE AVOIDED HER KISS...
IF I'D TRIED HARDER. MAYBE I WANTED TO KISS HER...
BECAUSE YOU WON'T KISS ME, AYU!
B-B...
BUT THAT'S NOT TRUE!
IT WAS JUST THAT ONE TIME!
YOU SURPRISED ME! AND, WELL...
ALL OUR FRIENDS WERE THERE!
AND I GUESS I PANICKED!

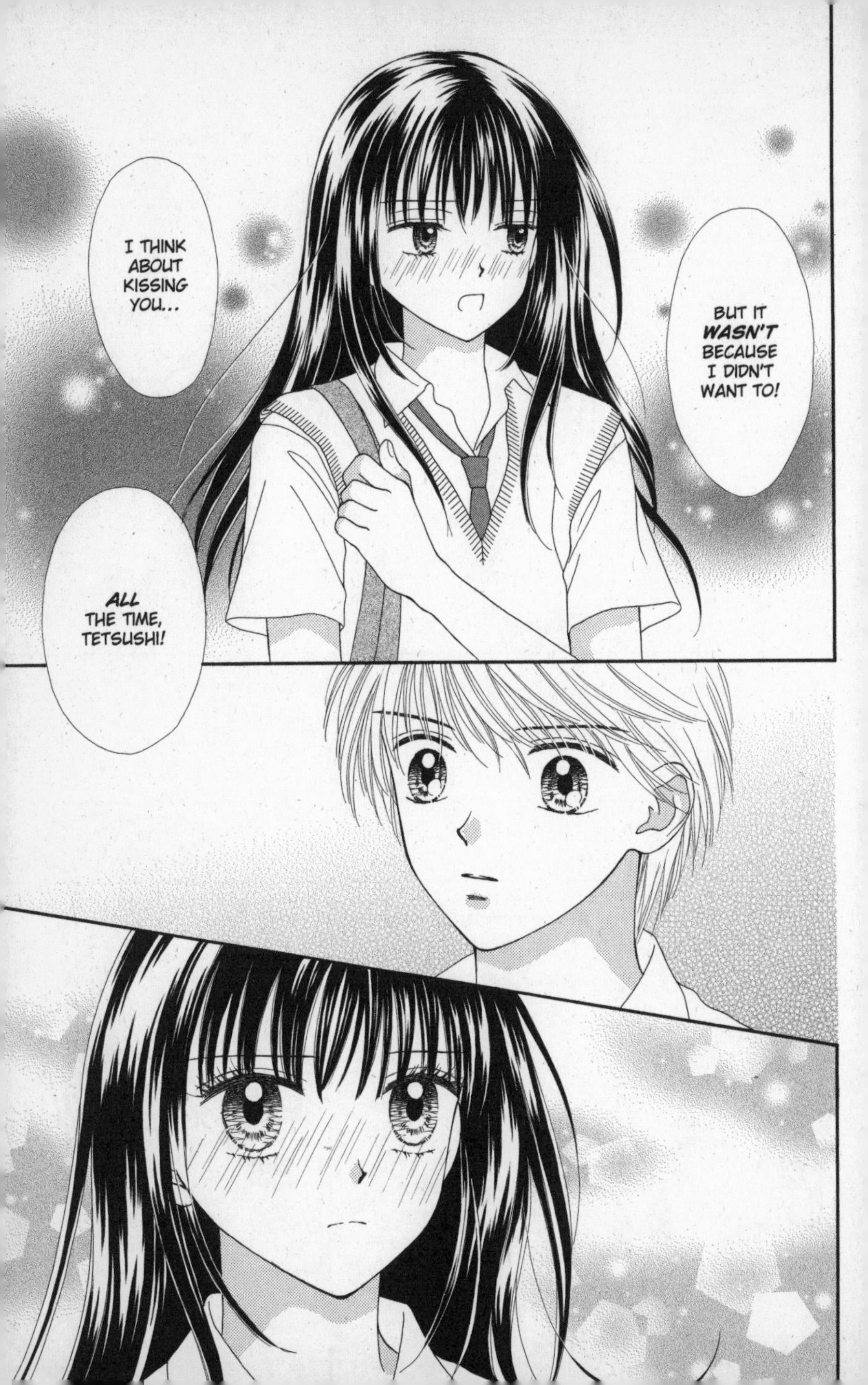
BUT IT **WASN'T** BECAUSE I DIDN'T WANT TO!
I THINK ABOUT KISSING YOU...
ALL THE TIME, TETSUSHI!

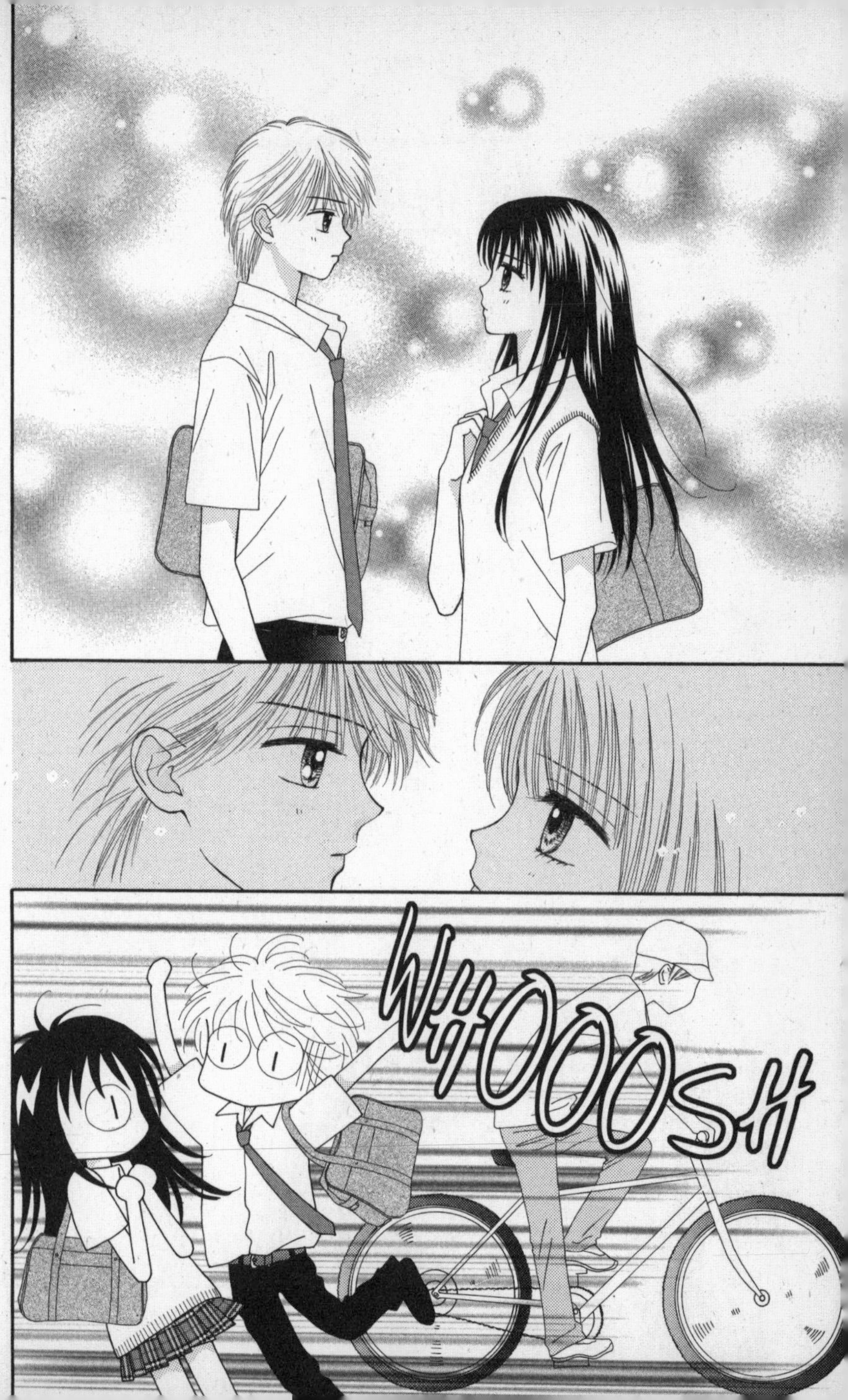
WHOOOOSH

FREE TALK 5

The thing I found most interesting about the anime version of Ultra Maniac was how surprised I was when I watched the finished results. Sometimes I'd read a script and be sure that it was going to be a great episode. But then I'd see it and be disappointed. And the opposite happened, too! Sometimes I'd read a script that didn't seem so good, but the finished anime turned out to be great!

I didn't have this sort of experience with the anime of Marmalade Boy. The difference between the quality of the script and the completed episode didn't vary that much—even though each episode is influenced by the personality and style of the different directors.

The first part of Ultra Maniac was basically a comedy. So my reaction to the anime probably depended on whether the director's humor and timing synched with what I liked.

Anime is different from manga in that you can't "read" it at your own pace. But in manga an artist can "speed up" a story or slow it down by the size and number of the panels as well as the amount of dialog used. So I guess "direction" is pretty important for manga too.

There's a scene in Episode 21 of the anime during which Ayu and Tetsushi finally get together. In the scene, it's fall and the sun is setting. The main theme song is playing. And the performances of the voice actors are outstanding. I thought this was a lot better than the manga. It was a beautiful piece of direction.

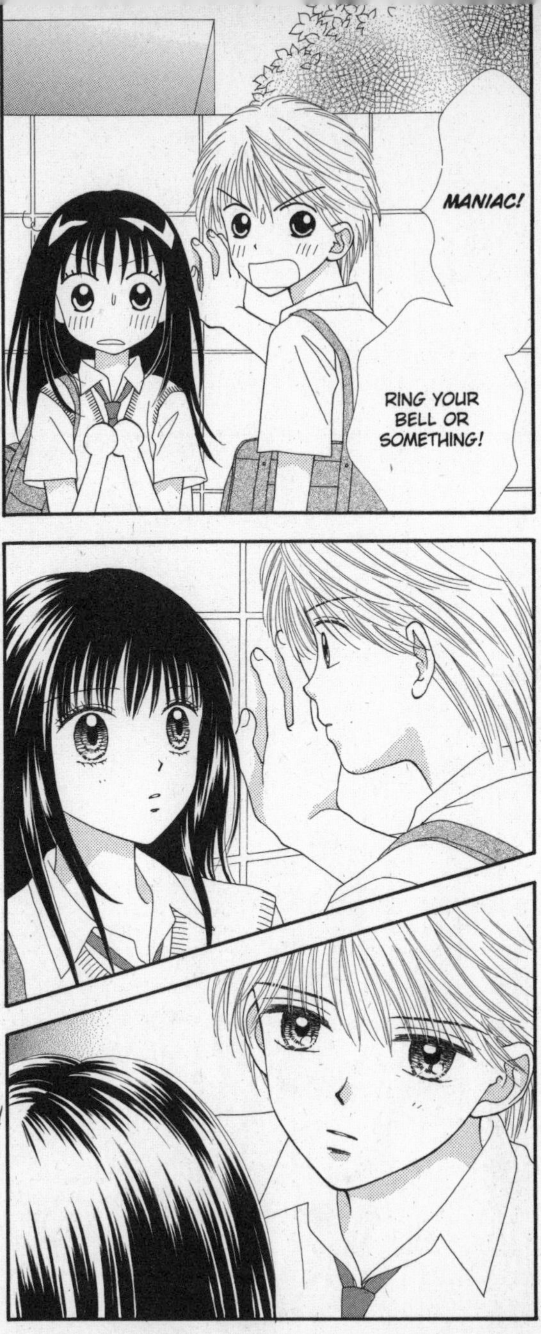
MANIAC!
RING YOUR BELL OR SOMETHING!

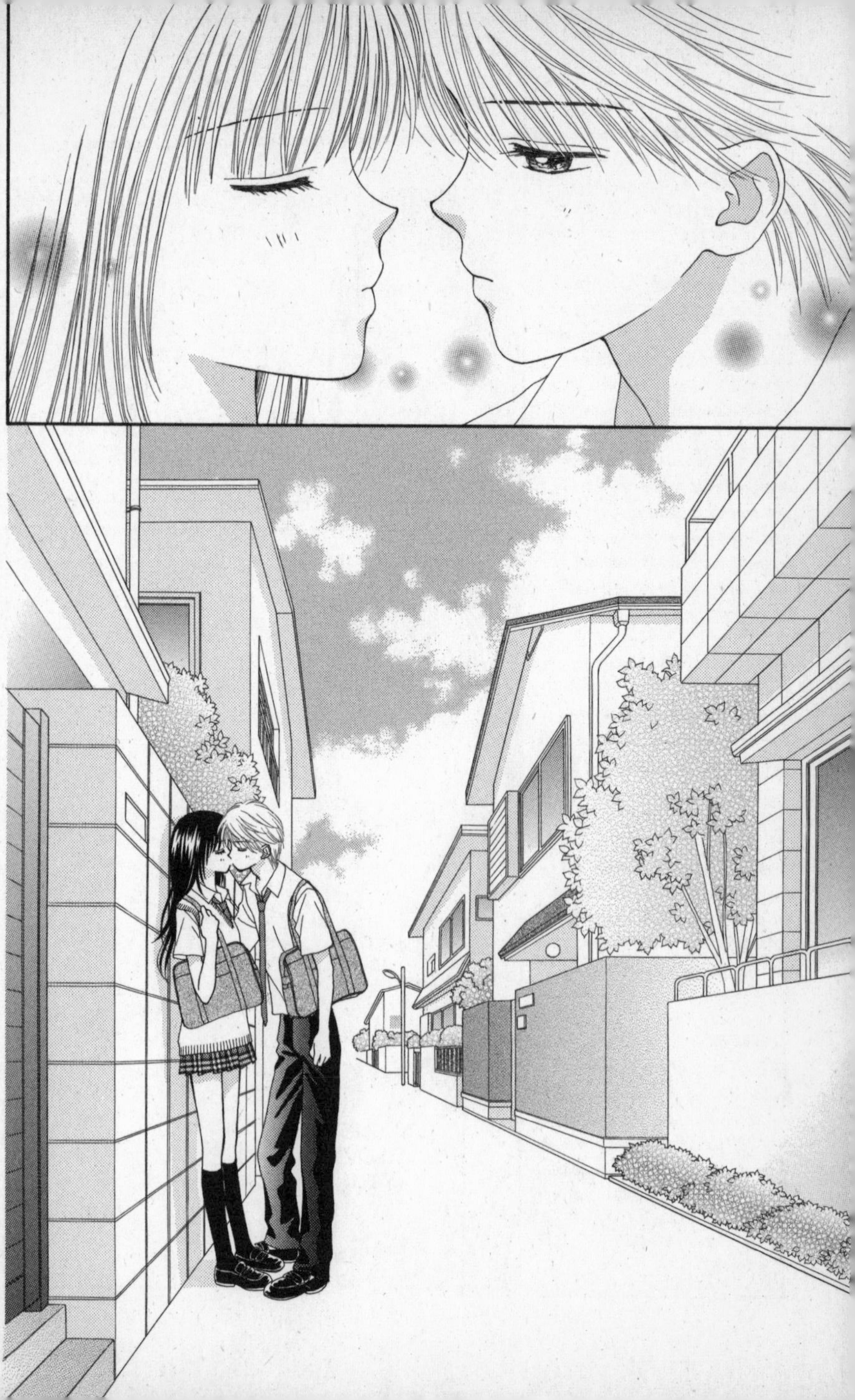

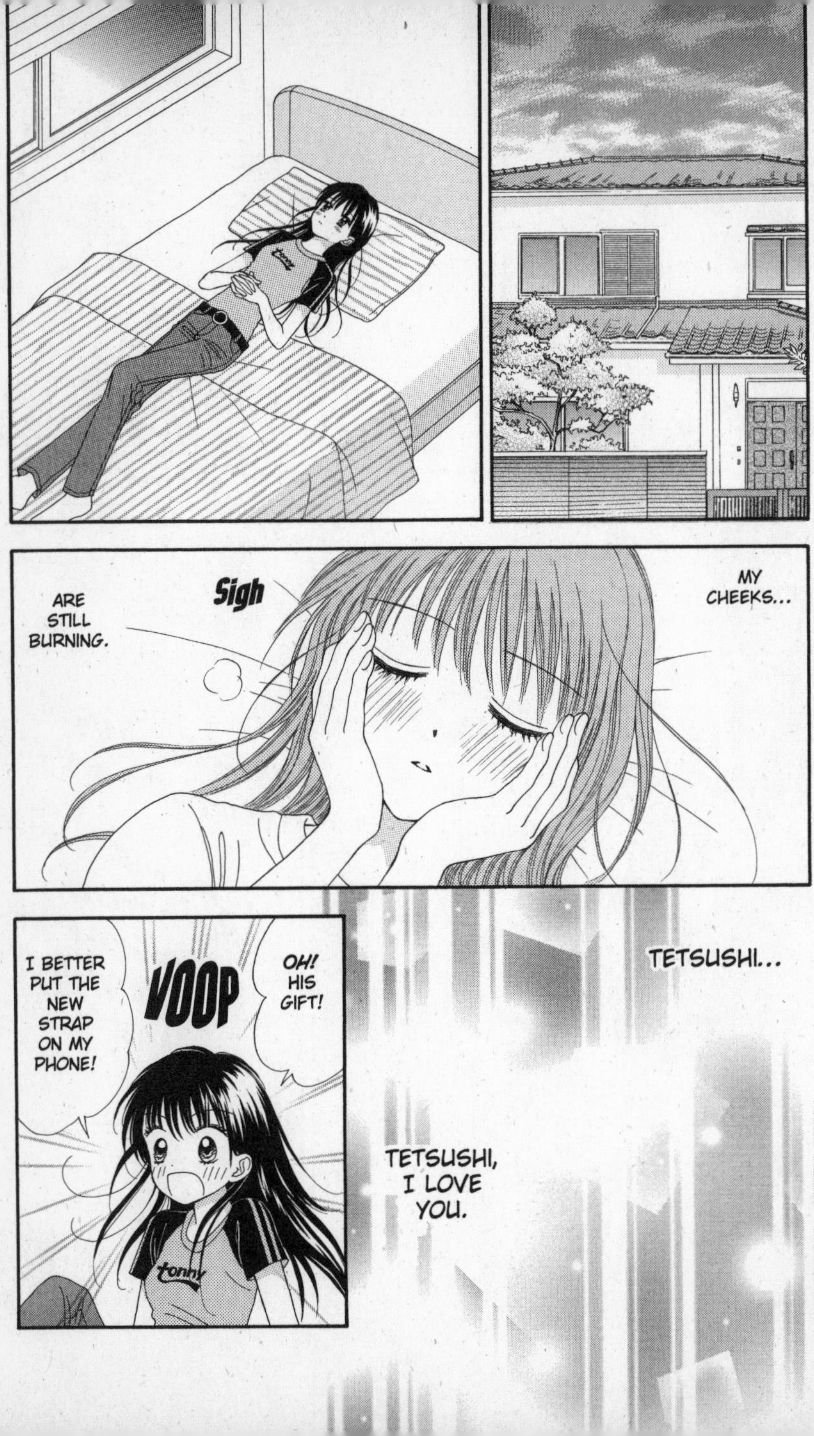
MY CHEEKS...
Sigh
ARE STILL BURNING.
TETSUSHI...
TETSUSHI, I LOVE YOU.
OH! HIS GIFT!
VOOP
I BETTER PUT THE NEW STRAP ON MY PHONE!

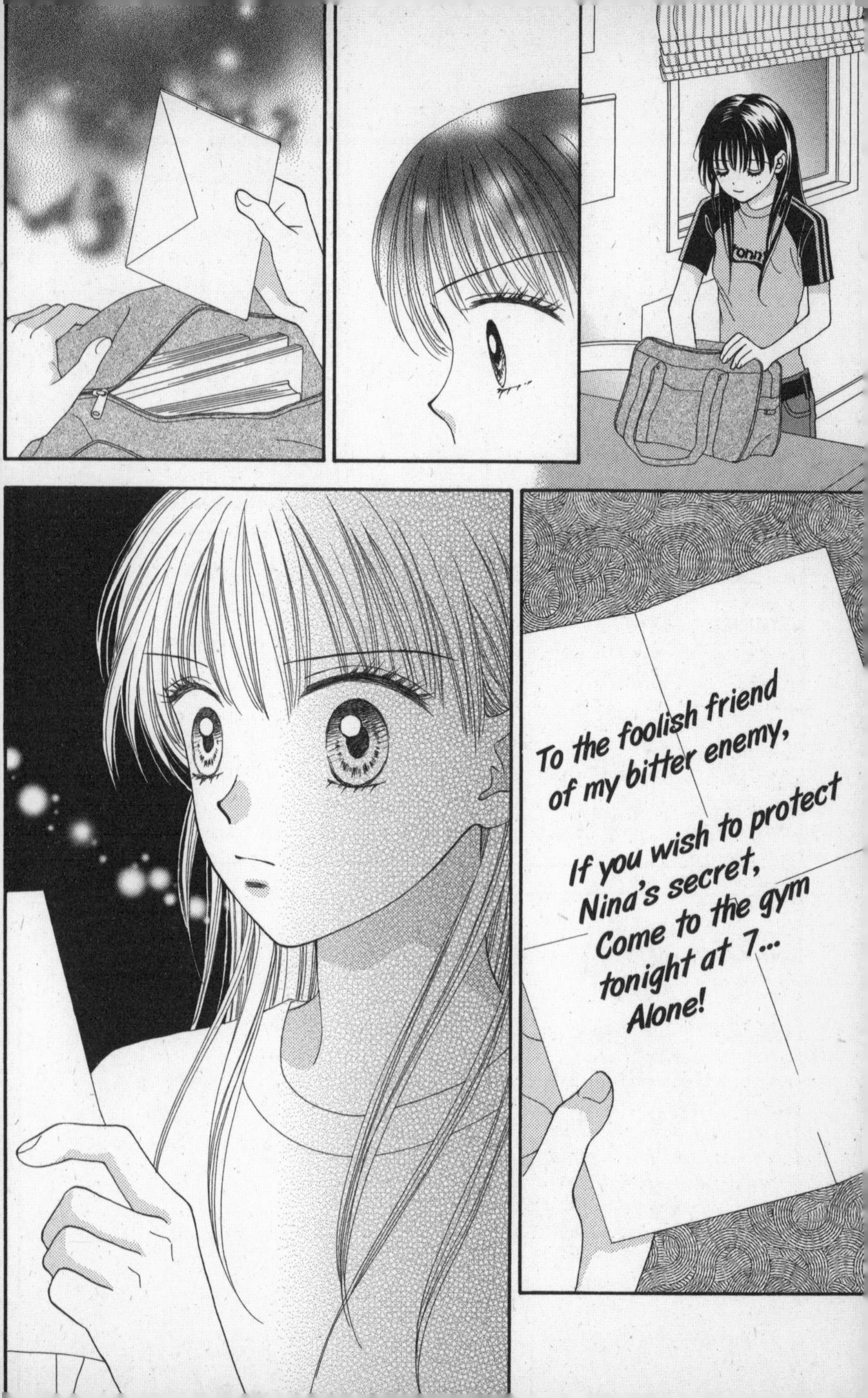
To the foolish friend of my bitter enemy,
If you wish to protect Nina's secret, Come to the gym tonight at 7... Alone!

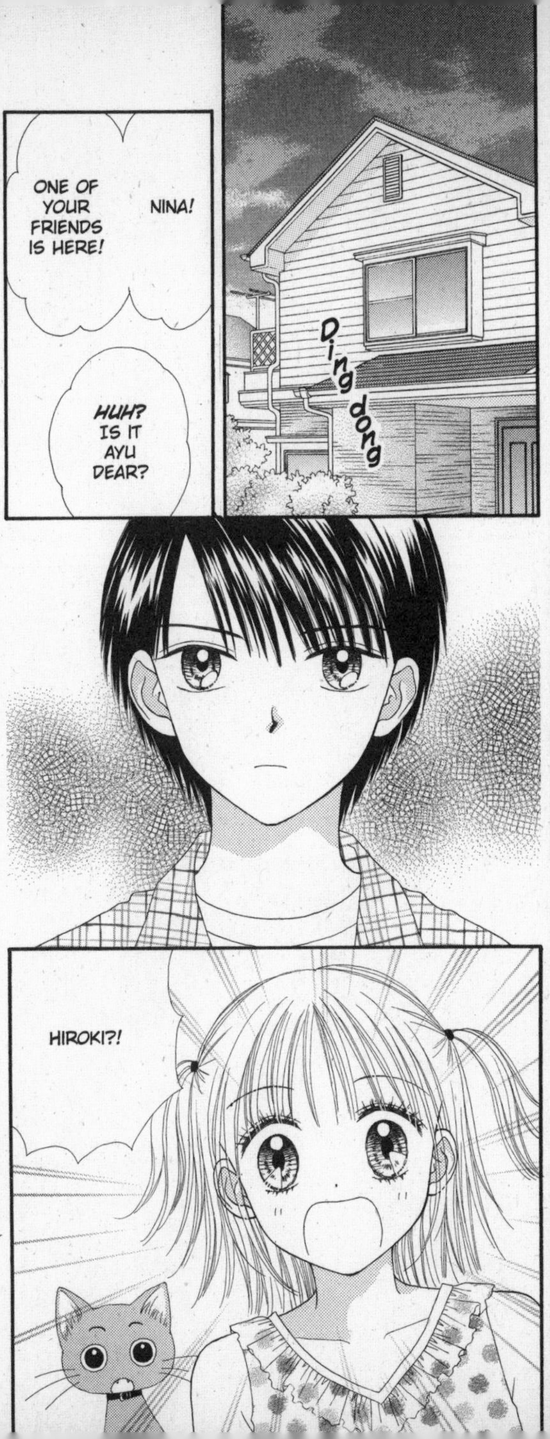
Ding dong
NINA!
ONE OF YOUR FRIENDS IS HERE!
HUH? IS IT AYU DEAR?
HIROKI?!

FREE TALK 6

In Episode 11 of the anime, an original character named "Sebastian" appears. The voice actor who plays him is Takuma Takewaka and he's a favorite of mine. When the American TV series **Dawson's Creek** was dubbed for Japan, Takuma did the voice for Dawson's friend, Pacey.

I was watching Episode 11, saying "Wow, it's really Pacey. It's Pacey's voice!" ♡

I was really enjoying myself, when lo and behold, Episodes 18 and 23 featured Tokuyoshi Kawashima who dubbed the Japanese voice of Dawson!

Mr. Kawashima's role in the anime was of a club owner with a Mohawk. So, unfortunately, he didn't have too many scenes . . .

I'm looking forward to the new episodes of **Dawson's Creek** they're going to be showing on Wowow (a cable network in Japan).

Also, the host-family mom in **Ultra Maniac** is played by Yumi Shinsui, who does a voice for V.I.P.—another American TV show that I like. So I was really happy.

By the way, in Episode 11 (where the character Sebastian shows up) there's a scene where Hiroki gets his face caught in a door and smashed. The person who smashes him is Ayu. She's trying to guard Nina's secret, but it's pretty hysterical because she does some really awful things to boys (other than Tetsushi) without any concern. I laughed out loud at this scene, but I wonder: Will Hiroki's fans be upset? (Ha ha!)

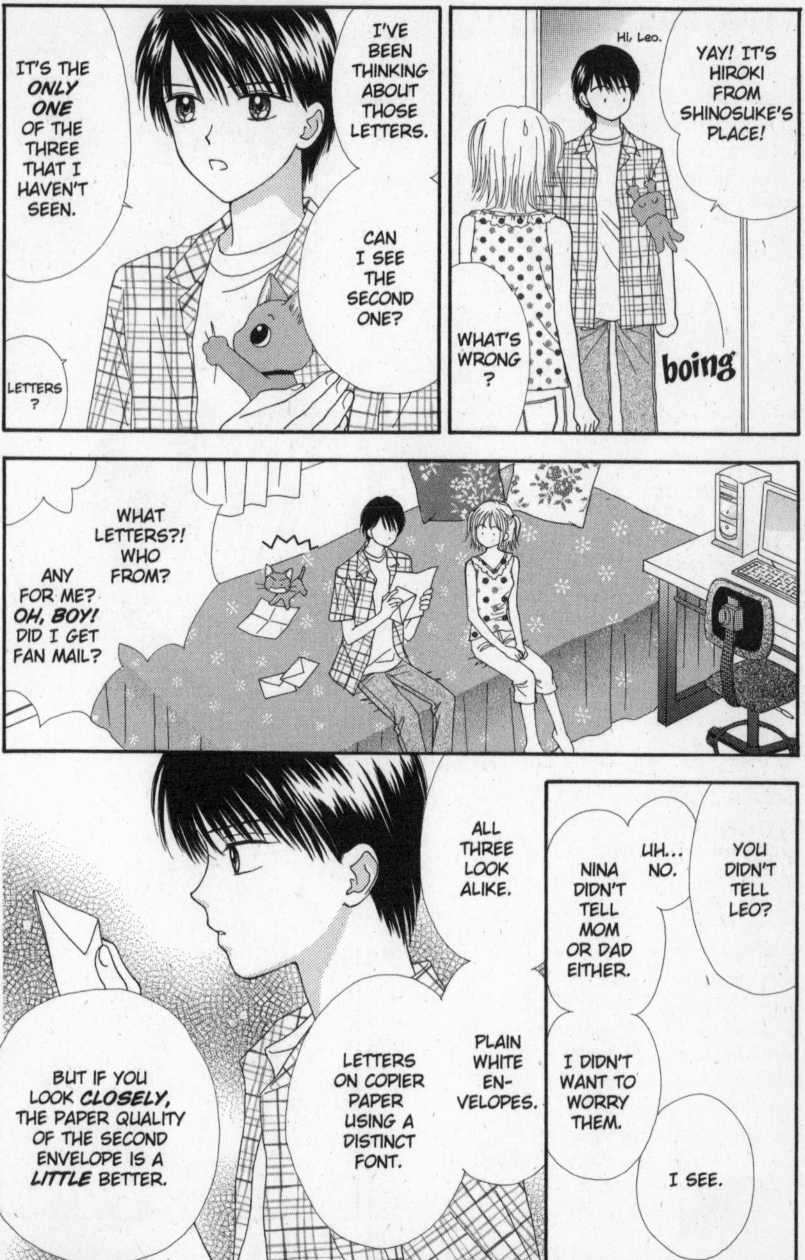
YAY! IT'S HIROKI FROM SHINOSUKE'S PLACE!
Hi, Leo.
boing
WHAT'S WRONG?
I'VE BEEN THINKING ABOUT THOSE LETTERS.
IT'S THE ONLY ONE OF THE THREE THAT I HAVEN'T SEEN.
CAN I SEE THE SECOND ONE?
LETTERS?
WHAT LETTERS?! WHO FROM?
ANY FOR ME? OH, BOY! DID I GET FAN MAIL?
YOU DIDN'T TELL LEO?
UH... NO.
NINA DIDN'T TELL MOM OR DAD EITHER.
I DIDN'T WANT TO WORRY THEM.
I SEE.
ALL THREE LOOK ALIKE.
PLAIN WHITE EN-VELOPES.
LETTERS ON COPIER PAPER USING A DISTINCT FONT.
BUT IF YOU LOOK CLOSELY, THE PAPER QUALITY OF THE SECOND ENVELOPE IS A LITTLE BETTER.

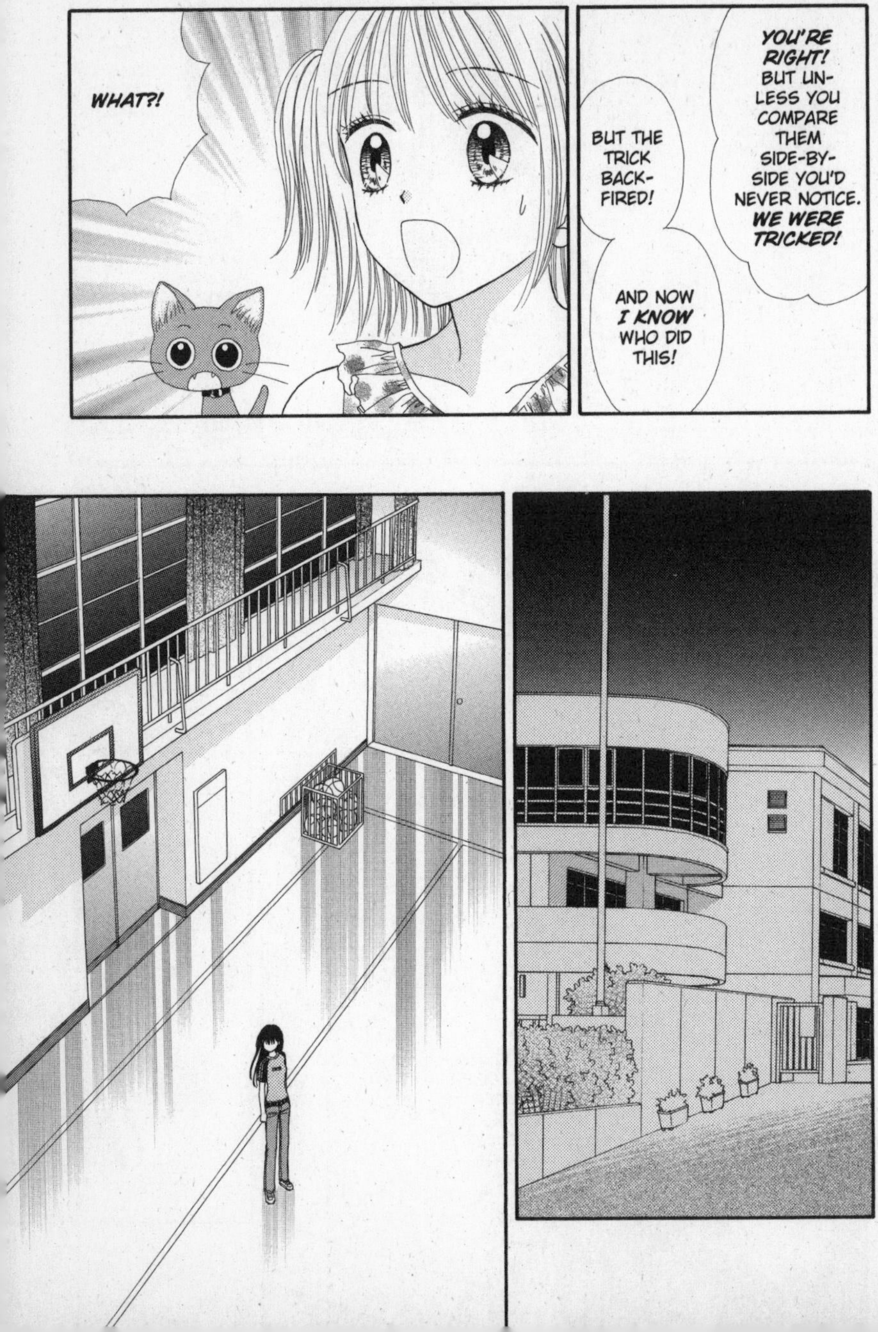
YOU'RE RIGHT! BUT UN-LESS YOU COMPARE THEM SIDE-BY-SIDE YOU'D NEVER NOTICE. WE WERE TRICKED!
BUT THE TRICK BACK-FIRED!
AND NOW I KNOW WHO DID THIS!
WHAT?!

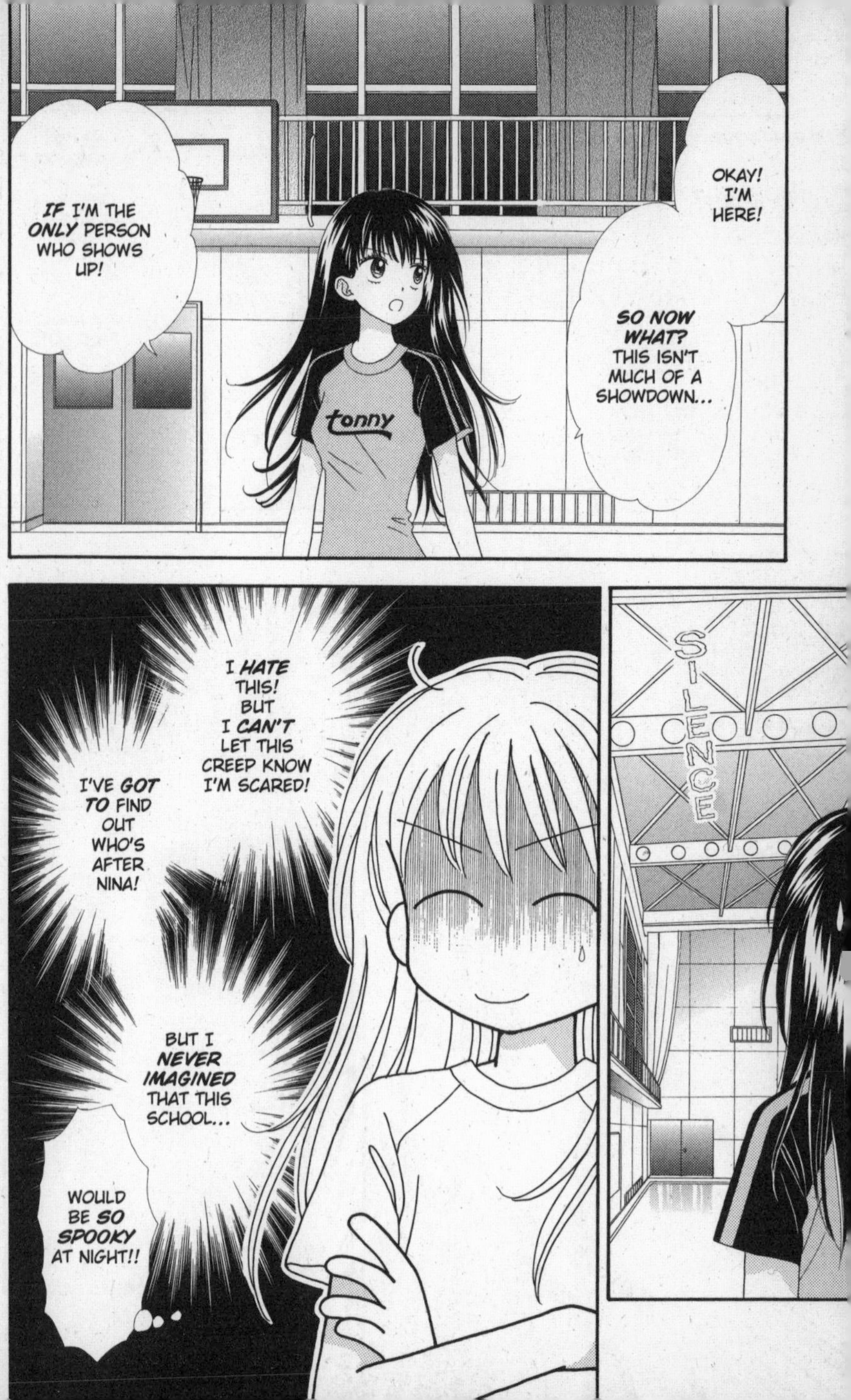
OKAY! I'M HERE!
SO NOW WHAT? THIS ISN'T MUCH OF A SHOWDOWN...
IF I'M THE ONLY PERSON WHO SHOWS UP!
tonny
SILENCE
I HATE THIS! BUT I CAN'T LET THIS CREEP KNOW I'M SCARED!
I'VE GOT TO FIND OUT WHO'S AFTER NINA!
BUT I NEVER IMAGINED THAT THIS SCHOOL...
WOULD BE SO SPOOKY AT NIGHT!!

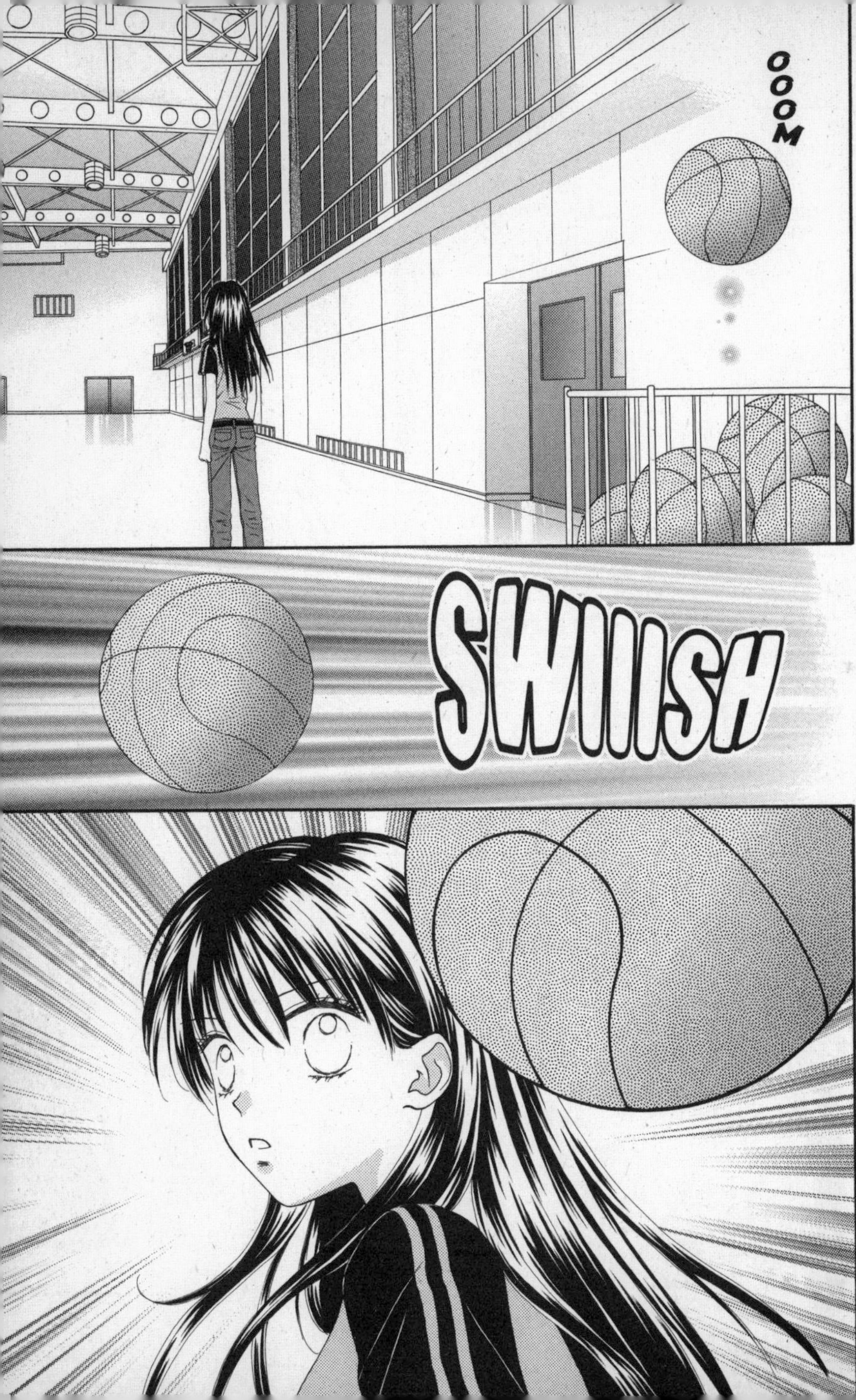
OOOM
SWIIISH

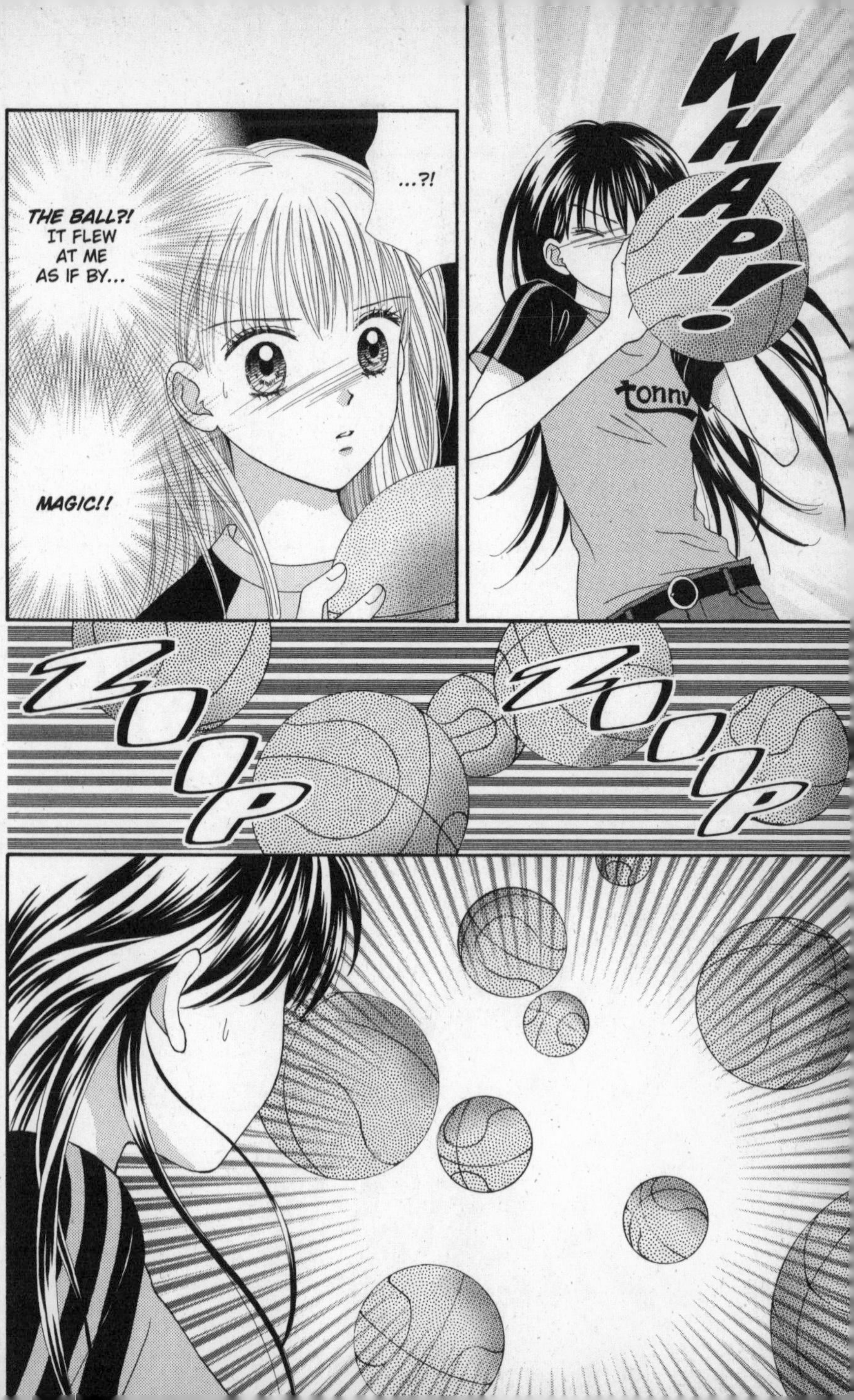
WHAP!
...?!
THE BALL?! IT FLEW AT ME AS IF BY...
MAGIC!!
ZOOOP
ZOOOP

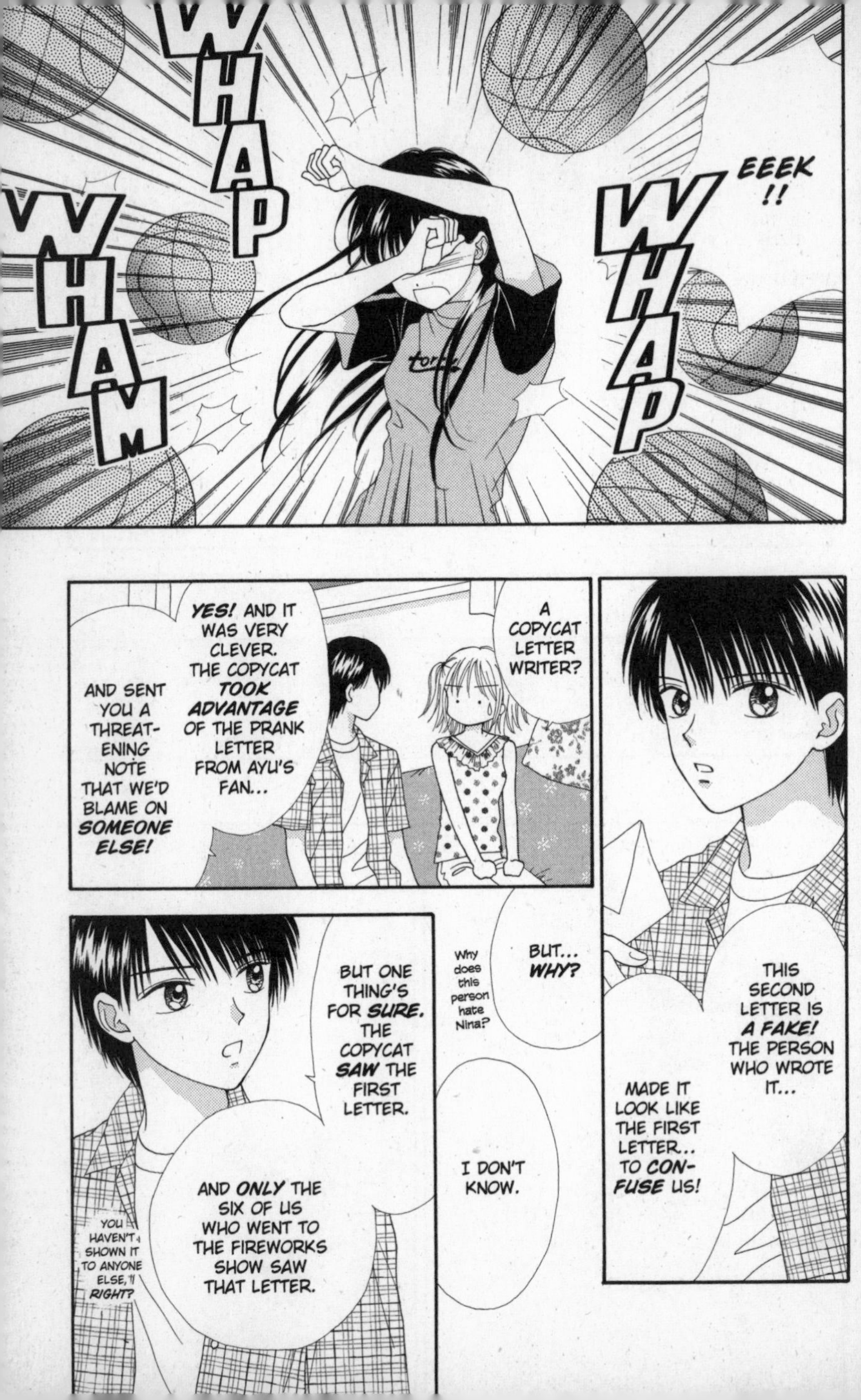
EEEK !!
WHAP
WHAP
WHAM
THIS SECOND LETTER IS A FAKE! THE PERSON WHO WROTE IT...
MADE IT LOOK LIKE THE FIRST LETTER... TO CONFUSE US!
A COPYCAT LETTER WRITER?
YES! AND IT WAS VERY CLEVER. THE COPYCAT TOOK ADVANTAGE OF THE PRANK LETTER FROM AYU'S FAN...
AND SENT YOU A THREAT-ENING NOTE THAT WE'D BLAME ON SOMEONE ELSE!
BUT... WHY?
Why does this person hate Nina?
I DON'T KNOW.
BUT ONE THING'S FOR SURE. THE COPYCAT SAW THE FIRST LETTER.
AND ONLY THE SIX OF US WHO WENT TO THE FIREWORKS SHOW SAW THAT LETTER.
YOU HAVEN'T SHOWN IT TO ANYONE ELSE, RIGHT?

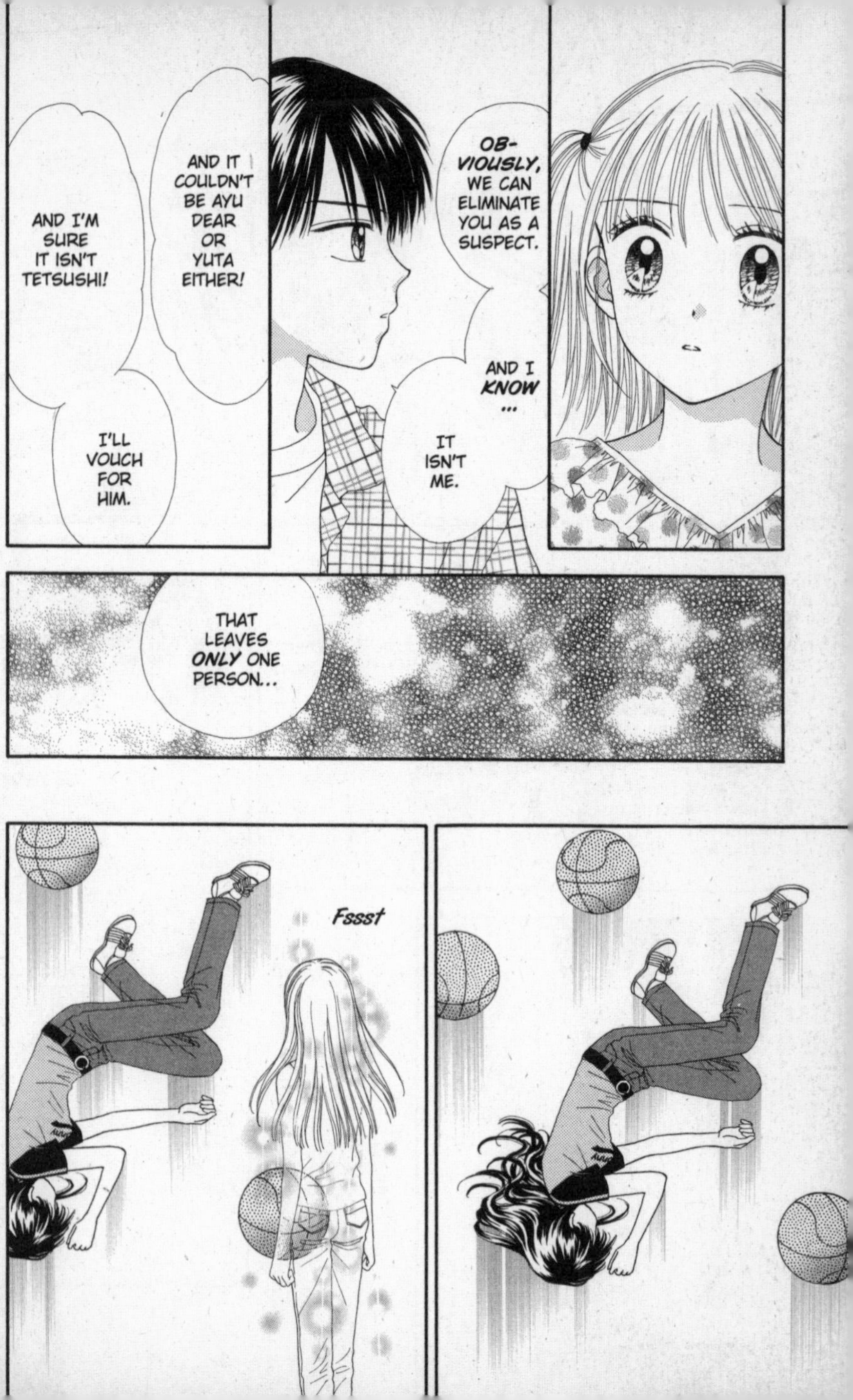
OB-VIOUSLY, WE CAN ELIMINATE YOU AS A SUSPECT.
AND I KNOW...
IT ISN'T ME.
AND IT COULDN'T BE AYU DEAR OR YUTA EITHER!
AND I'M SURE IT ISN'T TETSUSHI!
I'LL VOUCH FOR HIM.
THAT LEAVES ONLY ONE PERSON...
Fssst

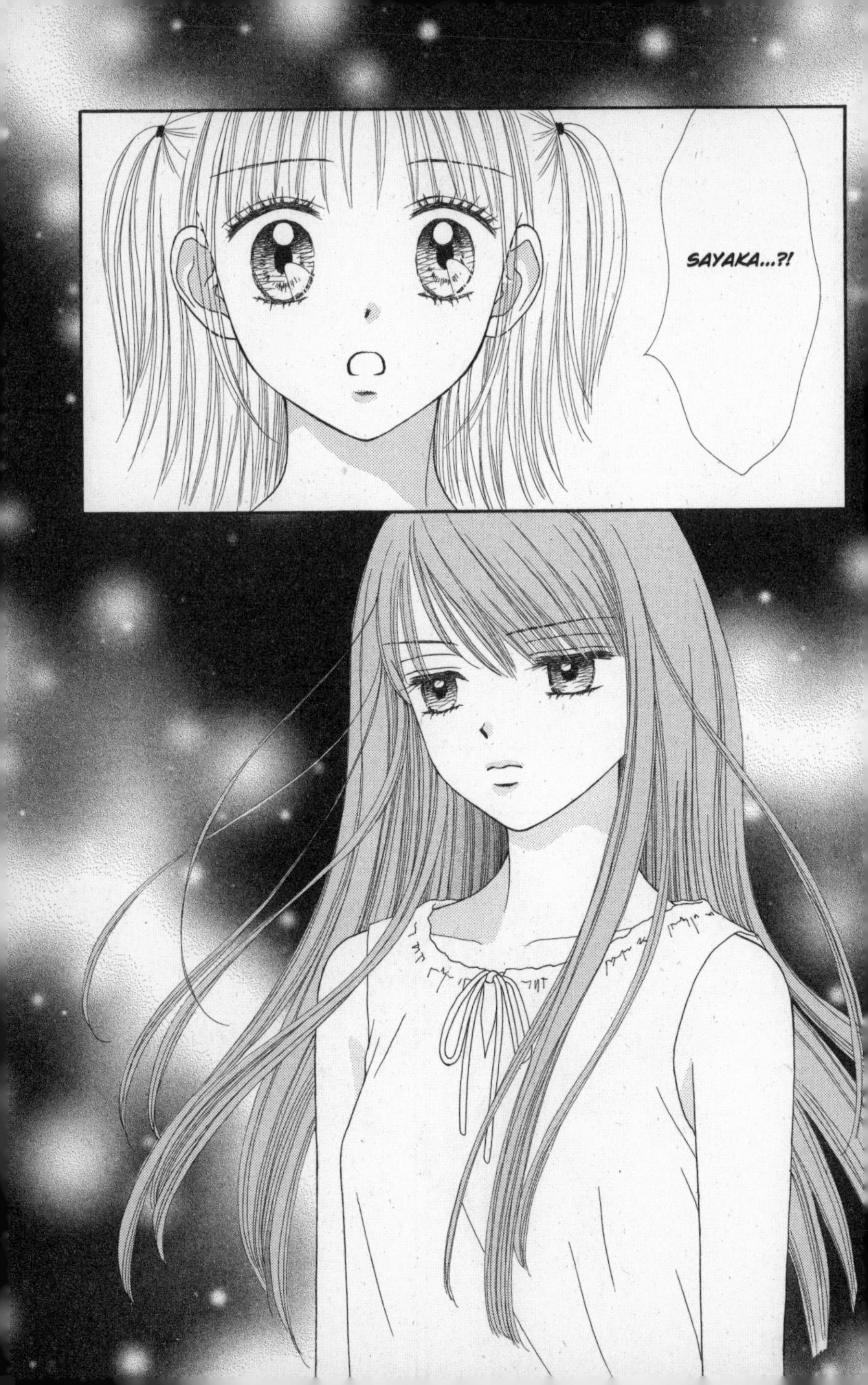
SAYAKA...?!

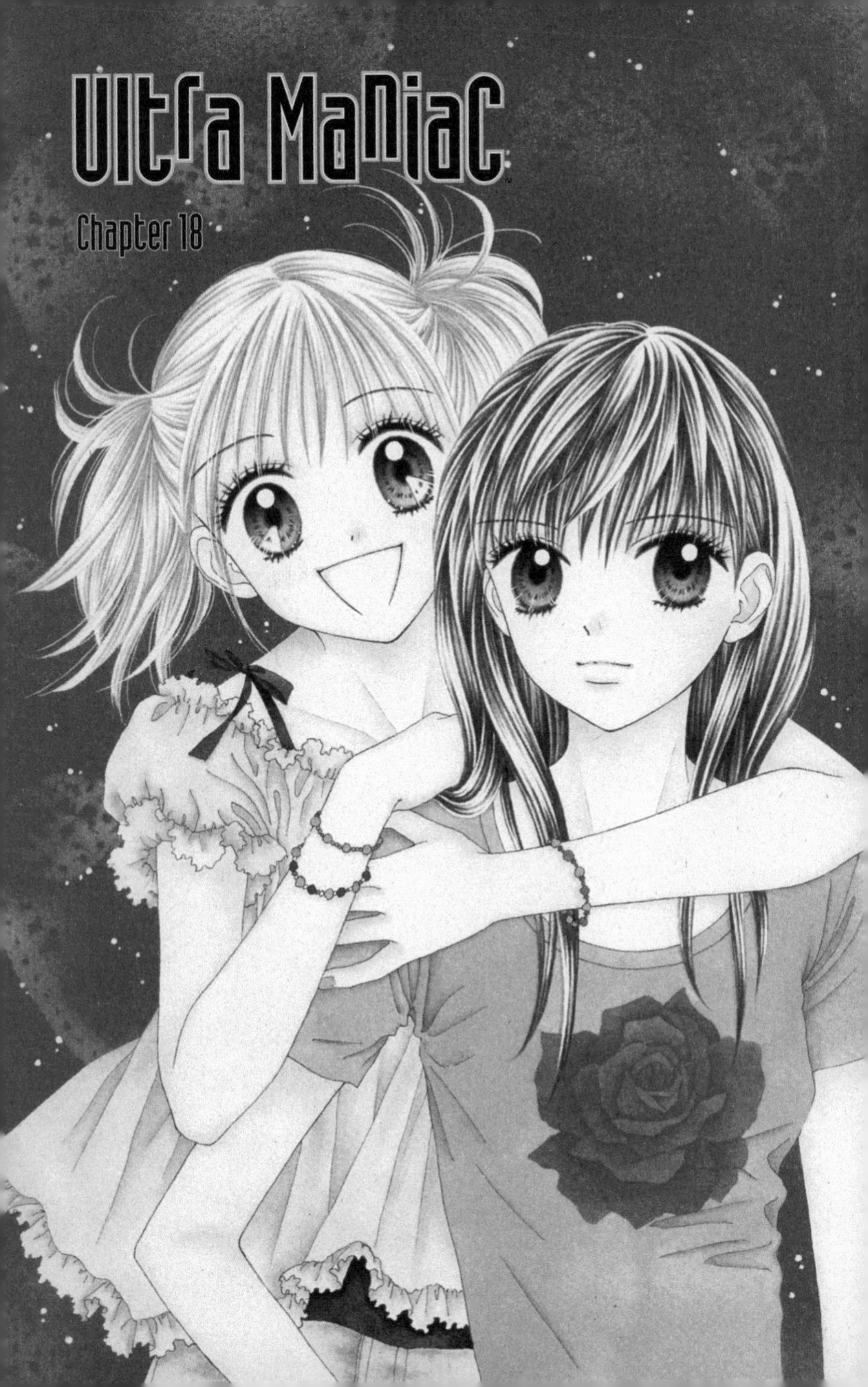
Ultra Maniac
Chapter 18

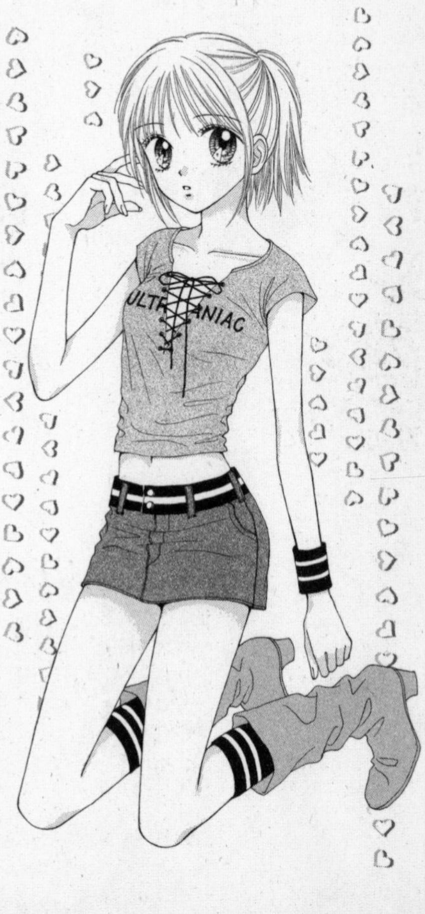
ULTR ANIAC

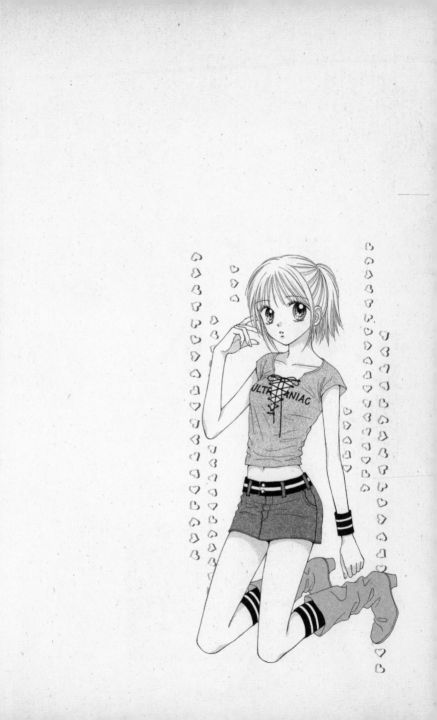

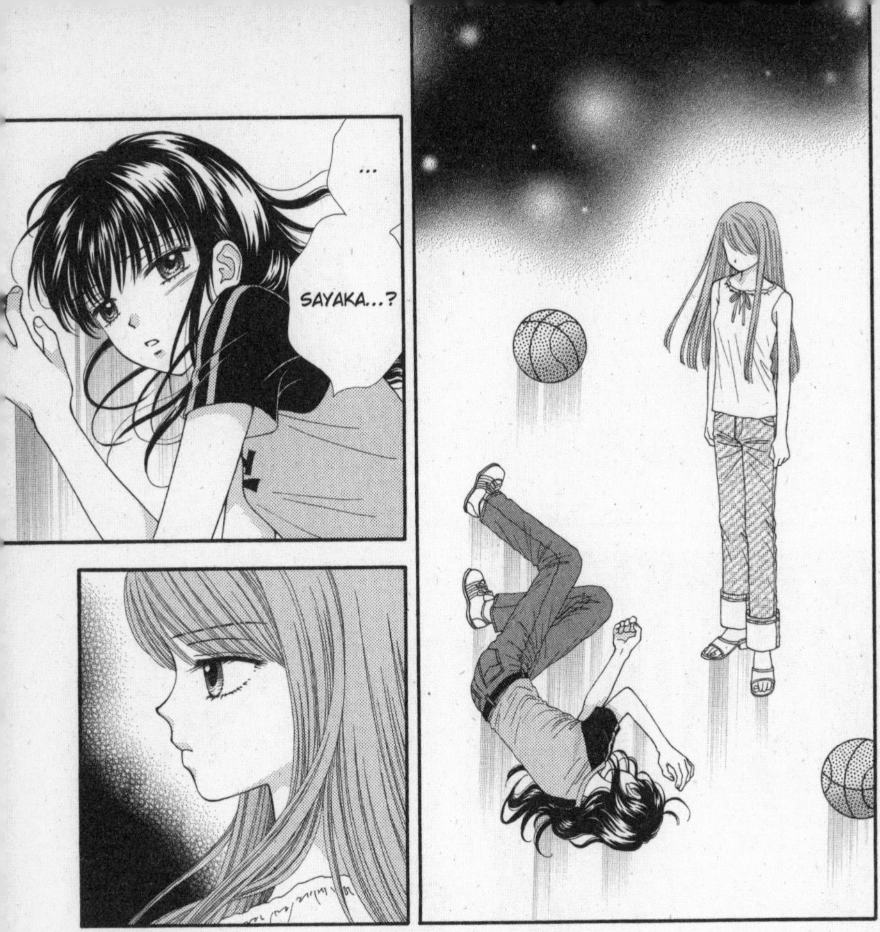
...
SAYAKA...?

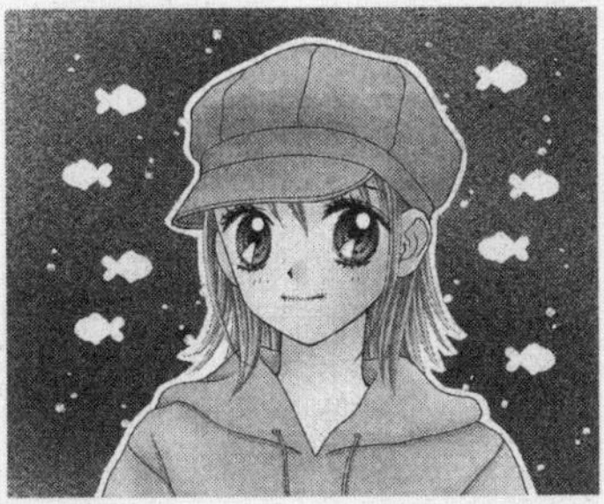

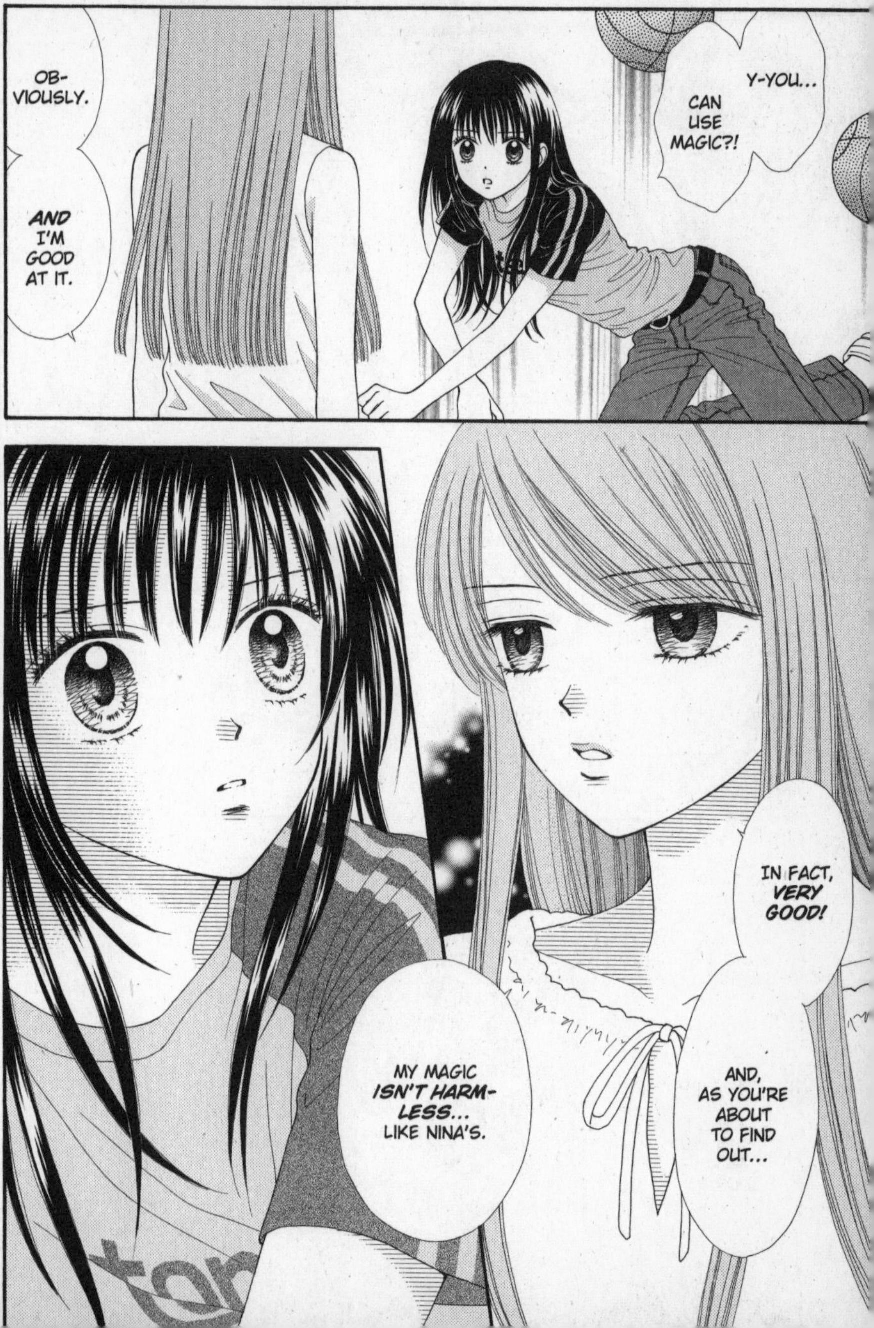
Y-YOU... CAN USE MAGIC?!
OB-VIOUSLY.
AND I'M GOOD AT IT.
IN FACT, VERY GOOD!
AND, AS YOU'RE ABOUT TO FIND OUT...
MY MAGIC ISN'T HARM-LESS... LIKE NINA'S.

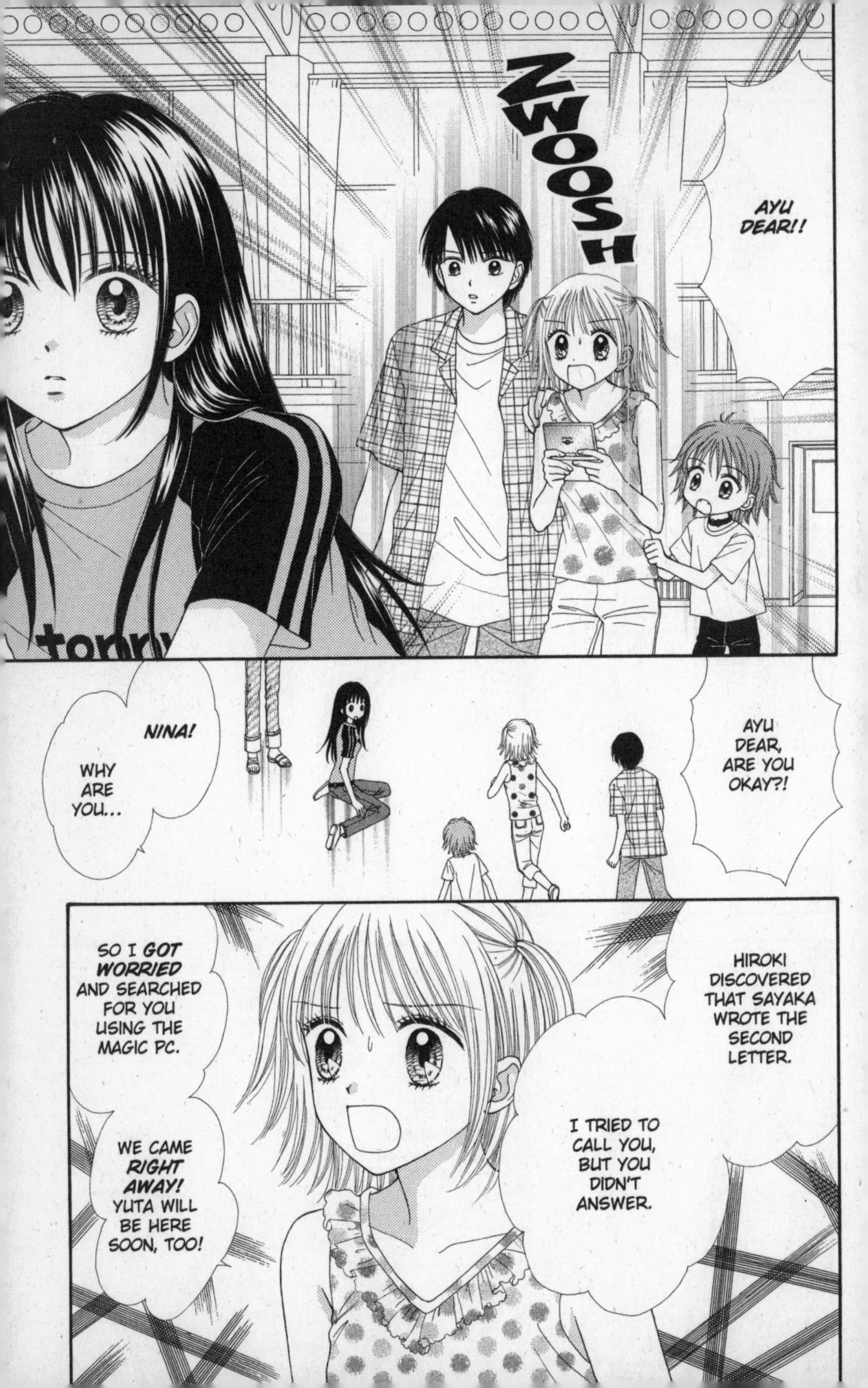
ZWOOSH
AYU DEAR!!
AYU DEAR, ARE YOU OKAY?!
NINA! WHY ARE YOU...
HIROKI DISCOVERED THAT SAYAKA WROTE THE SECOND LETTER.
I TRIED TO CALL YOU, BUT YOU DIDN'T ANSWER.
SO I GOT WORRIED AND SEARCHED FOR YOU USING THE MAGIC PC.
WE CAME RIGHT AWAY! YUTA WILL BE HERE SOON, TOO!

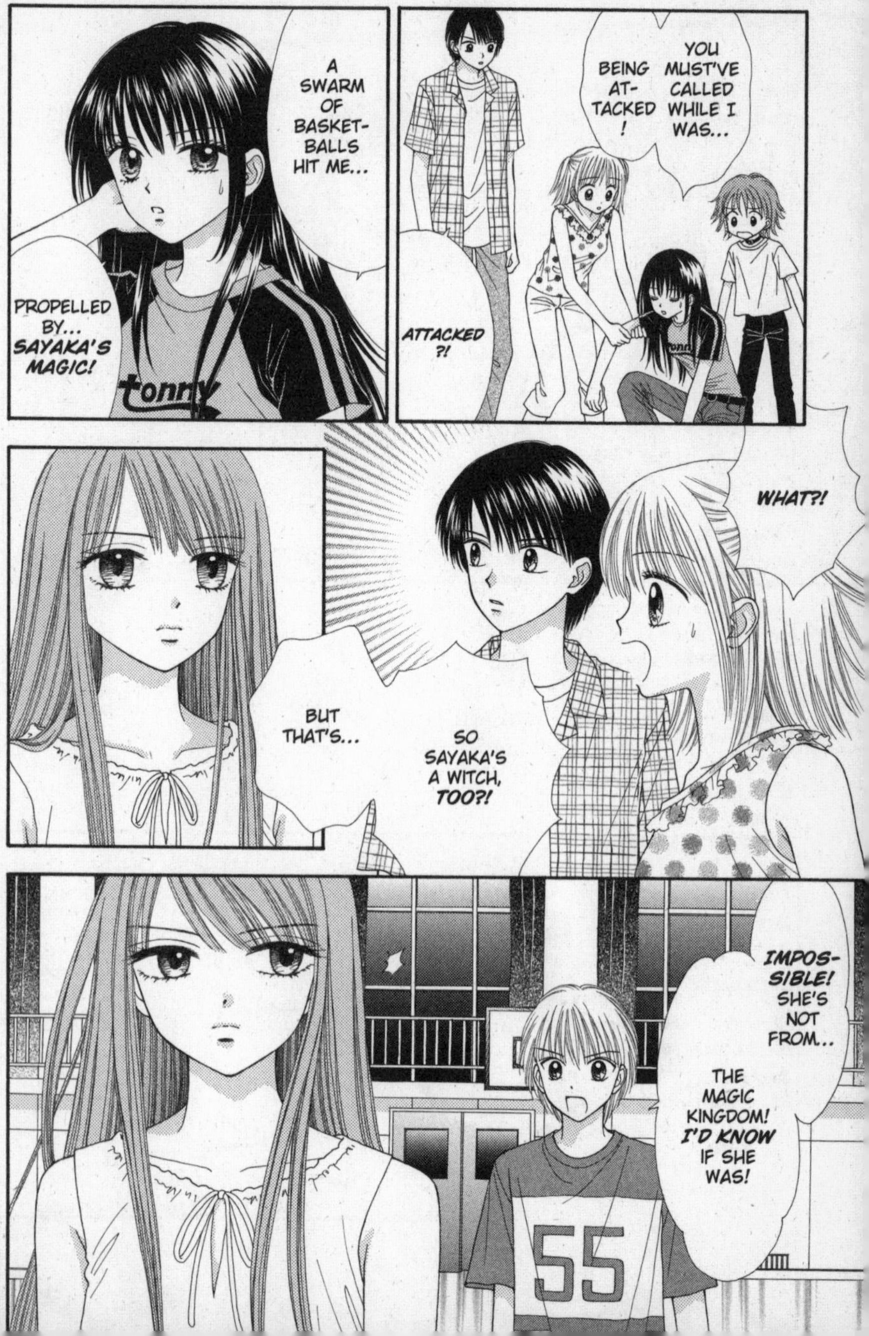
YOU MUST'VE CALLED WHILE I WAS...
BEING AT-TACKED!
ATTACKED?!
A SWARM OF BASKET-BALLS HIT ME...
PROPELLED BY... SAYAKA'S MAGIC!
WHAT?!
SO SAYAKA'S A WITCH, TOO?!
BUT THAT'S...
IMPOS-SIBLE! SHE'S NOT FROM...
THE MAGIC KINGDOM! I'D KNOW IF SHE WAS!

FREE TALK 7

Anime Episode 17 was a story about Ayu and Hiroki's pets. The exciting thing for me was that Ryutaro Okiai (who played Yuu from *Marmalade Boy*) was voicing Shinosuke.

This is the third time I've had one of my works animated, but this was the first time I've had voice actors from old series working on a new series. And it made me **really** happy.

Oddly enough, Mr. Okiai's voice seemed a little more childish than when he played Yuu. So it didn't sound like the same actor at all. Or should I say it didn't seem like Mr. Okiai at all?

Since it was for the part of a cat, obviously there were scenes that called for "meows." I guess Mr. Okiai did those, too. Reiko Takagi who did the part of Leo did say that she "had gotten the part because she was good at doing a cat's meow."

It must be hard for voice actors and actresses because they have to be able to do animal sounds, too. A chameleon shows up in the anime version of *Ultra Maniac* too, but I wonder: Do chameleons really say "ruu—"?

The part of Ruru the chameleon is played by Eiji Takemoto, who also does the voice of the principal. Unlike the principal (and the chameleon), he's actually a good-looking guy.

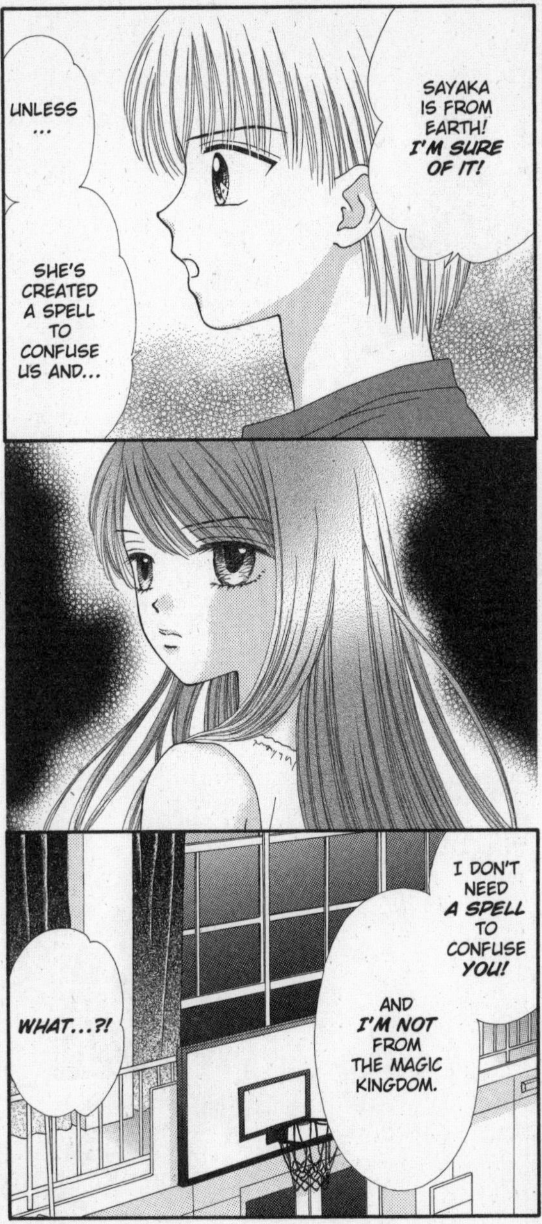
SAYAKA IS FROM EARTH! I'M SURE OF IT!
UNLESS ...
SHE'S CREATED A SPELL TO CONFUSE US AND...
I DON'T NEED A SPELL TO CONFUSE YOU!
AND I'M NOT FROM THE MAGIC KINGDOM.
WHAT...?!

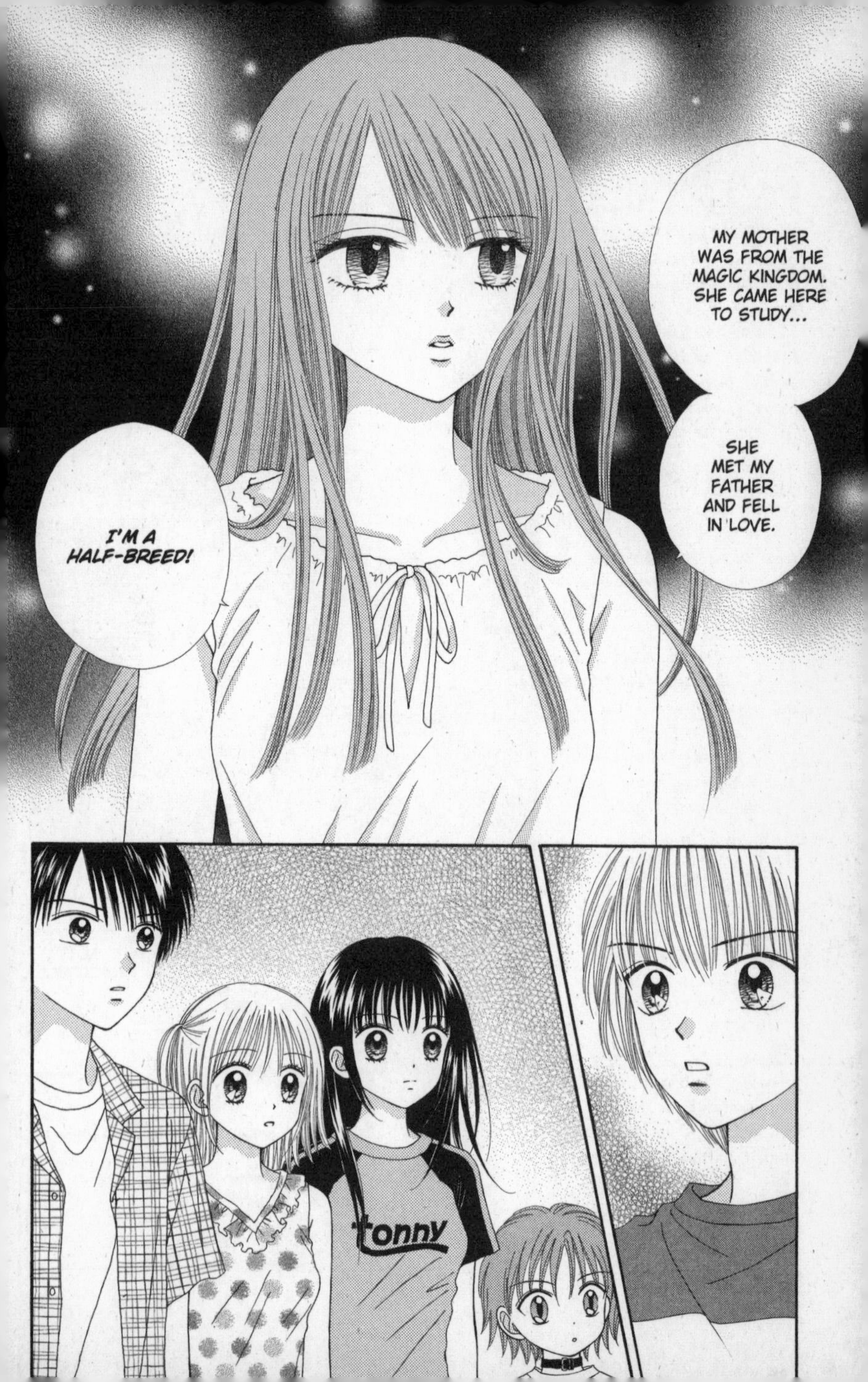
MY MOTHER WAS FROM THE MAGIC KINGDOM. SHE CAME HERE TO STUDY...
SHE MET MY FATHER AND FELL IN LOVE.
I'M A HALF-BREED!
tonny

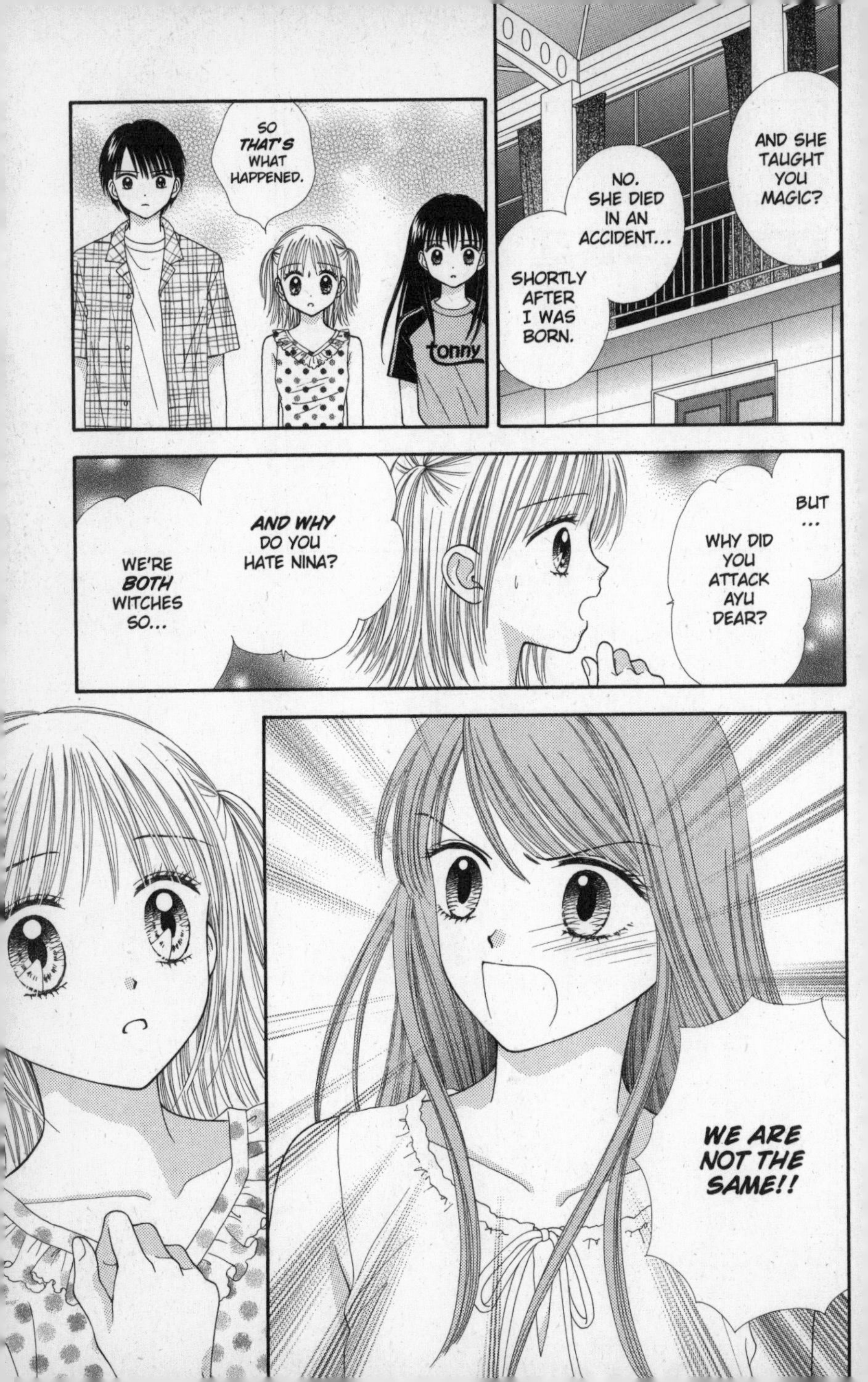
AND SHE TAUGHT YOU MAGIC?
NO. SHE DIED IN AN ACCIDENT...
SHORTLY AFTER I WAS BORN.
SO THAT'S WHAT HAPPENED.
BUT ...
WHY DID YOU ATTACK AYU DEAR?
AND WHY DO YOU HATE NINA?
WE'RE BOTH WITCHES SO...
WE ARE NOT THE SAME!!
tonny

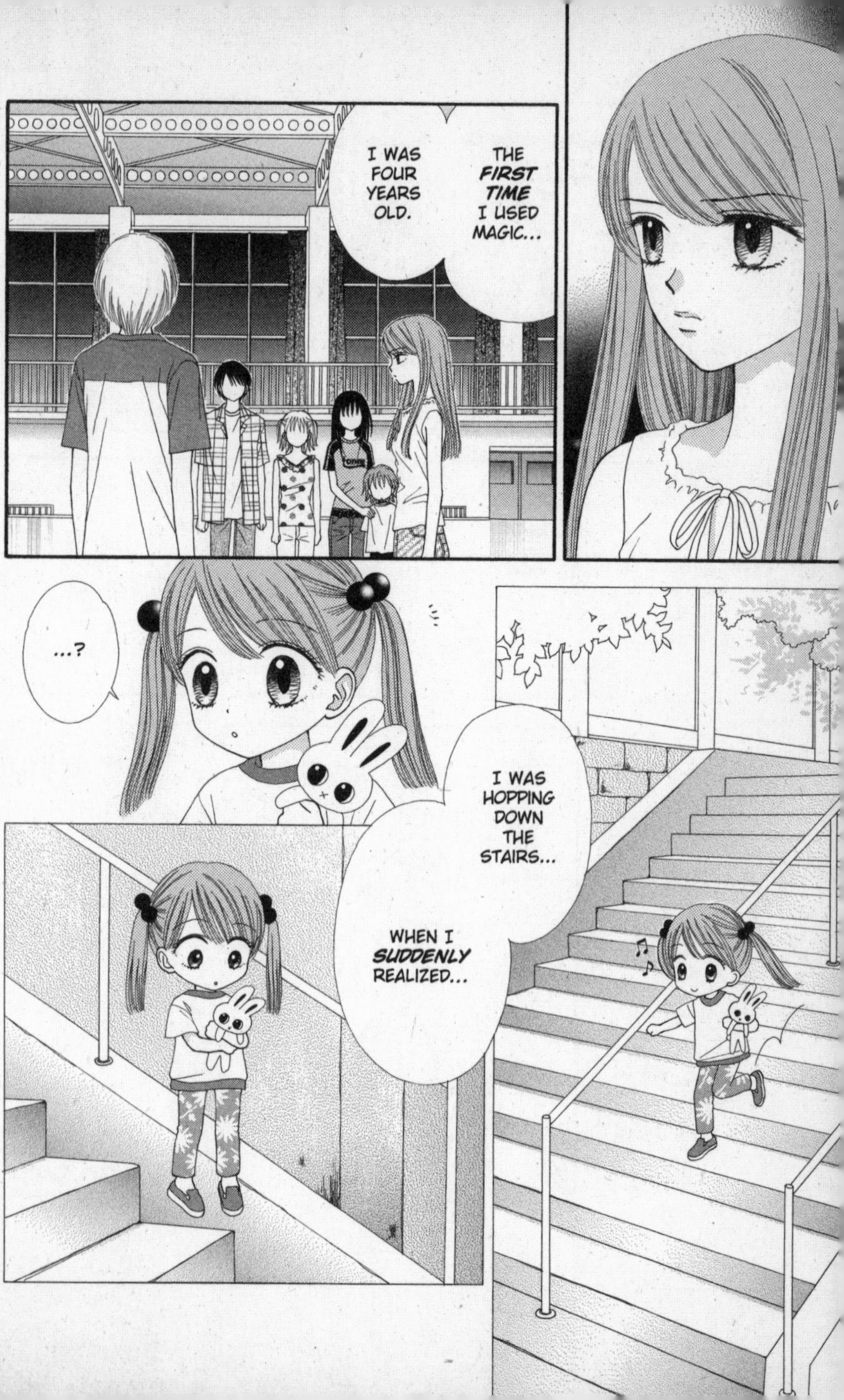
THE FIRST TIME I USED MAGIC...
I WAS FOUR YEARS OLD.
I WAS HOPPING DOWN THE STAIRS...
WHEN I SUDDENLY REALIZED...
...?

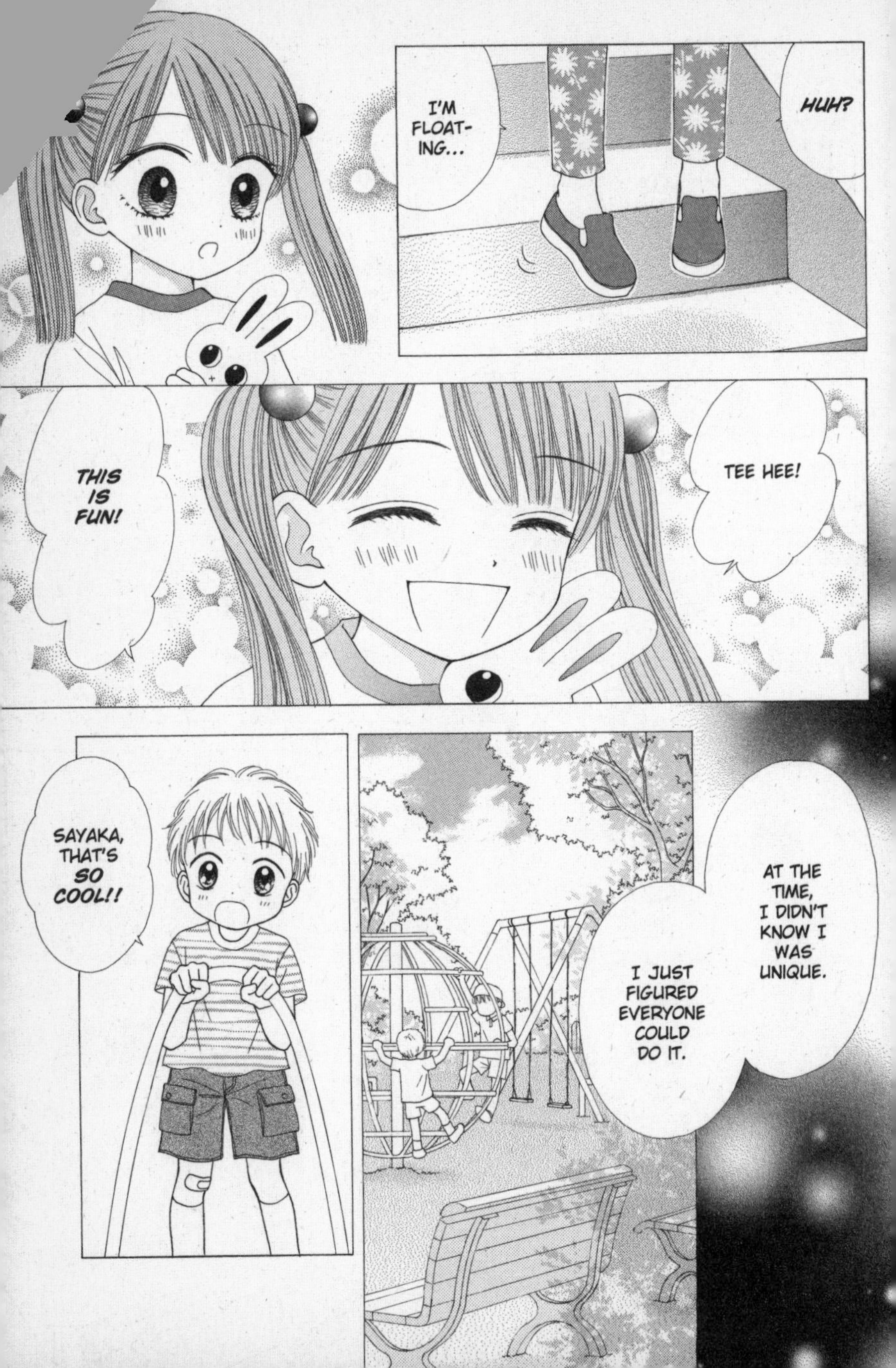
HUH?
I'M FLOATING...
TEE HEE!
THIS IS FUN!
AT THE TIME, I DIDN'T KNOW I WAS UNIQUE.
I JUST FIGURED EVERYONE COULD DO IT.
SAYAKA, THAT'S SO COOL!!

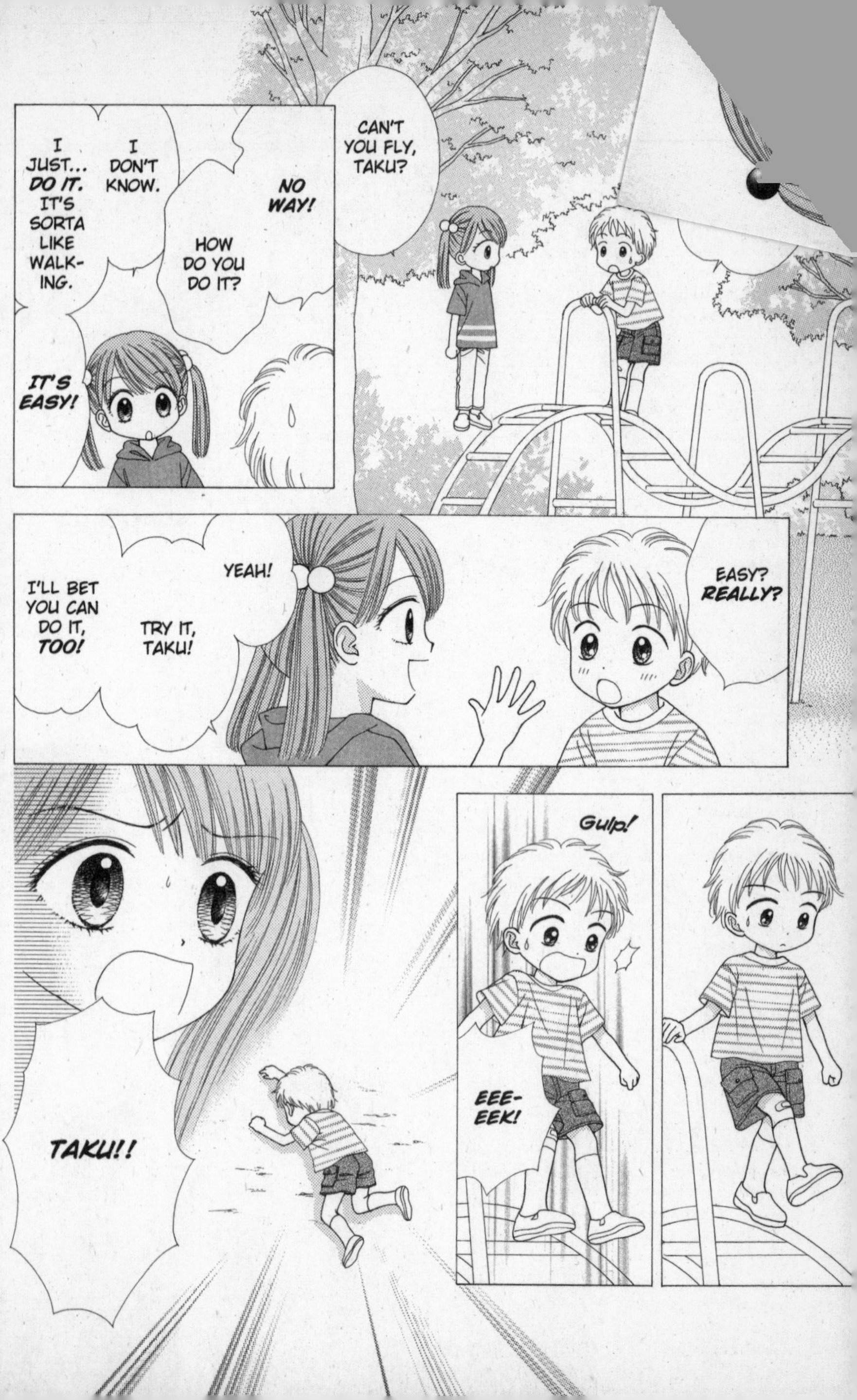
CAN'T YOU FLY, TAKU?
NO WAY!
HOW DO YOU DO IT?
I DON'T KNOW.
I JUST... DO IT. IT'S SORTA LIKE WALKING.
IT'S EASY!
EASY? REALLY?
YEAH!
TRY IT, TAKU!
I'LL BET YOU CAN DO IT, TOO!
Gulp!
EEE-EEK!
TAKU!!

FREE TALK 8

*My Free Talks about the Ultra Maniac anime have gone on longer than I expected. For people who haven't seen them, or have no interest in them, I apologize. Or maybe I should just say . . . **please see them!** ♡*

Hmm, as long as I'm pleading with you to check out more Ultra Maniac stuff, I might as well go all the way. There's an anime merchandise shop called Animate which sells backboards, memo paper, pins, mirrors, cell phone straps, and mini-hand towels. So, if you get a chance, check out all the cool Ultra Maniac stuff! ♡

I can't imagine there's anything else I forgot to write about during these anime articles . . .

Oh! But I did...

I forgot I wasn't able to completely finish writing about Maya's song in my notes about the Ultra Maniac CD. The song is sung by the actress who voiced Maya (Saeko Chiba.) Ms. Chiba's rendition of the song has a very mysterious and haunting quality. I highly recommend it!

By the way, one of the other actresses (Yuri Horie) apparently likes manga and has read a lot of my work. So I was quite happy when she told me that she really likes my Maria and Sasa characters from Mint na Bokura (We are Mint). Also, Akemi Kanda said that if she wakes up late, she can't do the voice of Nina. So she woke up especially early for all the afureco recordings. So a big thank you to her and all the cast and production staff for their work on the anime.

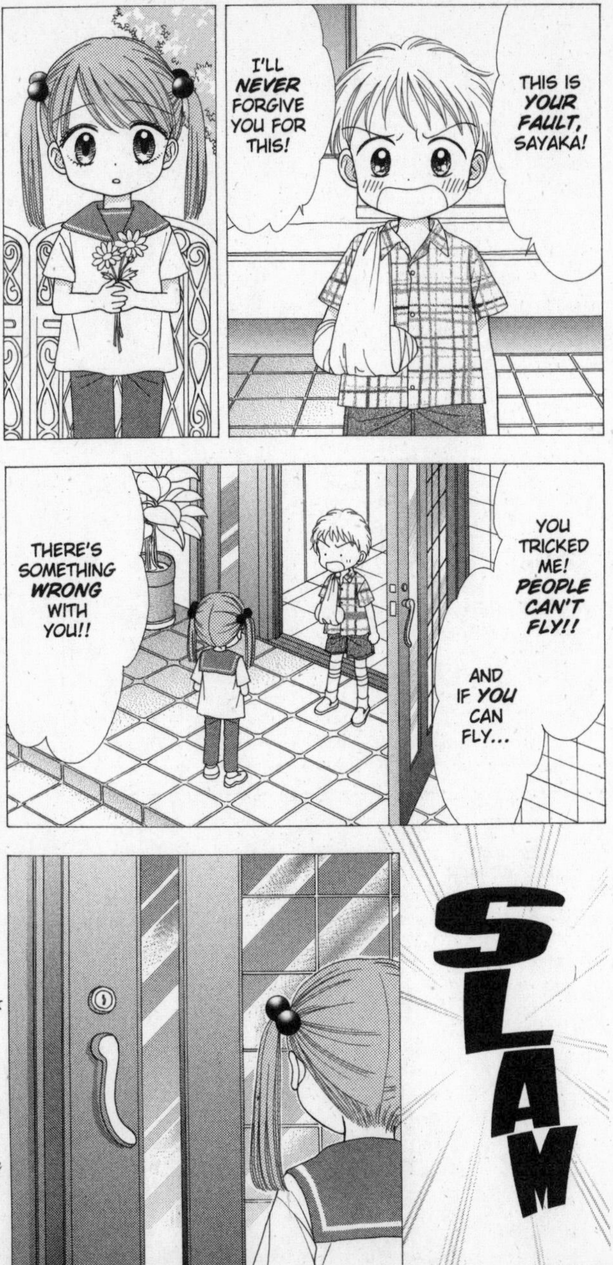

THIS IS YOUR FAULT, SAYAKA!
I'LL NEVER FORGIVE YOU FOR THIS!
YOU TRICKED ME! PEOPLE CAN'T FLY!!
AND IF YOU CAN FLY...
THERE'S SOMETHING WRONG WITH YOU!!
SLAM

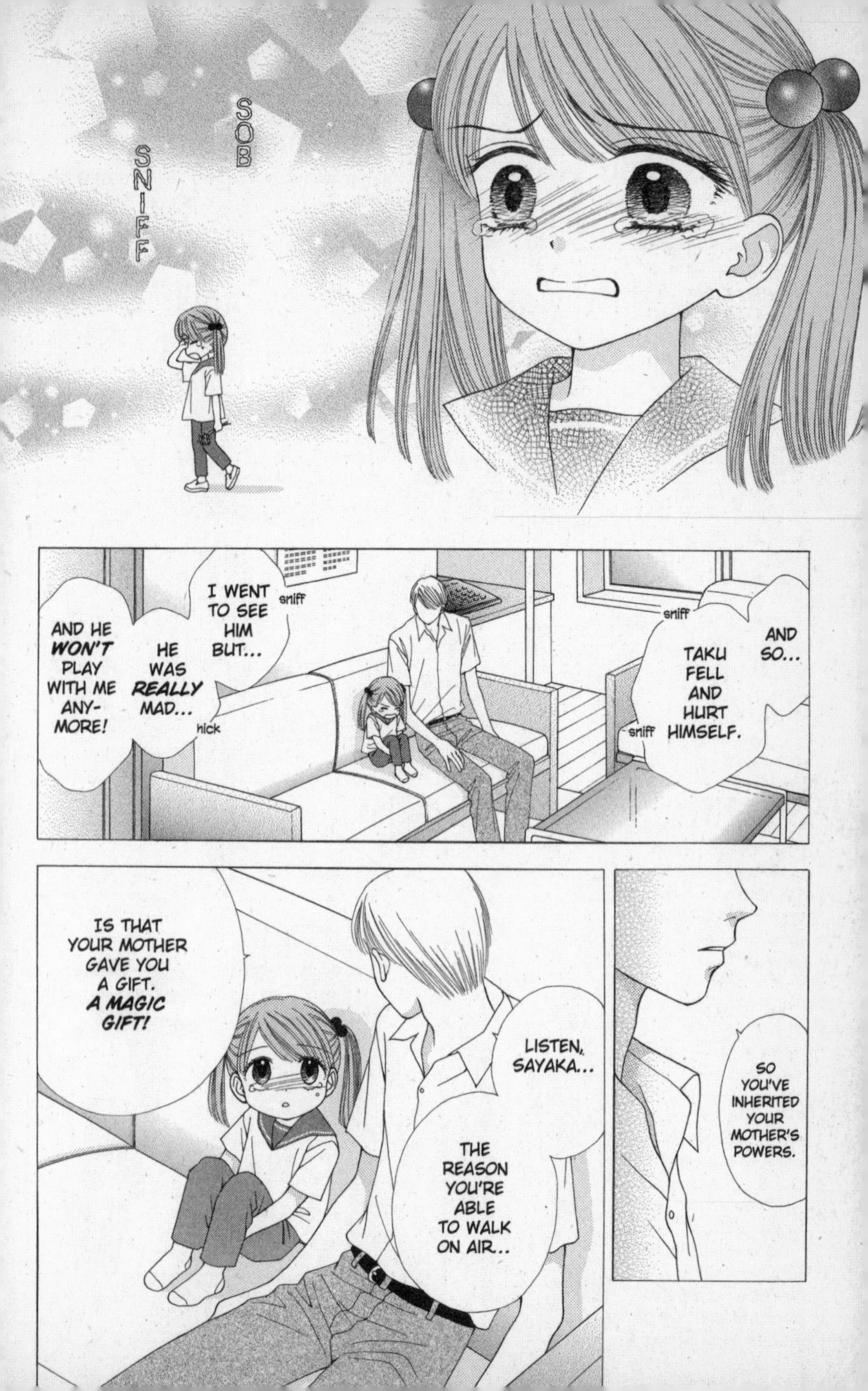
SOB
SNIFF
sniff
AND SO... TAKU FELL AND HURT HIMSELF.
sniff
I WENT TO SEE HIM BUT...
sniff
HE WAS **REALLY** MAD...
hick
AND HE **WON'T** PLAY WITH ME ANY-MORE!
SO YOU'VE INHERITED YOUR MOTHER'S POWERS.
LISTEN, SAYAKA...
THE REASON YOU'RE ABLE TO WALK ON AIR...
IS THAT YOUR MOTHER GAVE YOU A GIFT. **A MAGIC GIFT!**

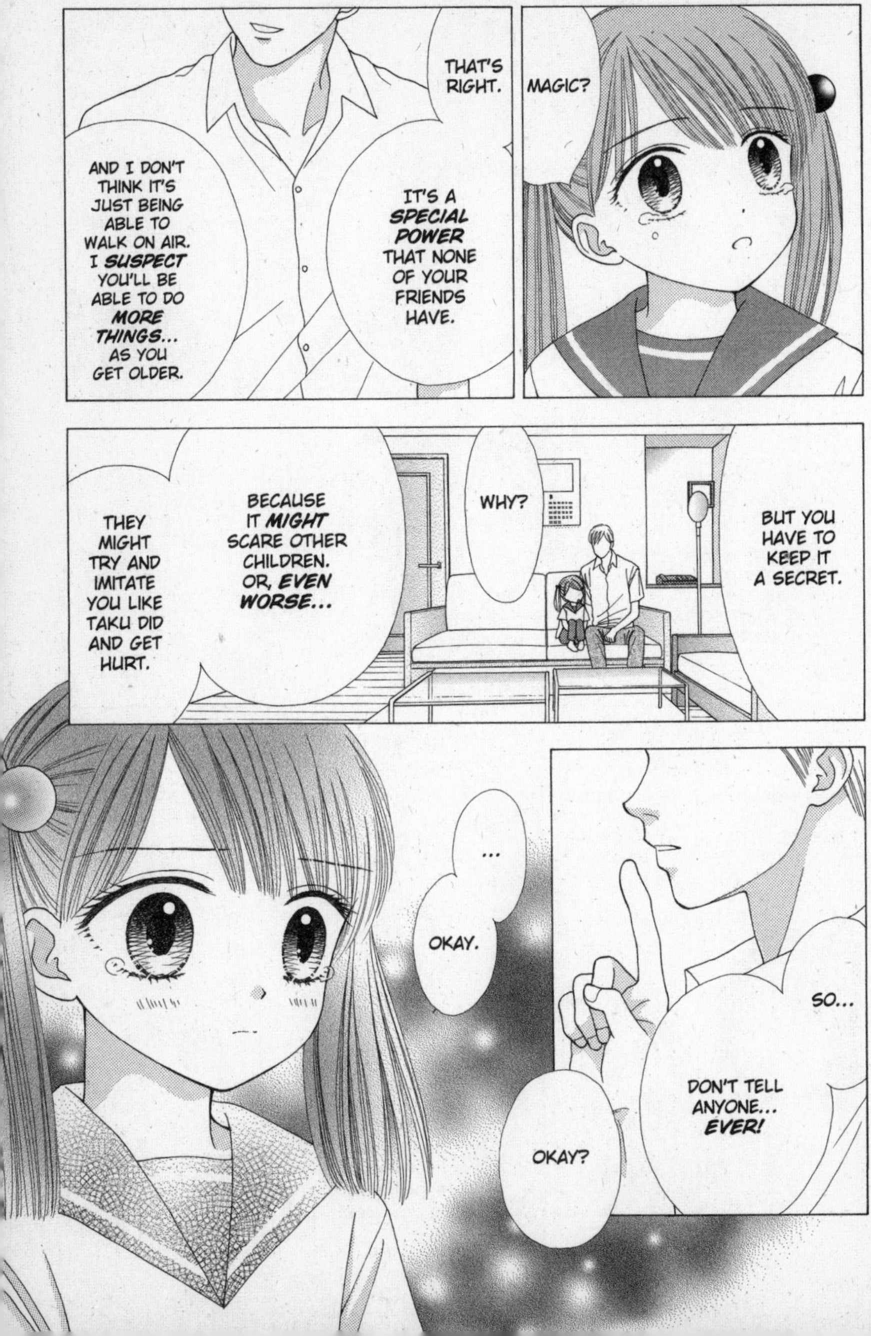
MAGIC?
THAT'S RIGHT.
IT'S A SPECIAL POWER THAT NONE OF YOUR FRIENDS HAVE.
AND I DON'T THINK IT'S JUST BEING ABLE TO WALK ON AIR. I SUSPECT YOU'LL BE ABLE TO DO MORE THINGS... AS YOU GET OLDER.
BUT YOU HAVE TO KEEP IT A SECRET.
WHY?
BECAUSE IT MIGHT SCARE OTHER CHILDREN. OR, EVEN WORSE...
THEY MIGHT TRY AND IMITATE YOU LIKE TAKU DID AND GET HURT.
SO...
DON'T TELL ANYONE... EVER!
OKAY?
...
OKAY.

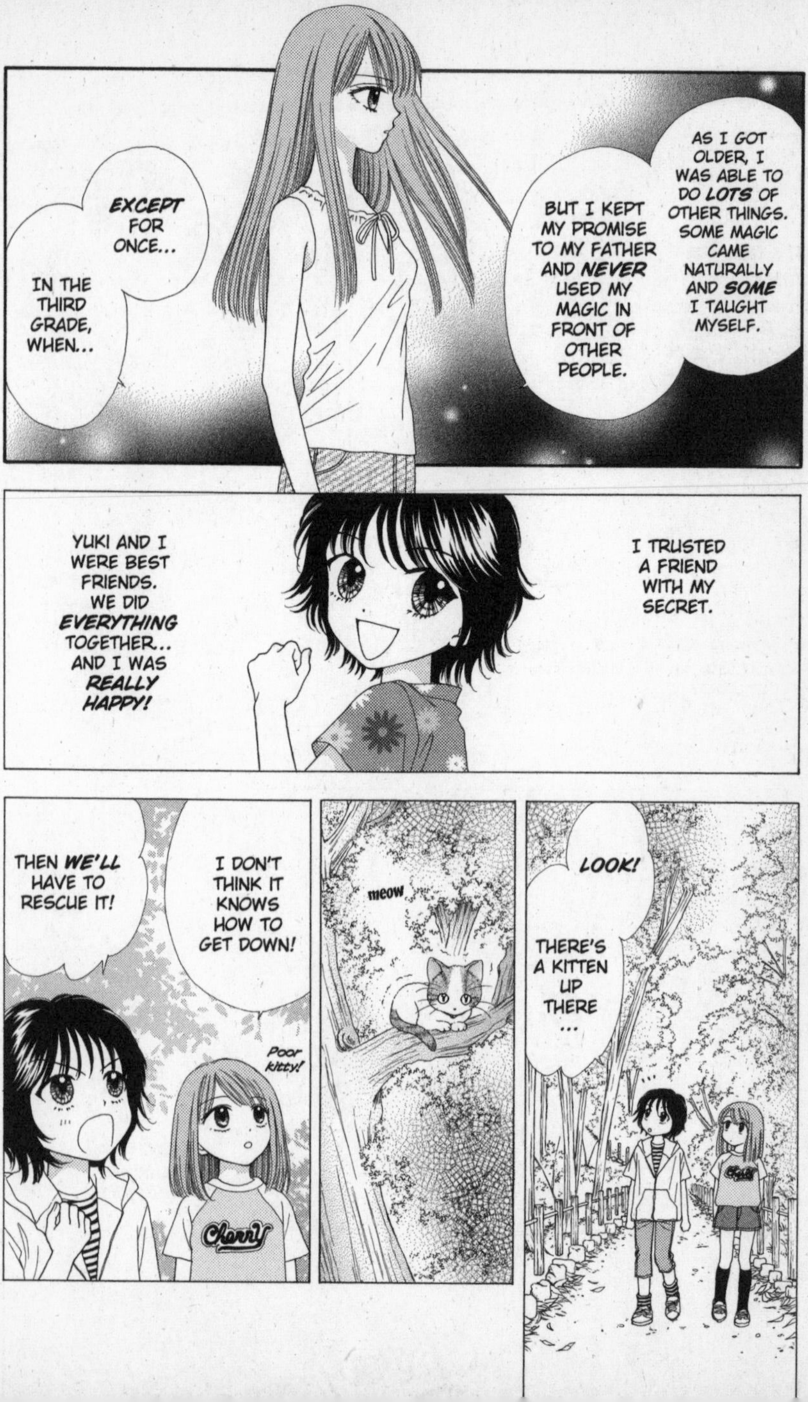
AS I GOT OLDER, I WAS ABLE TO DO LOTS OF OTHER THINGS. SOME MAGIC CAME NATURALLY AND SOME I TAUGHT MYSELF.
BUT I KEPT MY PROMISE TO MY FATHER AND NEVER USED MY MAGIC IN FRONT OF OTHER PEOPLE.
EXCEPT FOR ONCE...
IN THE THIRD GRADE, WHEN...
I TRUSTED A FRIEND WITH MY SECRET.
YUKI AND I WERE BEST FRIENDS. WE DID EVERYTHING TOGETHER... AND I WAS REALLY HAPPY!
LOOK!
THERE'S A KITTEN UP THERE ...
...
meow
I DON'T THINK IT KNOWS HOW TO GET DOWN!
Poor kitty!
THEN WE'LL HAVE TO RESCUE IT!

FREE TALK 9

The complete compilation of *Marmalade Boy* is coming out soon! YAY!

It's supposed to appear in February but (as I write this) there isn't much time left. Nothing's really been decided yet, so I wonder if it's going to make it? I admit that I'm a little worried...

I've completed the cover art, but I haven't met with the designer yet. So I don't know what's going to happen. But I'm going to do my best.

This summer, for the first time in years, I got to draw Yuu and Miki from *Marmalade Boy*. It was for a special colored insert to go with the *Marmalade Boy* anime DVD set. The insert was for people who bought both Volumes 2 and 3.

I was able to draw Yuu pretty easily. But Miki was really hard and while I was drawing her I had to look at the *Marmalade Boy Illustration Collection* so that she'd look right. I guess my art style has changed since I first drew her.

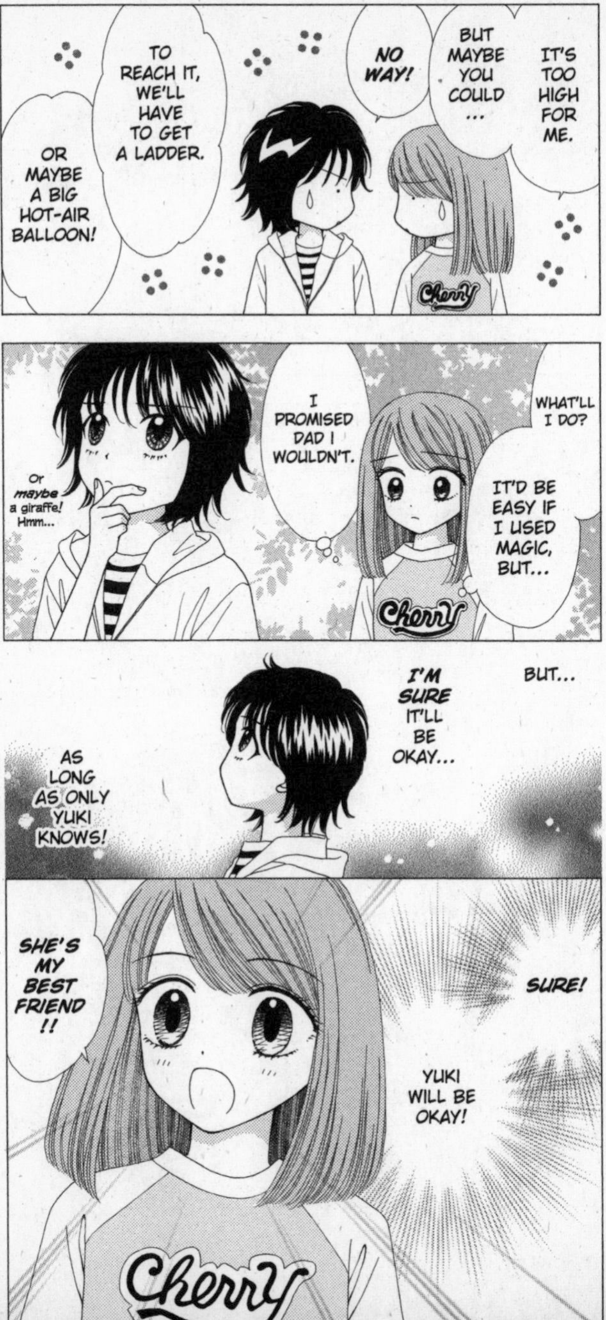
IT'S TOO HIGH FOR ME.
BUT MAYBE YOU COULD ...
NO WAY!
TO REACH IT, WE'LL HAVE TO GET A LADDER.
OR MAYBE A BIG HOT-AIR BALLOON!
WHAT'LL I DO?
IT'D BE EASY IF I USED MAGIC, BUT...
I PROMISED DAD I WOULDN'T.
Or maybe a giraffe! Hmm...
BUT...
I'M SURE IT'LL BE OKAY...
AS LONG AS ONLY YUKI KNOWS!
SURE!
YUKI WILL BE OKAY!
SHE'S MY BEST FRIEND!!

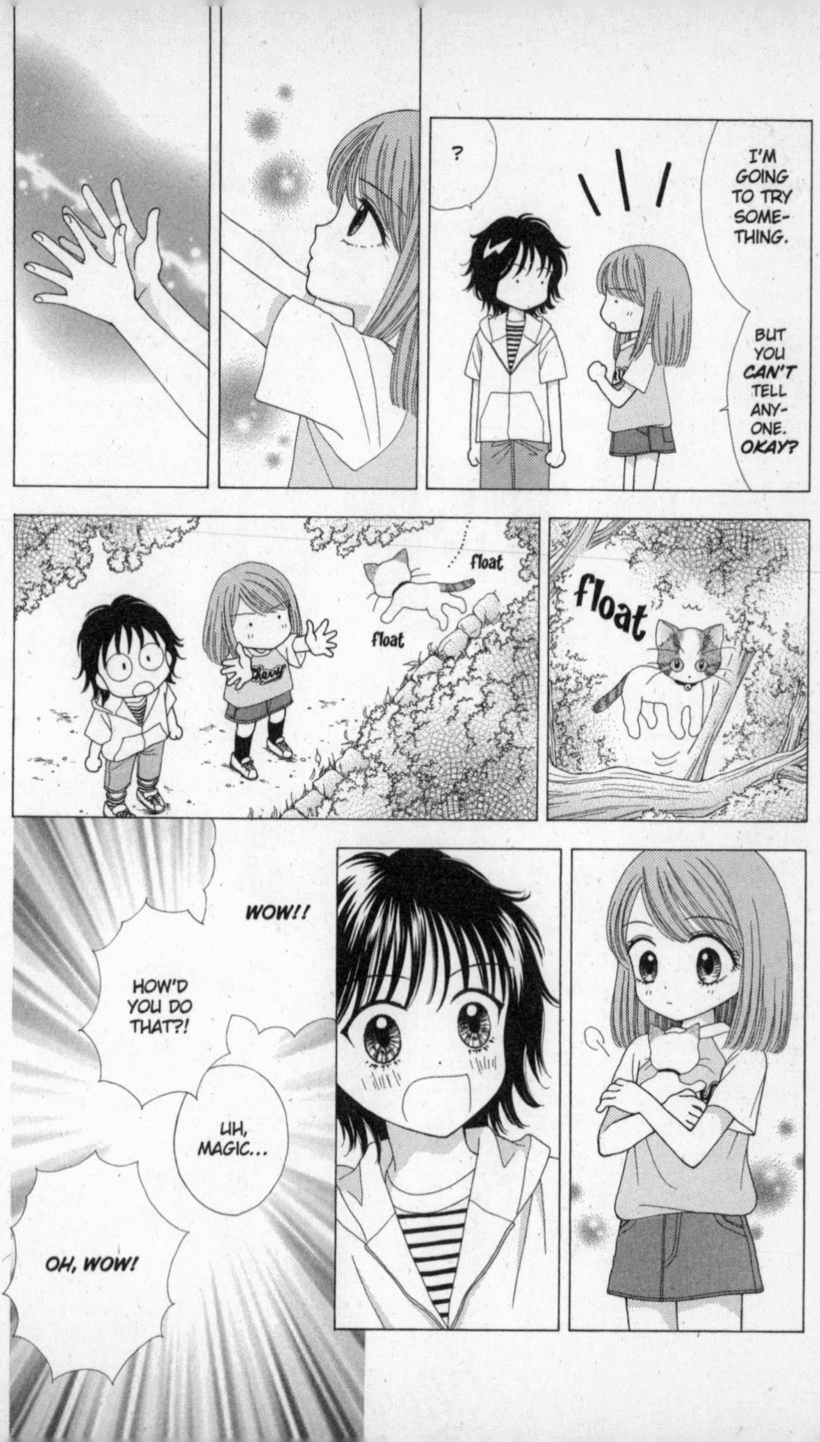
I'M GOING TO TRY SOMETHING.
BUT YOU CAN'T TELL ANYONE. OKAY?
?
float
float
float
WOW!!
HOW'D YOU DO THAT?!
UH, MAGIC...
OH, WOW!

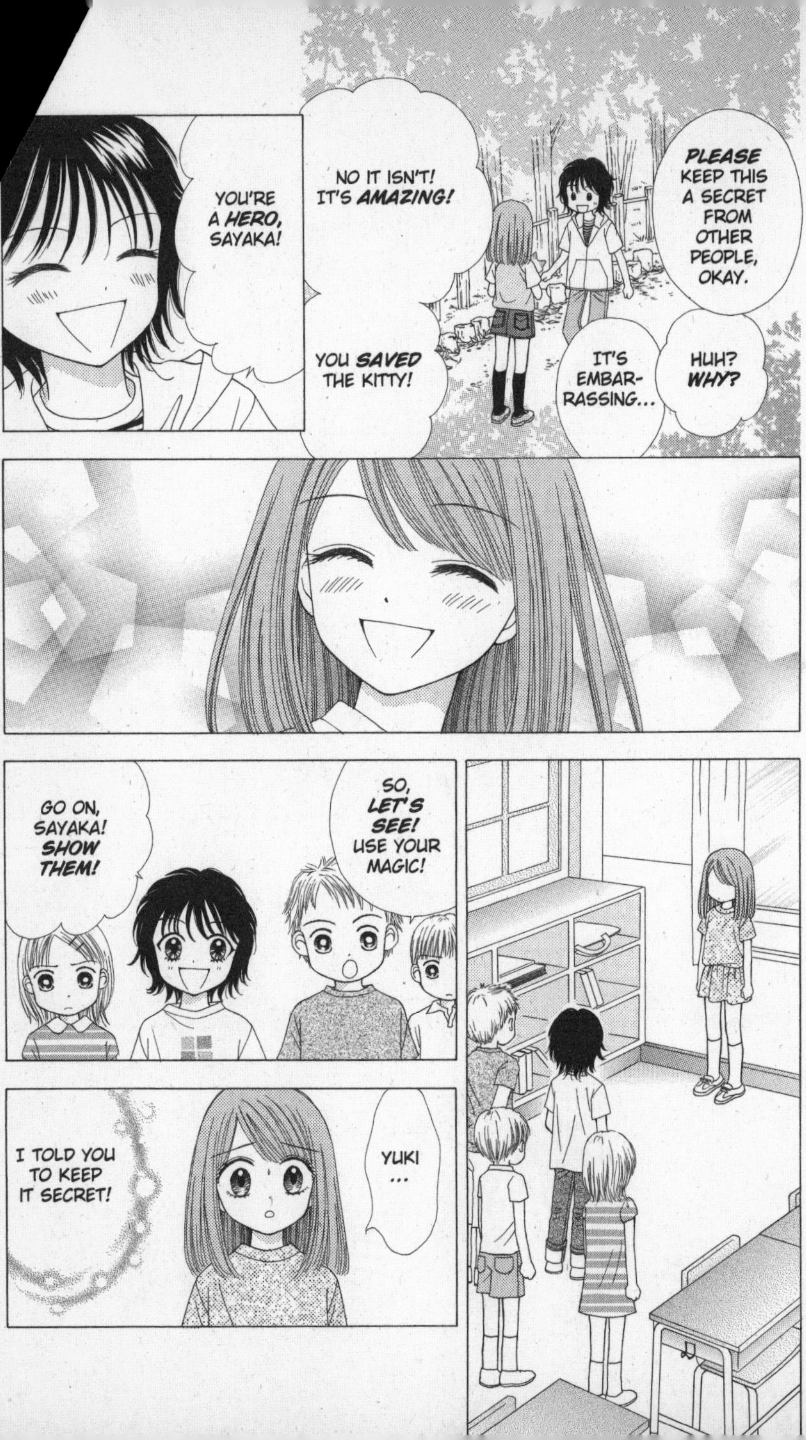
PLEASE KEEP THIS A SECRET FROM OTHER PEOPLE, OKAY.
HUH? WHY?
IT'S EMBARRASSING...
NO IT ISN'T! IT'S AMAZING!
YOU SAVED THE KITTY!
YOU'RE A HERO, SAYAKA!
SO, LET'S SEE! USE YOUR MAGIC!
GO ON, SAYAKA! SHOW THEM!
YUKI ...
I TOLD YOU TO KEEP IT SECRET!

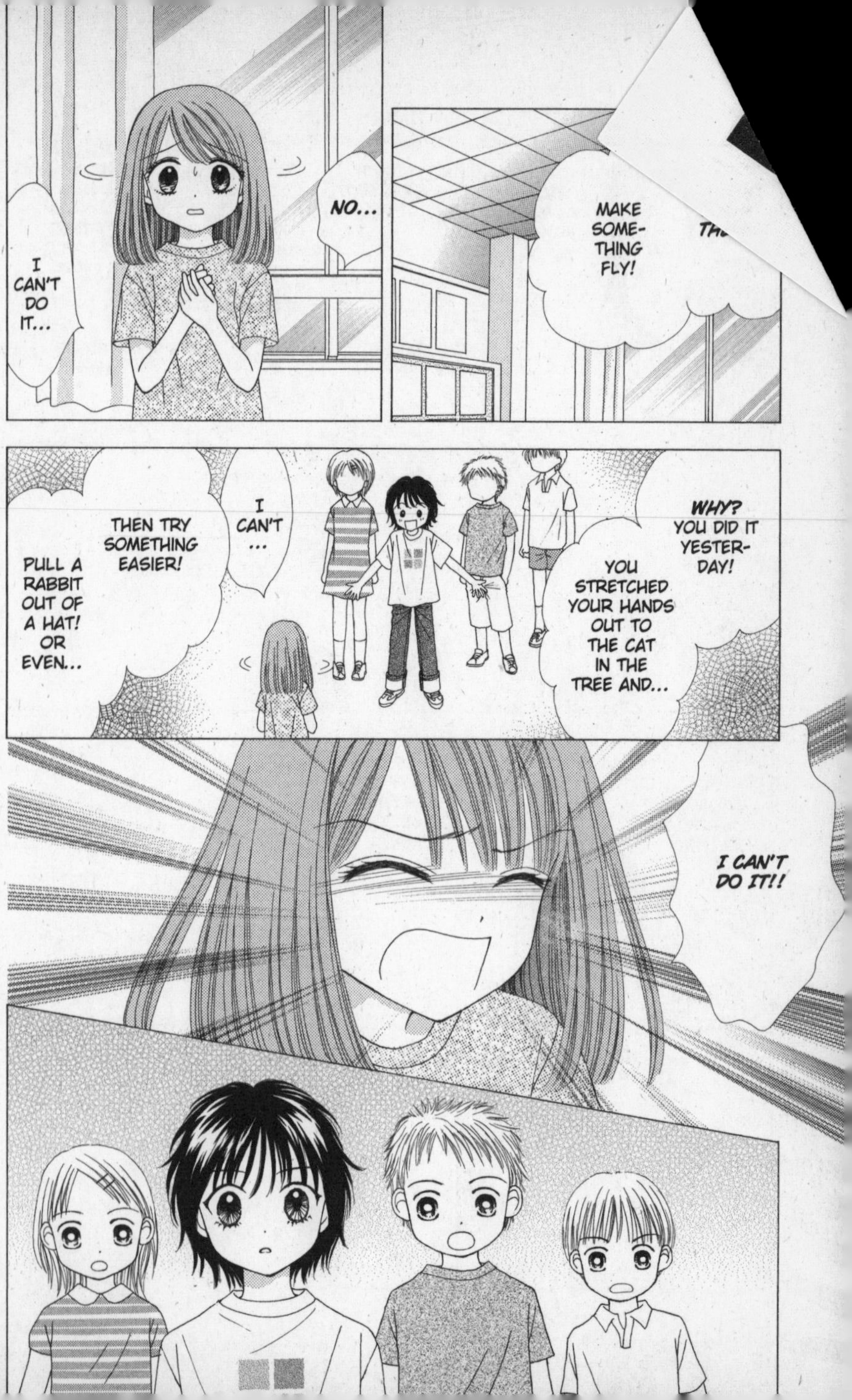
MAKE SOMETHING FLY!
NO...
I CAN'T DO IT...
WHY? YOU DID IT YESTERDAY!
YOU STRETCHED YOUR HANDS OUT TO THE CAT IN THE TREE AND...
I CAN'T ...
THEN TRY SOMETHING EASIER!
PULL A RABBIT OUT OF A HAT! OR EVEN...
I CAN'T DO IT!!

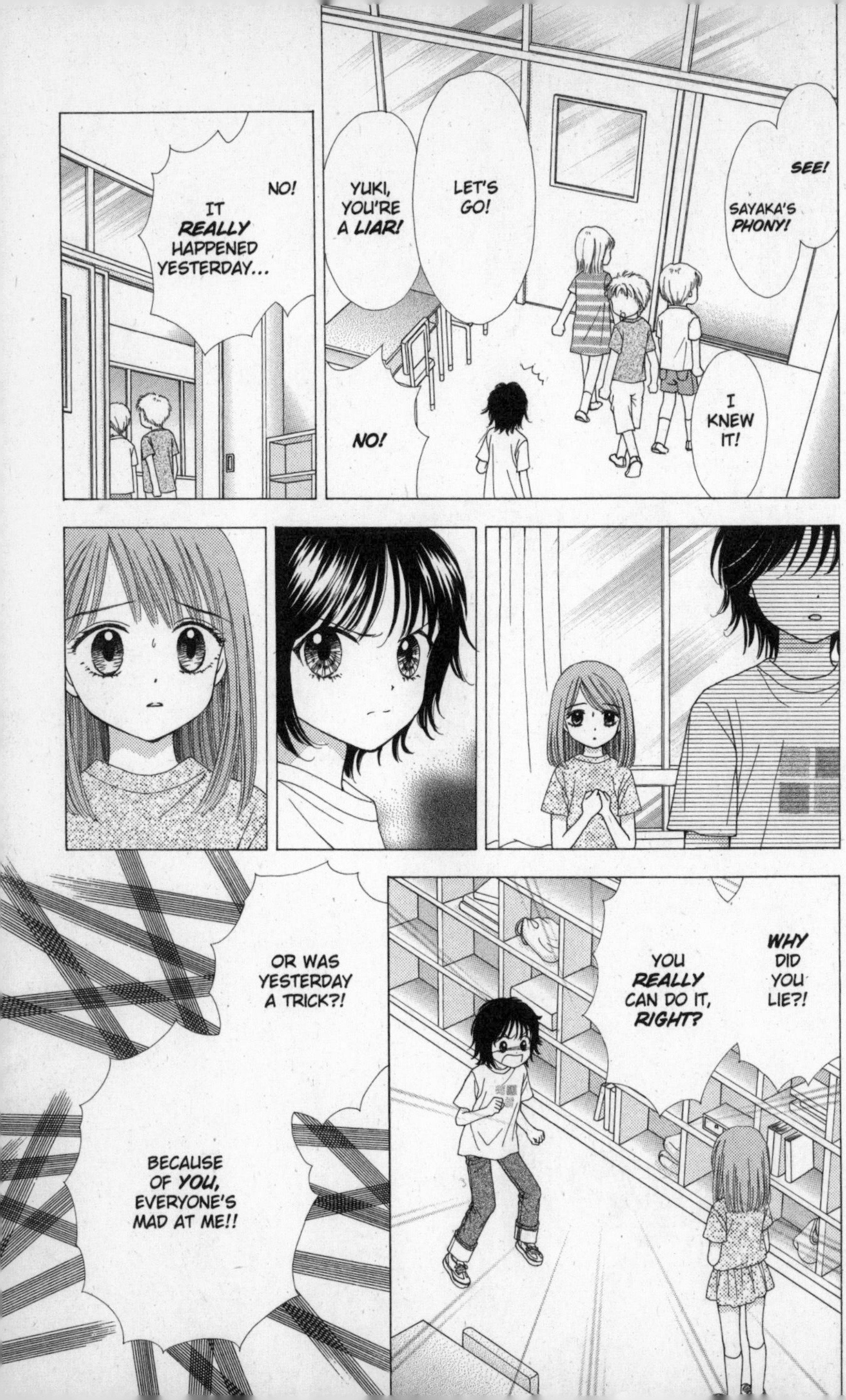
SEE!
SAYAKA'S PHONY!
LET'S GO!
YUKI, YOU'RE A LIAR!
I KNEW IT!
NO!
NO! IT REALLY HAPPENED YESTERDAY...
WHY DID YOU LIE?!
YOU REALLY CAN DO IT, RIGHT?
OR WAS YESTERDAY A TRICK?!
BECAUSE OF YOU, EVERYONE'S MAD AT ME!!

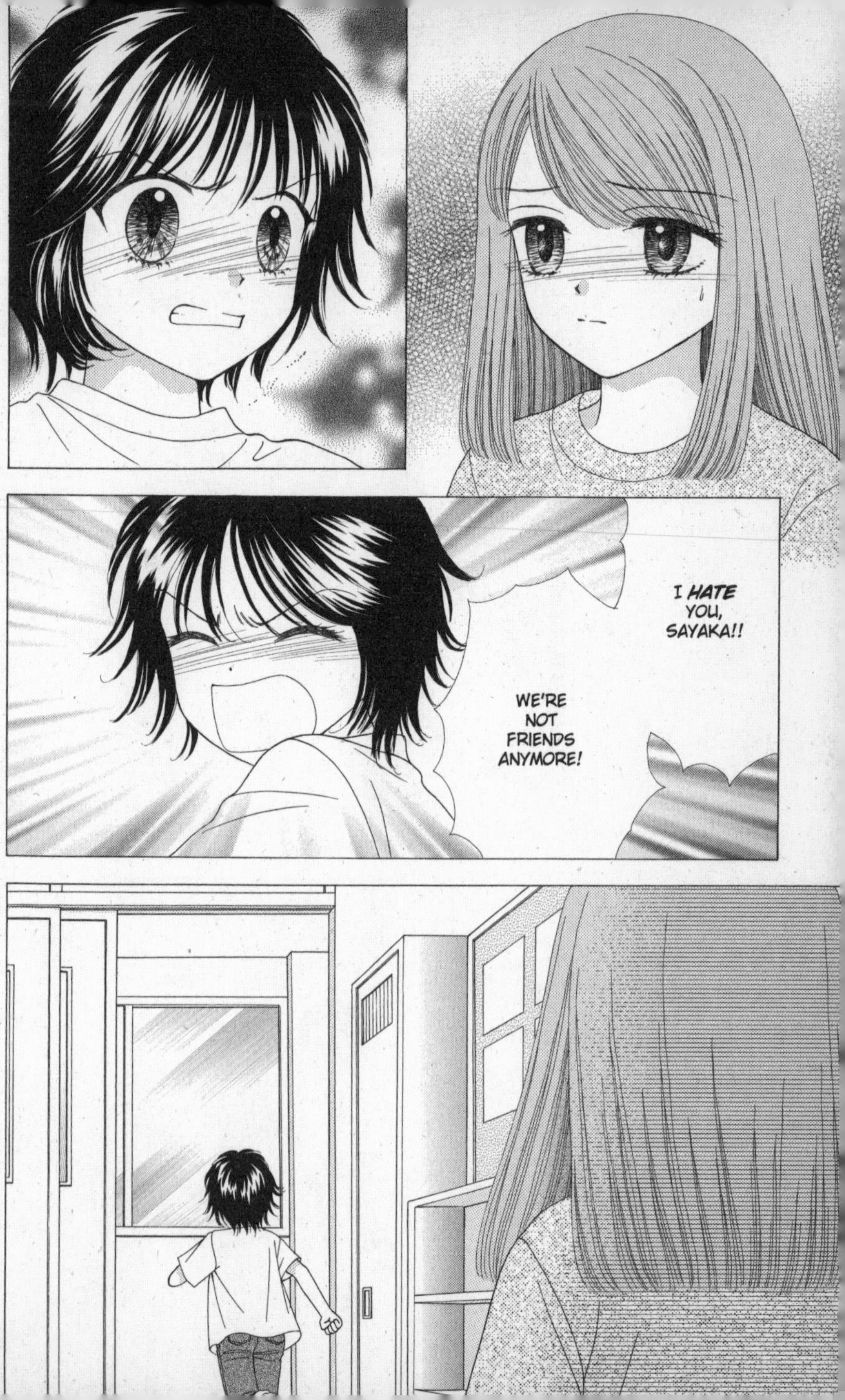
I HATE YOU, SAYAKA!!
WE'RE NOT FRIENDS ANYMORE!

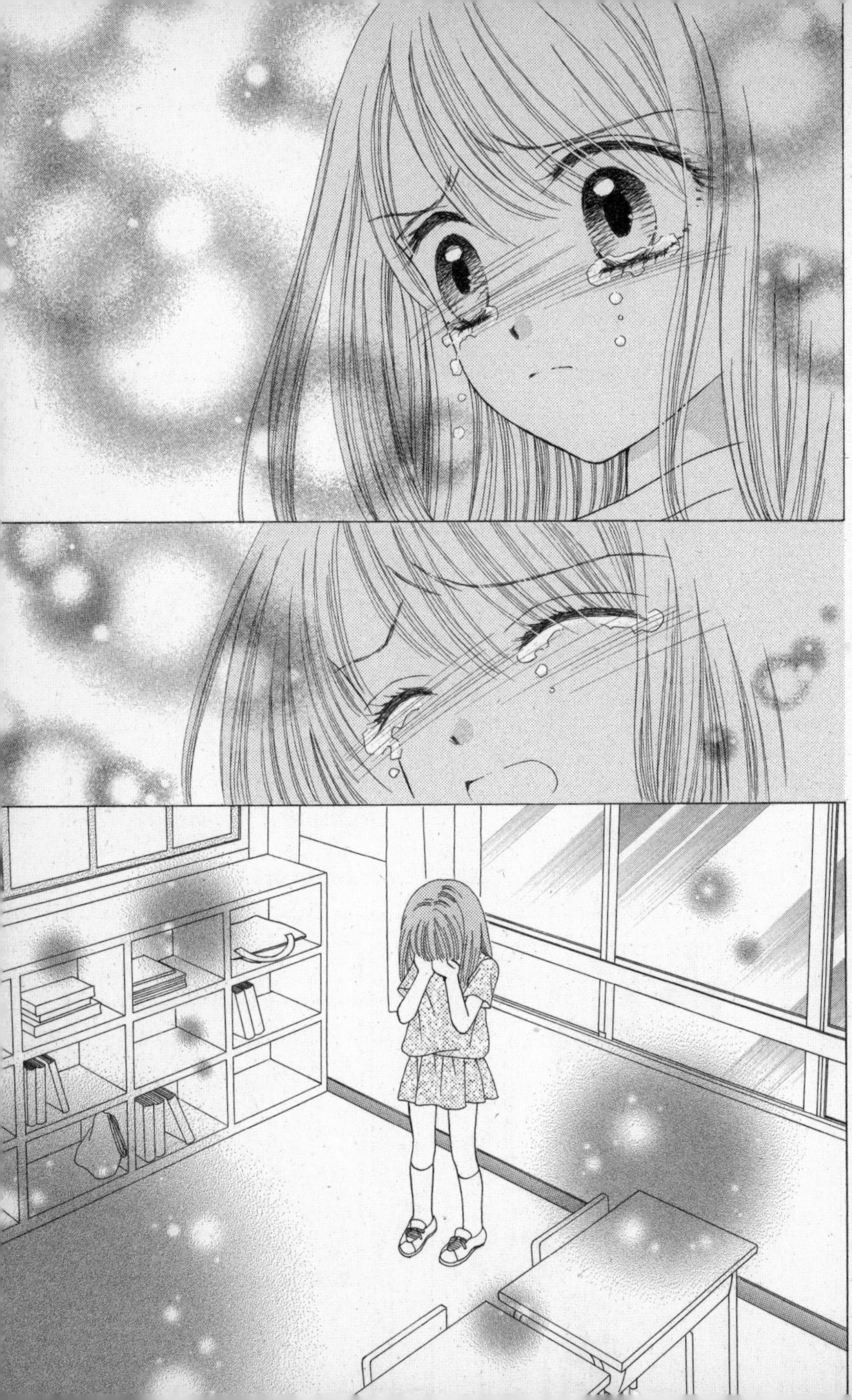

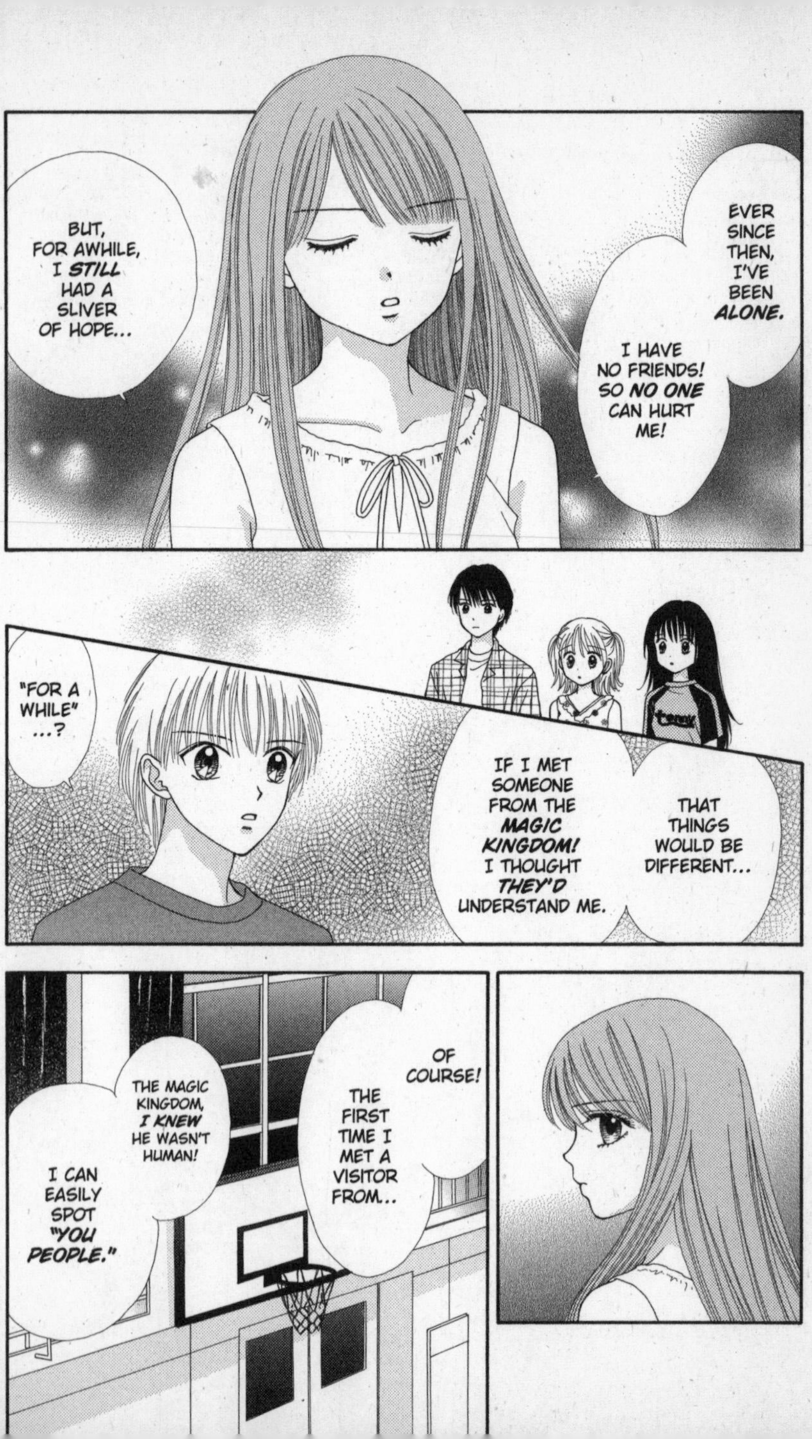
EVER SINCE THEN, I'VE BEEN *ALONE.*
I HAVE NO FRIENDS! SO *NO ONE* CAN HURT ME!
BUT, FOR AWHILE, I *STILL* HAD A SLIVER OF HOPE...
THAT THINGS WOULD BE DIFFERENT...
IF I MET SOMEONE FROM THE *MAGIC KINGDOM!* I THOUGHT *THEY'D* UNDERSTAND ME.
"FOR A WHILE"...?
OF COURSE!
THE FIRST TIME I MET A VISITOR FROM...
THE MAGIC KINGDOM, *I KNEW* HE WASN'T HUMAN!
I CAN EASILY SPOT *"YOU PEOPLE."*

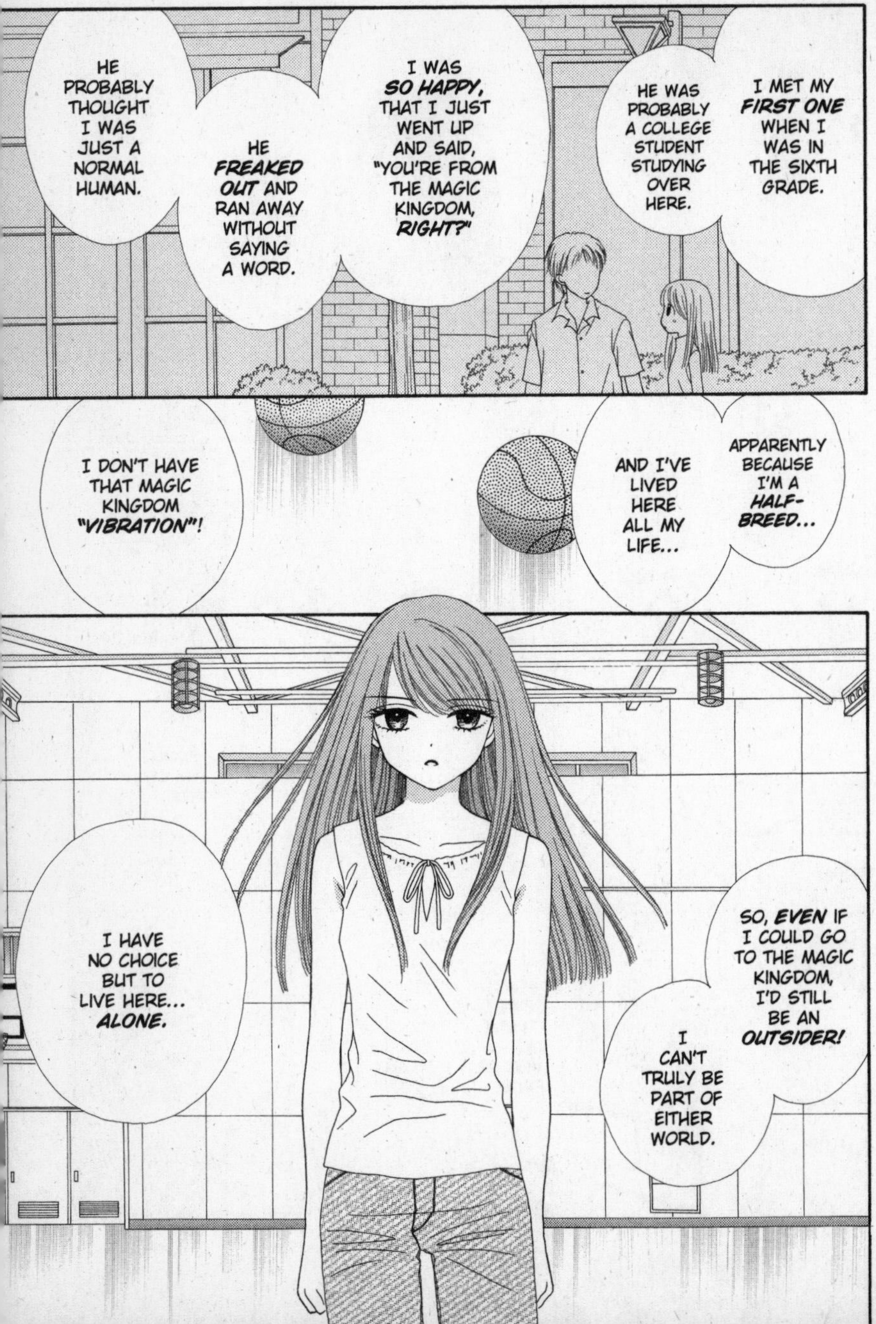
I MET MY FIRST ONE WHEN I WAS IN THE SIXTH GRADE.
HE WAS PROBABLY A COLLEGE STUDENT STUDYING OVER HERE.
I WAS SO HAPPY, THAT I JUST WENT UP AND SAID, "YOU'RE FROM THE MAGIC KINGDOM, RIGHT?"
HE FREAKED OUT AND RAN AWAY WITHOUT SAYING A WORD.
HE PROBABLY THOUGHT I WAS JUST A NORMAL HUMAN.
APPARENTLY BECAUSE I'M A HALF-BREED...
AND I'VE LIVED HERE ALL MY LIFE...
I DON'T HAVE THAT MAGIC KINGDOM "VIBRATION"!
SO, EVEN IF I COULD GO TO THE MAGIC KINGDOM, I'D STILL BE AN OUTSIDER!
I CAN'T TRULY BE PART OF EITHER WORLD.
I HAVE NO CHOICE BUT TO LIVE HERE... ALONE.

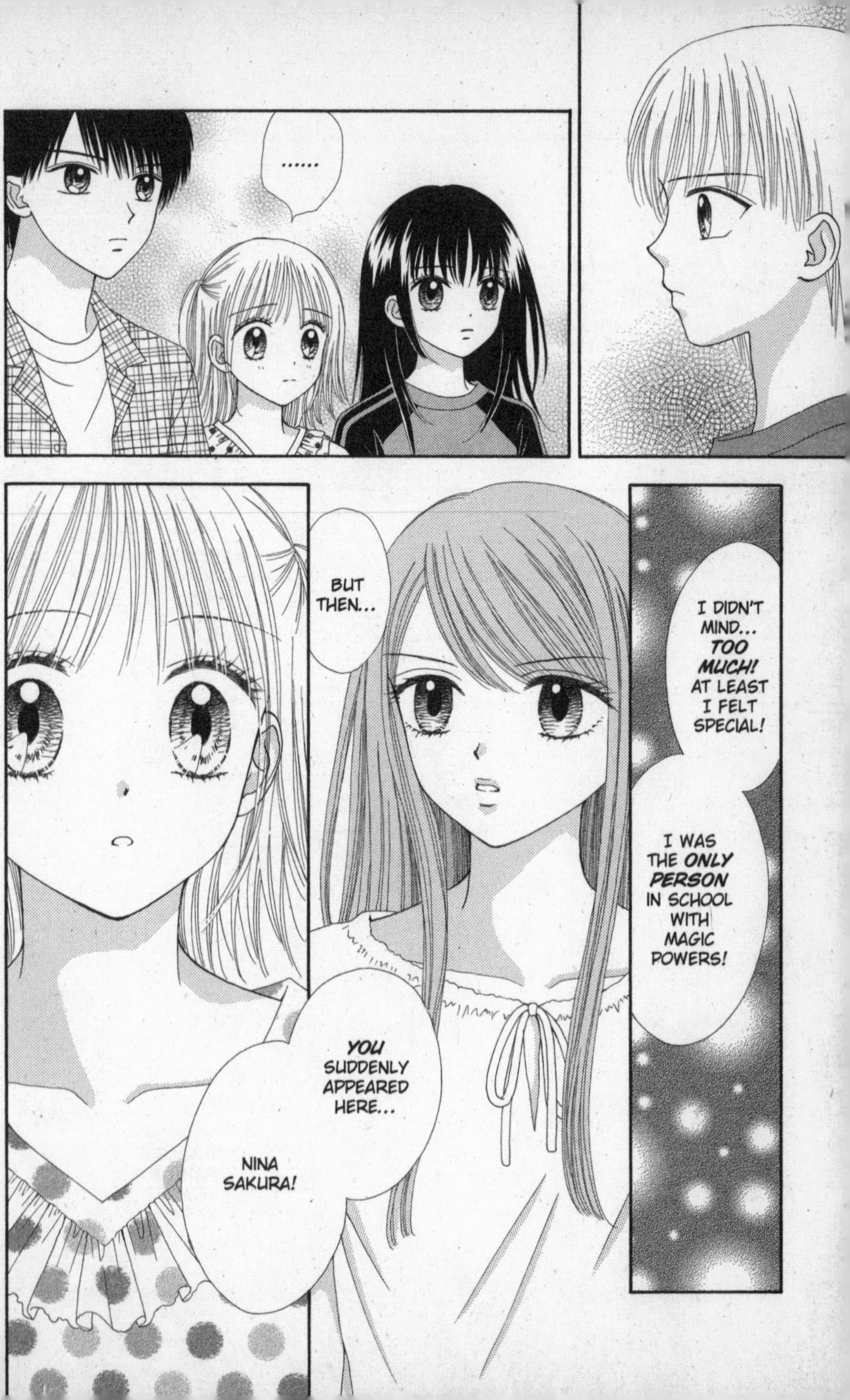

......
I DIDN'T MIND... ***TOO MUCH!*** AT LEAST I FELT SPECIAL!
I WAS THE ***ONLY PERSON*** IN SCHOOL WITH MAGIC POWERS!
BUT THEN...
YOU SUDDENLY APPEARED HERE...
NINA SAKURA!

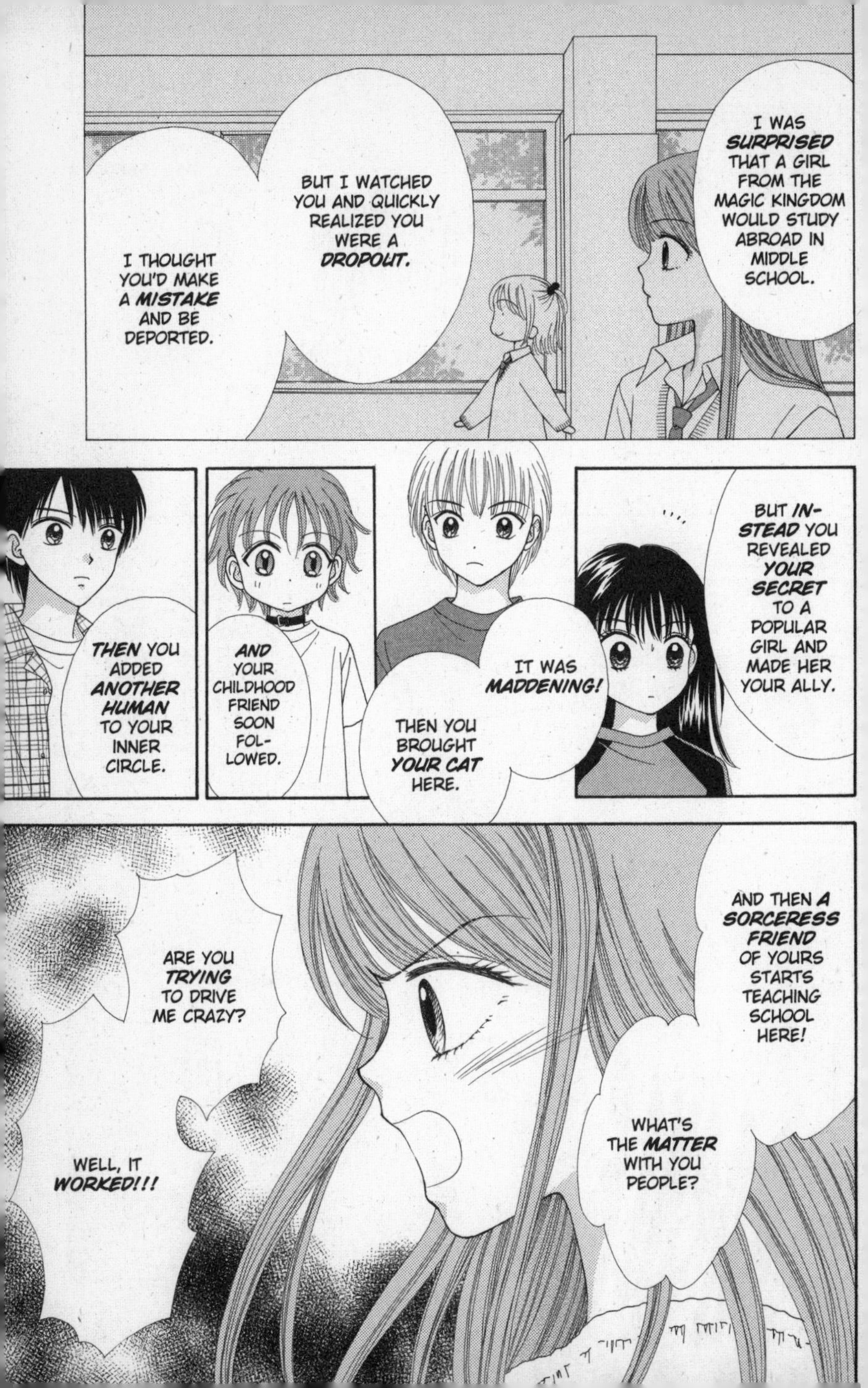

I WAS SURPRISED THAT A GIRL FROM THE MAGIC KINGDOM WOULD STUDY ABROAD IN MIDDLE SCHOOL.
BUT I WATCHED YOU AND QUICKLY REALIZED YOU WERE A DROPOUT.
I THOUGHT YOU'D MAKE A MISTAKE AND BE DEPORTED.
...
BUT INSTEAD YOU REVEALED YOUR SECRET TO A POPULAR GIRL AND MADE HER YOUR ALLY.
IT WAS MADDENING!
THEN YOU BROUGHT YOUR CAT HERE.
AND YOUR CHILDHOOD FRIEND SOON FOLLOWED.
THEN YOU ADDED ANOTHER HUMAN TO YOUR INNER CIRCLE.
AND THEN A SORCERESS FRIEND OF YOURS STARTS TEACHING SCHOOL HERE!
WHAT'S THE MATTER WITH YOU PEOPLE?
ARE YOU TRYING TO DRIVE ME CRAZY?
WELL, IT WORKED!!!

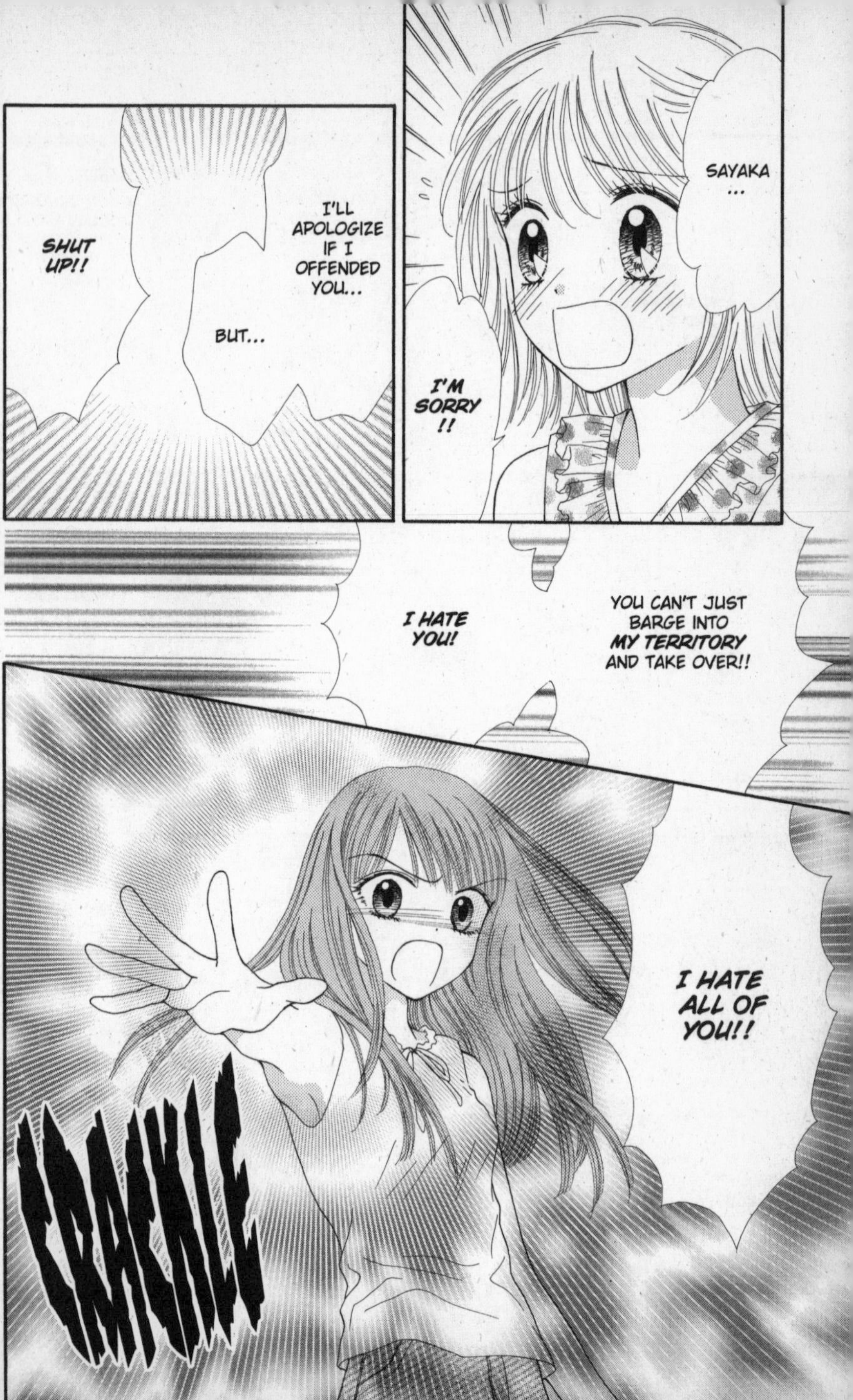
SAYAKA ...
I'M SORRY !!
I'LL APOLOGIZE IF I OFFENDED YOU...
BUT...
SHUT UP!!
YOU CAN'T JUST BARGE INTO MY TERRITORY AND TAKE OVER!!
I HATE YOU!
I HATE ALL OF YOU!!
CRACKLE

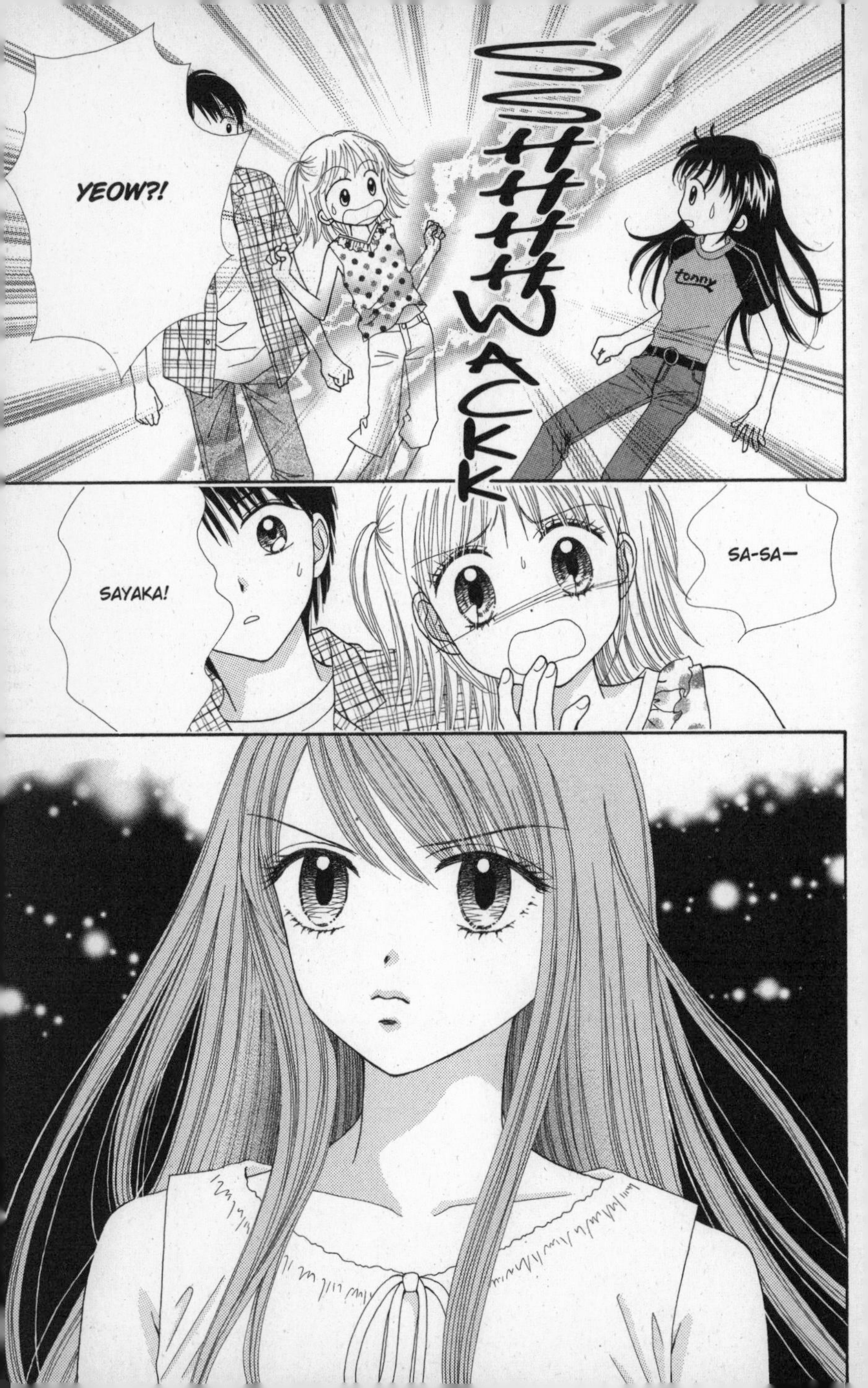
SMMMMWACKK
YEOW?!
SA-SA—
SAYAKA!

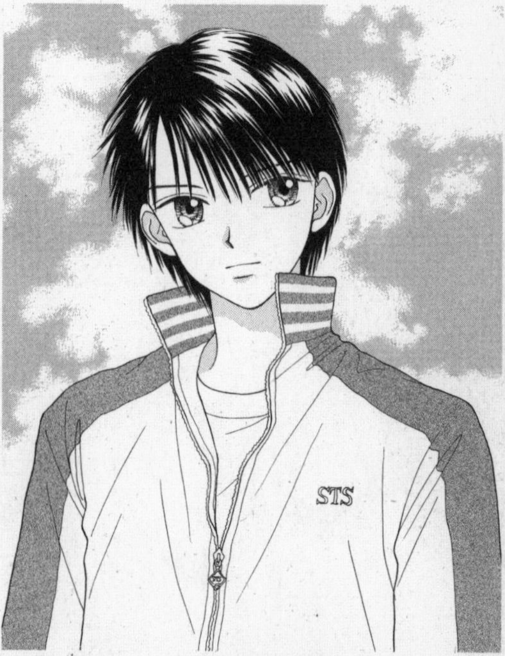
STS

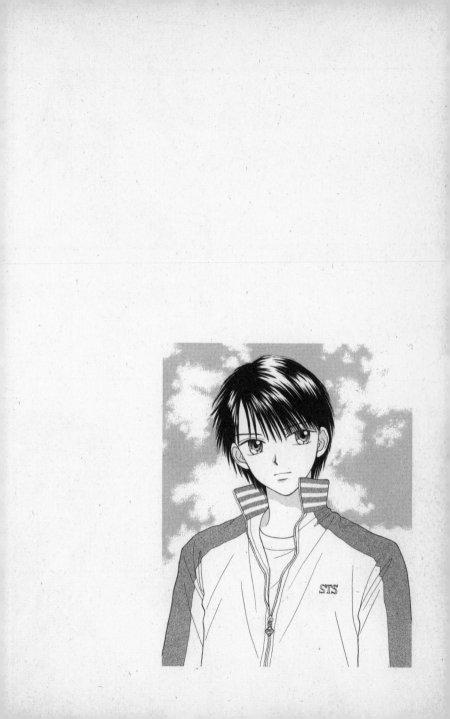

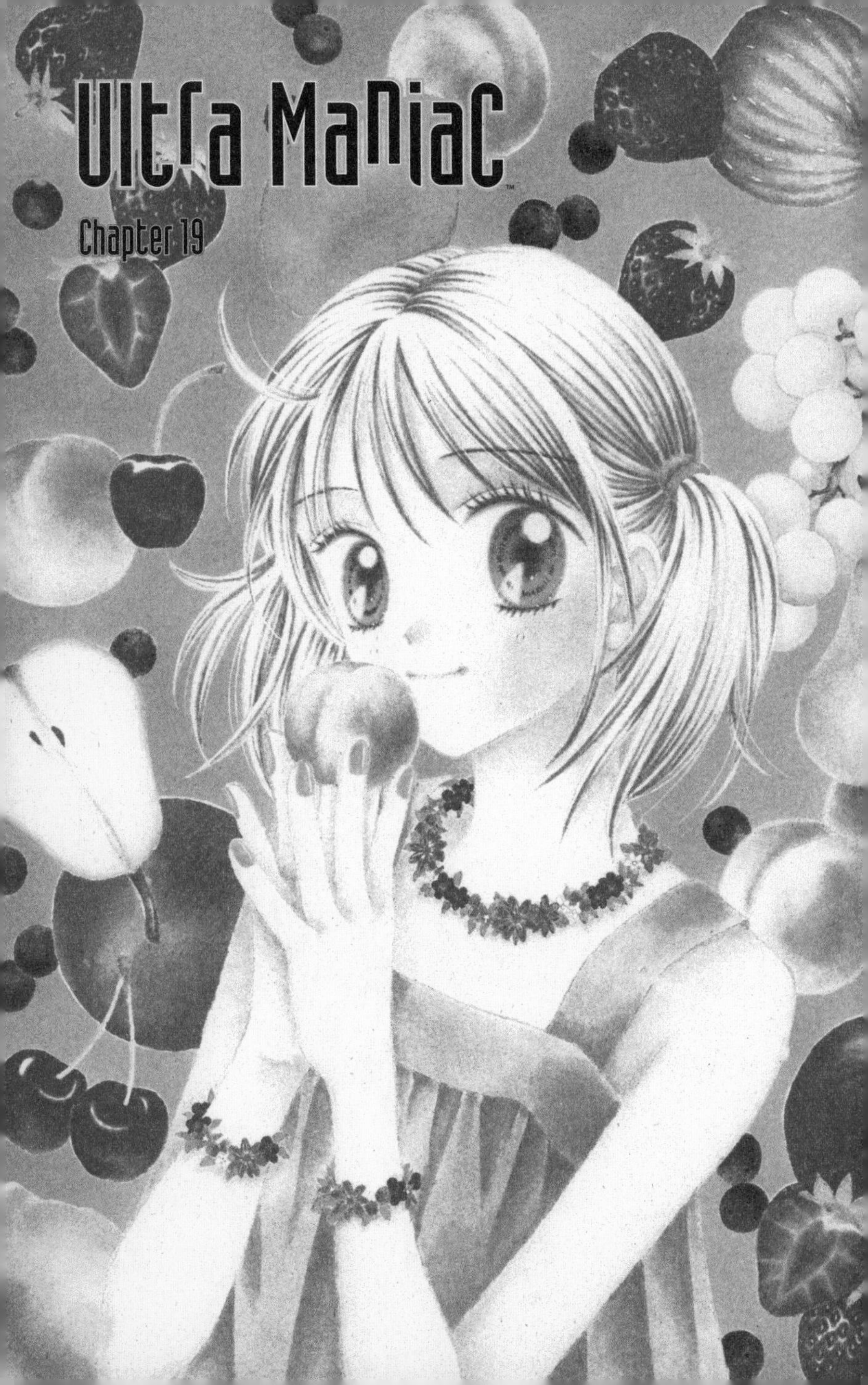
Ultra Maniac™
Chapter 19

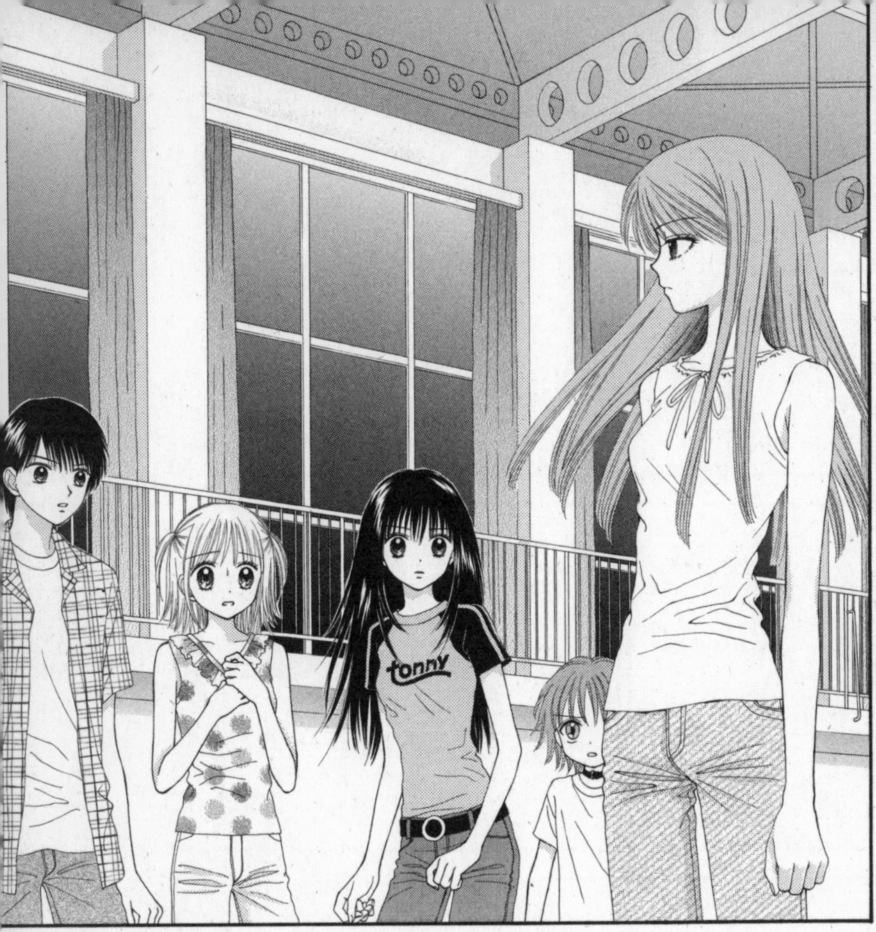
tonny

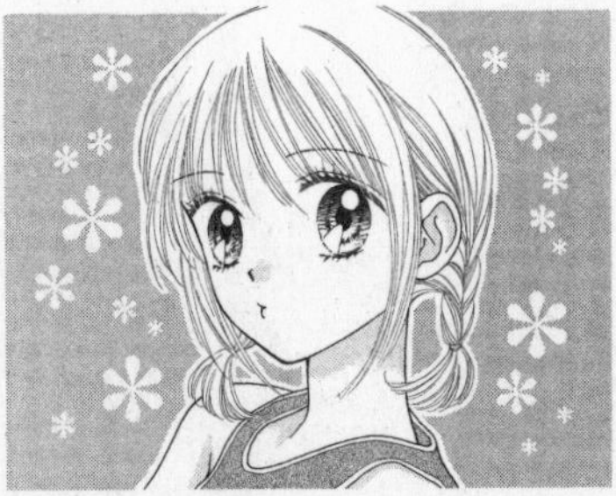

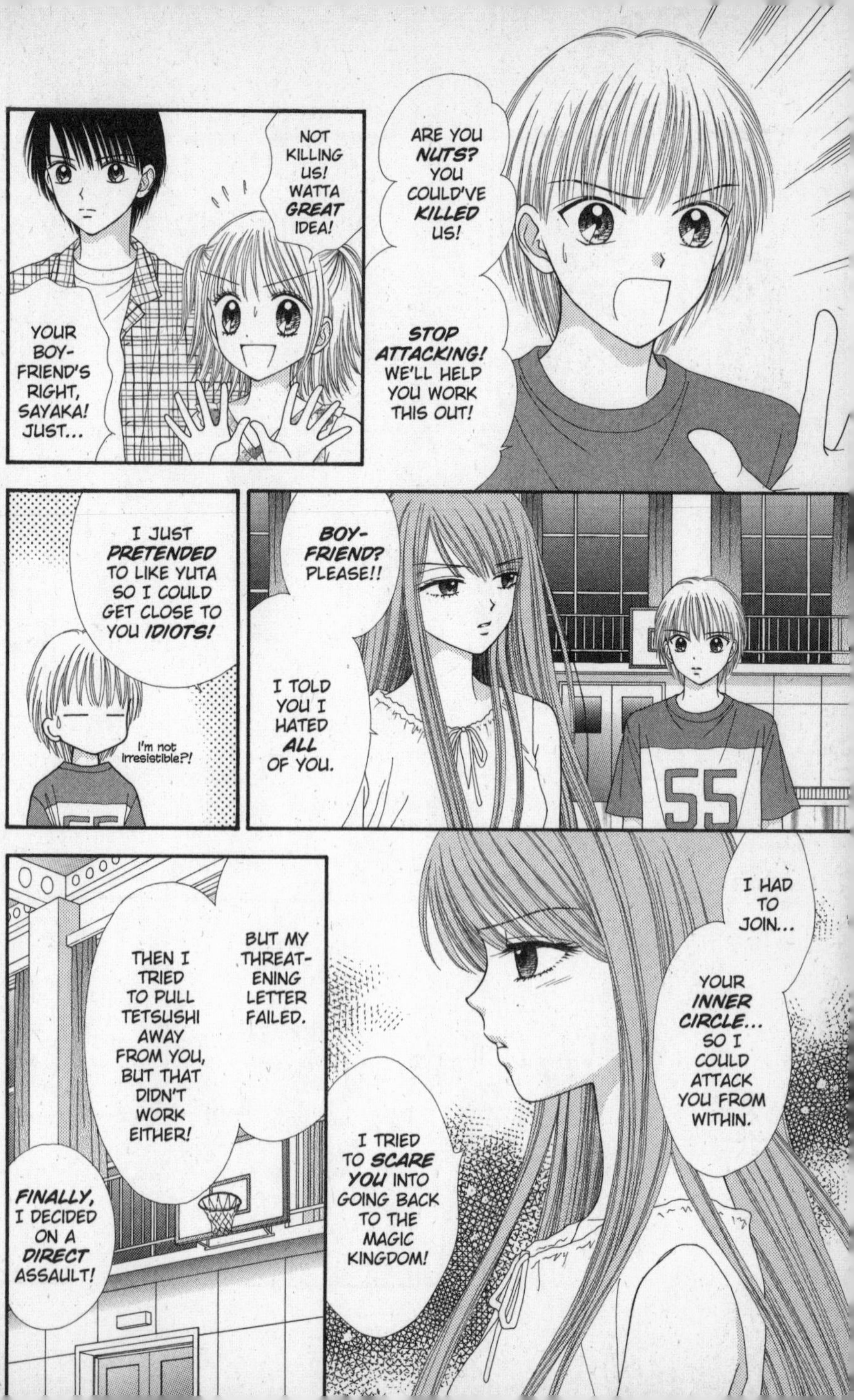
ARE YOU NUTS? YOU COULD'VE KILLED US!
STOP ATTACKING! WE'LL HELP YOU WORK THIS OUT!
NOT KILLING US! WATTA GREAT IDEA!
YOUR BOY-FRIEND'S RIGHT, SAYAKA! JUST...
BOY-FRIEND? PLEASE!!
I TOLD YOU I HATED ALL OF YOU.
I JUST PRETENDED TO LIKE YUTA SO I COULD GET CLOSE TO YOU IDIOTS!
I'm not irresistible?!
I HAD TO JOIN...
YOUR INNER CIRCLE... SO I COULD ATTACK YOU FROM WITHIN.
I TRIED TO SCARE YOU INTO GOING BACK TO THE MAGIC KINGDOM!
BUT MY THREAT-ENING LETTER FAILED.
THEN I TRIED TO PULL TETSUSHI AWAY FROM YOU, BUT THAT DIDN'T WORK EITHER!
FINALLY, I DECIDED ON A DIRECT ASSAULT!

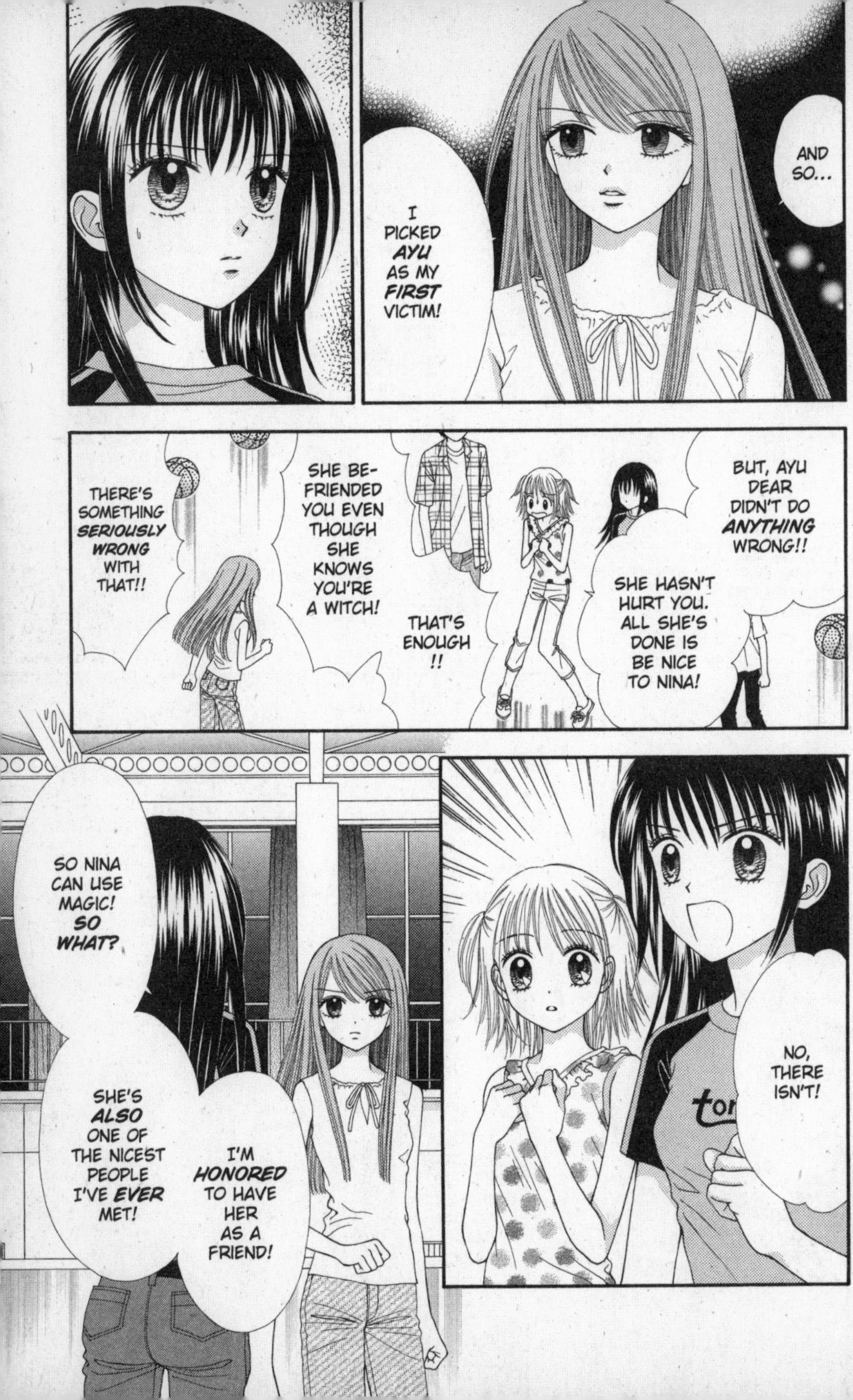
AND SO...
I PICKED AYU AS MY FIRST VICTIM!
BUT, AYU DEAR DIDN'T DO ANYTHING WRONG!!
SHE HASN'T HURT YOU. ALL SHE'S DONE IS BE NICE TO NINA!
THAT'S ENOUGH !!
SHE BE-FRIENDED YOU EVEN THOUGH SHE KNOWS YOU'RE A WITCH!
THERE'S SOMETHING SERIOUSLY WRONG WITH THAT!!
NO, THERE ISN'T!
SO NINA CAN USE MAGIC! SO WHAT?
SHE'S ALSO ONE OF THE NICEST PEOPLE I'VE EVER MET!
I'M HONORED TO HAVE HER AS A FRIEND!

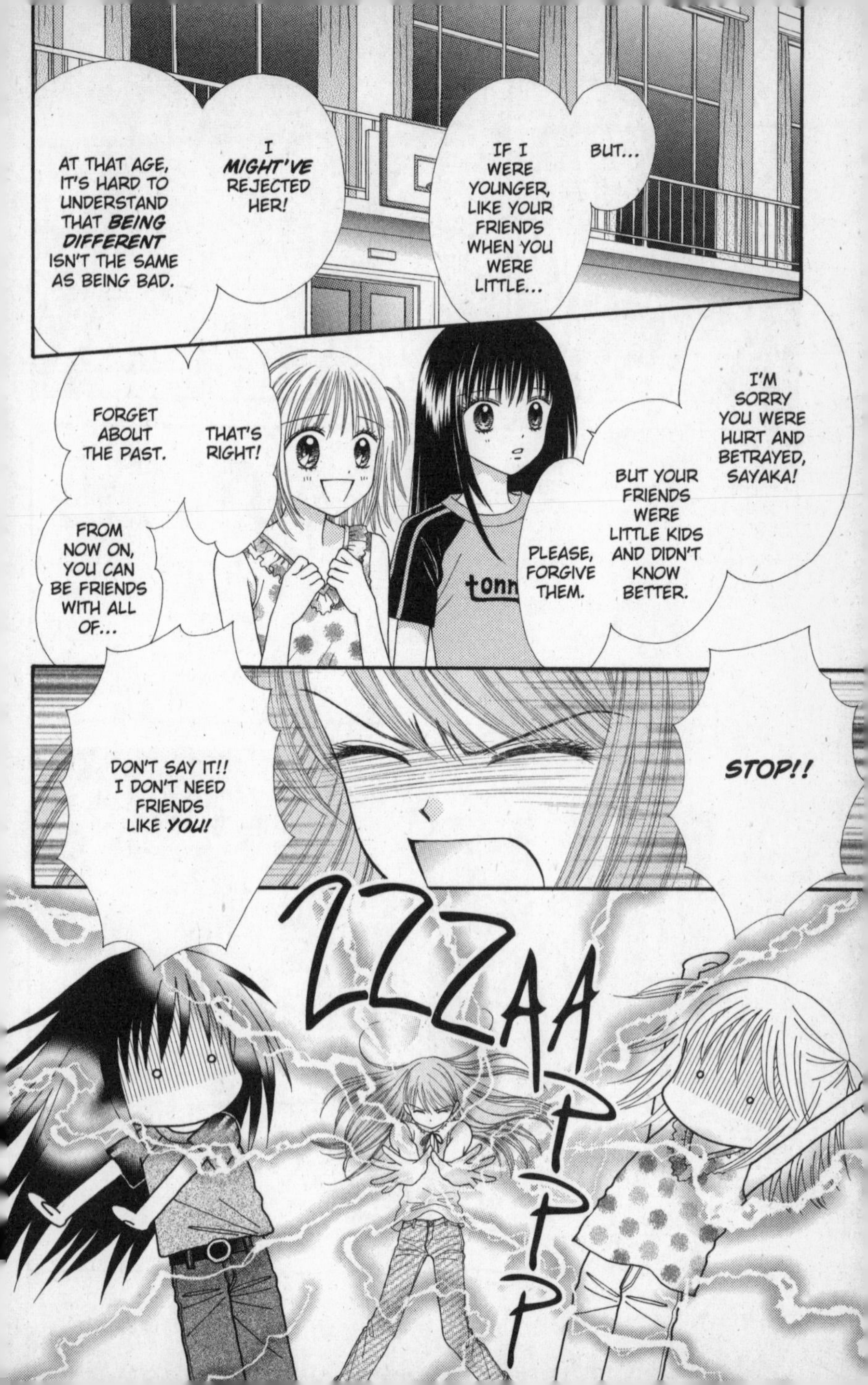
BUT...
IF I WERE YOUNGER, LIKE YOUR FRIENDS WHEN YOU WERE LITTLE...
I *MIGHT'VE* REJECTED HER!
AT THAT AGE, IT'S HARD TO UNDERSTAND THAT *BEING DIFFERENT* ISN'T THE SAME AS BEING BAD.
I'M SORRY YOU WERE HURT AND BETRAYED, SAYAKA!
BUT YOUR FRIENDS WERE LITTLE KIDS AND DIDN'T KNOW BETTER.
PLEASE, FORGIVE THEM.
THAT'S RIGHT!
FORGET ABOUT THE PAST.
FROM NOW ON, YOU CAN BE FRIENDS WITH ALL OF...
STOP!!
DON'T SAY IT!! I DON'T NEED FRIENDS LIKE *YOU!*
ZZZAAPPP

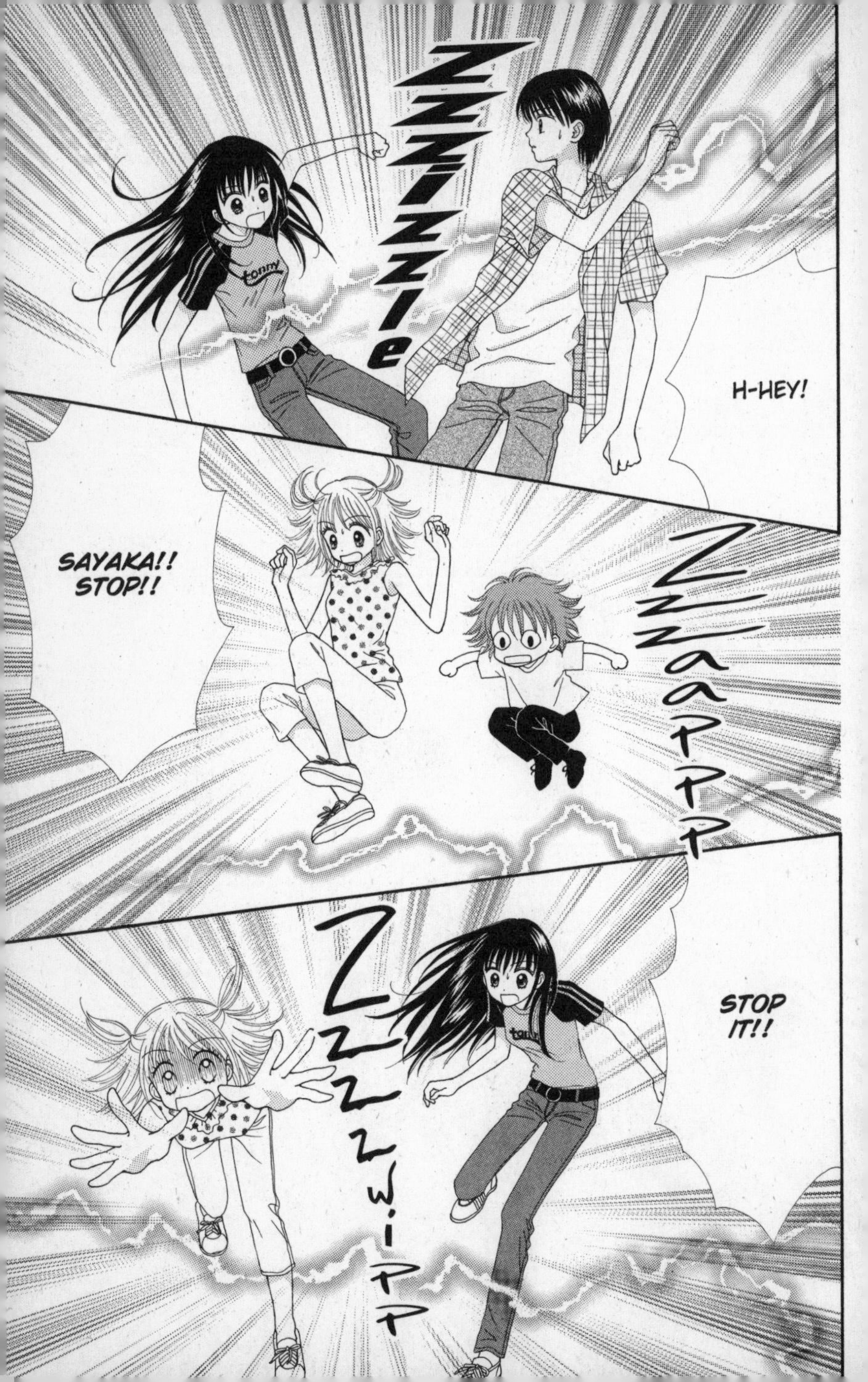
H-HEY!
ZZZIZZIE
SAYAKA!! STOP!!
ZZZAAPPP
STOP IT!!
ZZZZWIPP

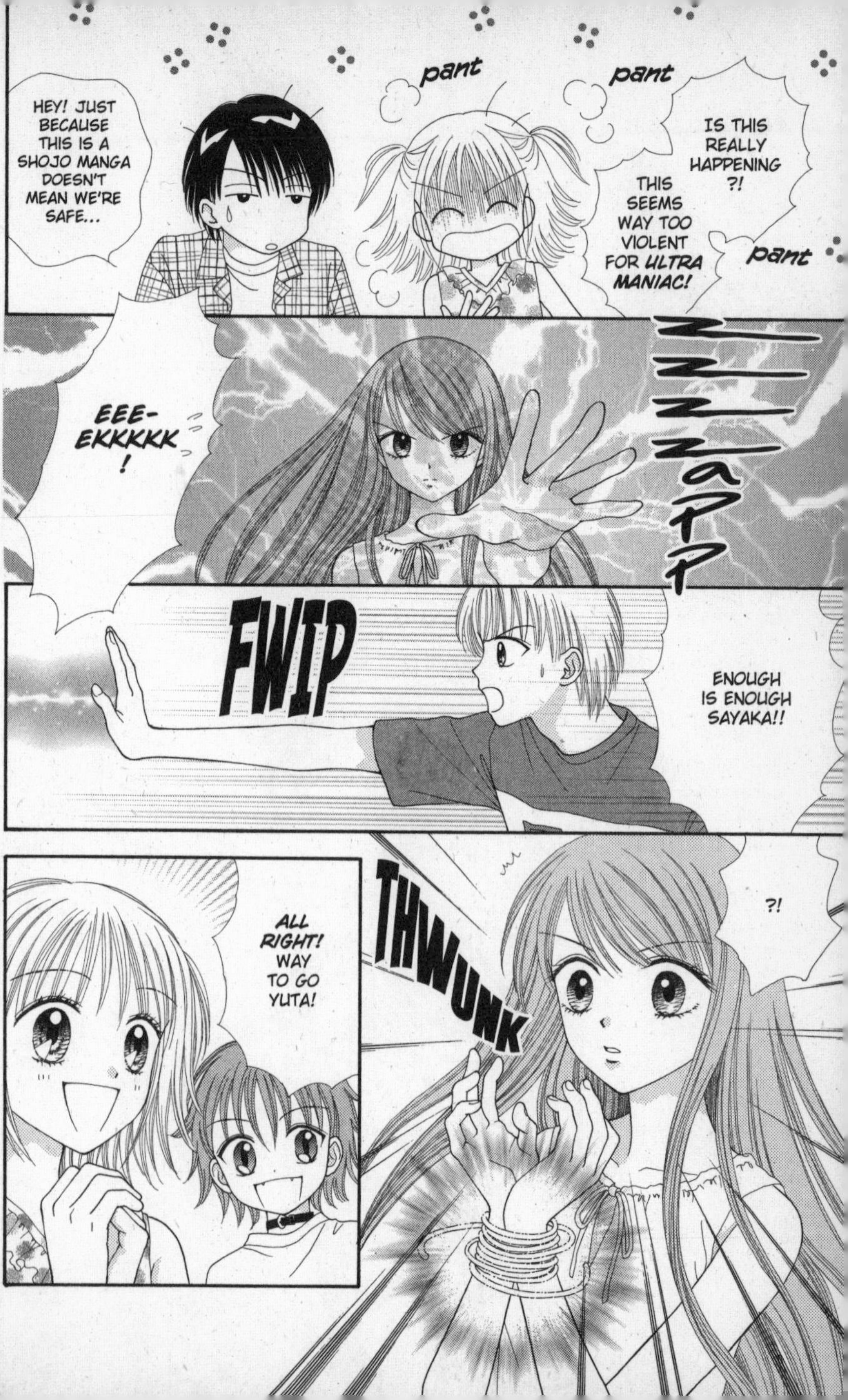
pant
pant
IS THIS REALLY HAPPENING?!
THIS SEEMS WAY TOO VIOLENT FOR *ULTRA MANIAC!*
pant
HEY! JUST BECAUSE THIS IS A SHOJO MANGA DOESN'T MEAN WE'RE SAFE...
ZZZZaPP
EEE-EKKKKK!
ENOUGH IS ENOUGH SAYAKA!!
FWIP
?!
THWUNK
ALL RIGHT! WAY TO GO YUTA!

FREE TALK 10

With the **Marmalade Boy** *DVD Box set, vocal collection CD and the complete collection being released, I started feeling pretty nostalgic for* **Marmalade Boy.** *So I called up Hiromi Seki (the producer of the* **Marmalade Boy** *anime) and asked her if she'd be interested in getting together.*

Then Hiromi called up Mariko Koda (the voice actress who played Miki in **Marmalade Boy***) and invited her to come along, too. We had lunch together yesterday and had a great time.*

I've met Mariko a number of times, but I've never eaten with her before in private. Prior to this, I've always assumed Mariko was a prim and proper lady. But she's actually quite a tomboy! (Laughs!)

She really opened up and it was a lot of fun.

She even gave me some really good African herbal tea!♡

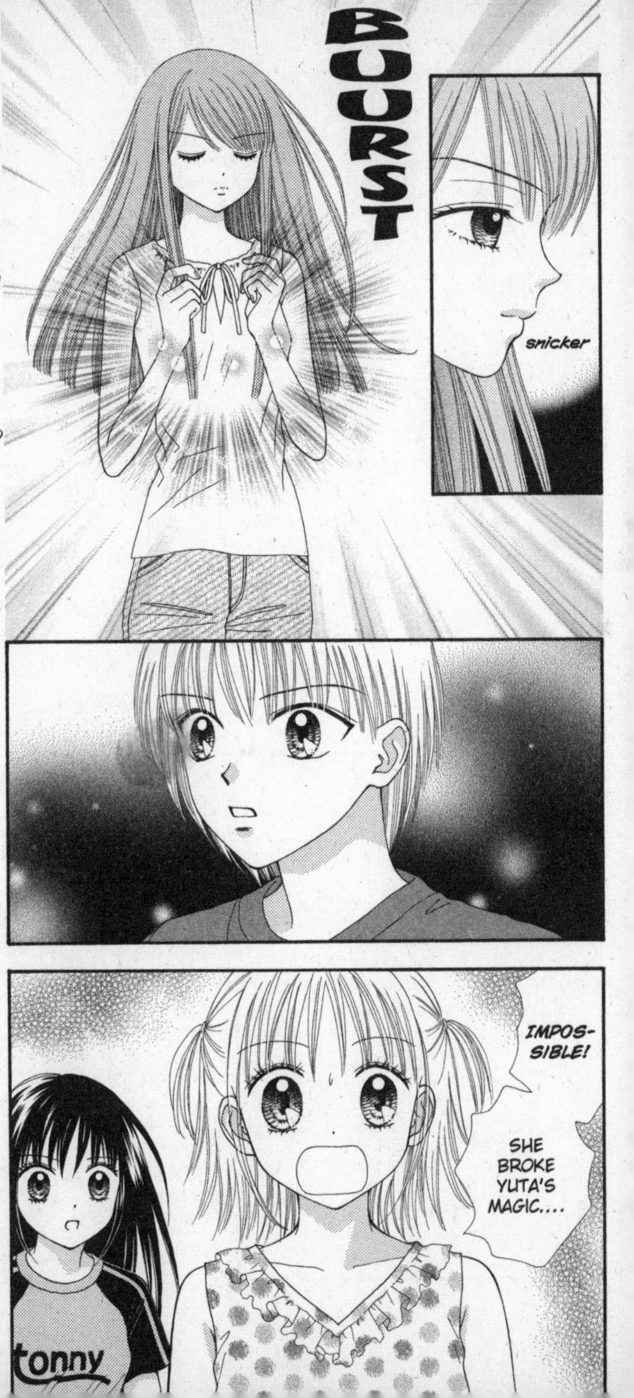
snicker
BURST
IMPOS-SIBLE!
SHE BROKE YUTA'S MAGIC....

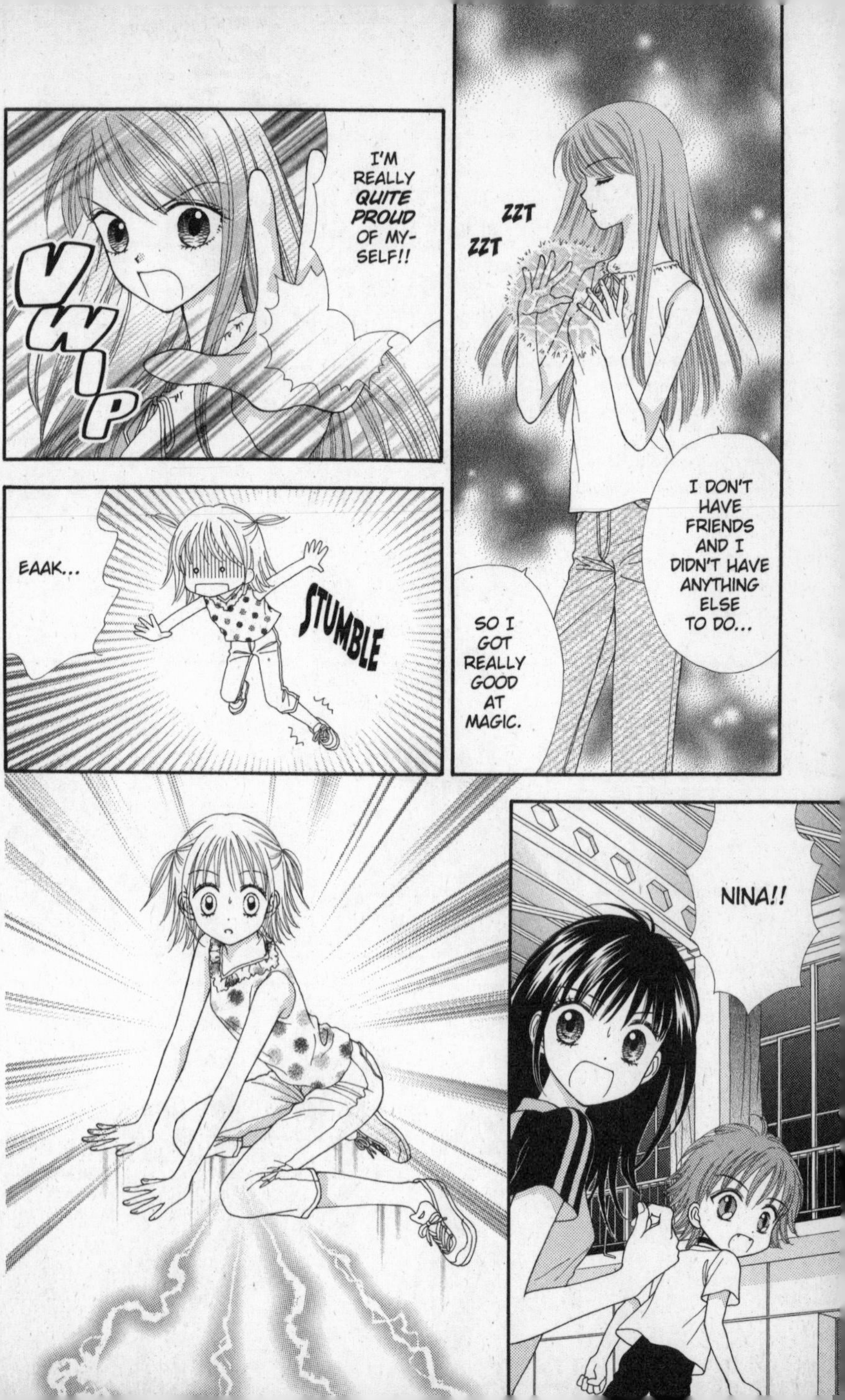
ZZT
ZZT
I DON'T HAVE FRIENDS AND I DIDN'T HAVE ANYTHING ELSE TO DO...
SO I GOT REALLY GOOD AT MAGIC.
I'M REALLY QUITE PROUD OF MY-SELF!!
VWIP
EAAK...
STUMBLE
NINA!!

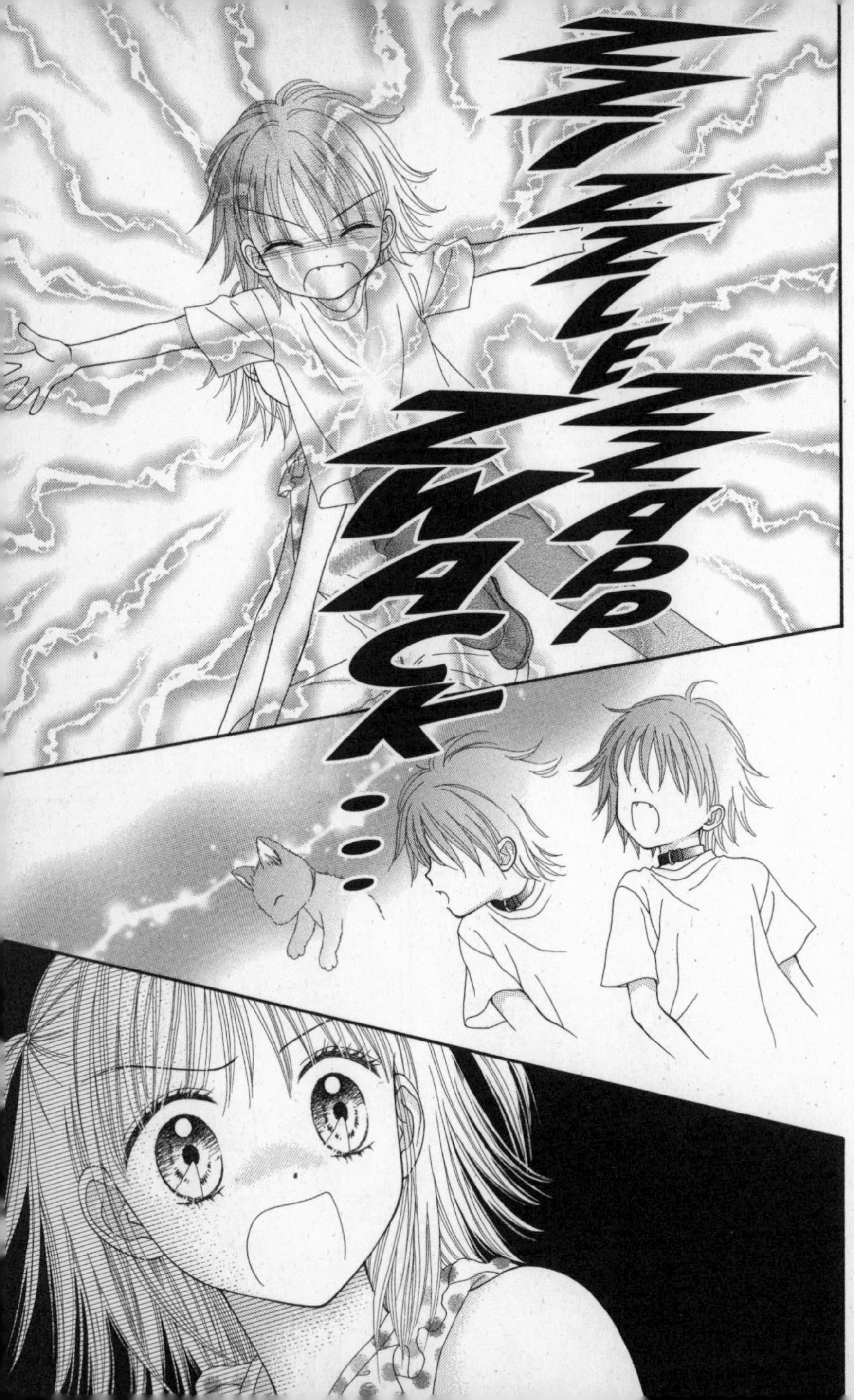
ZZZZZZZZZAPP
ZWACK....

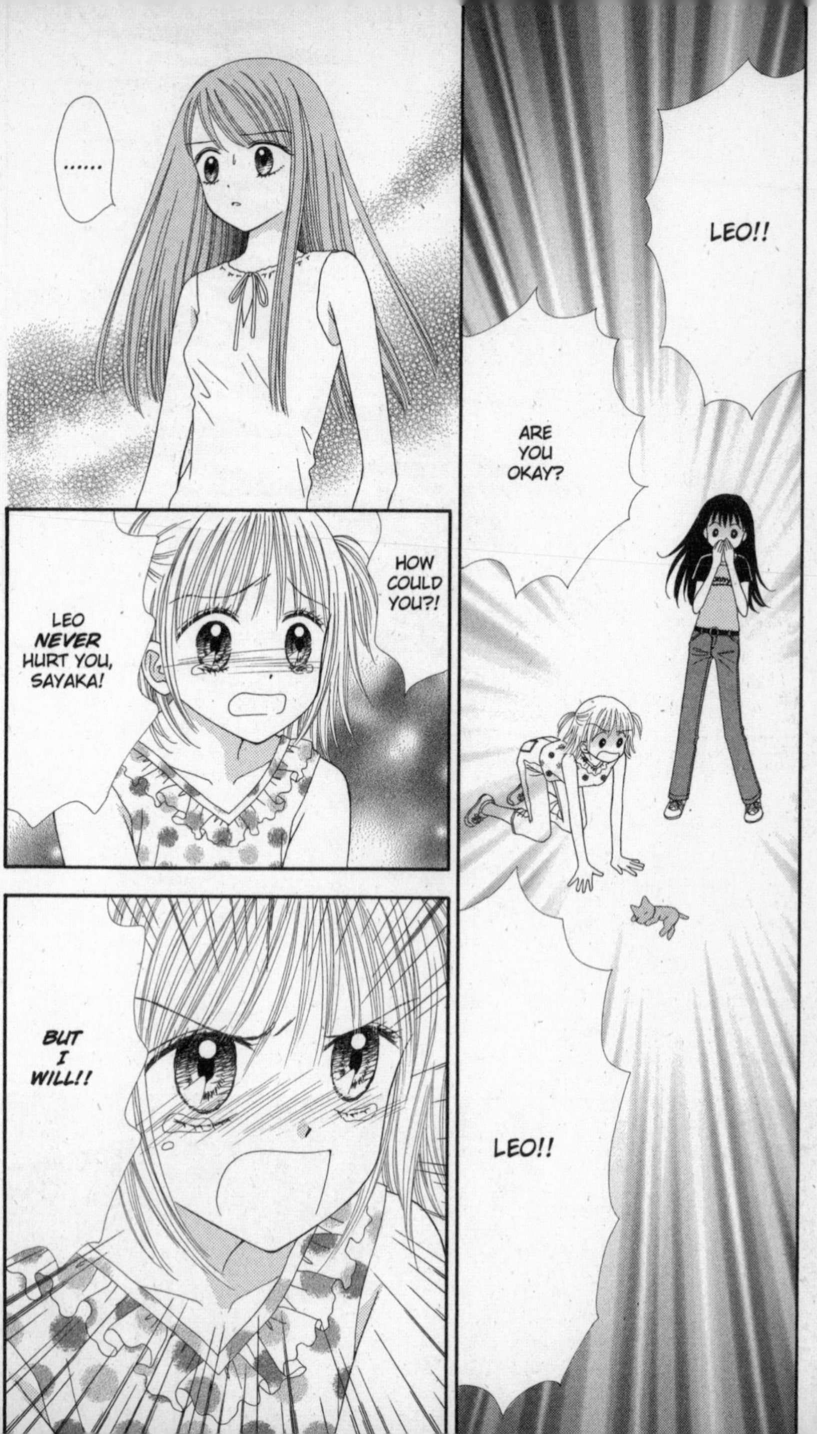
LEO!!
ARE YOU OKAY?
LEO!!
......
HOW COULD YOU?!
LEO ***NEVER*** HURT YOU, SAYAKA!
BUT I WILL!!

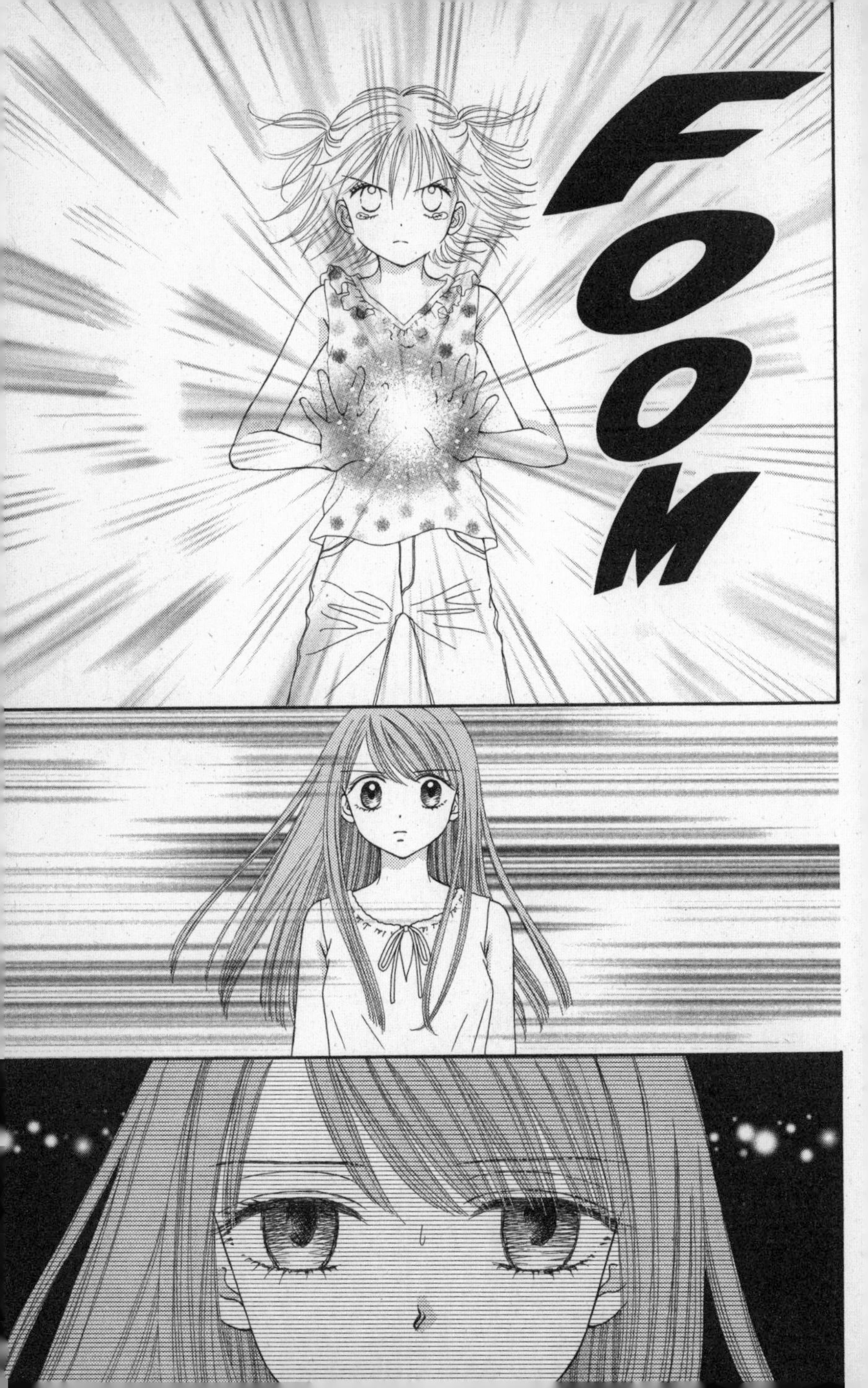
FOOM

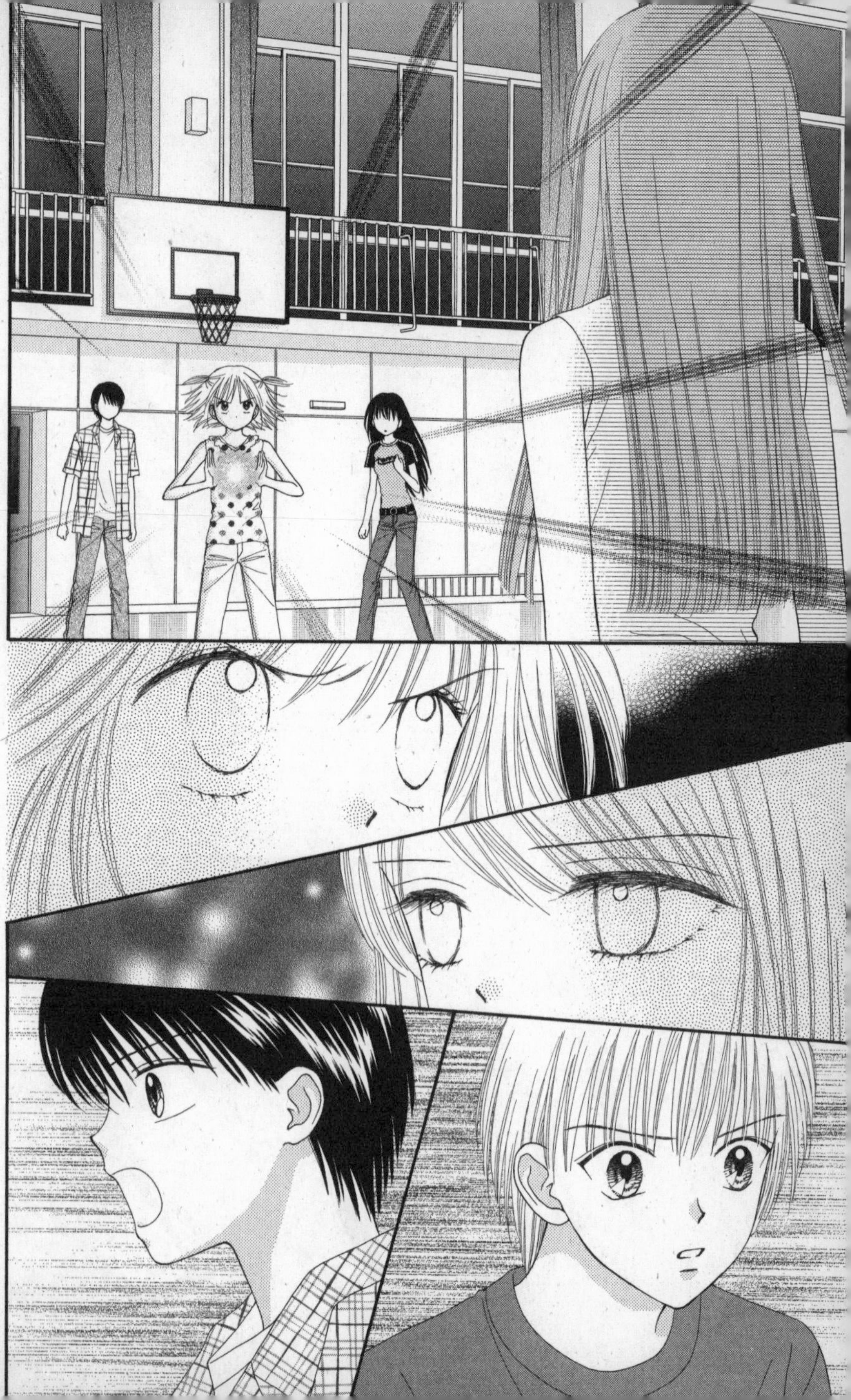

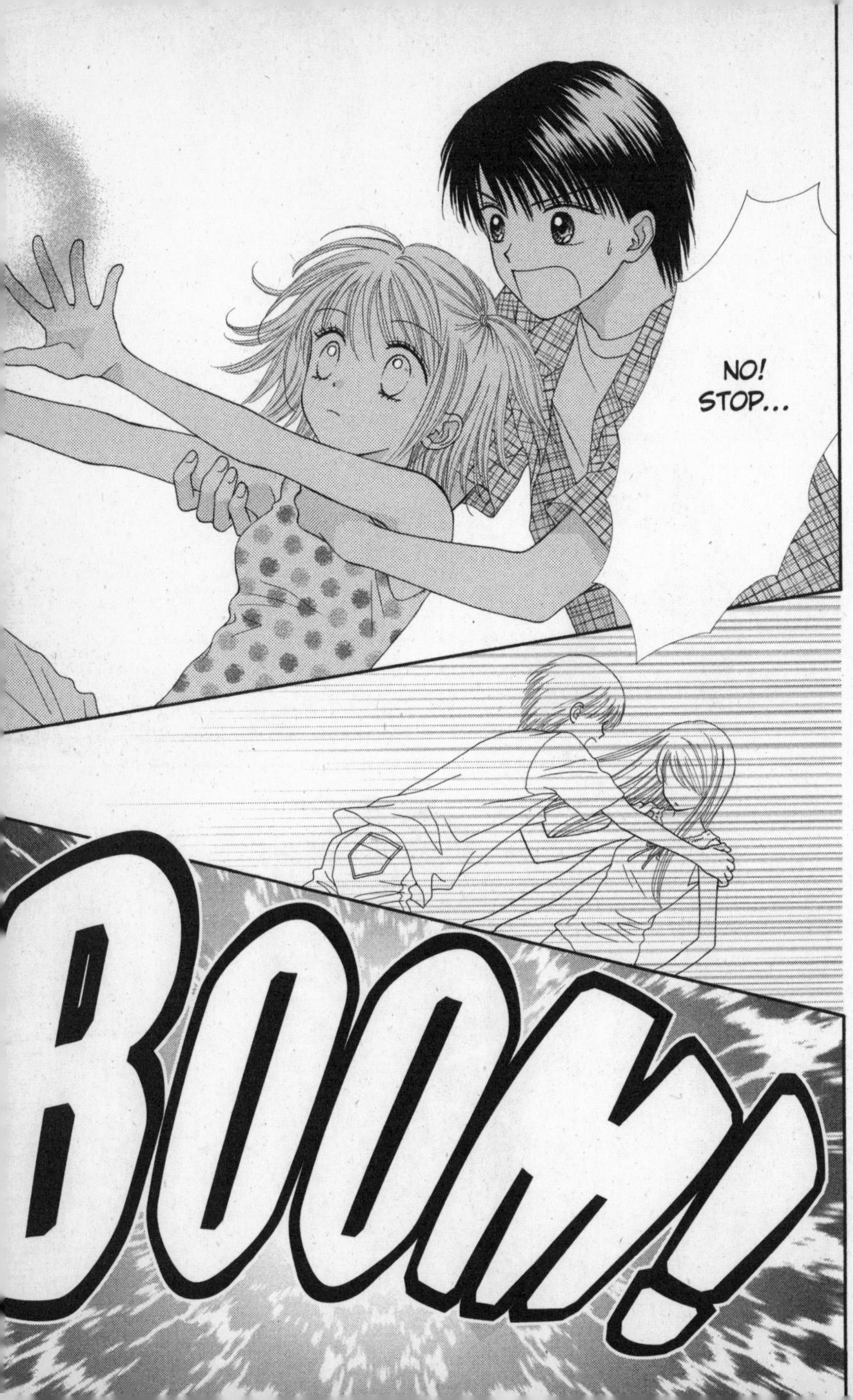
NO!
STOP...
BOOM!

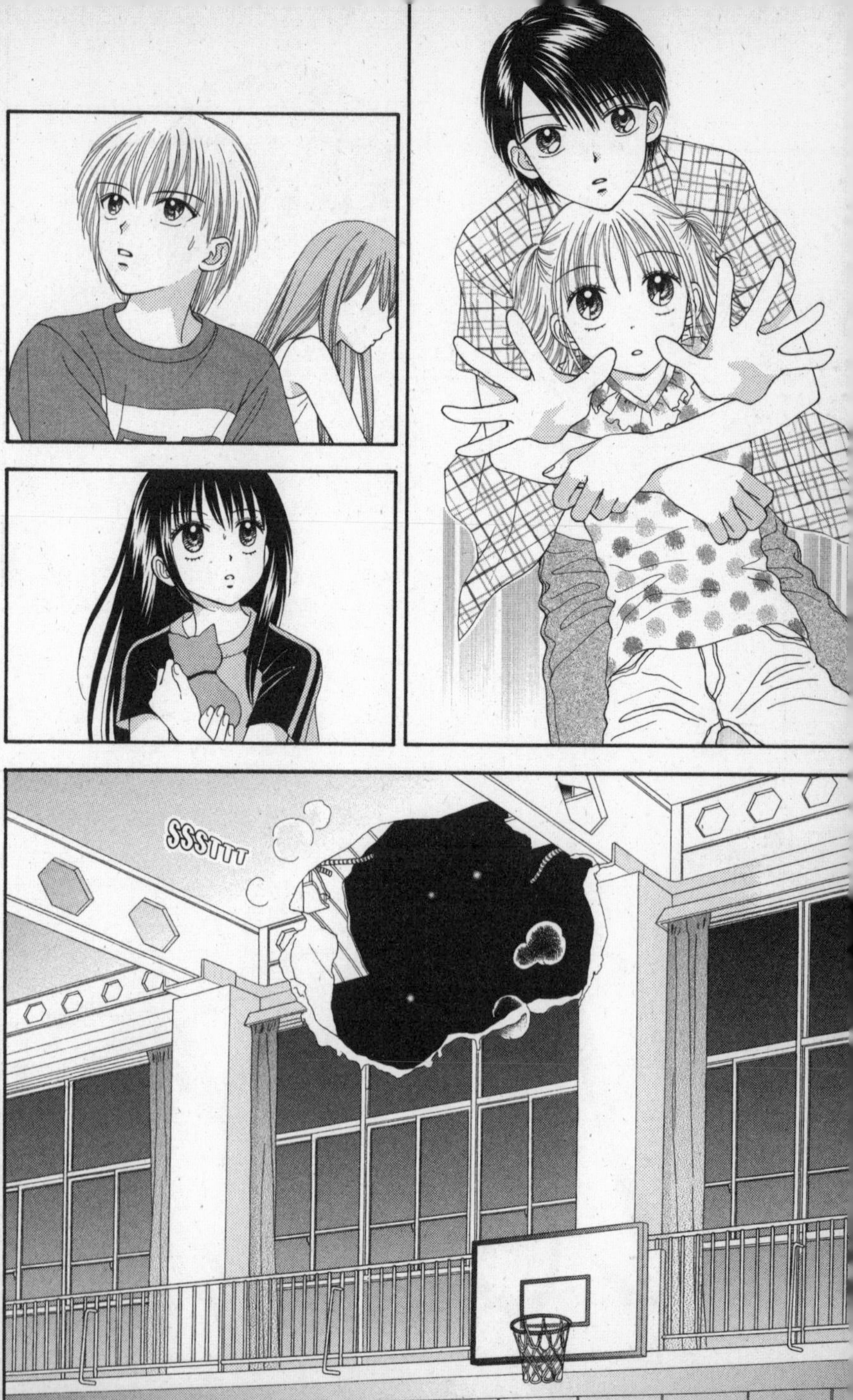
SSSTTT

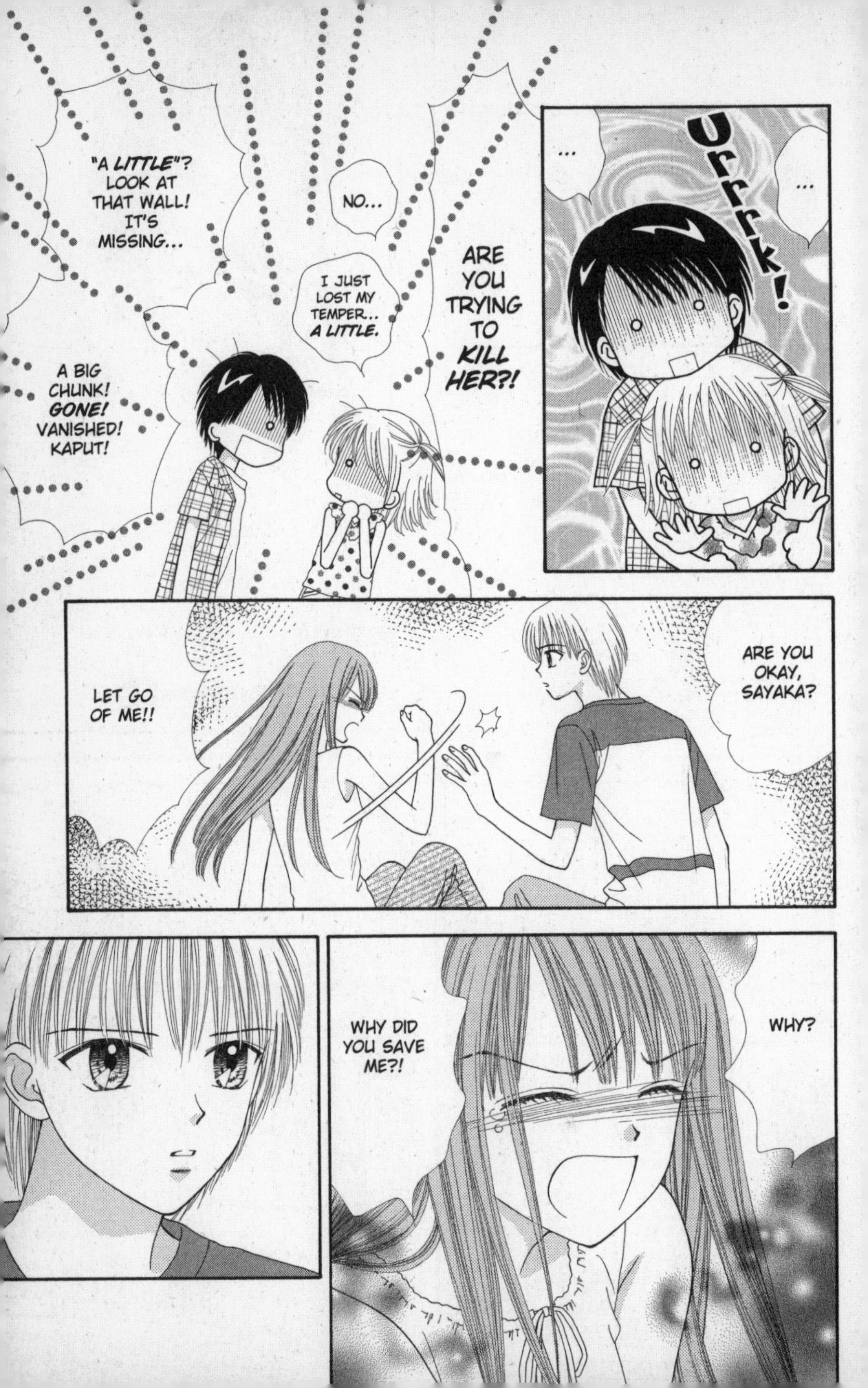

URRRK!
...
...
ARE YOU TRYING TO *KILL HER?!*
NO...
I JUST LOST MY TEMPER... *A LITTLE.*
"A *LITTLE*"? LOOK AT THAT WALL! IT'S MISSING...
A BIG CHUNK! *GONE!* VANISHED! KAPUT!
ARE YOU OKAY, SAYAKA?
LET GO OF ME!!
WHY?
WHY DID YOU SAVE ME?!

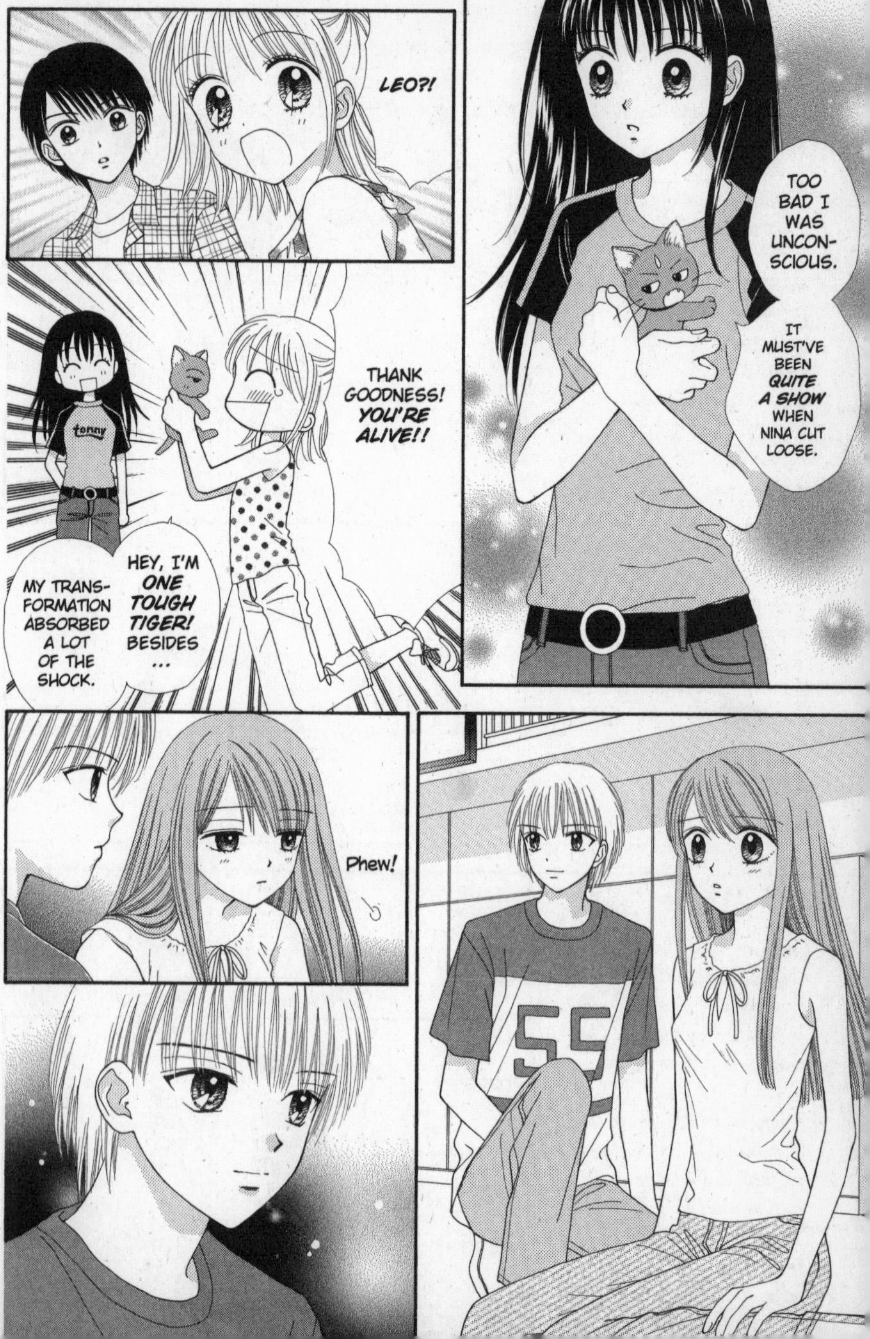
TOO BAD I WAS UNCONSCIOUS.
IT MUST'VE BEEN QUITE A SHOW WHEN NINA CUT LOOSE.
LEO?!
THANK GOODNESS! YOU'RE ALIVE!!
HEY, I'M ONE TOUGH TIGER! BESIDES ...
MY TRANSFORMATION ABSORBED A LOT OF THE SHOCK.
Phew!

FREE TALK 11

Changing the topic . . . I set up and sold things at a flea market for the first time.

Friends gave me lots of useful tips about selling in flea markets. So it was pretty easy. But, in some ways, the flea market was quite different from what I expected.

I thought it was going to be an easy-going, simple, cozy affair, but actually it was . . . sort of terrifying. (Laughs.) Especially first thing in the morning.

In fact, the real frenzy was before we officially opened. People barged in and tried to buy stuff before I was finished setting up. All of them were giving off this powerful "I'm going to get the best bargain!" or "I'll find the diamond in the rough!" energy. It was incredible.

I thought a cute girl would buy my Prada shoes. (I really liked the design, but the arch didn't fit so I only wore them once.) Or buy my Gucci enamel loafers and Anna Sui sandals. But all three were bought (prior to opening) by a middle-aged woman. She didn't even try them on!

I suspect she isn't going to wear them herself. I'll bet she's going to sell them...maybe on an on-line auction. Oh, well. Everything sold well and there were lots of nice people, too. So I think I'll do it again.

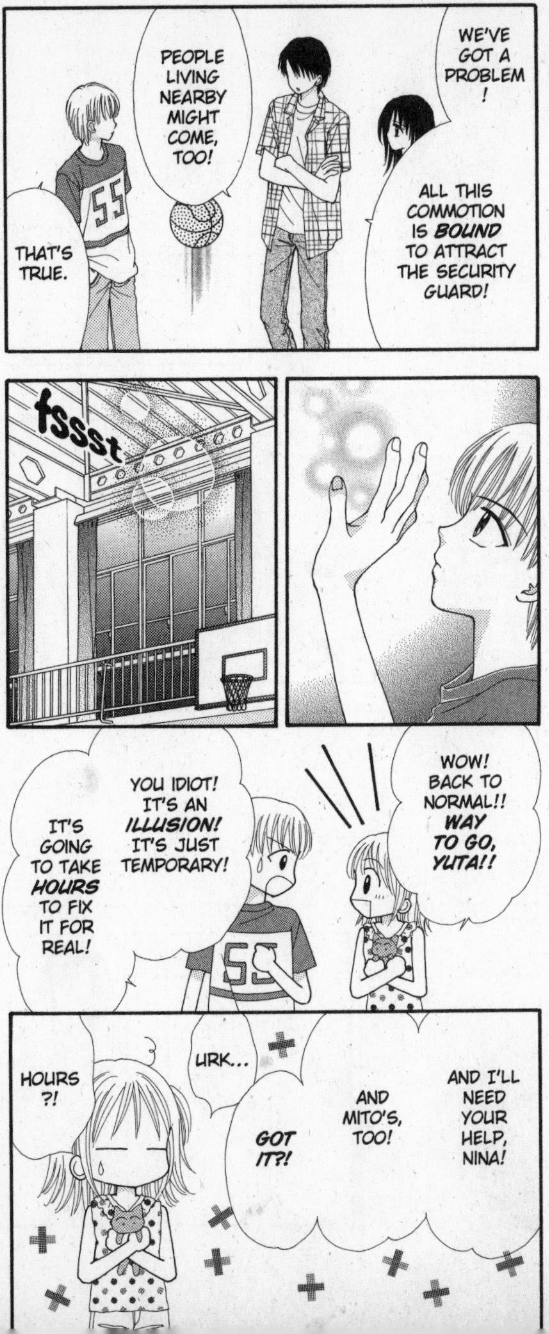
WE'VE GOT A PROBLEM!
ALL THIS COMMOTION IS BOUND TO ATTRACT THE SECURITY GUARD!
PEOPLE LIVING NEARBY MIGHT COME, TOO!
THAT'S TRUE.
fssst
WOW! BACK TO NORMAL!! WAY TO GO, YUTA!!
YOU IDIOT! IT'S AN ILLUSION! IT'S JUST TEMPORARY!
IT'S GOING TO TAKE HOURS TO FIX IT FOR REAL!
AND I'LL NEED YOUR HELP, NINA!
AND MITO'S, TOO!
GOT IT?!
URK...
HOURS?!

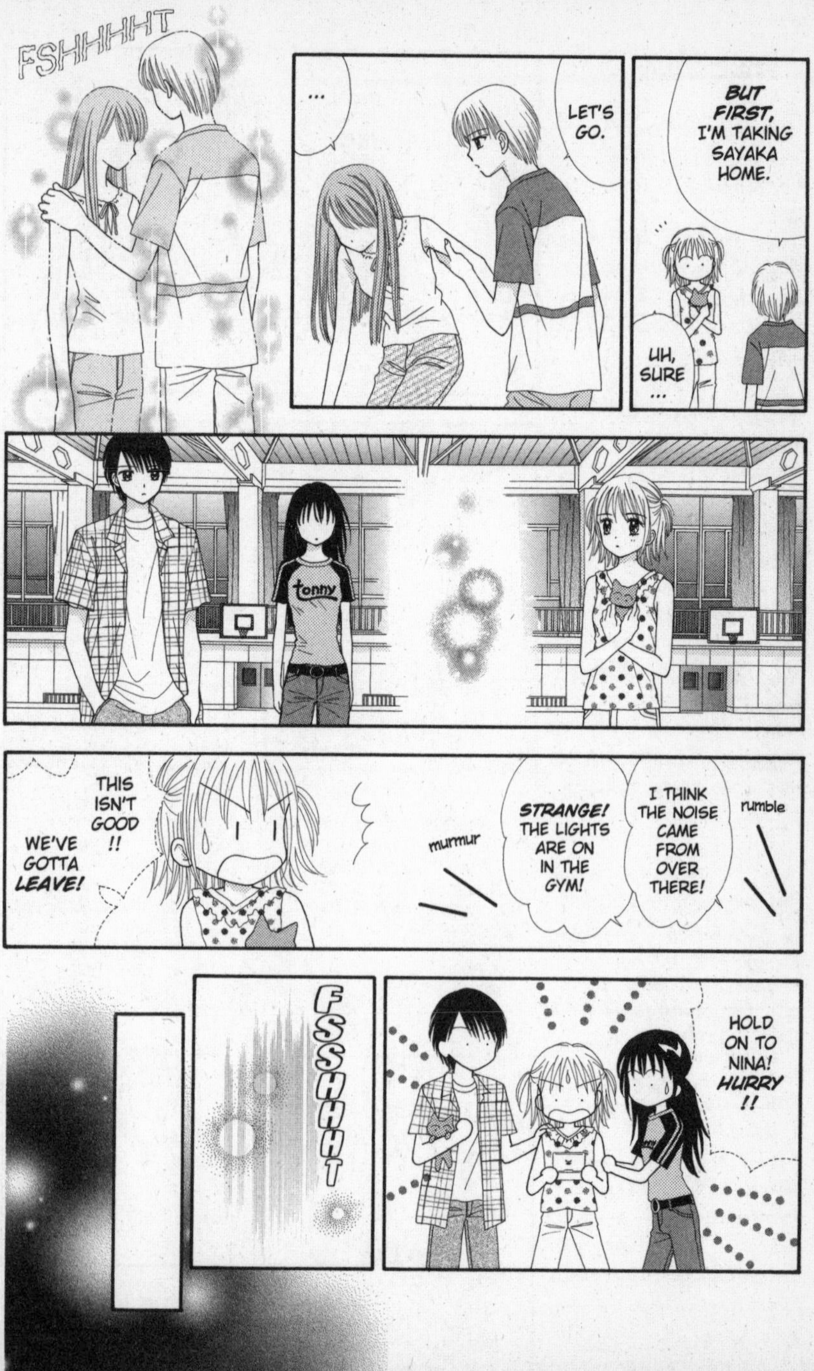
BUT FIRST, I'M TAKING SAYAKA HOME.
...
UH, SURE ...
LET'S GO.
...
FSHHHHT
tonny
rumble
I THINK THE NOISE CAME FROM OVER THERE!
STRANGE! THE LIGHTS ARE ON IN THE GYM!
murmur
THIS ISN'T GOOD !!
WE'VE GOTTA LEAVE!
HOLD ON TO NINA! HURRY !!
FSSHHHT

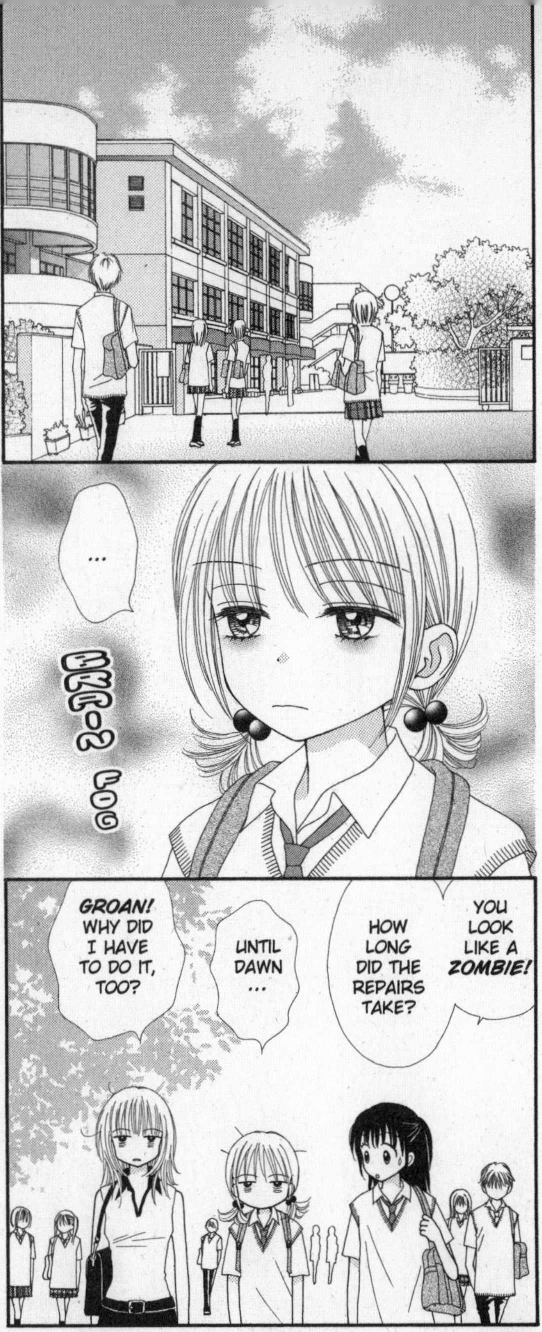
...
BRAIN FOG
YOU LOOK LIKE A ZOMBIE!
HOW LONG DID THE REPAIRS TAKE?
UNTIL DAWN ...
GROAN! WHY DID I HAVE TO DO IT, TOO?

FREE TALK 12

"The Kenya Trip Chronicles" at the end of this volume was written right before the start of **Ultra Maniac**.

Usually, my manga essays are just written about events in my life. They don't depict other people as central characters. But on this trip, Ura (Satoru Hiura, creator of **Eb Star**) was the one saying funny things, and Miwa-pon (Miwa Ueda of **Peach Girl** fame) was doing all the funny things. I wasn't doing anything funny! So I wrote about all three of us. (Many thanks to Ura and Miwa-pon for allowing me to do that!)

Kenya was really amazing. I want to go again!! But it's so far . . .

I planned to finish off all the side stuff in the Free Talk this time, but I'm out of time. So I'll bring it to a close here.

If you'd like, please write and tell me what you think of **Ultra Maniac**. Mail to:

> Ultra Maniac c/o Shojo Beat
> VIZ Media
> P.O. Box 77010
> San Francisco, CA 94107

--Wataru Yoshizumi

And so, I'll talk to you later in Volume 5!

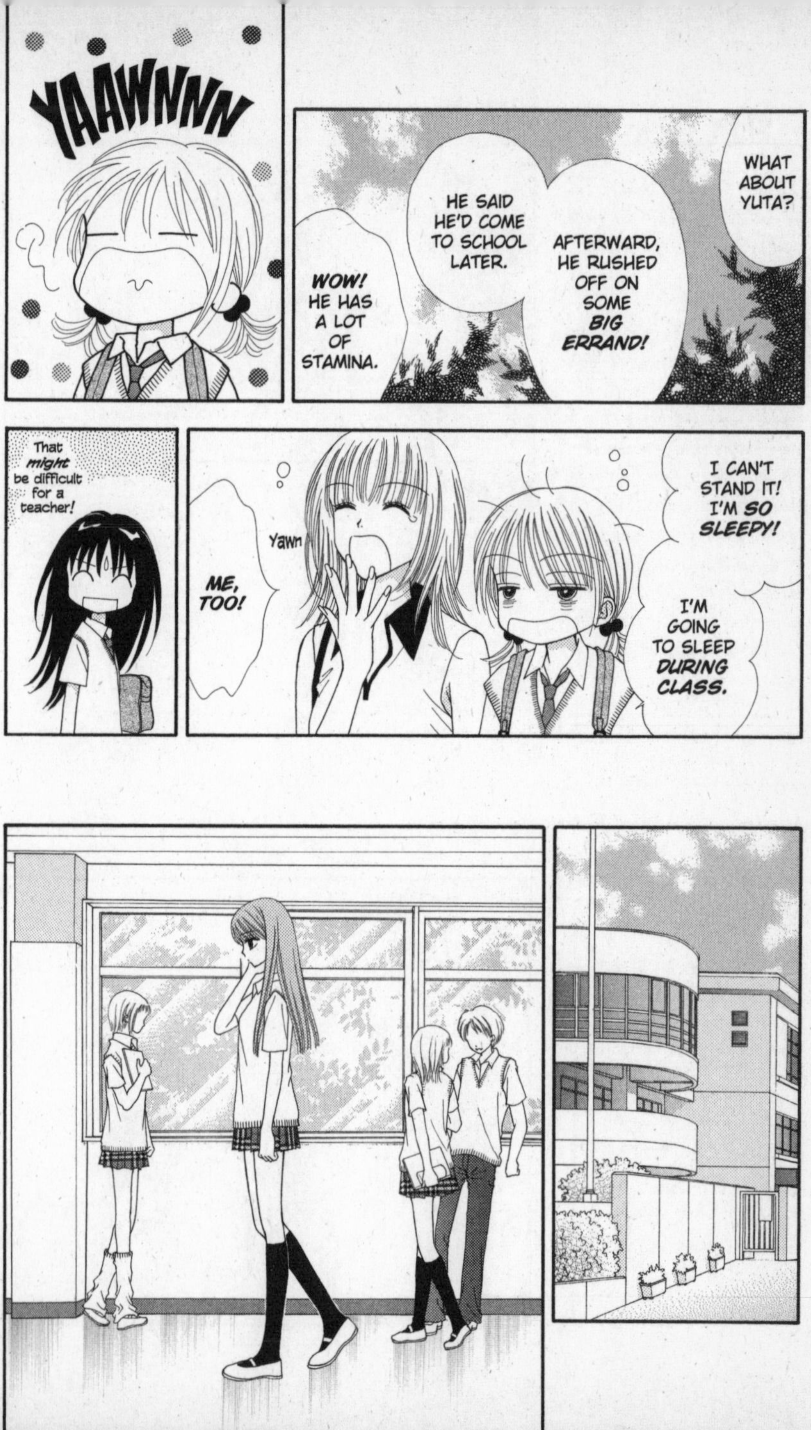
WHAT ABOUT YUTA?
HE SAID HE'D COME TO SCHOOL LATER.
AFTERWARD, HE RUSHED OFF ON SOME BIG ERRAND!
WOW! HE HAS A LOT OF STAMINA.
YAAWNNN
I CAN'T STAND IT! I'M SO SLEEPY!
I'M GOING TO SLEEP DURING CLASS.
Yawn
ME, TOO!
That might be difficult for a teacher!

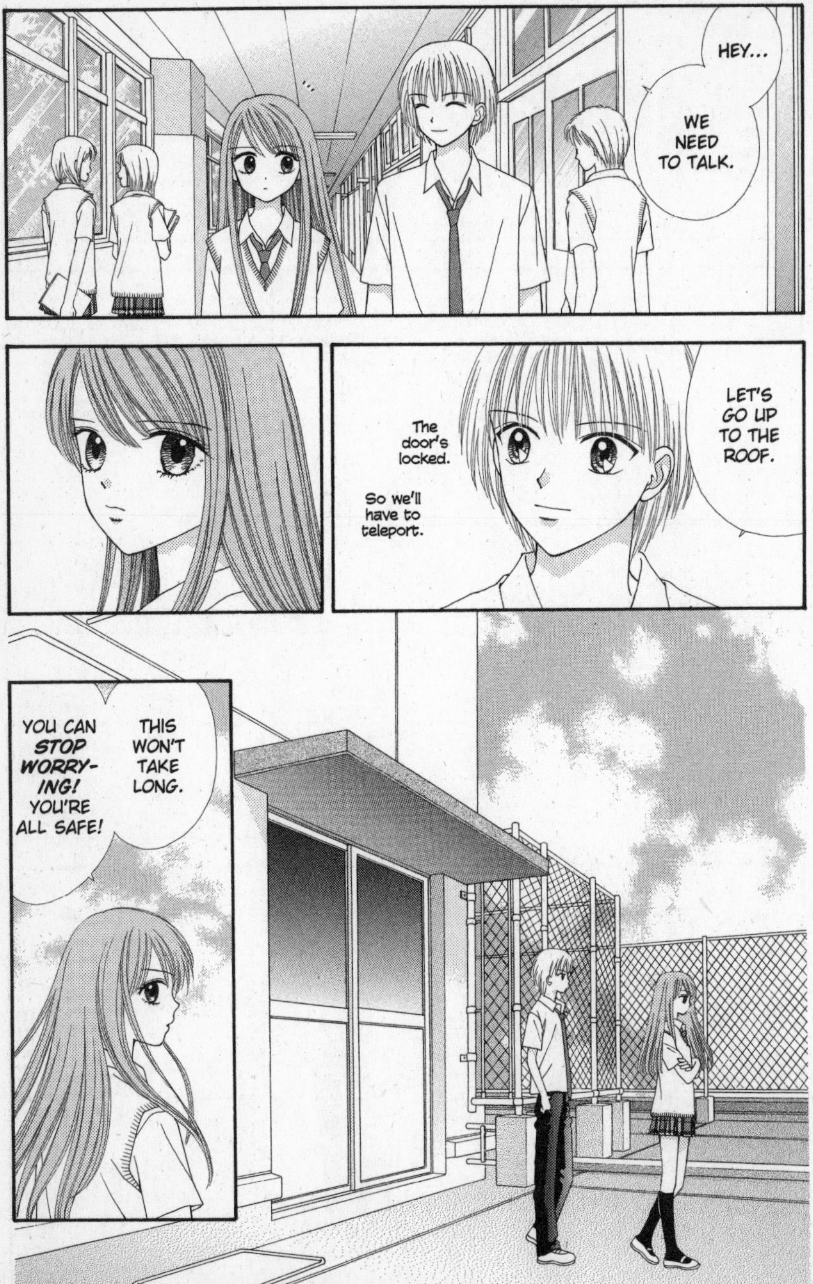
HEY...
WE NEED TO TALK.
LET'S GO UP TO THE ROOF.
The door's locked.
So we'll have to teleport.
THIS WON'T TAKE LONG.
YOU CAN *STOP WORRY-ING!* YOU'RE ALL SAFE!

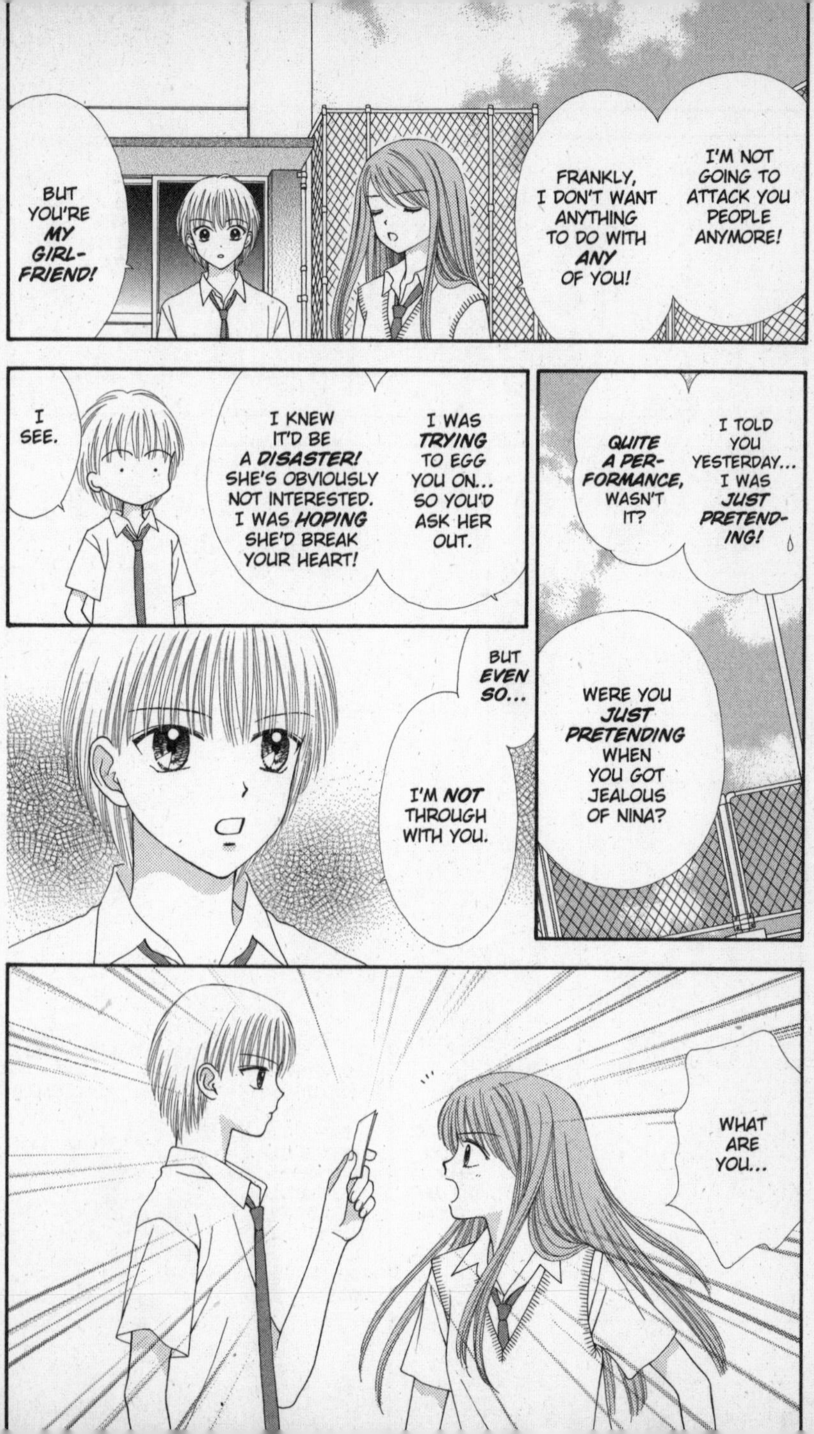

I'M NOT GOING TO ATTACK YOU PEOPLE ANYMORE!
FRANKLY, I DON'T WANT ANYTHING TO DO WITH ANY OF YOU!
BUT YOU'RE MY GIRL-FRIEND!
I TOLD YOU YESTERDAY... I WAS JUST PRETEND-ING!
QUITE A PER-FORMANCE, WASN'T IT?
WERE YOU JUST PRETENDING WHEN YOU GOT JEALOUS OF NINA?
I WAS TRYING TO EGG YOU ON... SO YOU'D ASK HER OUT.
I KNEW IT'D BE A DISASTER! SHE'S OBVIOUSLY NOT INTERESTED. I WAS HOPING SHE'D BREAK YOUR HEART!
I SEE.
BUT EVEN SO...
I'M NOT THROUGH WITH YOU.
WHAT ARE YOU...

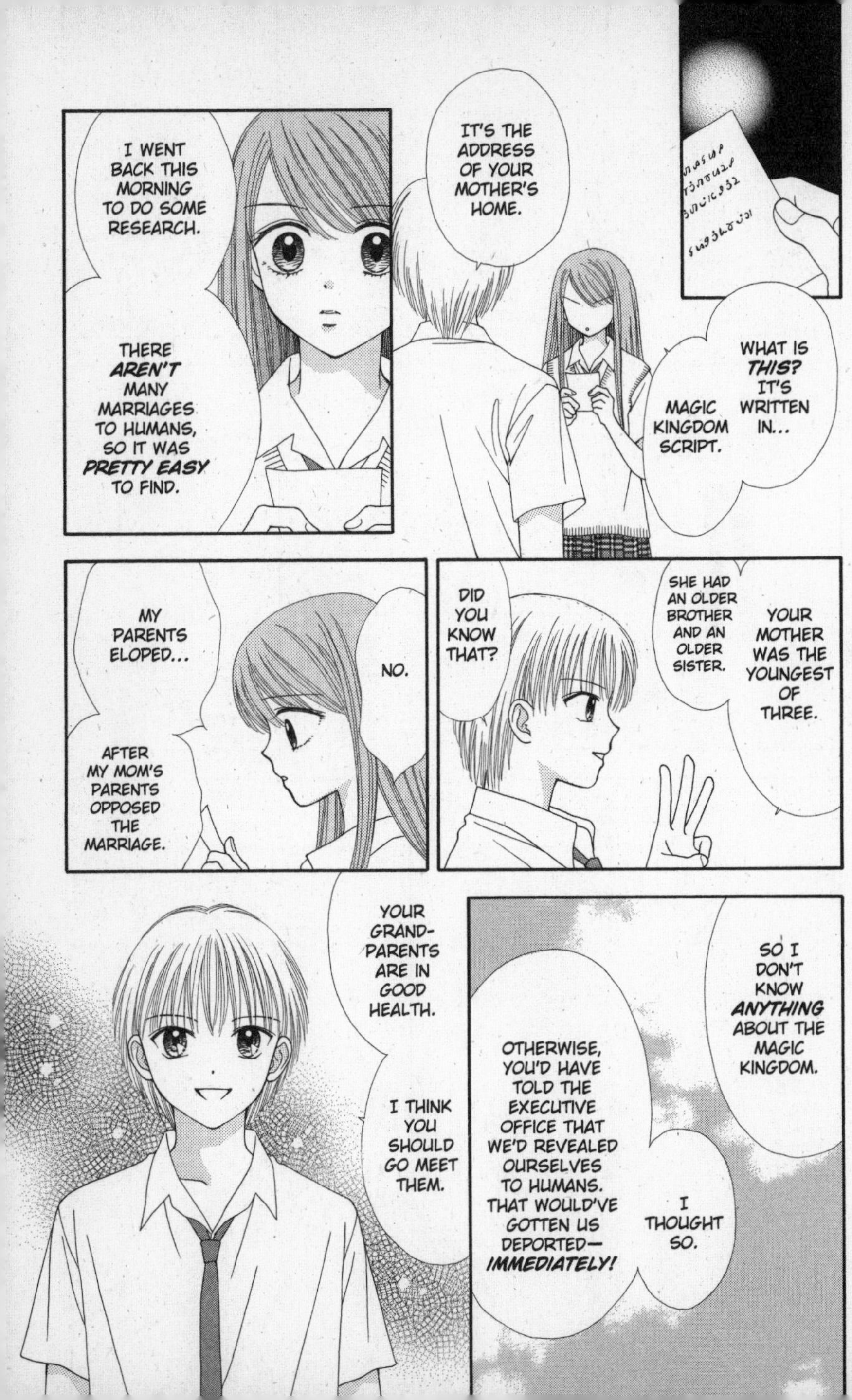
WHAT IS *THIS?* IT'S WRITTEN IN...
MAGIC KINGDOM SCRIPT.
IT'S THE ADDRESS OF YOUR MOTHER'S HOME.
I WENT BACK THIS MORNING TO DO SOME RESEARCH.
THERE *AREN'T* MANY MARRIAGES TO HUMANS, SO IT WAS *PRETTY EASY* TO FIND.
YOUR MOTHER WAS THE YOUNGEST OF THREE.
SHE HAD AN OLDER BROTHER AND AN OLDER SISTER.
DID YOU KNOW THAT?
NO.
MY PARENTS ELOPED...
AFTER MY MOM'S PARENTS OPPOSED THE MARRIAGE.
SO I DON'T KNOW *ANYTHING* ABOUT THE MAGIC KINGDOM.
I THOUGHT SO.
OTHERWISE, YOU'D HAVE TOLD THE EXECUTIVE OFFICE THAT WE'D REVEALED OURSELVES TO HUMANS. THAT WOULD'VE GOTTEN US DEPORTED—*IMMEDIATELY!*
YOUR GRAND-PARENTS ARE IN GOOD HEALTH.
I THINK YOU SHOULD GO MEET THEM.

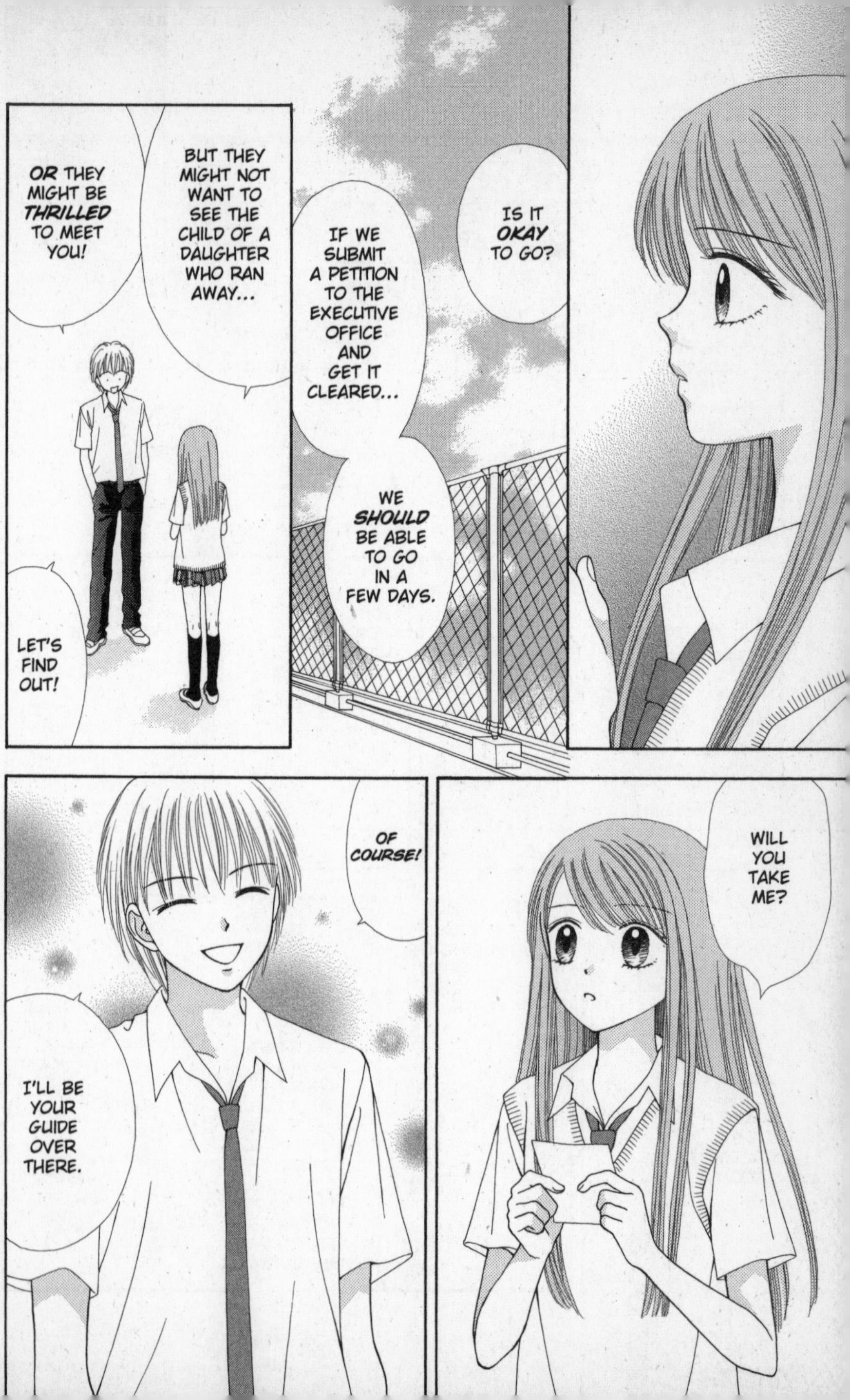
IS IT OKAY TO GO?
IF WE SUBMIT A PETITION TO THE EXECUTIVE OFFICE AND GET IT CLEARED...
WE SHOULD BE ABLE TO GO IN A FEW DAYS.
BUT THEY MIGHT NOT WANT TO SEE THE CHILD OF A DAUGHTER WHO RAN AWAY...
OR THEY MIGHT BE THRILLED TO MEET YOU!
LET'S FIND OUT!
WILL YOU TAKE ME?
OF COURSE!
I'LL BE YOUR GUIDE OVER THERE.

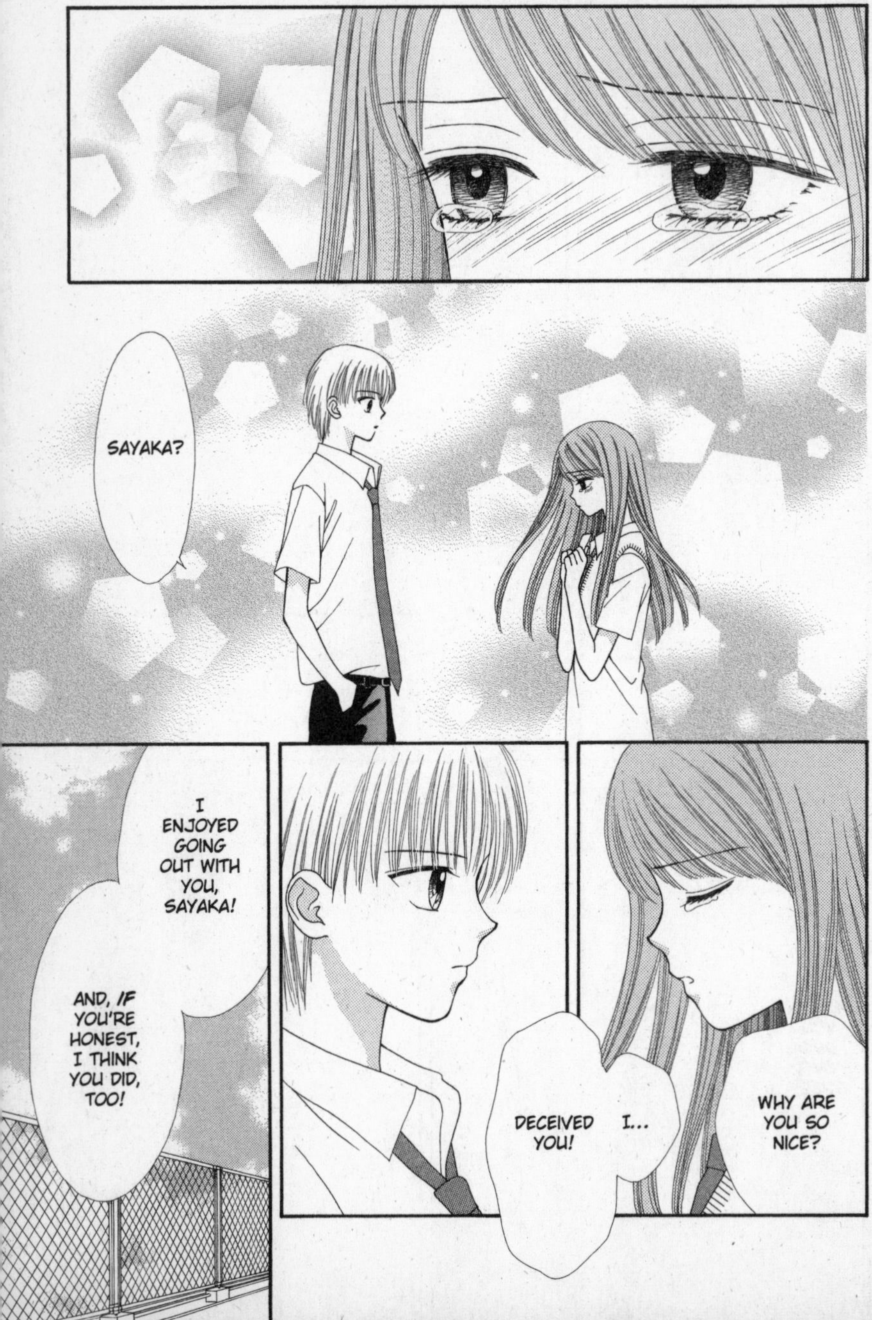
SAYAKA?
WHY ARE YOU SO NICE?
I...
DECEIVED YOU!
I ENJOYED GOING OUT WITH YOU, SAYAKA!
AND, *IF* YOU'RE HONEST, I THINK YOU DID, TOO!

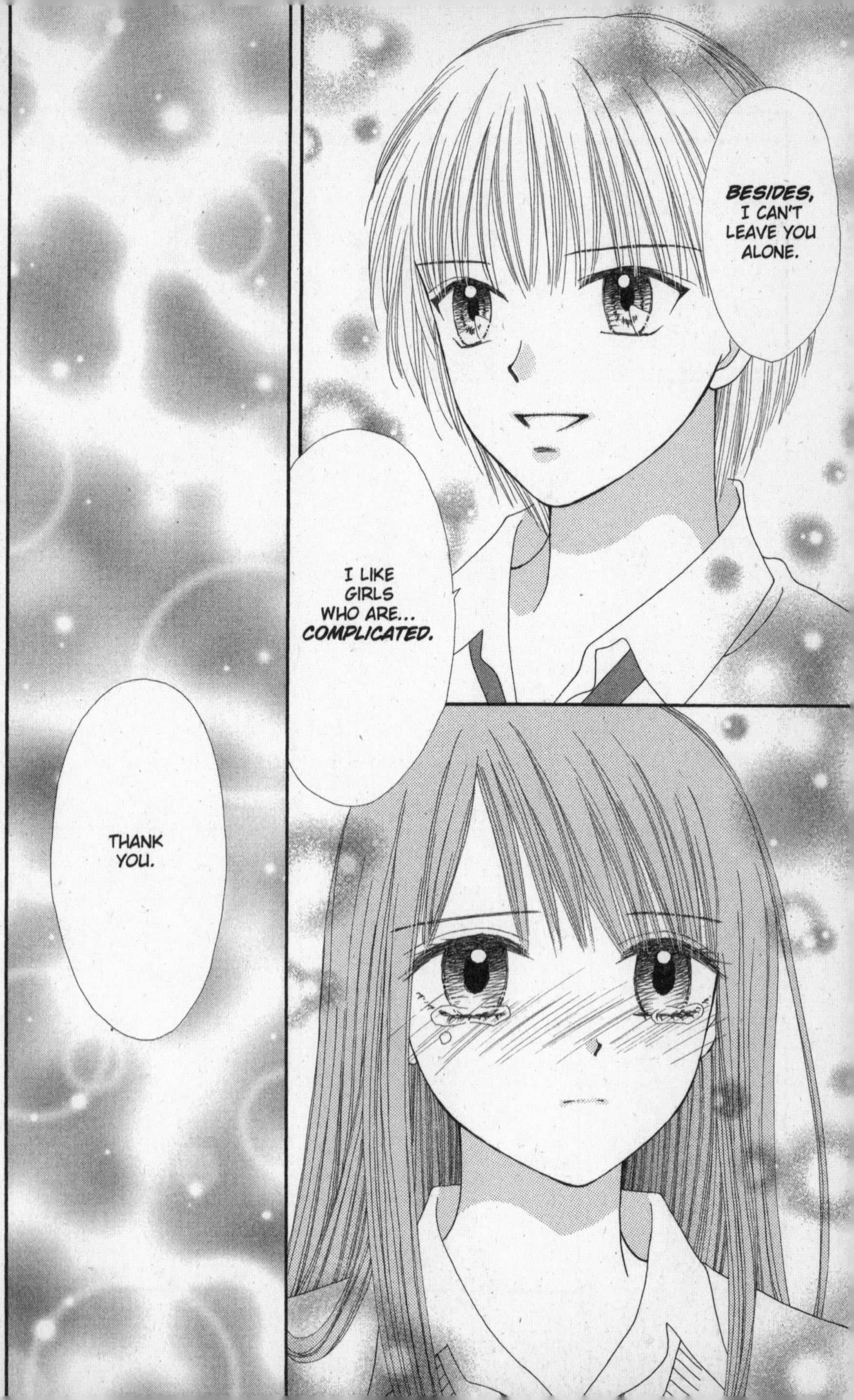
BESIDES, I CAN'T LEAVE YOU ALONE.
I LIKE GIRLS WHO ARE... COMPLICATED.
THANK YOU.

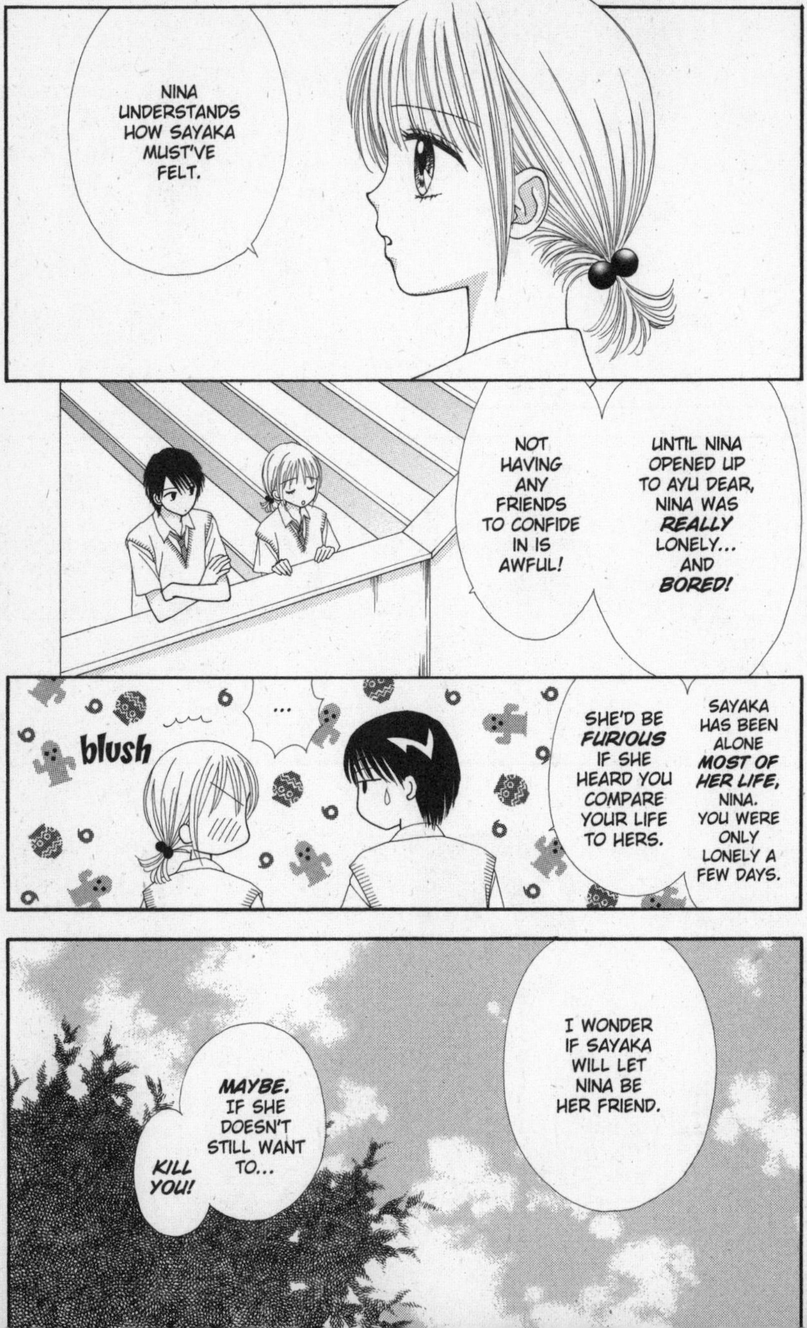
NINA UNDERSTANDS HOW SAYAKA MUST'VE FELT.
UNTIL NINA OPENED UP TO AYU DEAR, NINA WAS REALLY LONELY... AND BORED!
NOT HAVING ANY FRIENDS TO CONFIDE IN IS AWFUL!
SAYAKA HAS BEEN ALONE MOST OF HER LIFE, NINA. YOU WERE ONLY LONELY A FEW DAYS.
SHE'D BE FURIOUS IF SHE HEARD YOU COMPARE YOUR LIFE TO HERS.
...
blush
I WONDER IF SAYAKA WILL LET NINA BE HER FRIEND.
MAYBE. IF SHE DOESN'T STILL WANT TO... KILL YOU!

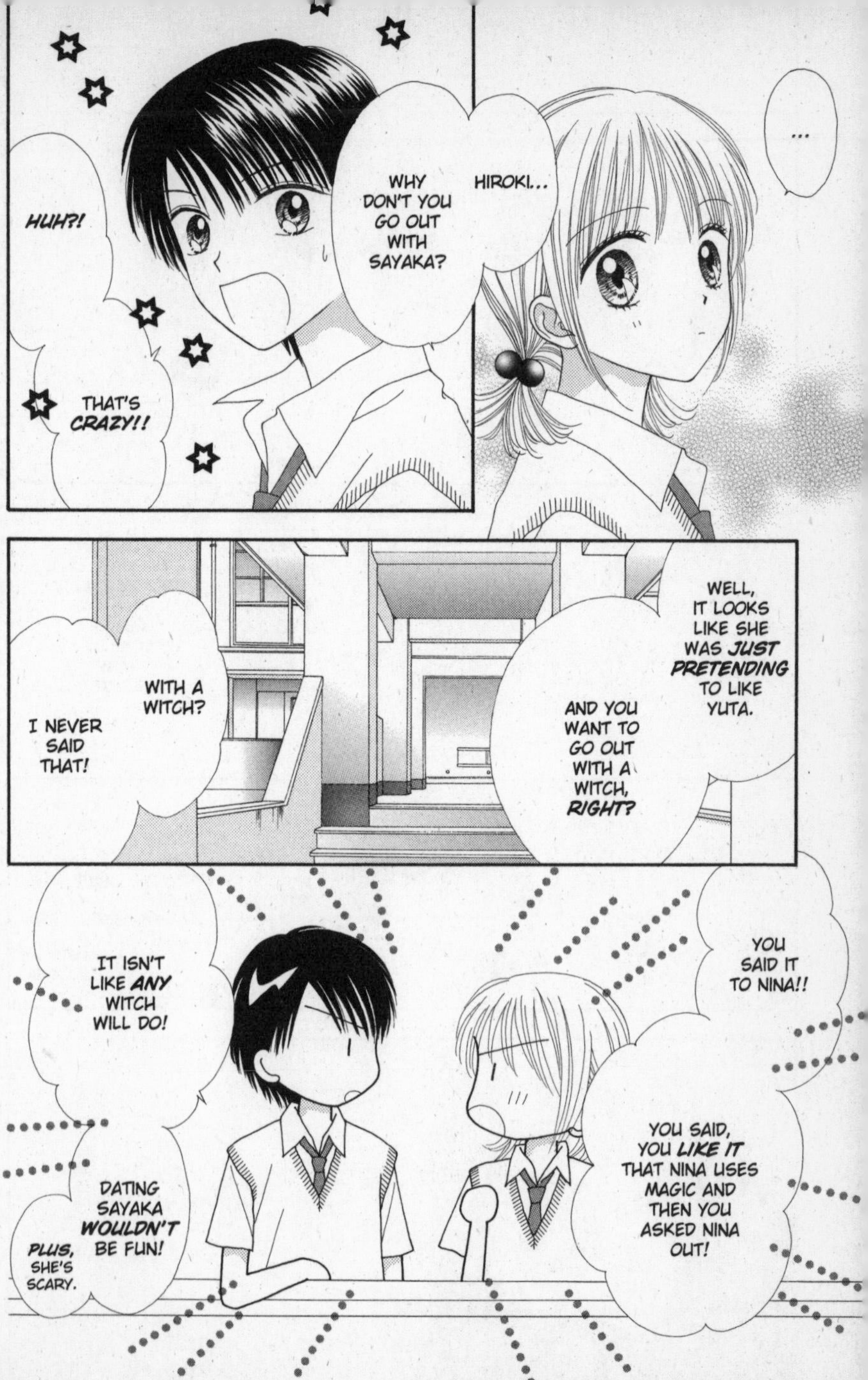
...
HIROKI...
WHY DON'T YOU GO OUT WITH SAYAKA?
HUH?!
THAT'S CRAZY!!
WELL, IT LOOKS LIKE SHE WAS JUST PRETENDING TO LIKE YUTA.
AND YOU WANT TO GO OUT WITH A WITCH, RIGHT?
WITH A WITCH?
I NEVER SAID THAT!
YOU SAID IT TO NINA!!
YOU SAID, YOU LIKE IT THAT NINA USES MAGIC AND THEN YOU ASKED NINA OUT!
IT ISN'T LIKE ANY WITCH WILL DO!
DATING SAYAKA WOULDN'T BE FUN!
PLUS, SHE'S SCARY.

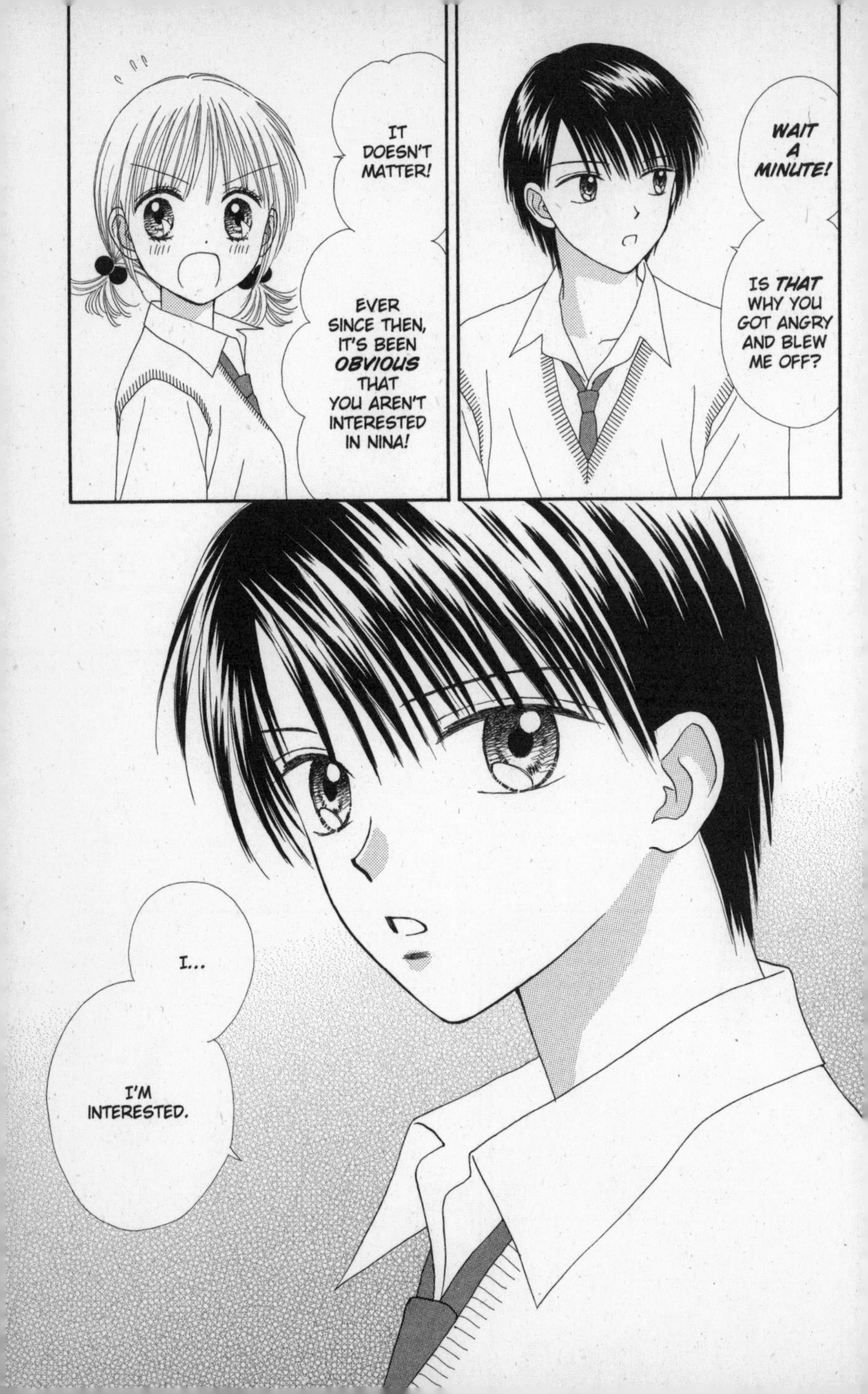
WAIT A MINUTE!
IS THAT WHY YOU GOT ANGRY AND BLEW ME OFF?
IT DOESN'T MATTER!
EVER SINCE THEN, IT'S BEEN OBVIOUS THAT YOU AREN'T INTERESTED IN NINA!
I...
I'M INTERESTED.

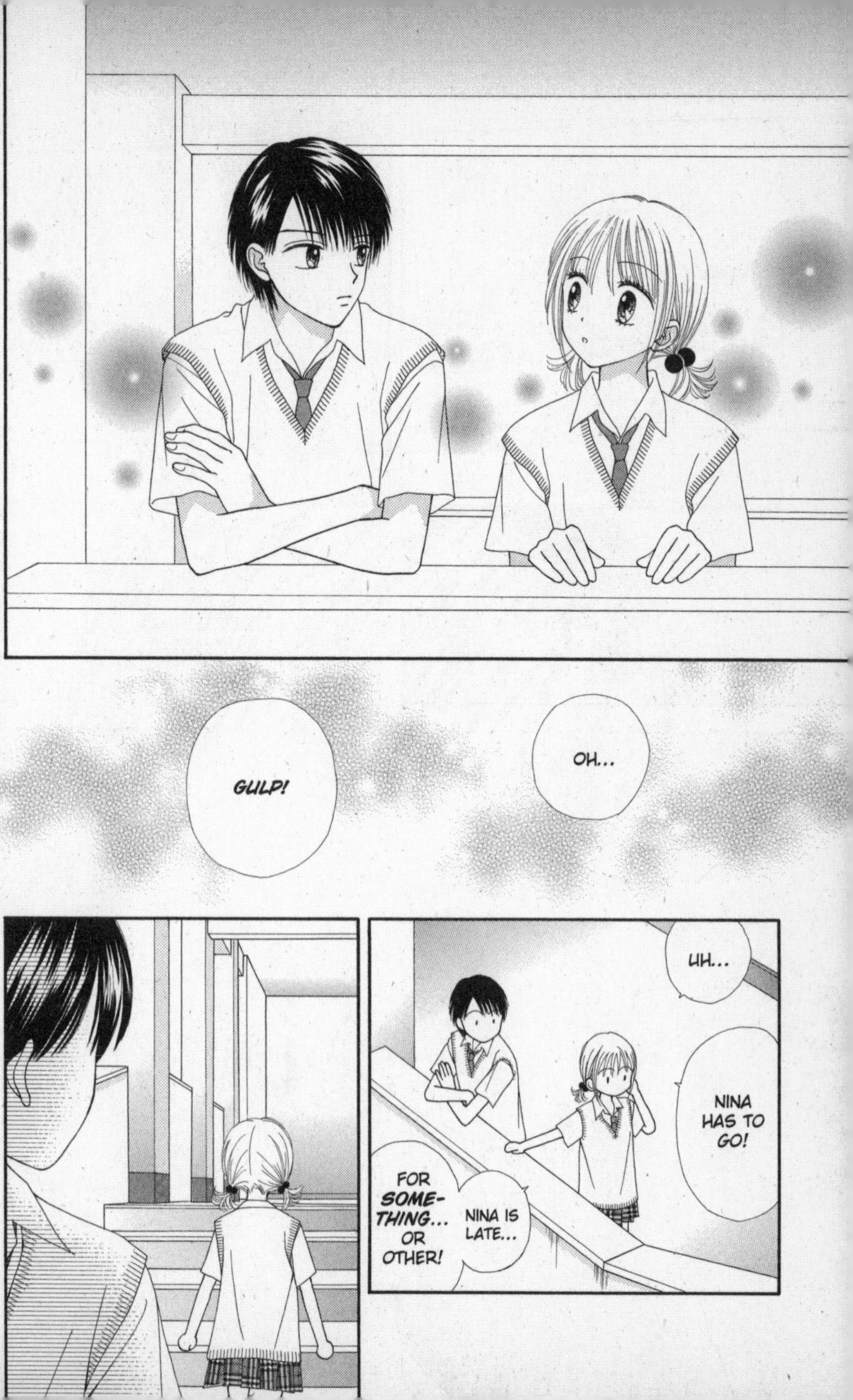
OH...
GULP!
UH...
NINA HAS TO GO!
NINA IS LATE...
FOR SOMETHING... OR OTHER!

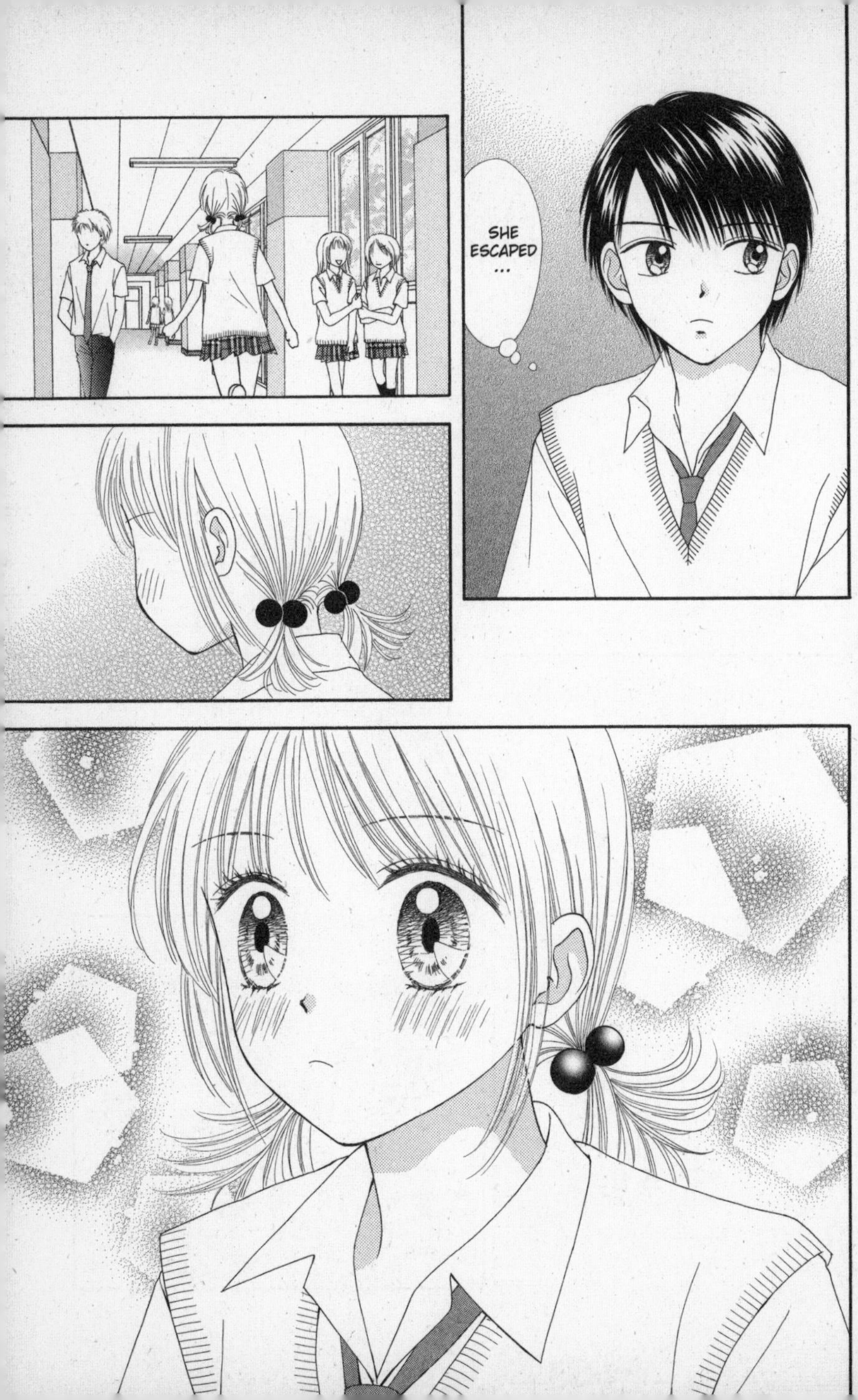
SHE ESCAPED ...

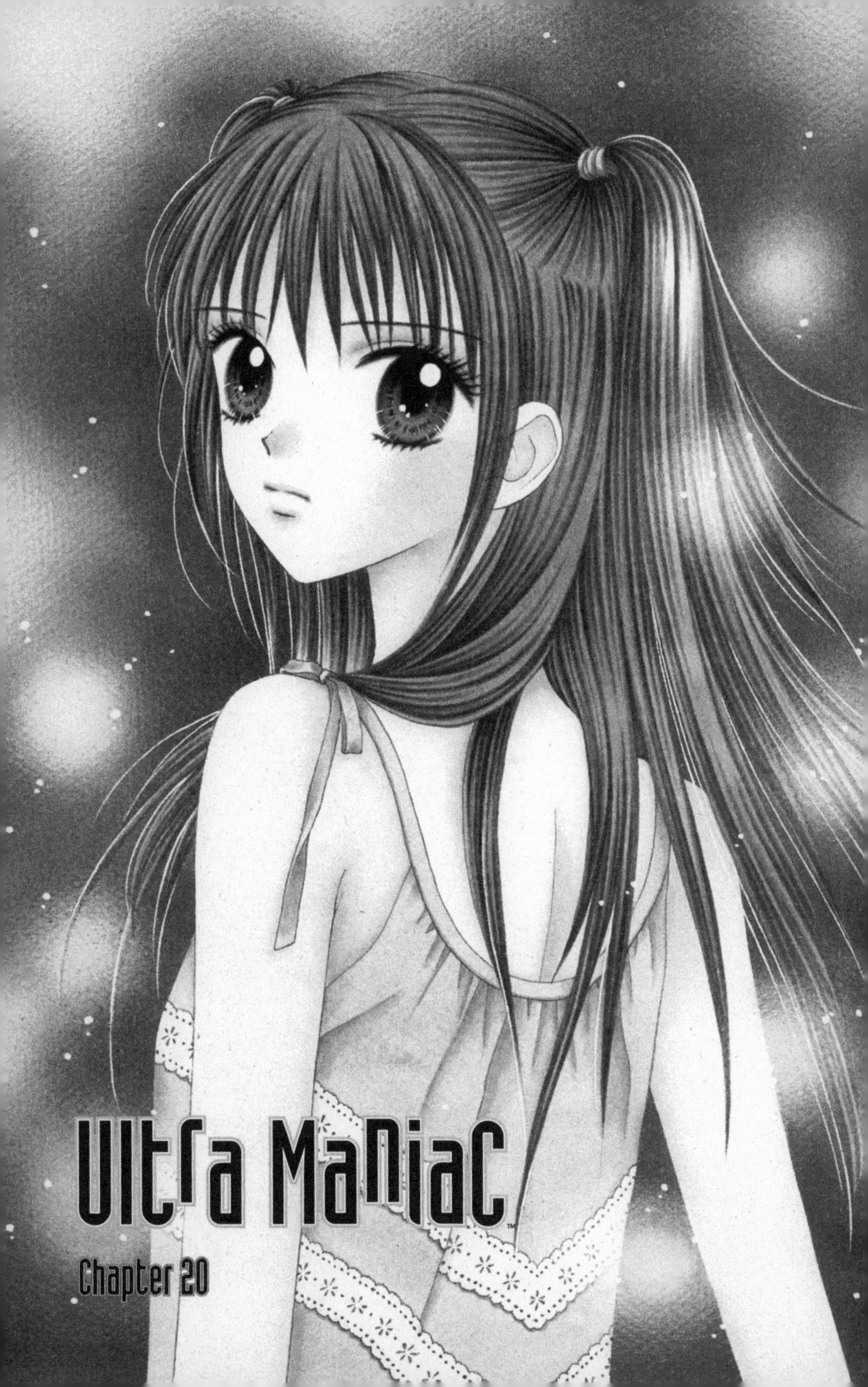
Ultra Maniac™
Chapter 20

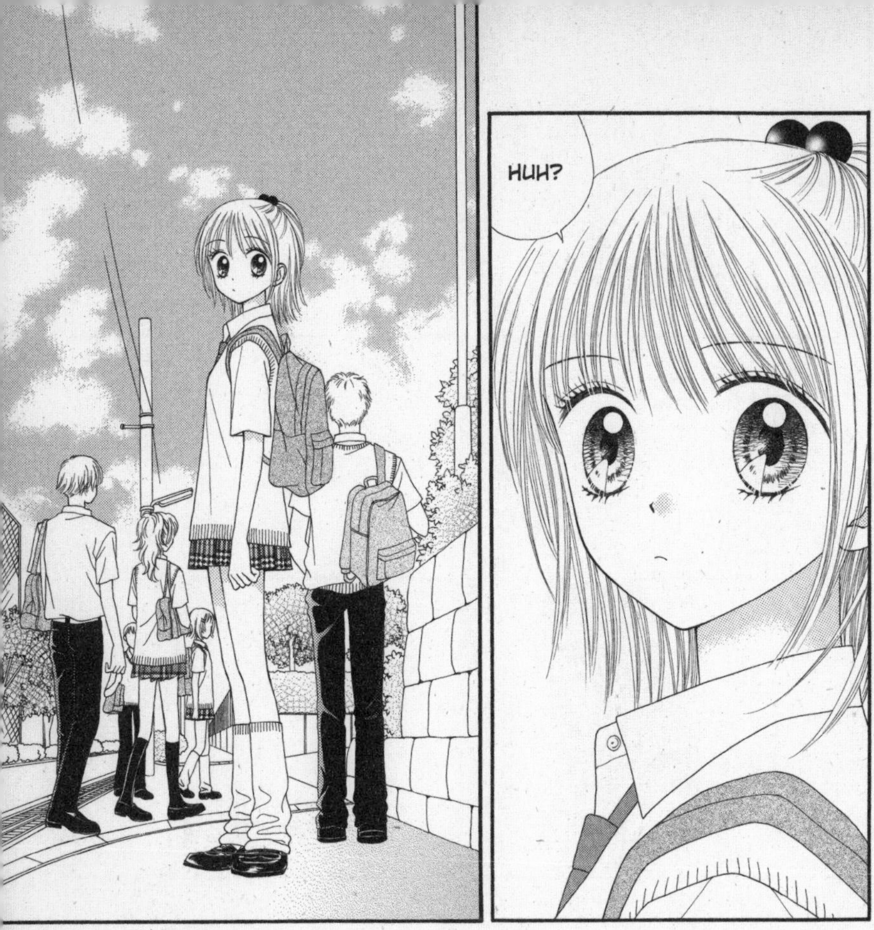
HUH?

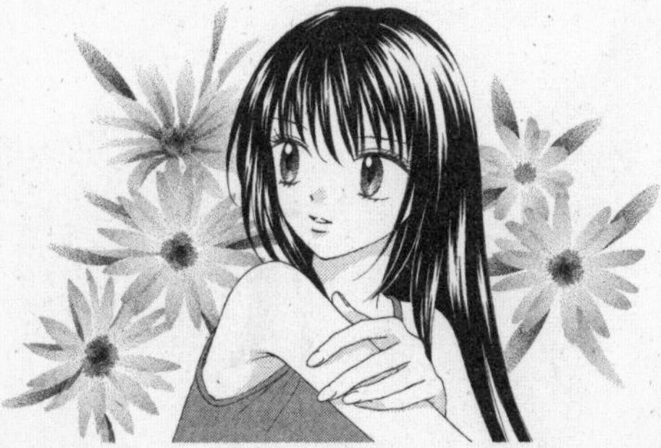

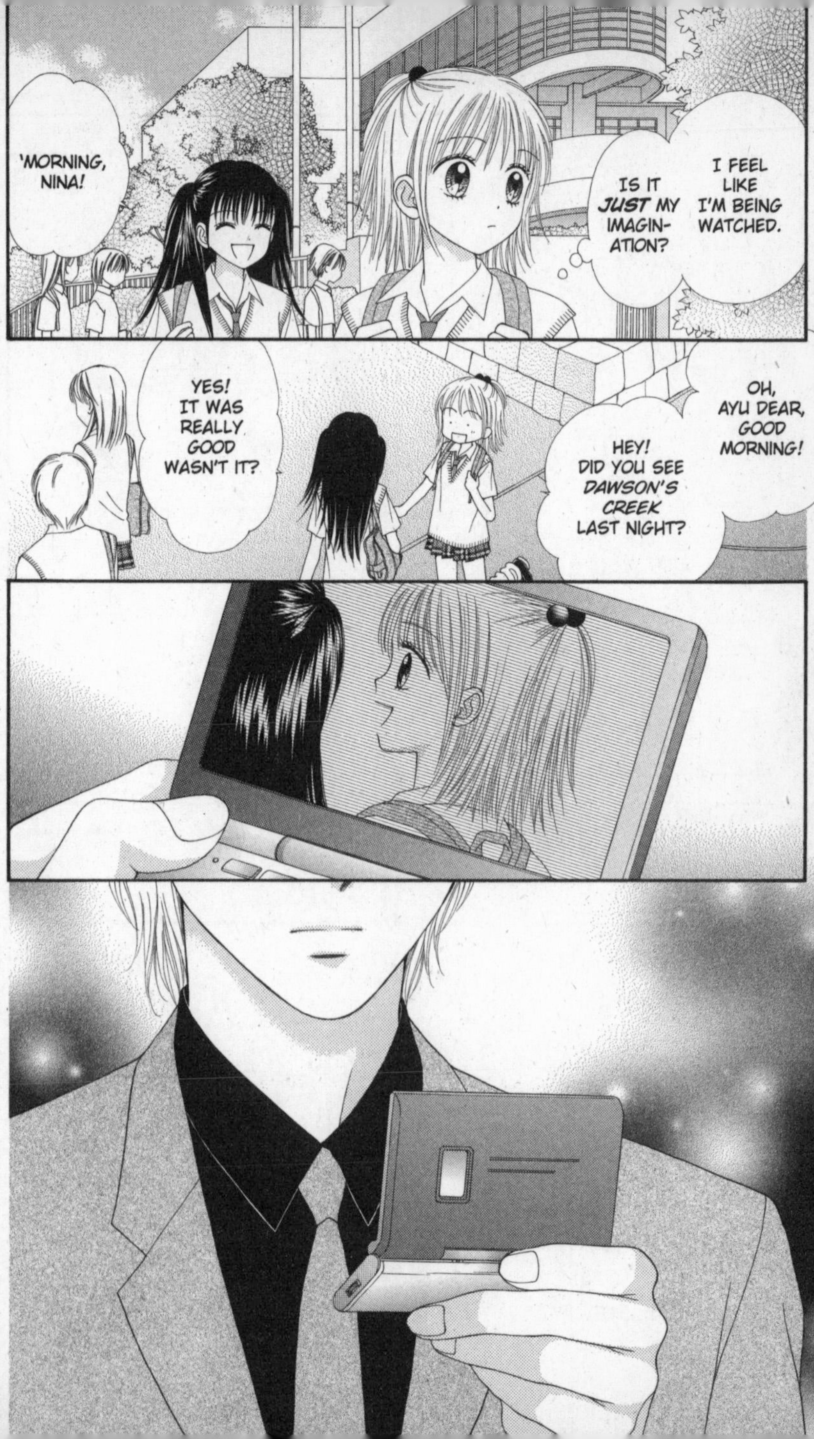

I FEEL LIKE I'M BEING WATCHED.
IS IT *JUST* MY IMAGINATION?
'MORNING, NINA!
OH, AYU DEAR, GOOD MORNING!
HEY! DID YOU SEE *DAWSON'S CREEK* LAST NIGHT?
YES! IT WAS REALLY GOOD WASN'T IT?

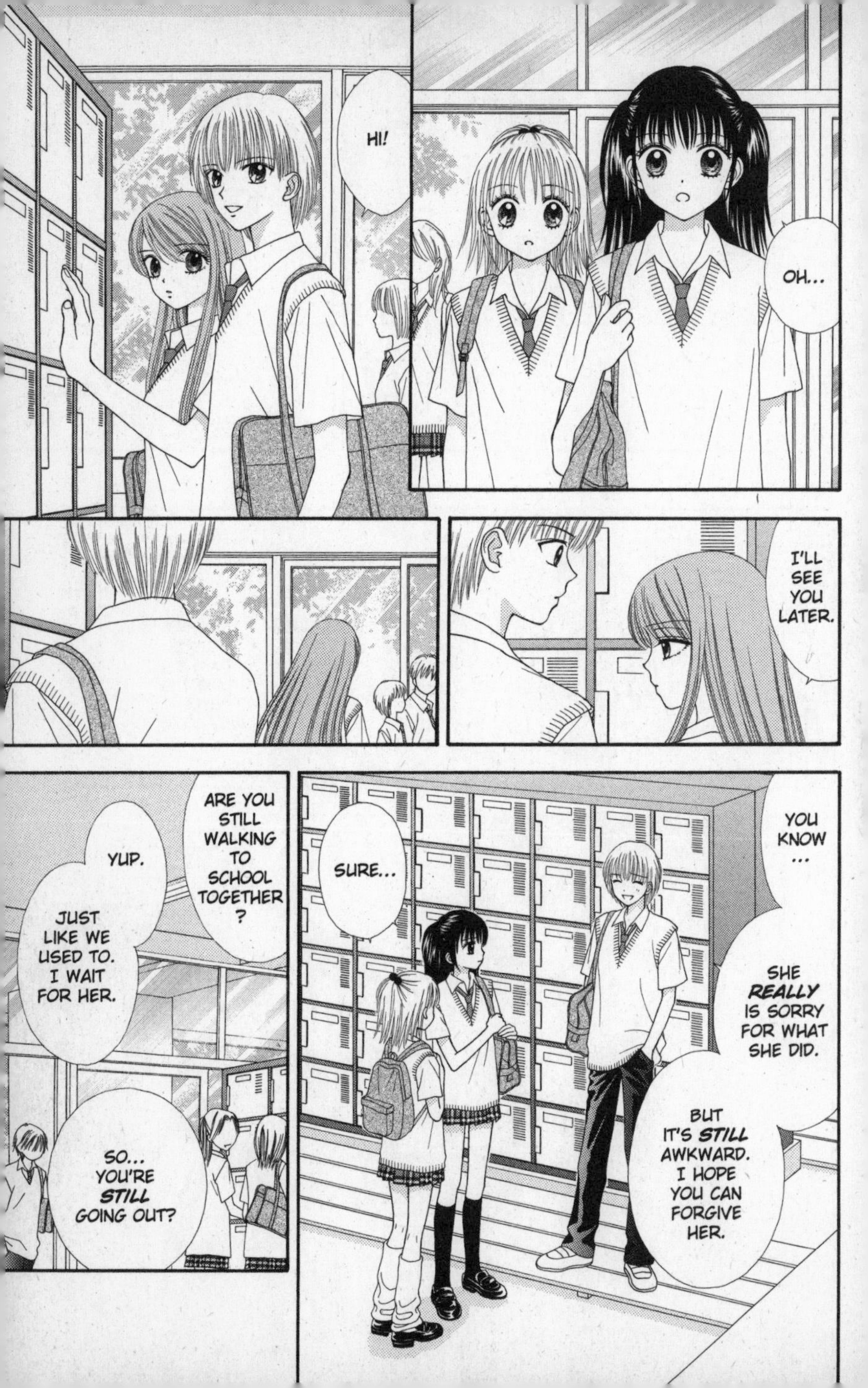
OH...
HI!
I'LL SEE YOU LATER.
YOU KNOW ...
SHE *REALLY* IS SORRY FOR WHAT SHE DID.
BUT IT'S *STILL* AWKWARD. I HOPE YOU CAN FORGIVE HER.
SURE...
ARE YOU STILL WALKING TO SCHOOL TOGETHER?
YUP.
JUST LIKE WE USED TO. I WAIT FOR HER.
SO... YOU'RE *STILL* GOING OUT?

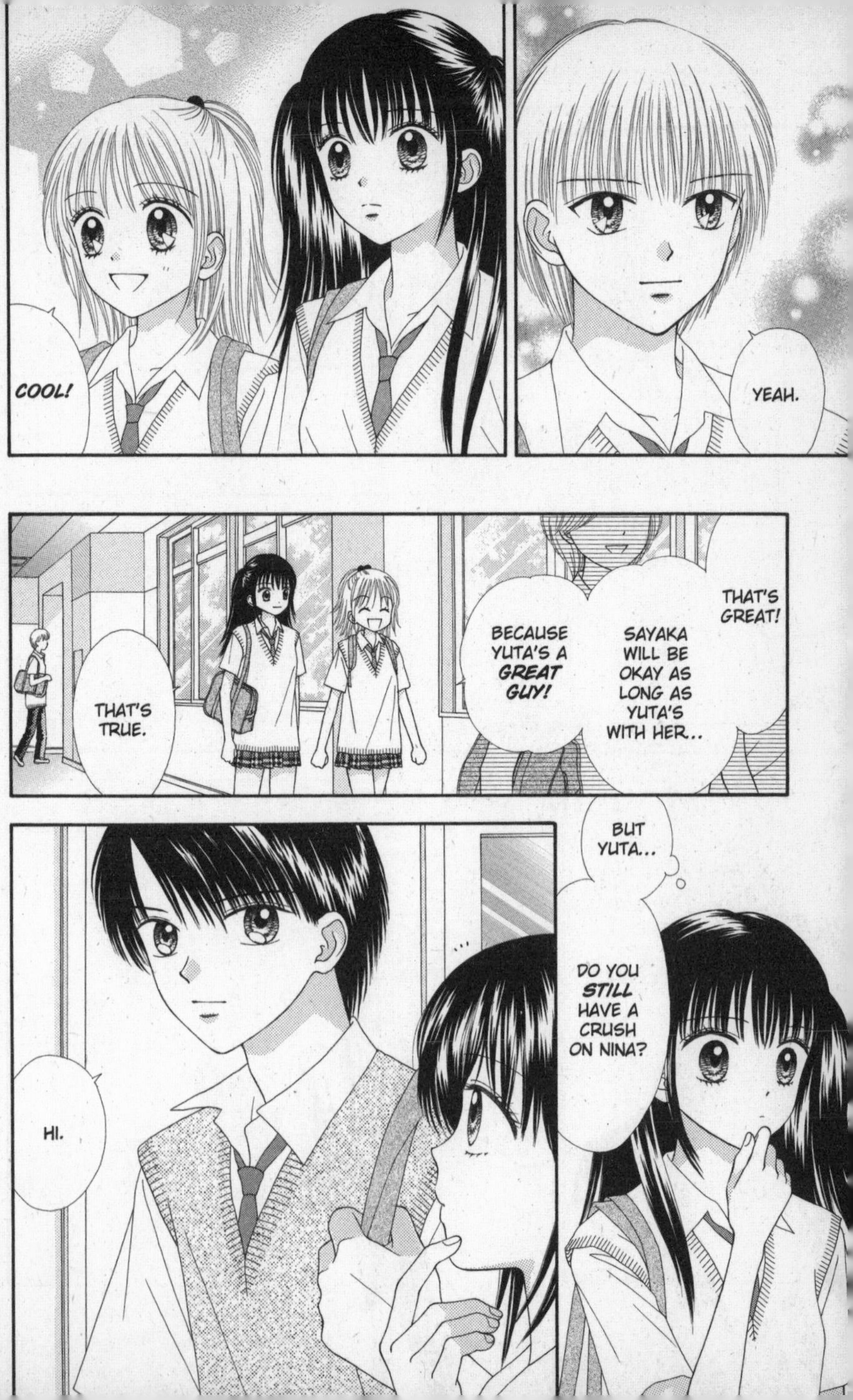
YEAH.
COOL!
THAT'S GREAT!
SAYAKA WILL BE OKAY AS LONG AS YUTA'S WITH HER..
BECAUSE YUTA'S A GREAT GUY!
THAT'S TRUE.
BUT YUTA...
DO YOU STILL HAVE A CRUSH ON NINA?
...
HI.

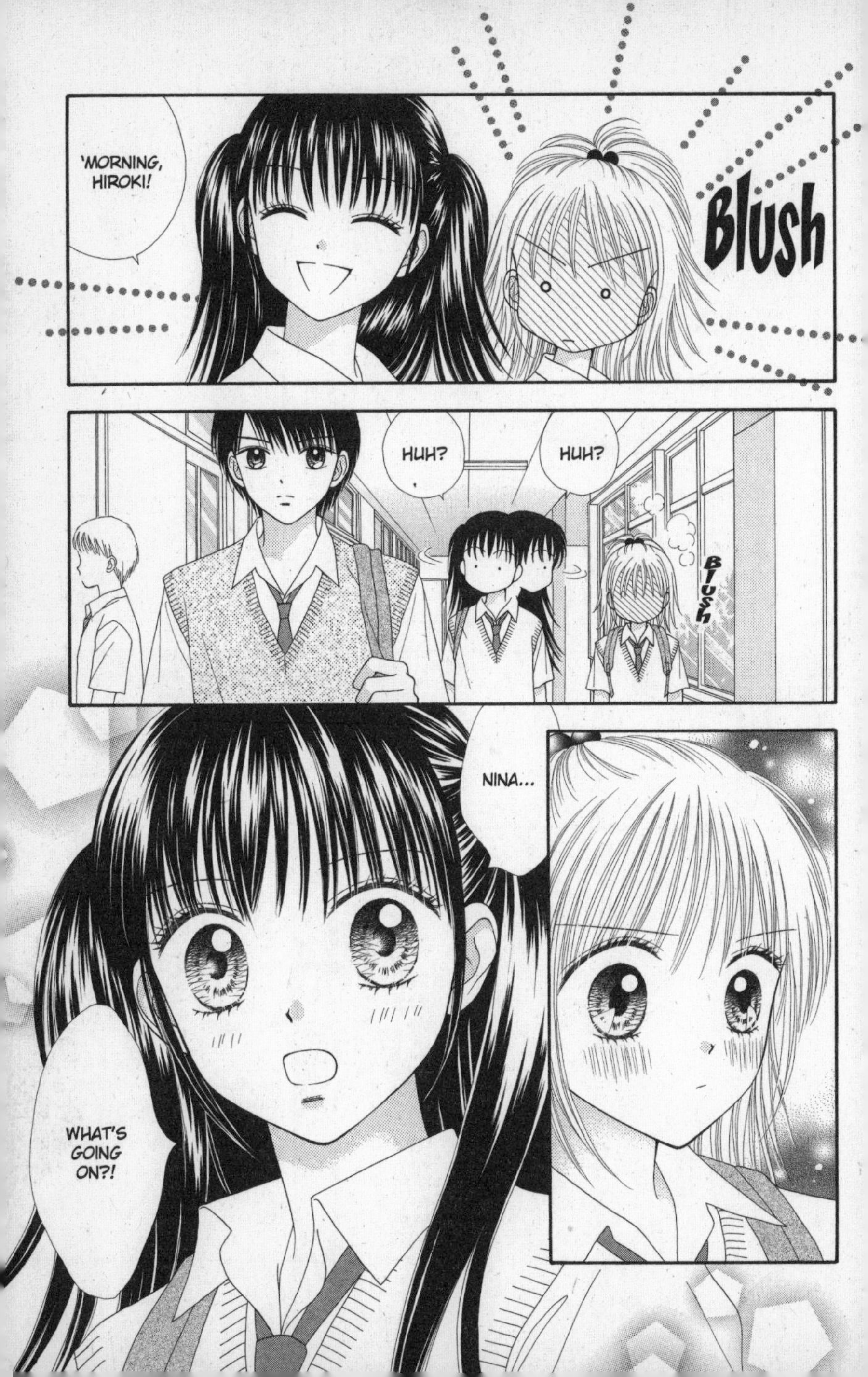
Blush
'MORNING, HIROKI!
HUH?
HUH?
BLUSH
NINA...
WHAT'S GOING ON?!

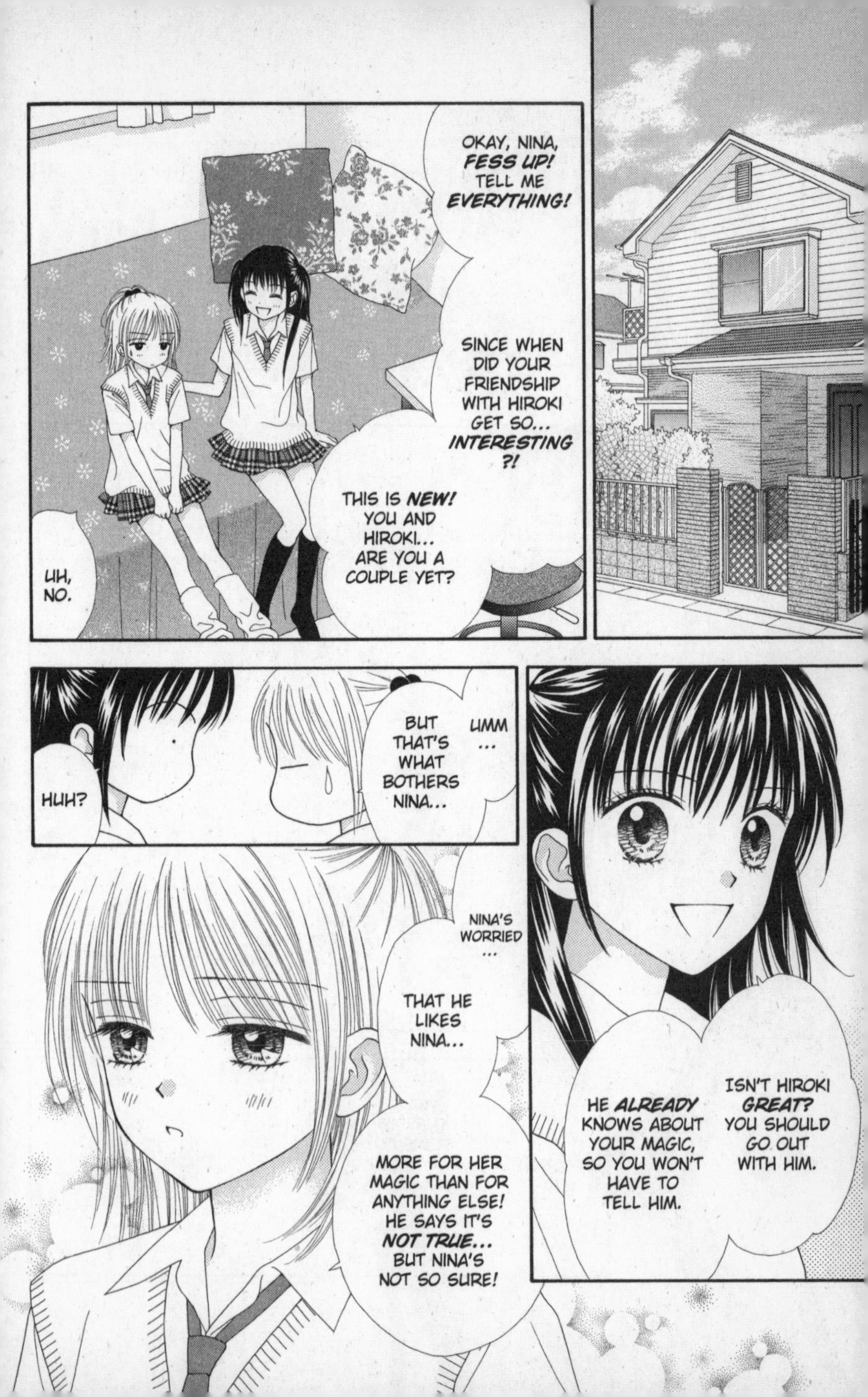

OKAY, NINA, FESS UP! TELL ME EVERYTHING!
SINCE WHEN DID YOUR FRIENDSHIP WITH HIROKI GET SO... INTERESTING?!
THIS IS NEW! YOU AND HIROKI... ARE YOU A COUPLE YET?
UH, NO.
ISN'T HIROKI GREAT? YOU SHOULD GO OUT WITH HIM.
HE ALREADY KNOWS ABOUT YOUR MAGIC, SO YOU WON'T HAVE TO TELL HIM.
UMM...
BUT THAT'S WHAT BOTHERS NINA...
HUH?
NINA'S WORRIED...
THAT HE LIKES NINA...
MORE FOR HER MAGIC THAN FOR ANYTHING ELSE! HE SAYS IT'S NOT TRUE... BUT NINA'S NOT SO SURE!

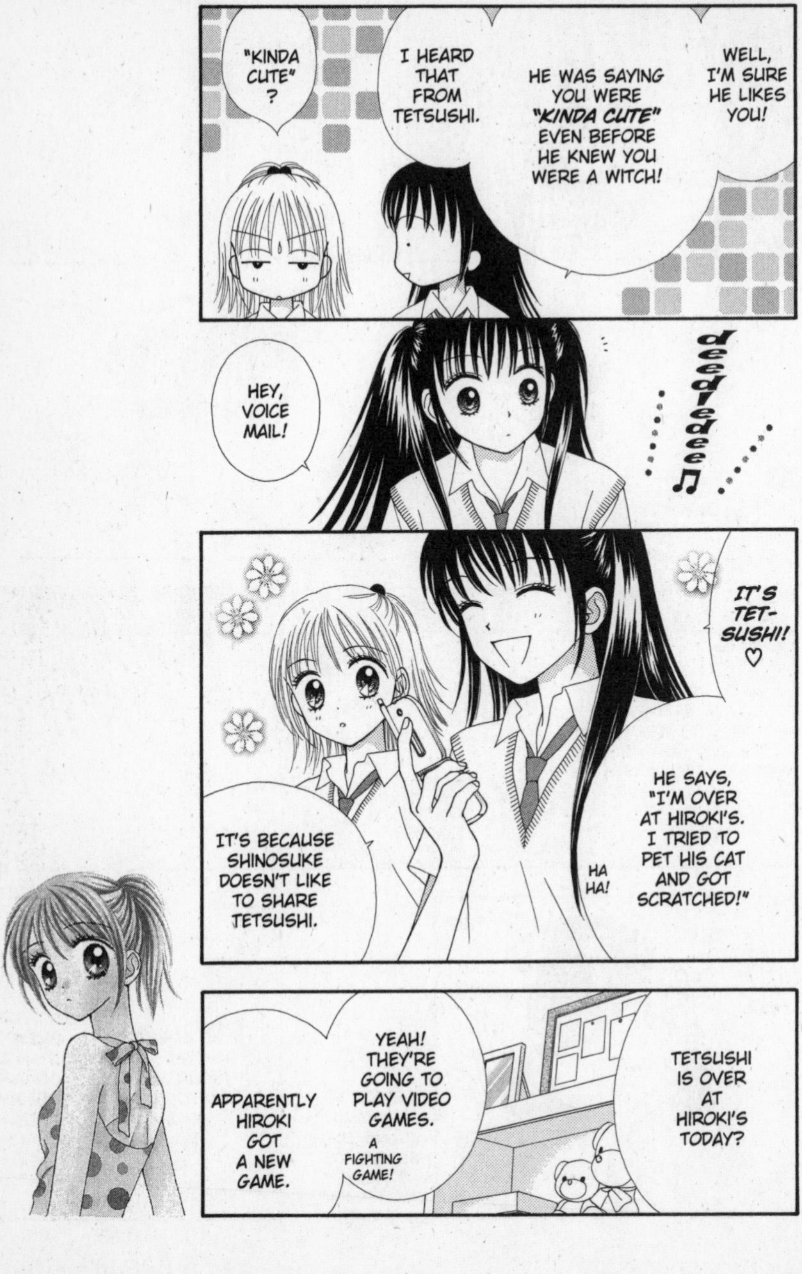
WELL, I'M SURE HE LIKES YOU!
HE WAS SAYING YOU WERE "KINDA CUTE" EVEN BEFORE HE KNEW YOU WERE A WITCH!
I HEARD THAT FROM TETSUSHI.
"KINDA CUTE"?
deedledee♫
HEY, VOICE MAIL!
IT'S TET-SUSHI! ♡
HE SAYS, "I'M OVER AT HIROKI'S. I TRIED TO PET HIS CAT AND GOT SCRATCHED!"
HA HA!
IT'S BECAUSE SHINOSUKE DOESN'T LIKE TO SHARE TETSUSHI.
TETSUSHI IS OVER AT HIROKI'S TODAY?
YEAH! THEY'RE GOING TO PLAY VIDEO GAMES.
A FIGHTING GAME!
APPARENTLY HIROKI GOT A NEW GAME.

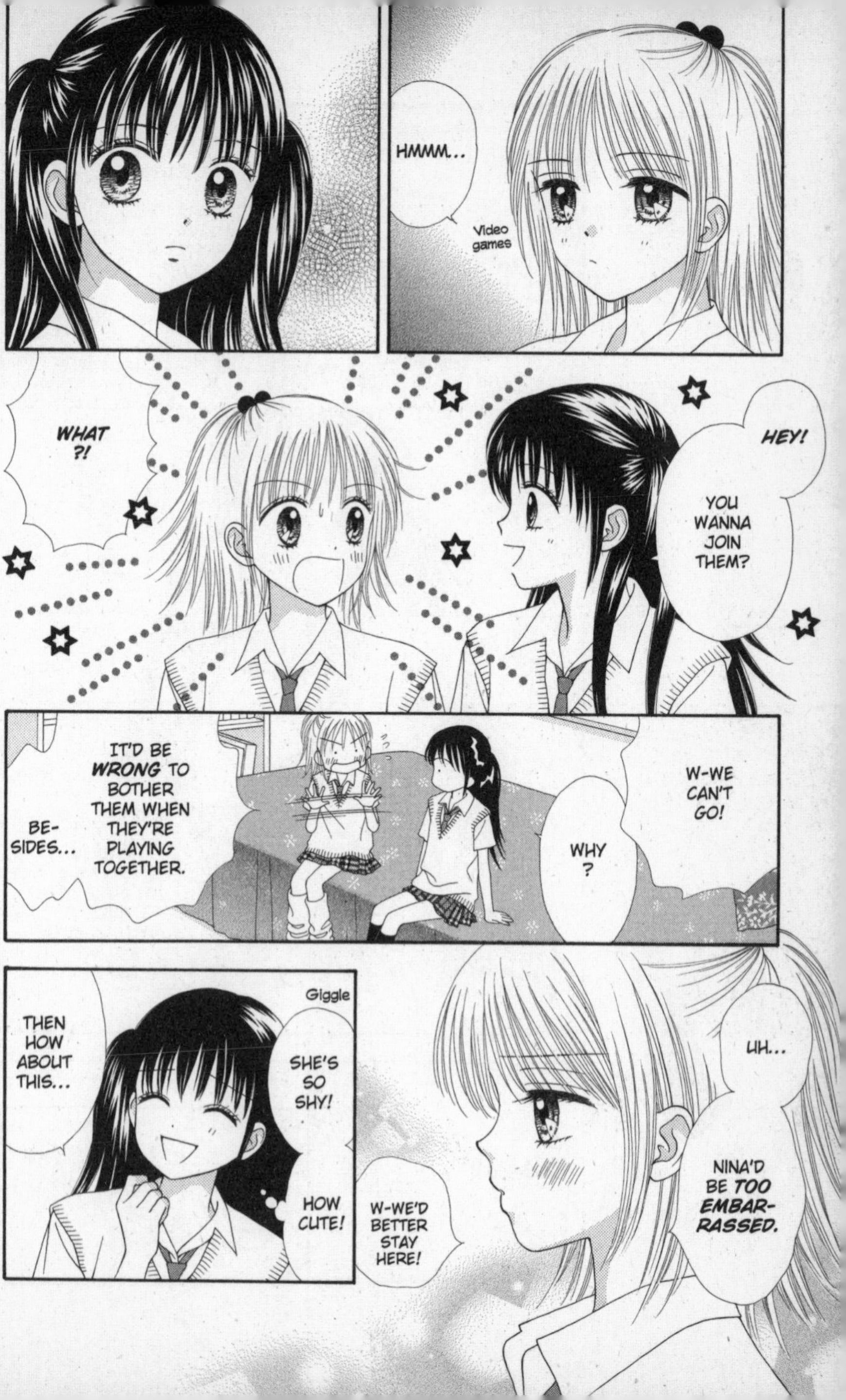
HMMM...
Video games
HEY!
YOU WANNA JOIN THEM?
WHAT ?!
W-WE CAN'T GO!
WHY ?
IT'D BE *WRONG* TO BOTHER THEM WHEN THEY'RE PLAYING TOGETHER.
BE-SIDES...
UH...
NINA'D BE *TOO EMBAR-RASSED.*
W-WE'D BETTER STAY HERE!
Giggle
SHE'S SO SHY!
HOW CUTE!
THEN HOW ABOUT THIS...

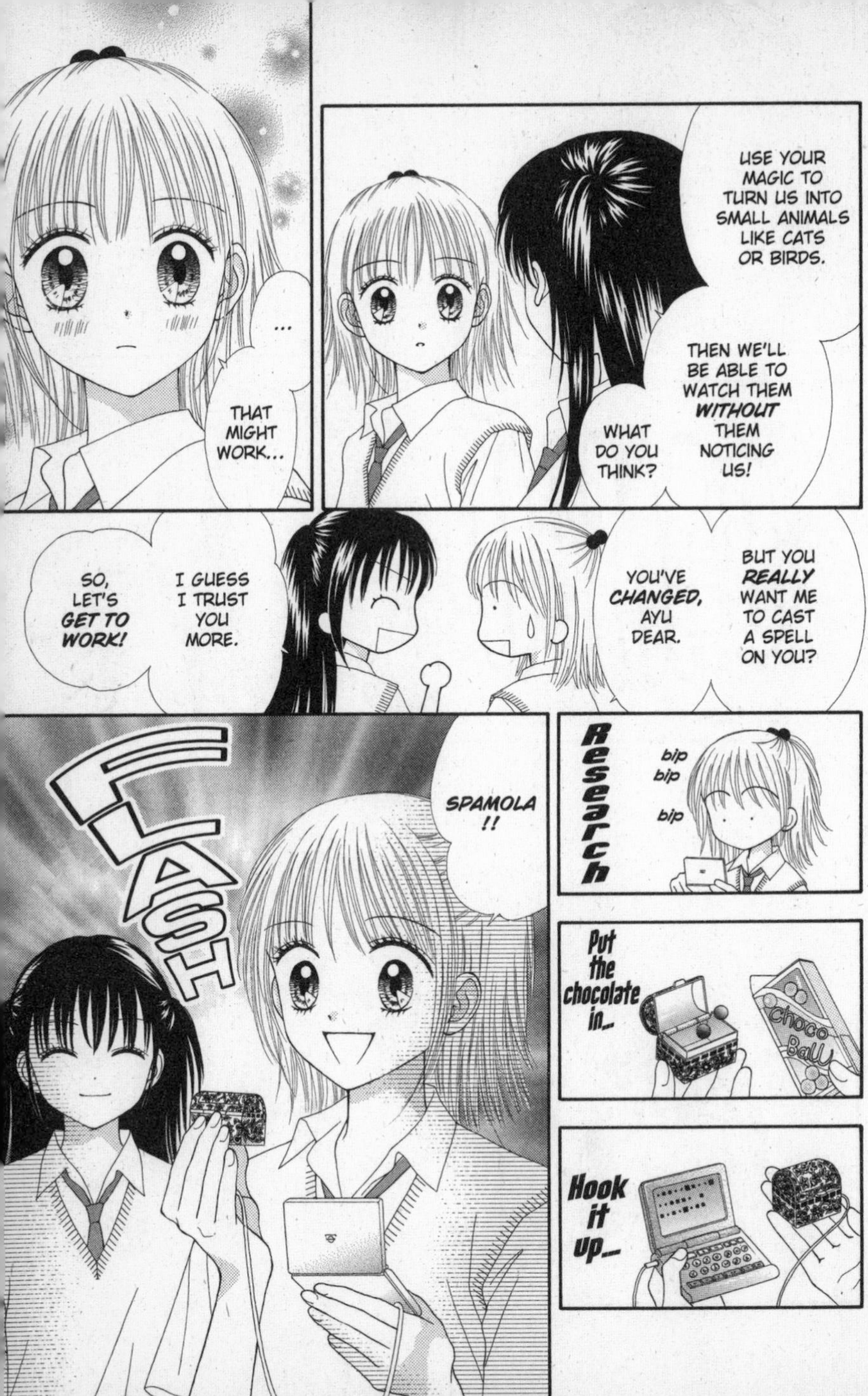
USE YOUR MAGIC TO TURN US INTO SMALL ANIMALS LIKE CATS OR BIRDS.
THEN WE'LL BE ABLE TO WATCH THEM ***WITHOUT*** THEM NOTICING US!
WHAT DO YOU THINK?
...
THAT MIGHT WORK...
BUT YOU ***REALLY*** WANT ME TO CAST A SPELL ON YOU?
YOU'VE ***CHANGED,*** AYU DEAR.
I GUESS I TRUST YOU MORE.
SO, LET'S ***GET TO WORK!***
Research
bip
bip
bip
Put the chocolate in...
Choco Ball
Hook it up...
SPAMOLA!!
FLASH

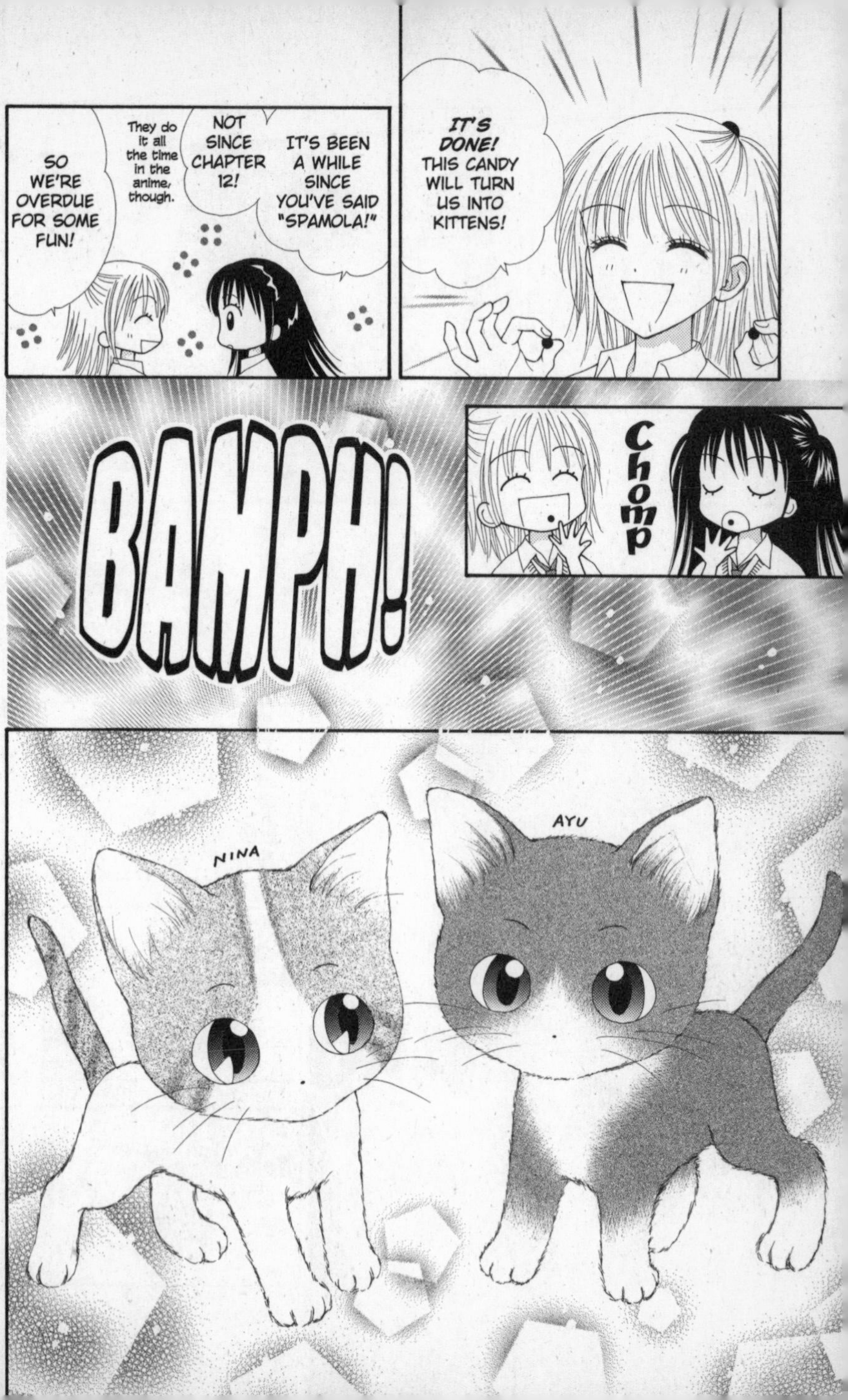
IT'S DONE! THIS CANDY WILL TURN US INTO KITTENS!
IT'S BEEN A WHILE SINCE YOU'VE SAID "SPAMOLA!"
NOT SINCE CHAPTER 12!
They do it all the time in the anime, though.
SO WE'RE OVERDUE FOR SOME FUN!
Chomp
BAMPH!
AYU
NINA

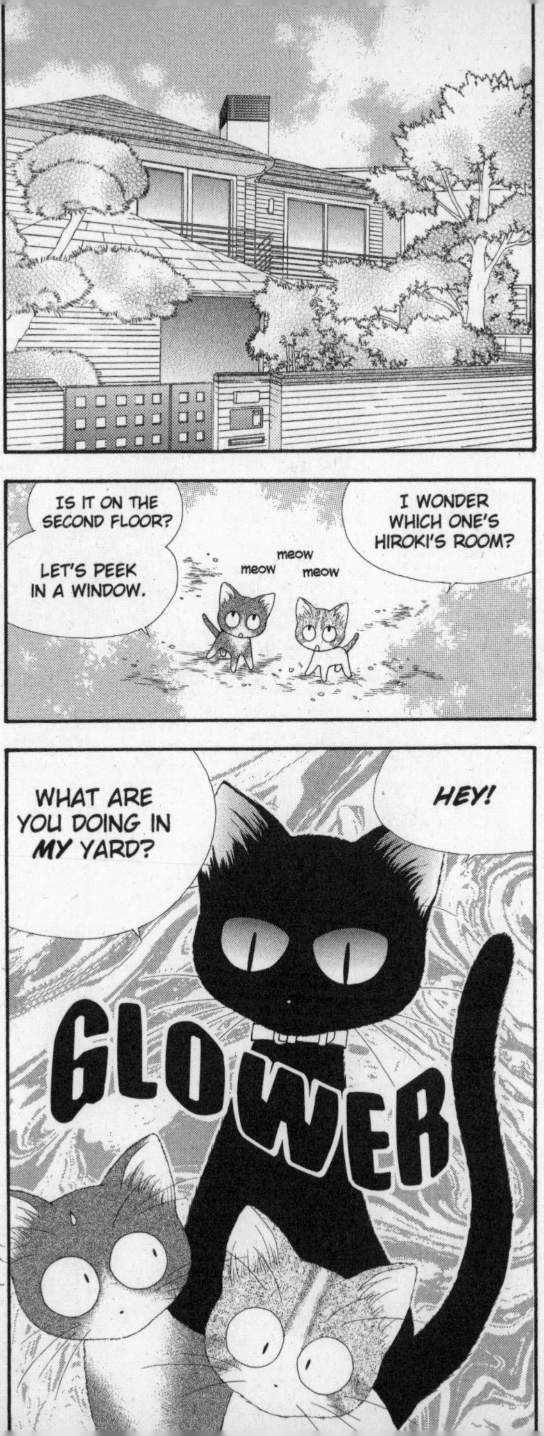
I WONDER WHICH ONE'S HIROKI'S ROOM?
meow
meow
meow
IS IT ON THE SECOND FLOOR?
LET'S PEEK IN A WINDOW.
HEY!
WHAT ARE YOU DOING IN *MY* YARD?
GLOWER

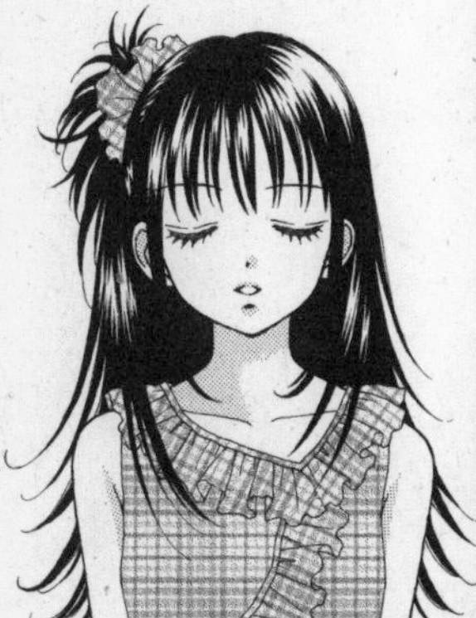

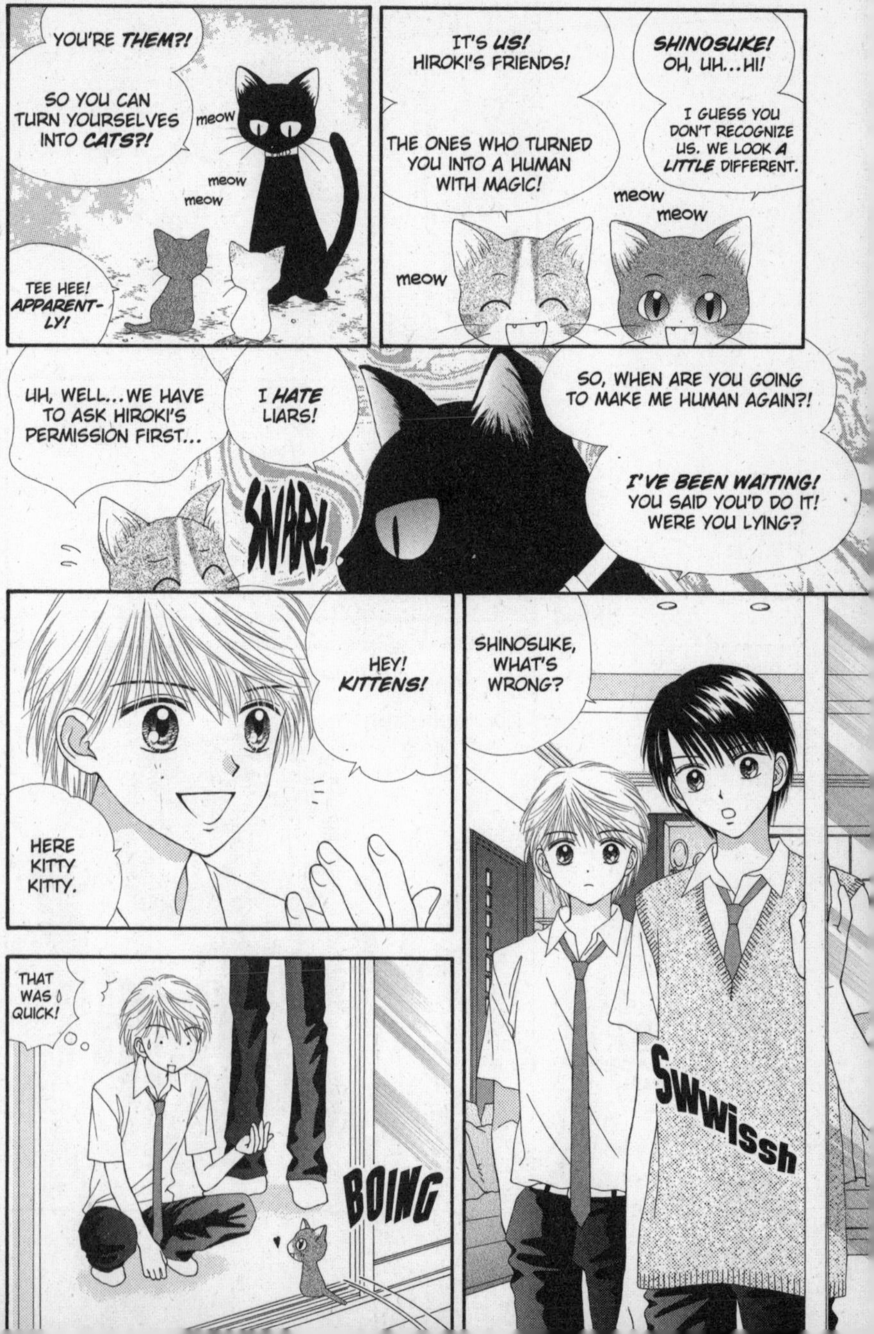
SHINOSUKE! OH, UH...HI!
I GUESS YOU DON'T RECOGNIZE US. WE LOOK A LITTLE DIFFERENT.
IT'S US! HIROKI'S FRIENDS!
THE ONES WHO TURNED YOU INTO A HUMAN WITH MAGIC!
meow
meow
meow
YOU'RE THEM?!
SO YOU CAN TURN YOURSELVES INTO CATS?!
meow
meow
meow
TEE HEE! APPARENTLY!
SO, WHEN ARE YOU GOING TO MAKE ME HUMAN AGAIN?!
I'VE BEEN WAITING! YOU SAID YOU'D DO IT! WERE YOU LYING?
SNARL
I HATE LIARS!
UH, WELL...WE HAVE TO ASK HIROKI'S PERMISSION FIRST...
SHINOSUKE, WHAT'S WRONG?
SWWISSH
HEY! KITTENS!
HERE KITTY KITTY.
THAT WAS QUICK!
BOING

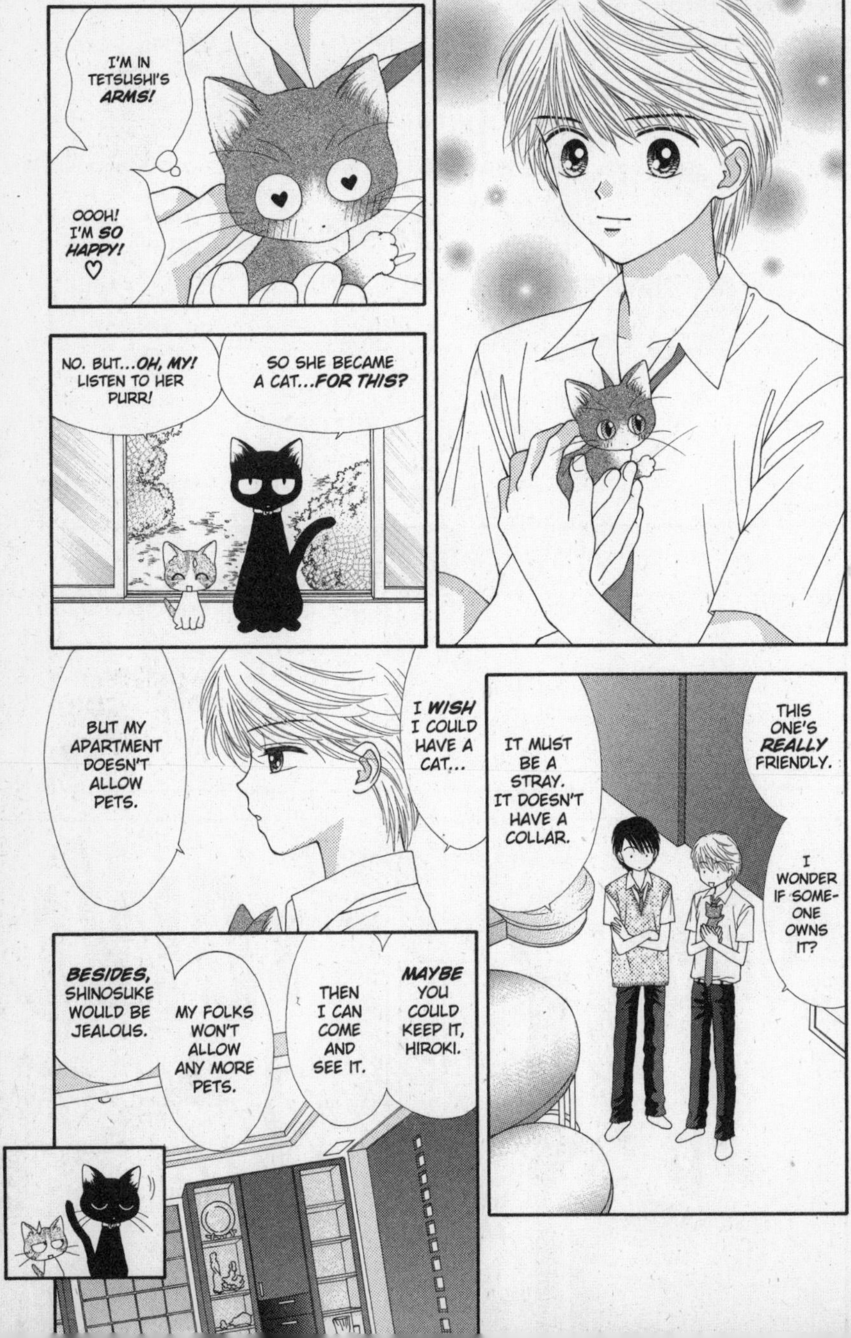
I'M IN TETSUSHI'S ARMS!
OOOH! I'M SO HAPPY! ♡
SO SHE BECAME A CAT...FOR THIS?
NO. BUT...OH, MY! LISTEN TO HER PURR!
THIS ONE'S REALLY FRIENDLY.
IT MUST BE A STRAY. IT DOESN'T HAVE A COLLAR.
I WONDER IF SOME-ONE OWNS IT?
I WISH I COULD HAVE A CAT...
BUT MY APARTMENT DOESN'T ALLOW PETS.
MAYBE YOU COULD KEEP IT, HIROKI.
THEN I CAN COME AND SEE IT.
MY FOLKS WON'T ALLOW ANY MORE PETS.
BESIDES, SHINOSUKE WOULD BE JEALOUS.

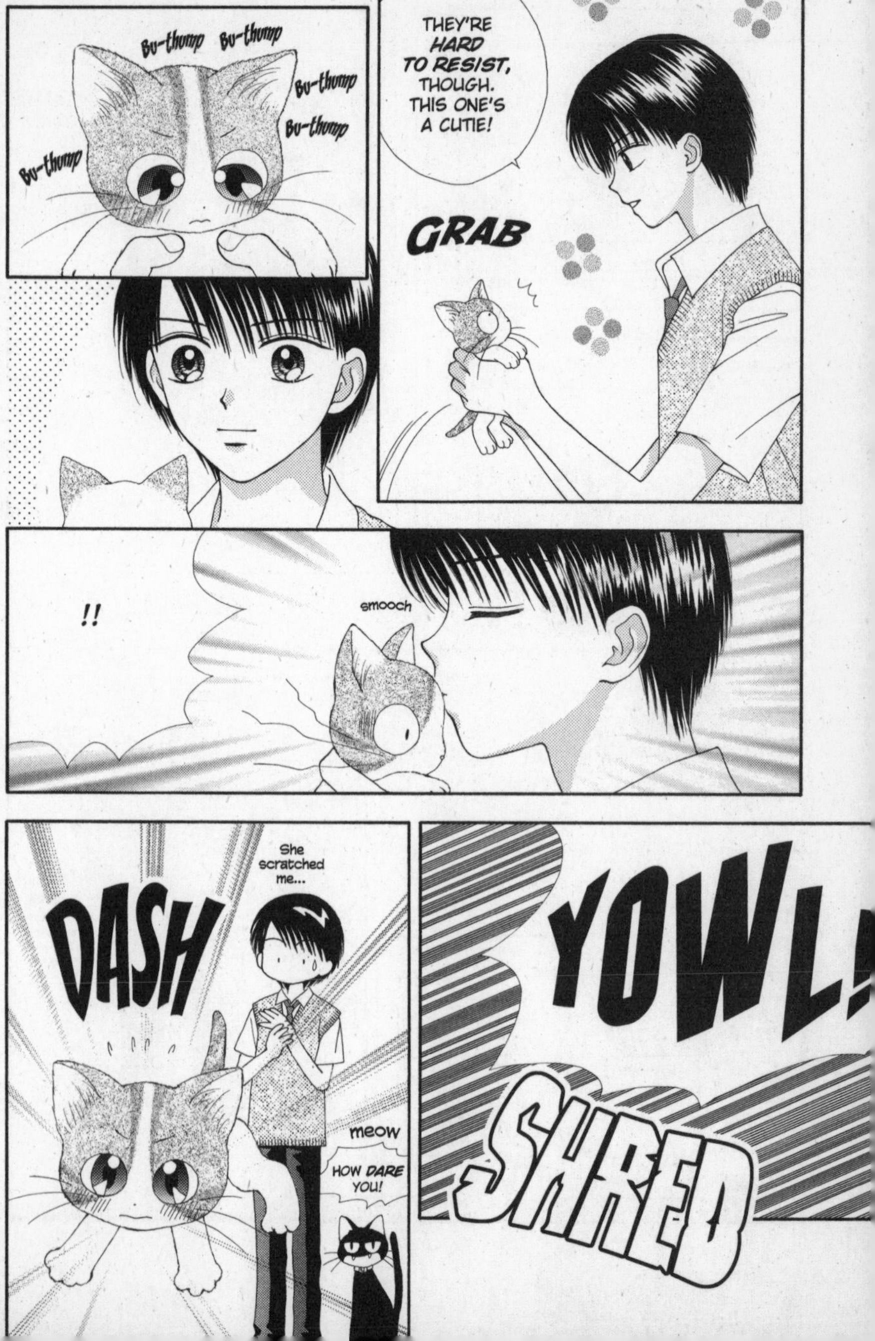
THEY'RE HARD TO RESIST, THOUGH. THIS ONE'S A CUTIE!
GRAB
Bu-thump Bu-thump
Bu-thump
Bu-thump
Bu-thump
smooch
!!
YOWL!
SHRED
She scratched me...
DASH
meow
HOW DARE YOU!

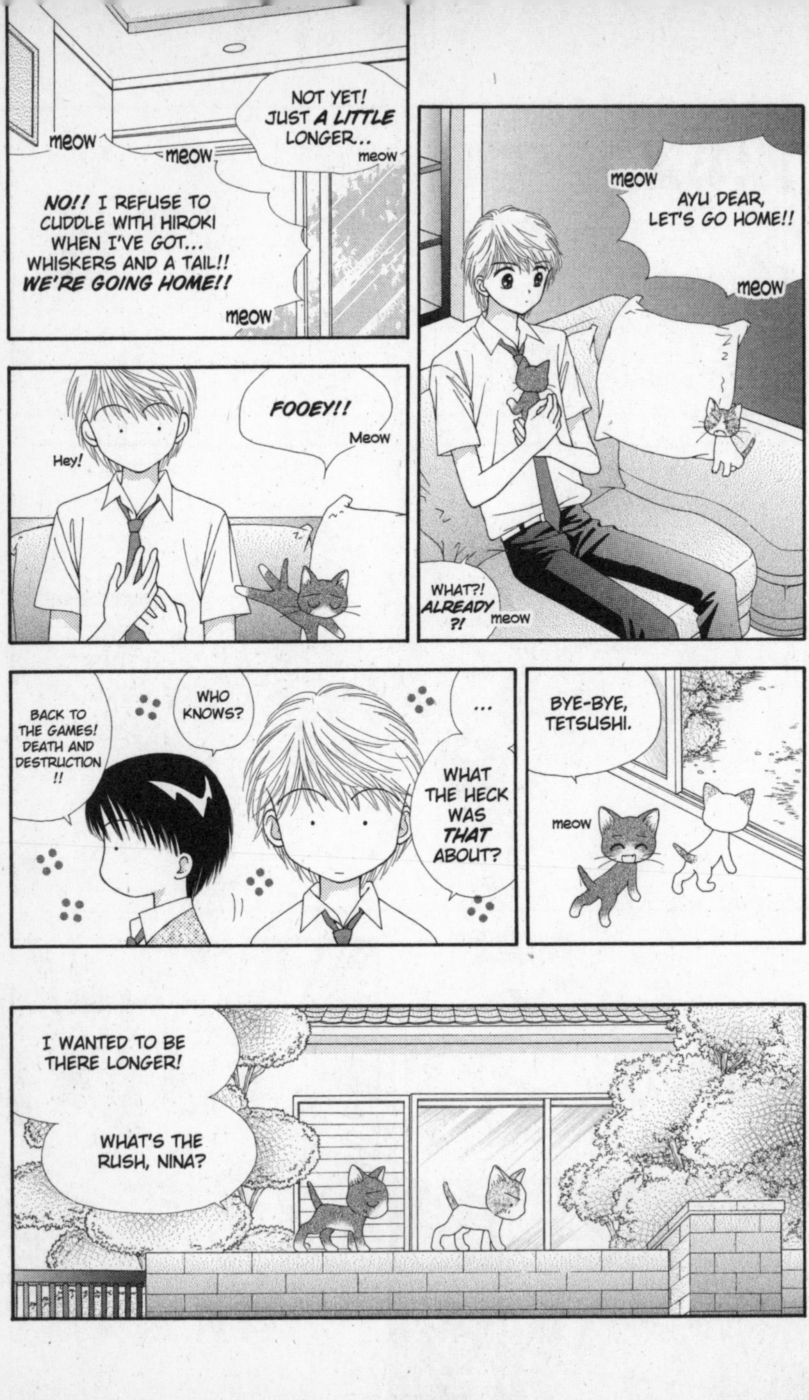
meow
AYU DEAR, LET'S GO HOME!!
meow
WHAT?! ALREADY ?!
meow
NOT YET! JUST A LITTLE LONGER...
meow
meow
meow
NO!! I REFUSE TO CUDDLE WITH HIROKI WHEN I'VE GOT... WHISKERS AND A TAIL!! WE'RE GOING HOME!!
meow
FOOEY!!
Meow
Hey!
BYE-BYE, TETSUSHI.
meow
...
WHAT THE HECK WAS THAT ABOUT?
WHO KNOWS?
BACK TO THE GAMES! DEATH AND DESTRUCTION!!
I WANTED TO BE THERE LONGER!
WHAT'S THE RUSH, NINA?

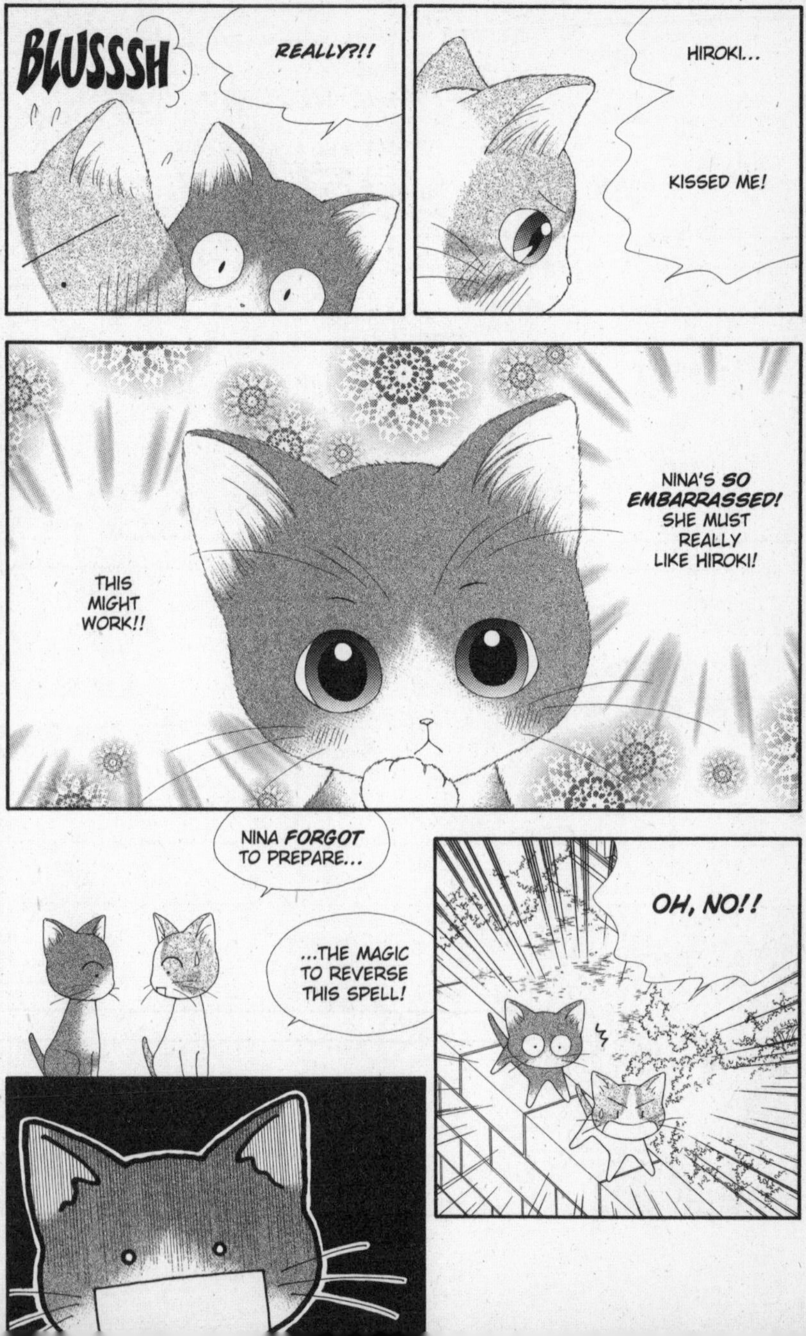
HIROKI...
KISSED ME!
BLUSSSH
REALLY?!!
NINA'S SO EMBARRASSED! SHE MUST REALLY LIKE HIROKI!
THIS MIGHT WORK!!
OH, NO!!
NINA FORGOT TO PREPARE...
...THE MAGIC TO REVERSE THIS SPELL!

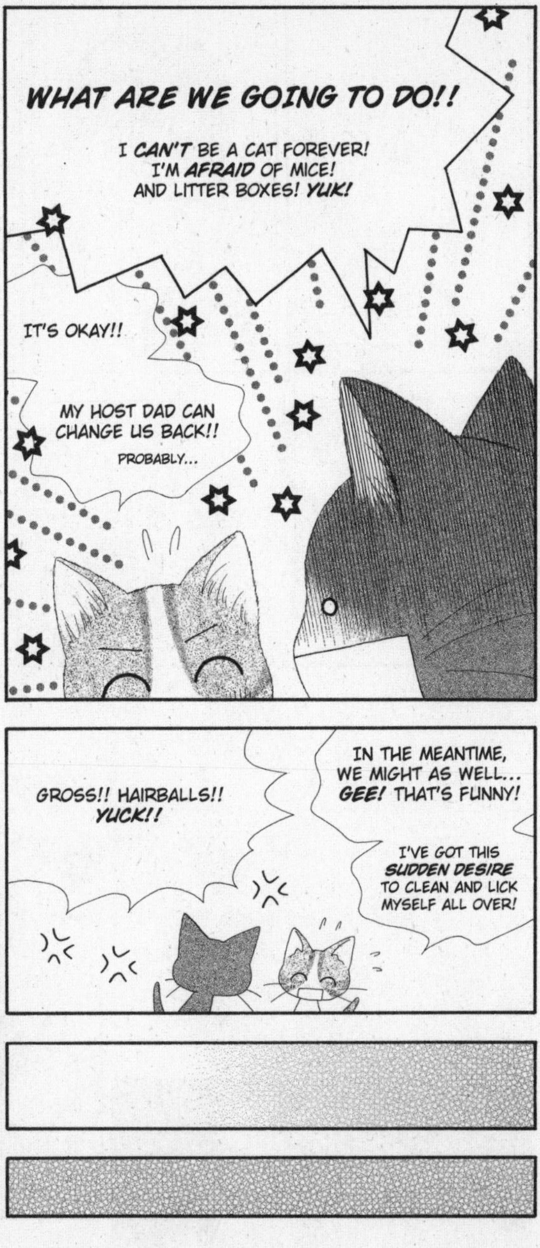
WHAT ARE WE GOING TO DO!!
I CAN'T BE A CAT FOREVER! I'M AFRAID OF MICE! AND LITTER BOXES! YUK!
IT'S OKAY!!
MY HOST DAD CAN CHANGE US BACK!!
PROBABLY...
IN THE MEANTIME, WE MIGHT AS WELL... GEE! THAT'S FUNNY!
I'VE GOT THIS SUDDEN DESIRE TO CLEAN AND LICK MYSELF ALL OVER!
GROSS!! HAIRBALLS!! YUCK!!

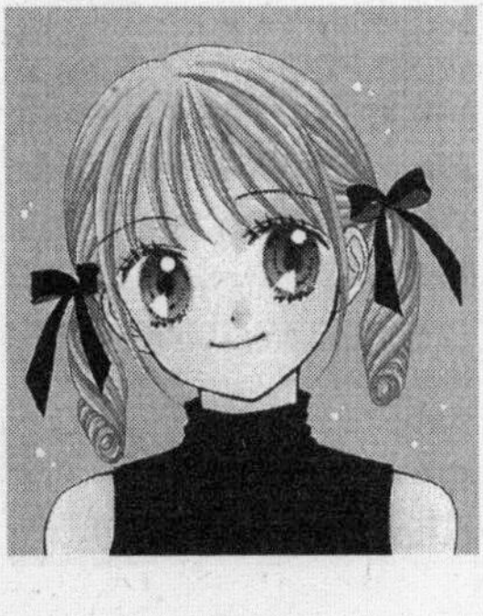

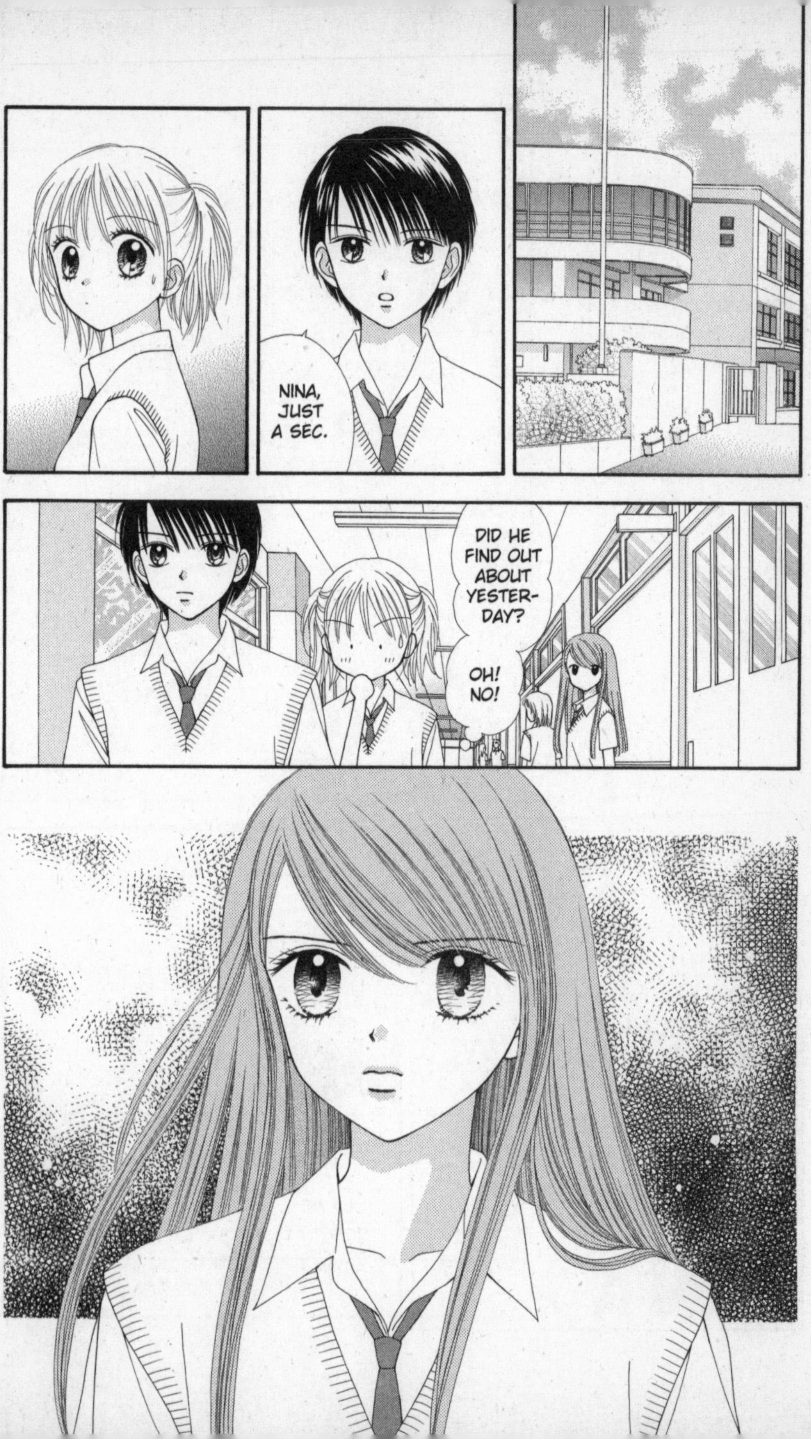
NINA, JUST A SEC.
DID HE FIND OUT ABOUT YESTER-DAY?
OH! NO!

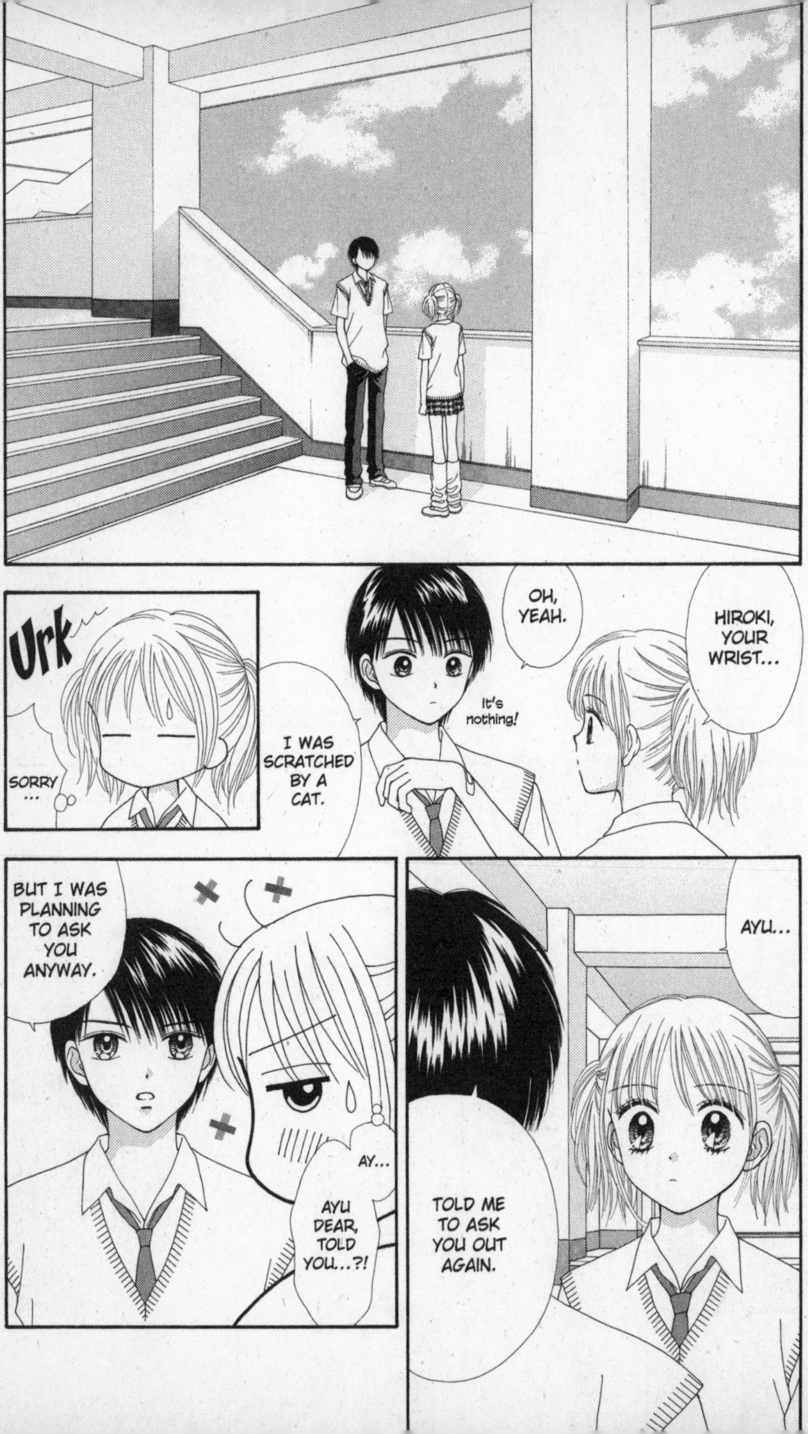
HIROKI, YOUR WRIST...
OH, YEAH.
It's nothing!
I WAS SCRATCHED BY A CAT.
Urk
SORRY...
AYU...
TOLD ME TO ASK YOU OUT AGAIN.
BUT I WAS PLANNING TO ASK YOU ANYWAY.
AY...
AYU DEAR, TOLD YOU...?!

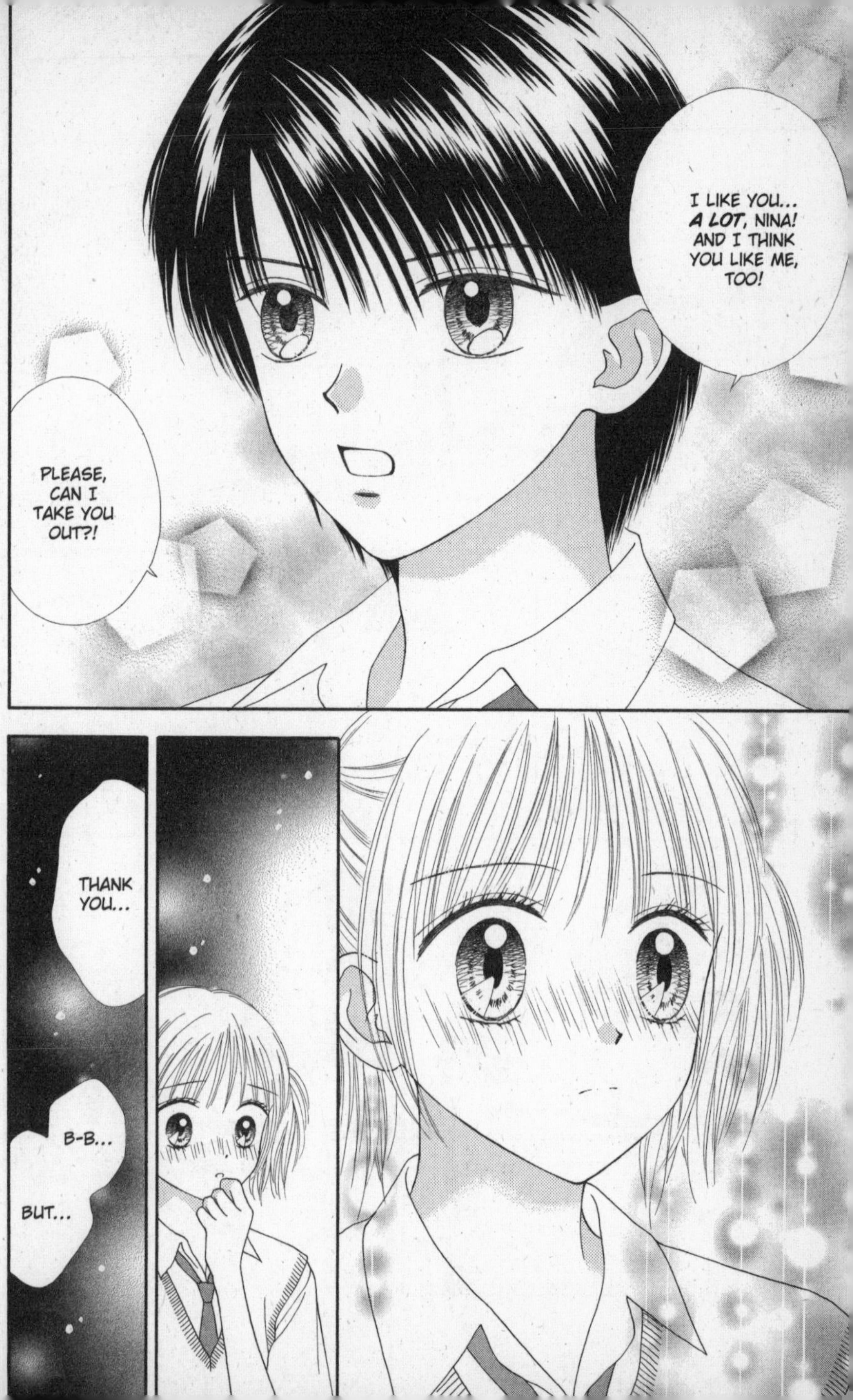
I LIKE YOU... **A LOT**, NINA! AND I THINK YOU LIKE ME, TOO!
PLEASE, CAN I TAKE YOU OUT?!
THANK YOU...
B-B...
BUT...

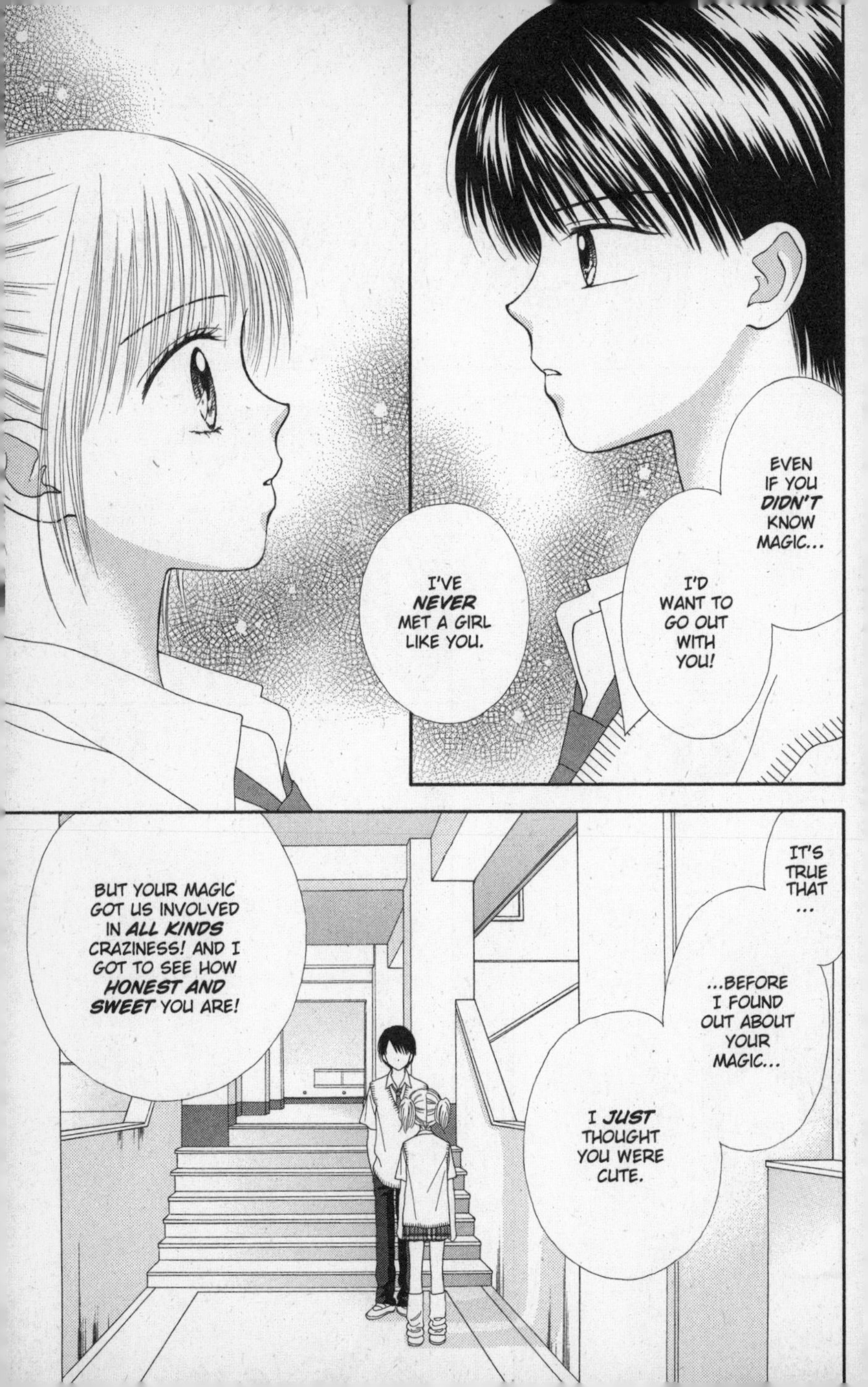
EVEN IF YOU DIDN'T KNOW MAGIC...
I'D WANT TO GO OUT WITH YOU!
I'VE NEVER MET A GIRL LIKE YOU.
IT'S TRUE THAT...
...BEFORE I FOUND OUT ABOUT YOUR MAGIC...
I JUST THOUGHT YOU WERE CUTE.
BUT YOUR MAGIC GOT US INVOLVED IN ALL KINDS CRAZINESS! AND I GOT TO SEE HOW HONEST AND SWEET YOU ARE!

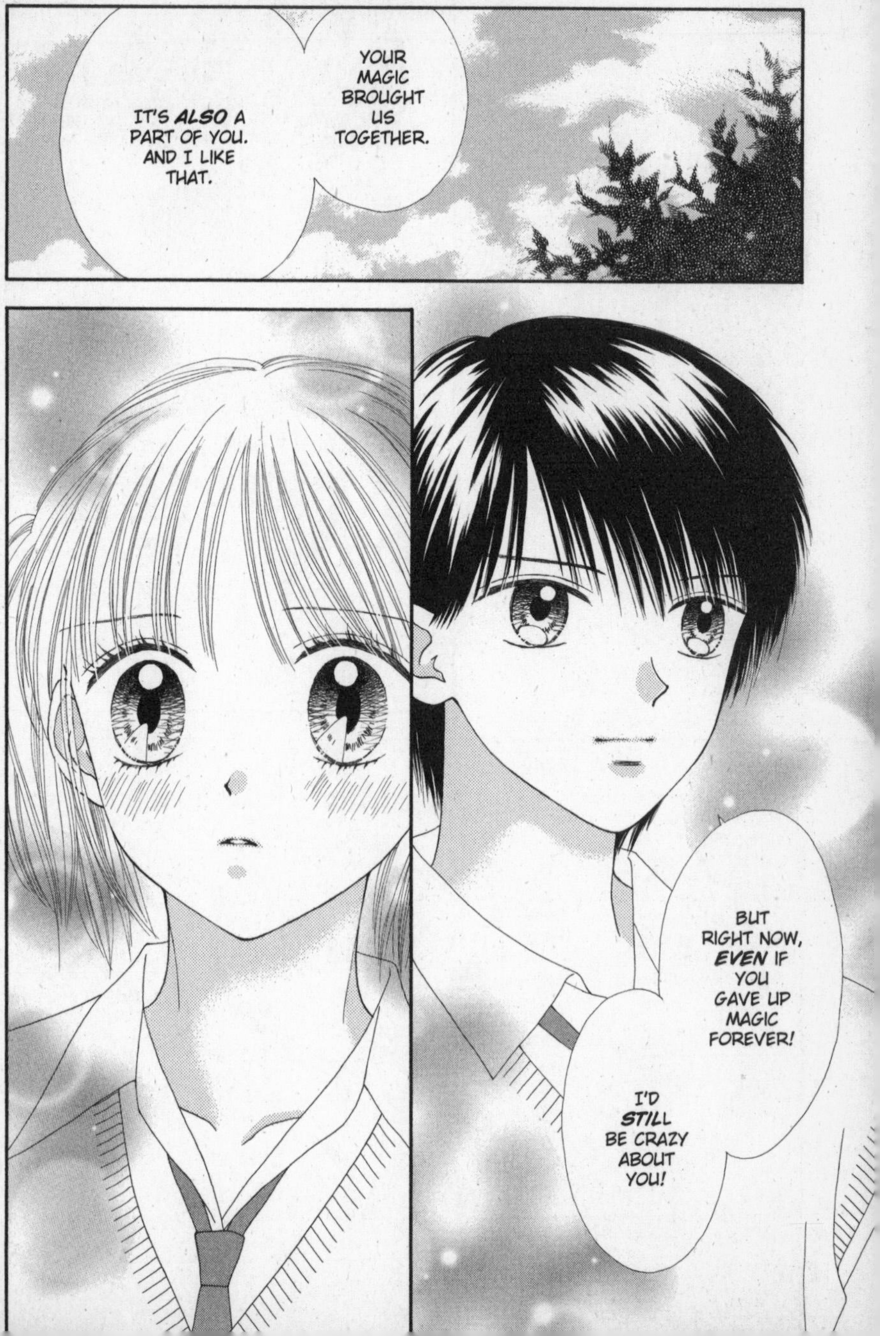
YOUR MAGIC BROUGHT US TOGETHER.
IT'S ALSO A PART OF YOU. AND I LIKE THAT.
BUT RIGHT NOW, EVEN IF YOU GAVE UP MAGIC FOREVER!
I'D STILL BE CRAZY ABOUT YOU!

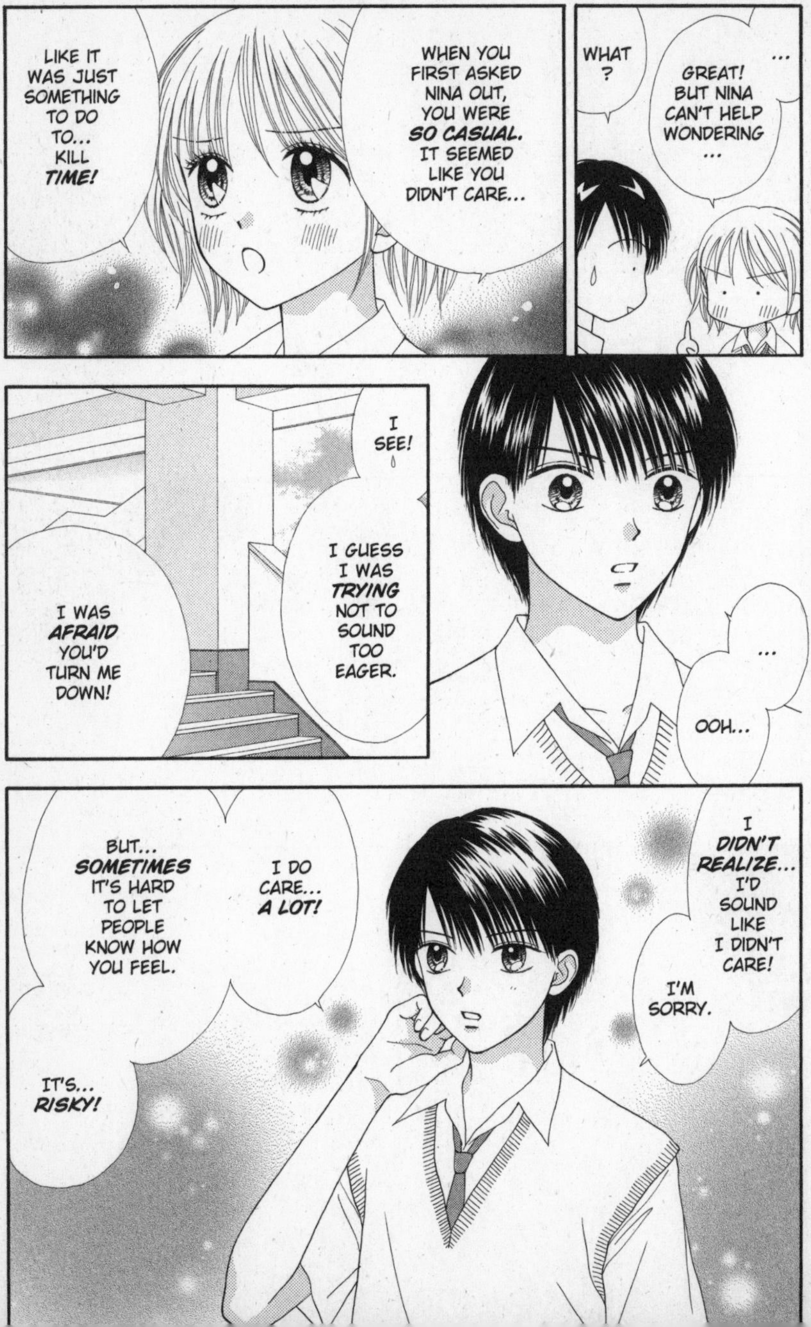
... GREAT! BUT NINA CAN'T HELP WONDERING ...
WHAT ?
WHEN YOU FIRST ASKED NINA OUT, YOU WERE SO CASUAL. IT SEEMED LIKE YOU DIDN'T CARE...
LIKE IT WAS JUST SOMETHING TO DO TO... KILL TIME!
...
OOH...
I SEE!
I GUESS I WAS TRYING NOT TO SOUND TOO EAGER.
I WAS AFRAID YOU'D TURN ME DOWN!
I DIDN'T REALIZE... I'D SOUND LIKE I DIDN'T CARE!
I'M SORRY.
I DO CARE... A LOT!
BUT... SOMETIMES IT'S HARD TO LET PEOPLE KNOW HOW YOU FEEL.
IT'S... RISKY!

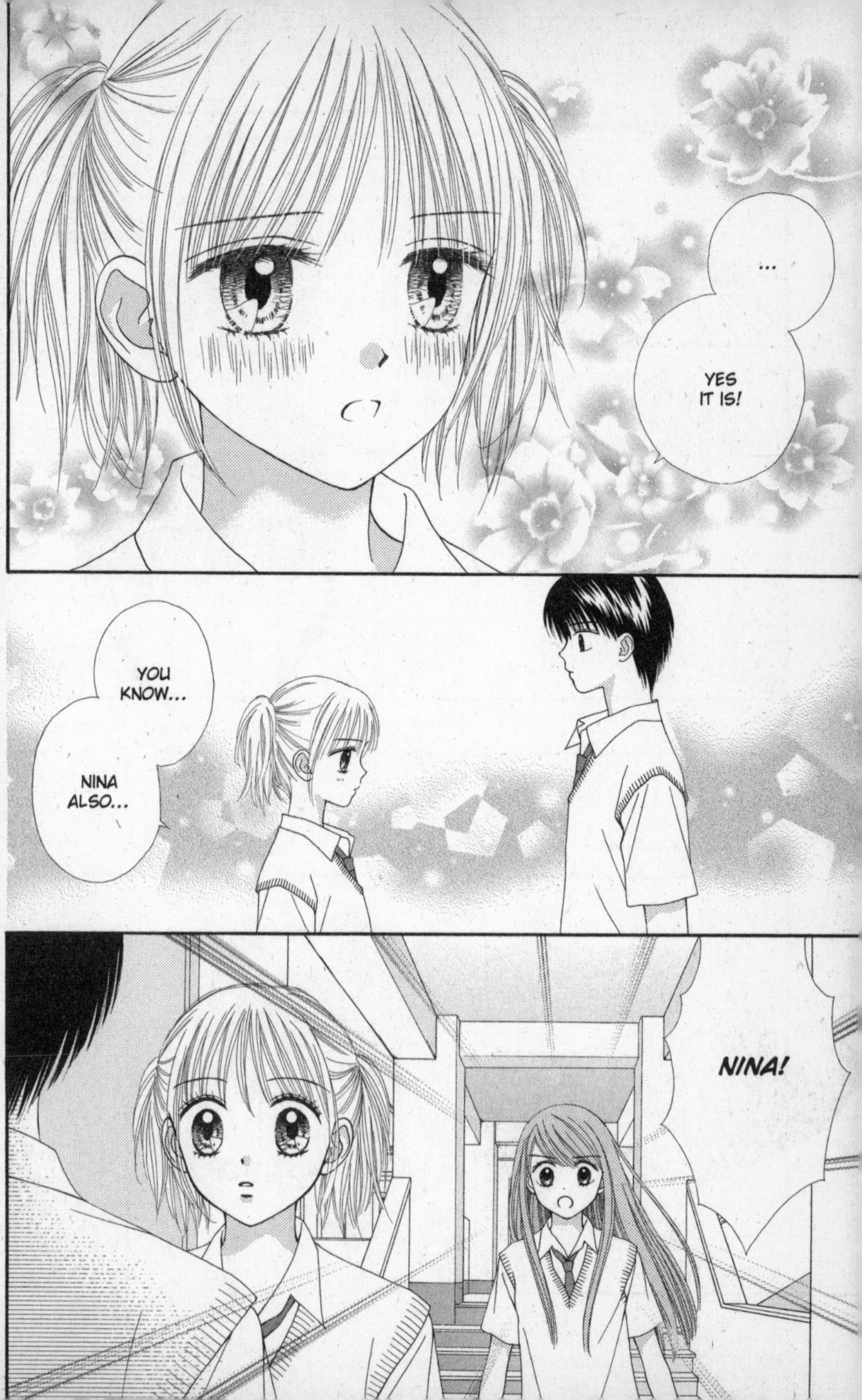
...
YES IT IS!
YOU KNOW...
NINA ALSO...
NINA!

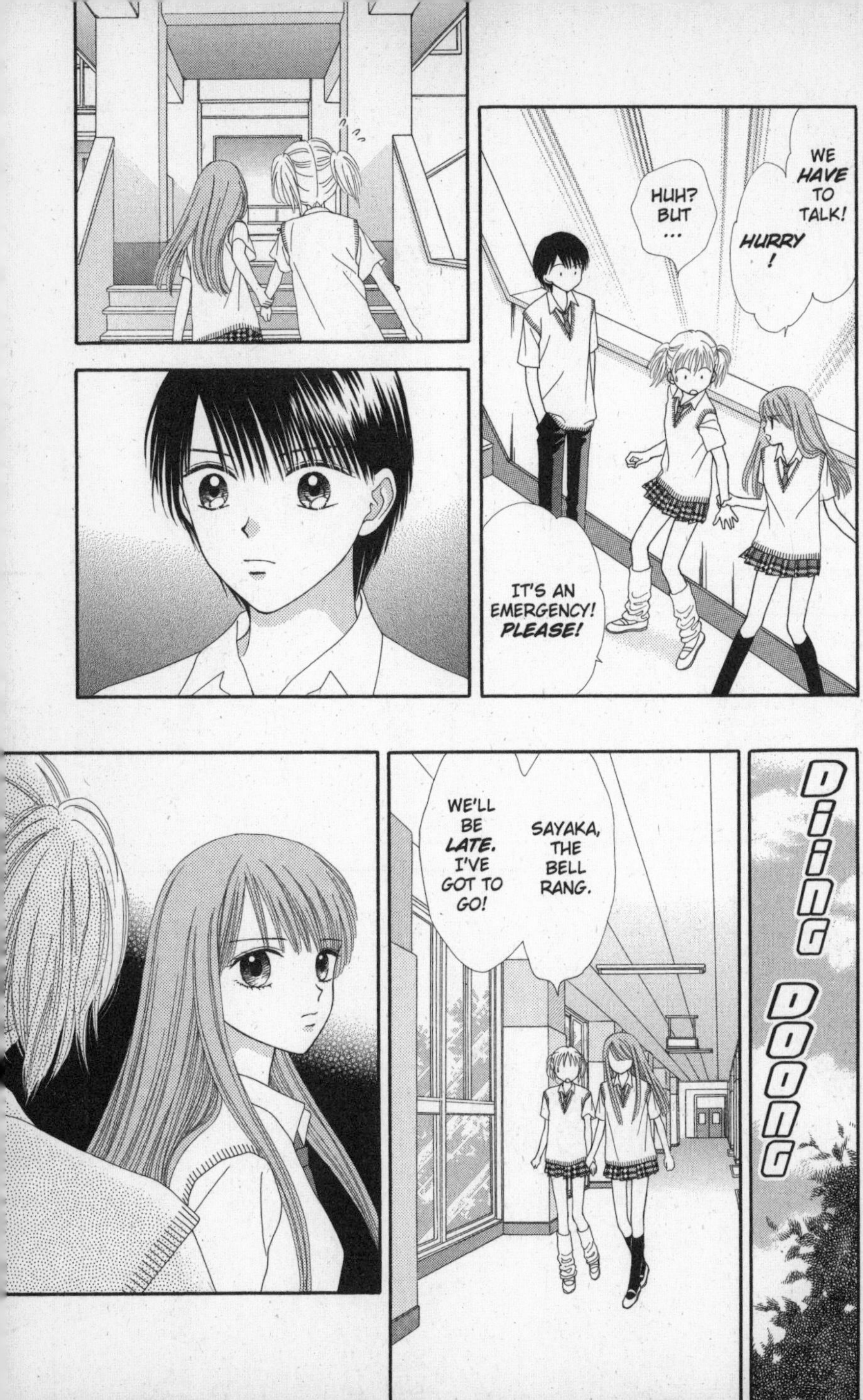
WE HAVE TO TALK! HURRY!
HUH? BUT ...
IT'S AN EMERGENCY! PLEASE!
DIIING DOOONG
SAYAKA, THE BELL RANG.
WE'LL BE LATE. I'VE GOT TO GO!

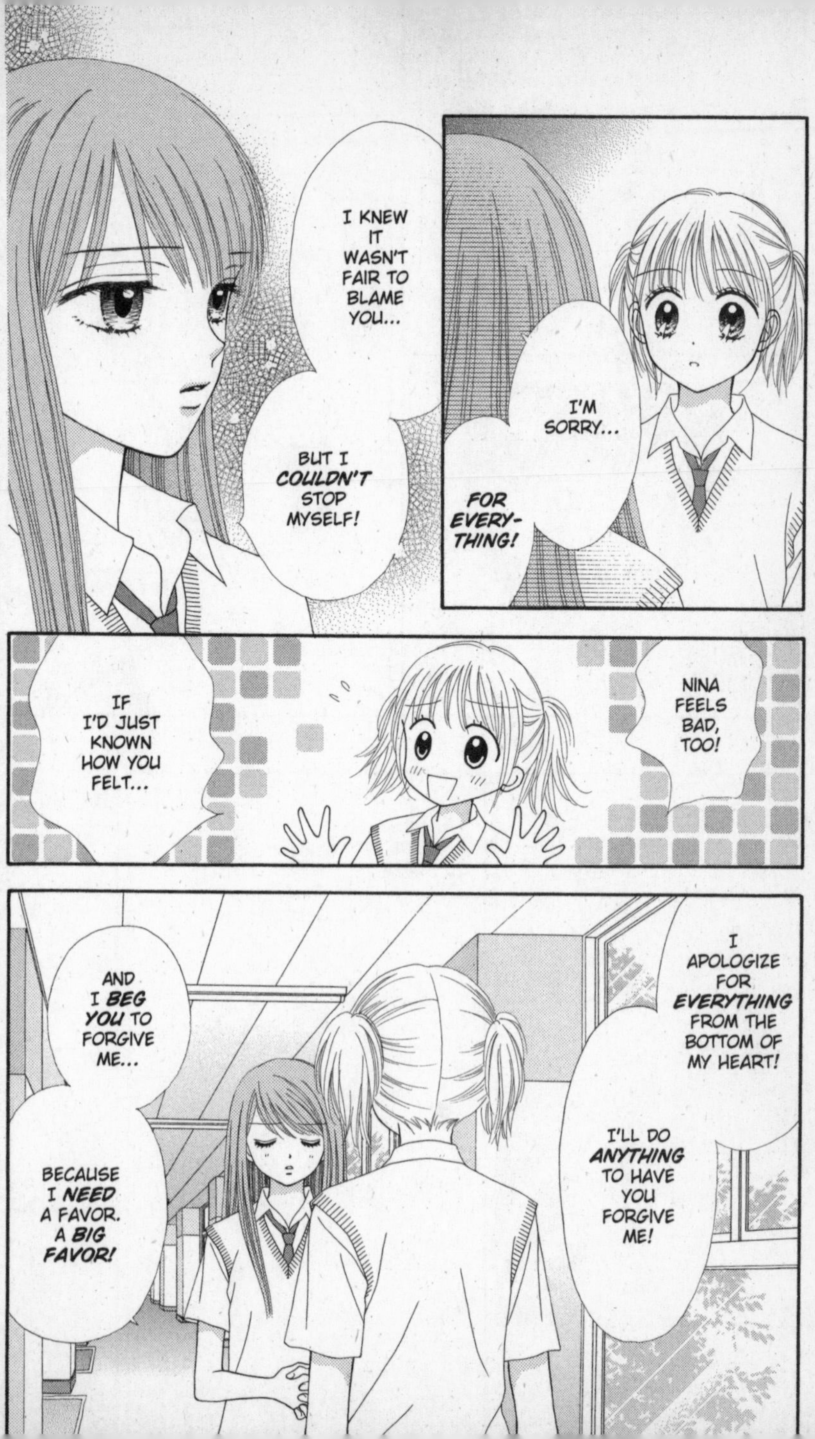
I'M SORRY...
FOR EVERYTHING!
I KNEW IT WASN'T FAIR TO BLAME YOU...
BUT I COULDN'T STOP MYSELF!
NINA FEELS BAD, TOO!
IF I'D JUST KNOWN HOW YOU FELT...
I APOLOGIZE FOR EVERYTHING FROM THE BOTTOM OF MY HEART!
I'LL DO ANYTHING TO HAVE YOU FORGIVE ME!
AND I BEG YOU TO FORGIVE ME...
BECAUSE I NEED A FAVOR. A BIG FAVOR!

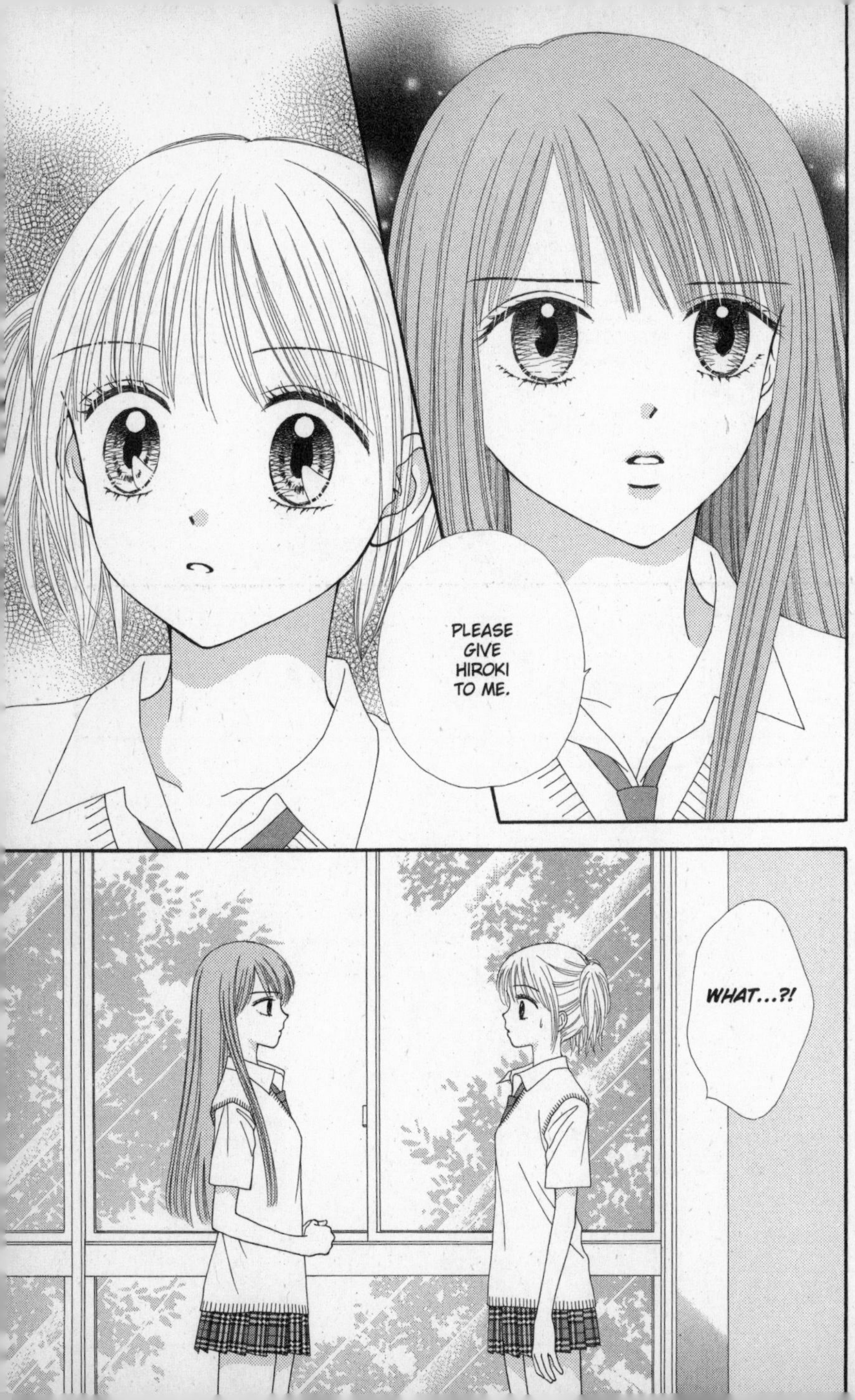
PLEASE GIVE HIROKI TO ME.
WHAT...?!

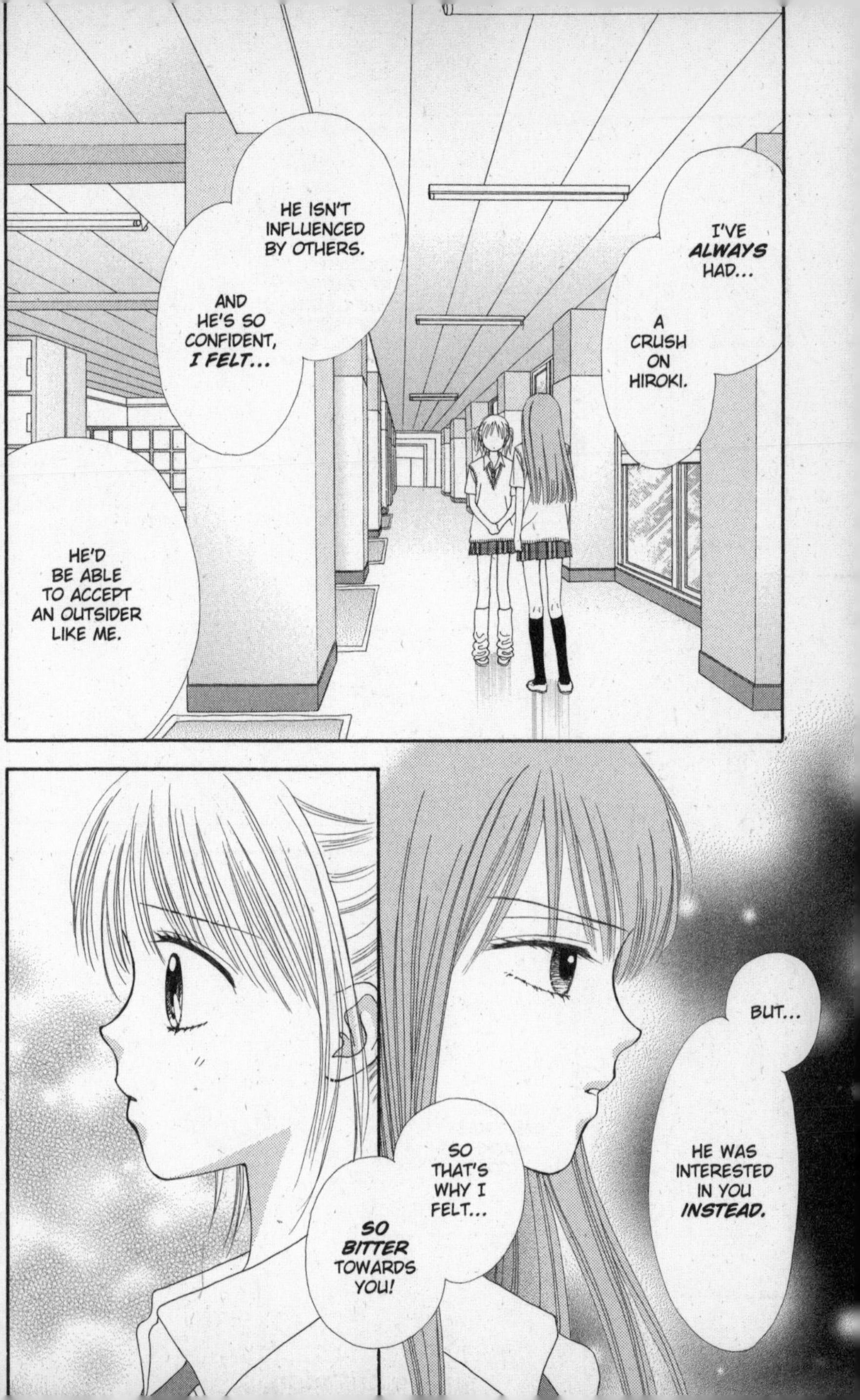
I'VE *ALWAYS* HAD...
A CRUSH ON HIROKI.
HE ISN'T INFLUENCED BY OTHERS.
AND HE'S SO CONFIDENT, *I FELT...*
HE'D BE ABLE TO ACCEPT AN OUTSIDER LIKE ME.
BUT...
HE WAS INTERESTED IN YOU *INSTEAD.*
SO THAT'S WHY I FELT...
SO BITTER TOWARDS YOU!

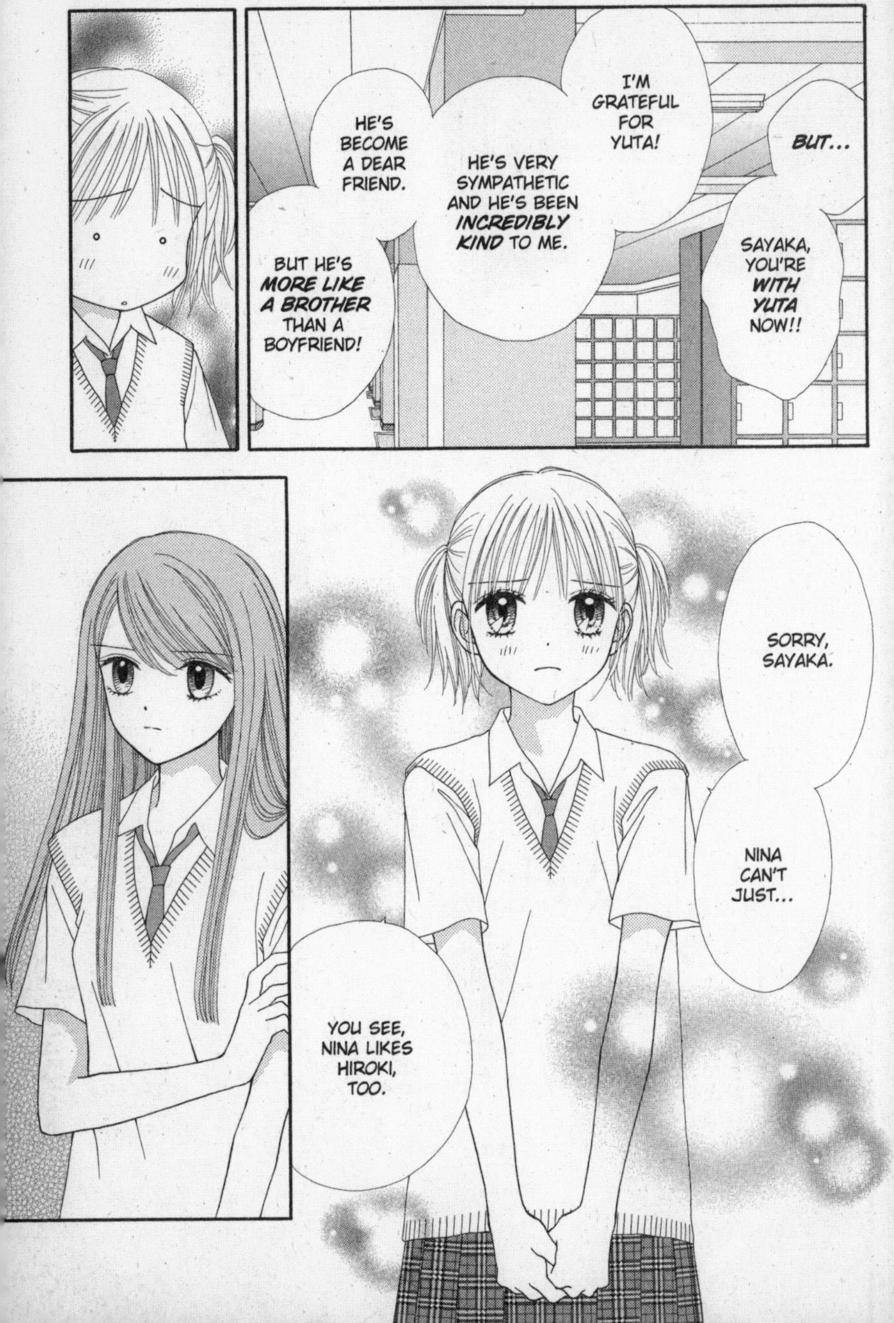
BUT...
SAYAKA, YOU'RE WITH YUTA NOW!!
I'M GRATEFUL FOR YUTA!
HE'S VERY SYMPATHETIC AND HE'S BEEN INCREDIBLY KIND TO ME.
HE'S BECOME A DEAR FRIEND.
BUT HE'S MORE LIKE A BROTHER THAN A BOYFRIEND!
SORRY, SAYAKA.
NINA CAN'T JUST...
YOU SEE, NINA LIKES HIROKI, TOO.

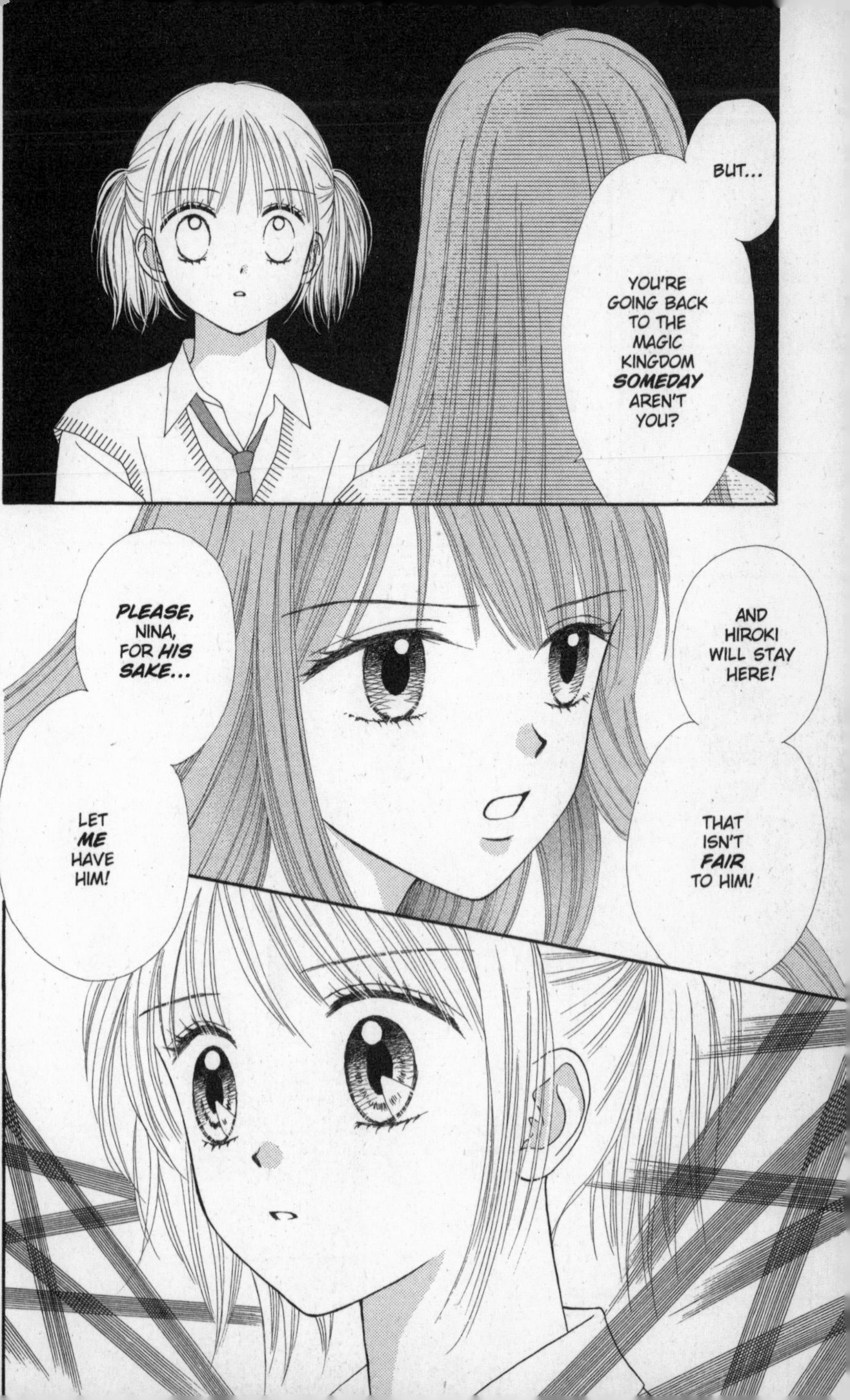
BUT...
YOU'RE GOING BACK TO THE MAGIC KINGDOM ***SOMEDAY*** AREN'T YOU?
AND HIROKI WILL STAY HERE!
THAT ISN'T ***FAIR*** TO HIM!
PLEASE, NINA, FOR ***HIS SAKE...***
LET ***ME*** HAVE HIM!

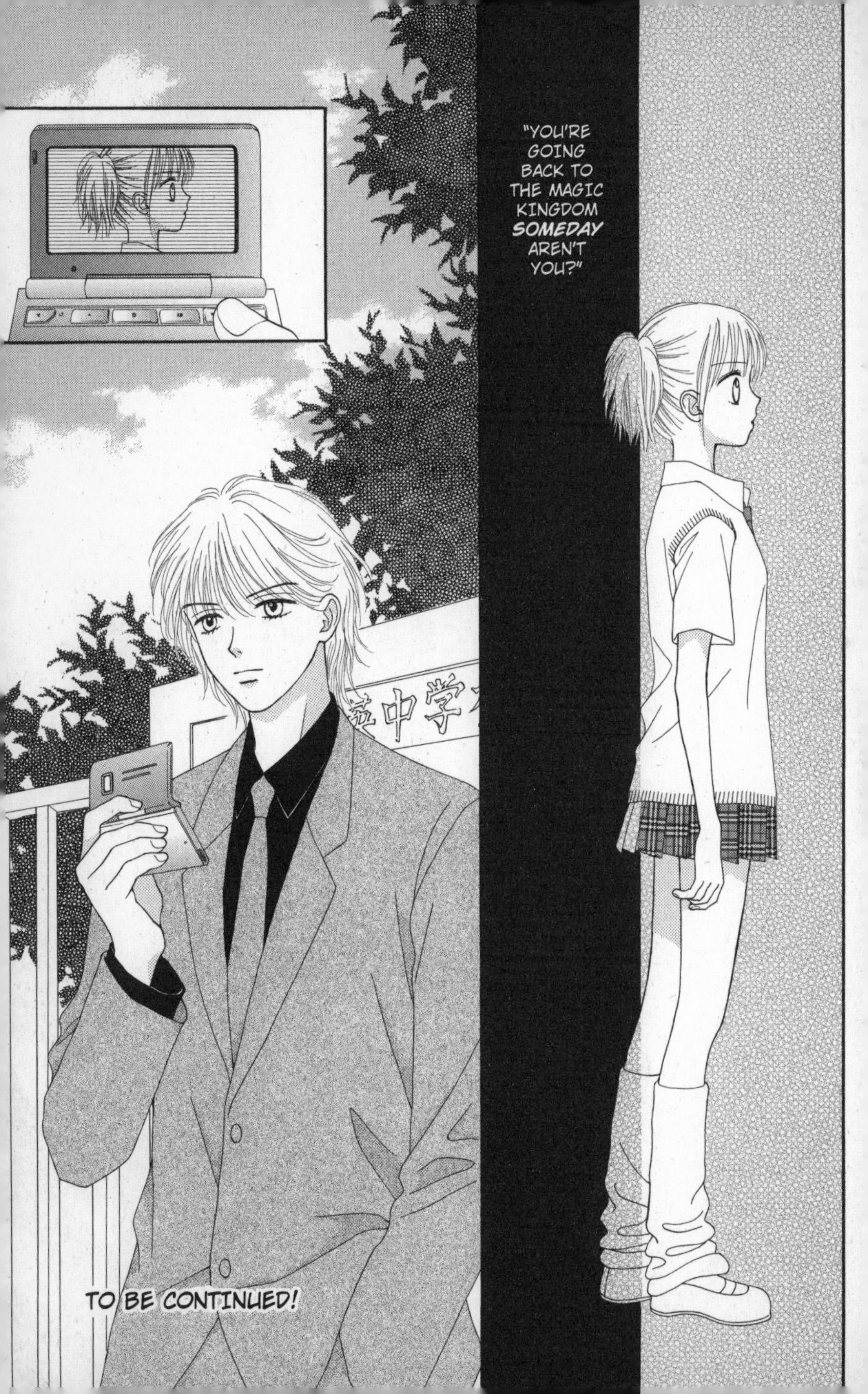
"YOU'RE GOING BACK TO THE MAGIC KINGDOM SOMEDAY AREN'T YOU?"
TO BE CONTINUED!

Bia Baridi!

Chronicles of the Kenya Trip.

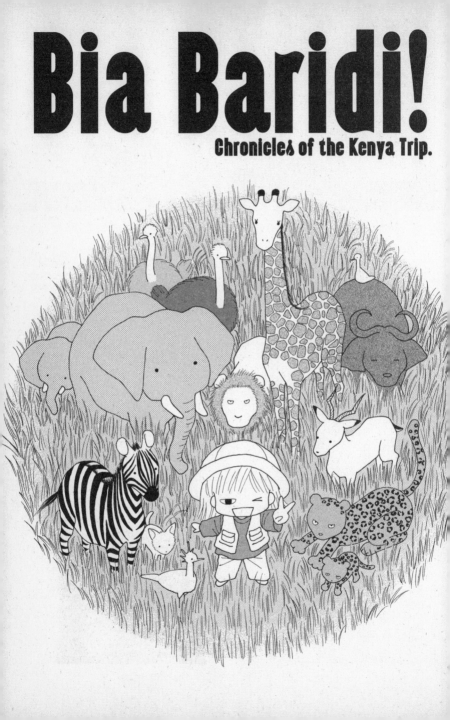

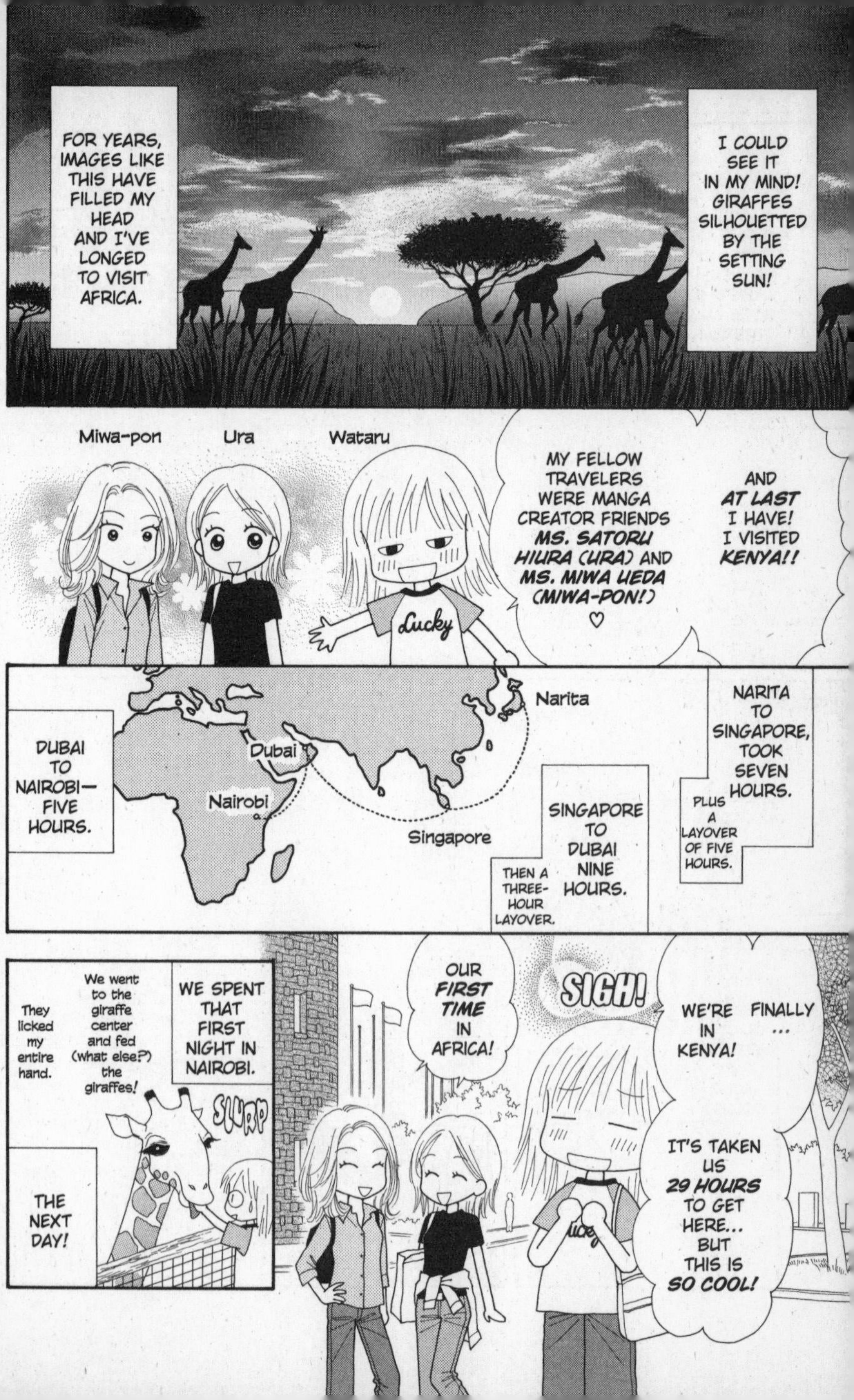
I COULD SEE IT IN MY MIND! GIRAFFES SILHOUETTED BY THE SETTING SUN!
FOR YEARS, IMAGES LIKE THIS HAVE FILLED MY HEAD AND I'VE LONGED TO VISIT AFRICA.
AND AT LAST I HAVE! I VISITED KENYA!!
MY FELLOW TRAVELERS WERE MANGA CREATOR FRIENDS MS. SATORU HIURA (URA) AND MS. MIWA UEDA (MIWA-PON!) ♡
Wataru
Ura
Miwa-pon
NARITA TO SINGAPORE, TOOK SEVEN HOURS.
PLUS A LAYOVER OF FIVE HOURS.
Narita
SINGAPORE TO DUBAI NINE HOURS.
THEN A THREE-HOUR LAYOVER.
Singapore
Dubai
Nairobi
DUBAI TO NAIROBI—FIVE HOURS.
FINALLY ...
WE'RE IN KENYA!
IT'S TAKEN US 29 HOURS TO GET HERE... BUT THIS IS SO COOL!
SIGH!
OUR FIRST TIME IN AFRICA!
WE SPENT THAT FIRST NIGHT IN NAIROBI.
We went to the giraffe center and fed (what else?) the giraffes!
They licked my entire hand.
SLURP
THE NEXT DAY!

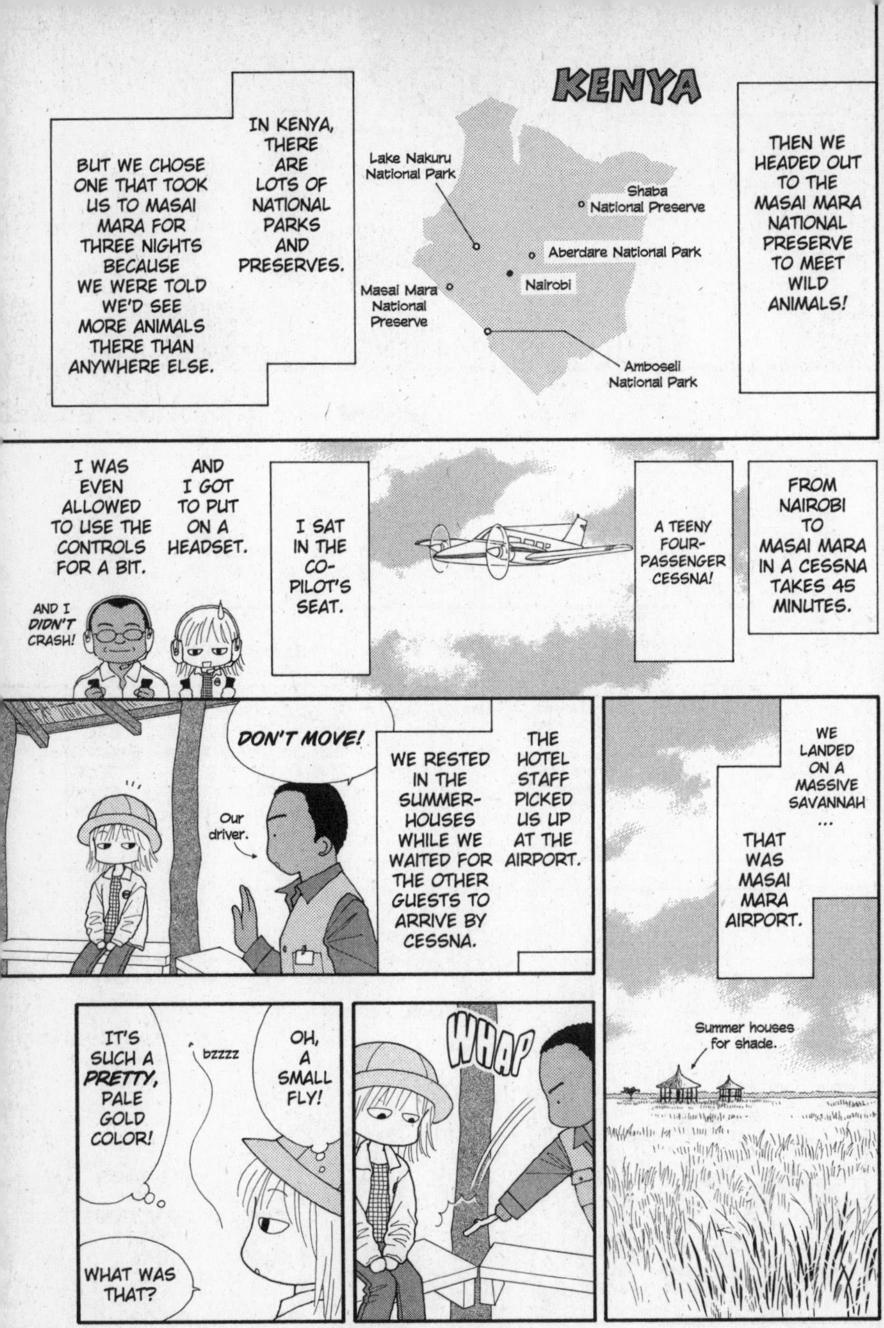
THEN WE HEADED OUT TO THE MASAI MARA NATIONAL PRESERVE TO MEET WILD ANIMALS!
KENYA
Shaba National Preserve
Lake Nakuru National Park
Aberdare National Park
Nairobi
Masai Mara National Preserve
Amboseli National Park
IN KENYA, THERE ARE LOTS OF NATIONAL PARKS AND PRESERVES.
BUT WE CHOSE ONE THAT TOOK US TO MASAI MARA FOR THREE NIGHTS BECAUSE WE WERE TOLD WE'D SEE MORE ANIMALS THERE THAN ANYWHERE ELSE.
FROM NAIROBI TO MASAI MARA IN A CESSNA TAKES 45 MINUTES.
A TEENY FOUR-PASSENGER CESSNA!
I SAT IN THE CO-PILOT'S SEAT.
AND I GOT TO PUT ON A HEADSET.
I WAS EVEN ALLOWED TO USE THE CONTROLS FOR A BIT.
AND I *DIDN'T* CRASH!
WE LANDED ON A MASSIVE SAVANNAH ...
THAT WAS MASAI MARA AIRPORT.
Summer houses for shade.
THE HOTEL STAFF PICKED US UP AT THE AIRPORT.
WE RESTED IN THE SUMMER-HOUSES WHILE WE WAITED FOR THE OTHER GUESTS TO ARRIVE BY CESSNA.
DON'T MOVE!
Our driver.
WHAP
OH, A SMALL FLY!
bzzzz
IT'S SUCH A *PRETTY*, PALE GOLD COLOR!
WHAT WAS THAT?

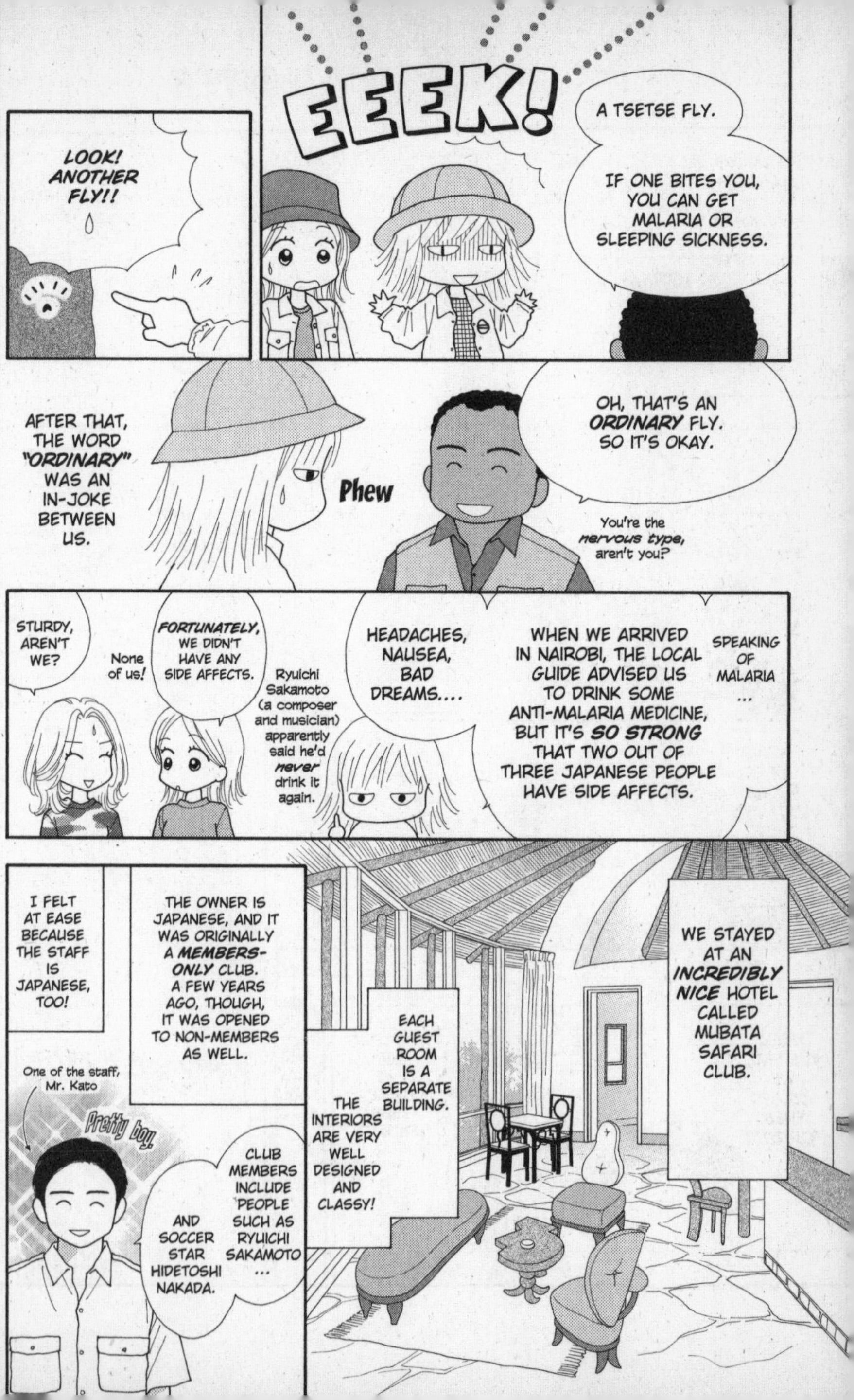

EEEK!
A TSETSE FLY.
IF ONE BITES YOU, YOU CAN GET MALARIA OR SLEEPING SICKNESS.
LOOK! ANOTHER FLY!!
OH, THAT'S AN ORDINARY FLY. SO IT'S OKAY.
You're the nervous type, aren't you?
Phew
AFTER THAT, THE WORD "ORDINARY" WAS AN IN-JOKE BETWEEN US.
SPEAKING OF MALARIA...
WHEN WE ARRIVED IN NAIROBI, THE LOCAL GUIDE ADVISED US TO DRINK SOME ANTI-MALARIA MEDICINE, BUT IT'S SO STRONG THAT TWO OUT OF THREE JAPANESE PEOPLE HAVE SIDE AFFECTS.
HEADACHES, NAUSEA, BAD DREAMS....
Ryuichi Sakamoto (a composer and musician) apparently said he'd never drink it again.
FORTUNATELY, WE DIDN'T HAVE ANY SIDE AFFECTS.
None of us!
STURDY, AREN'T WE?
WE STAYED AT AN INCREDIBLY NICE HOTEL CALLED MUBATA SAFARI CLUB.
EACH GUEST ROOM IS A SEPARATE BUILDING.
THE INTERIORS ARE VERY WELL DESIGNED AND CLASSY!
CLUB MEMBERS INCLUDE PEOPLE SUCH AS RYUICHI SAKAMOTO...
AND SOCCER STAR HIDETOSHI NAKADA.
Pretty boy.
One of the staff, Mr. Kato
THE OWNER IS JAPANESE, AND IT WAS ORIGINALLY A MEMBERS-ONLY CLUB. A FEW YEARS AGO, THOUGH, IT WAS OPENED TO NON-MEMBERS AS WELL.
I FELT AT EASE BECAUSE THE STAFF IS JAPANESE, TOO!

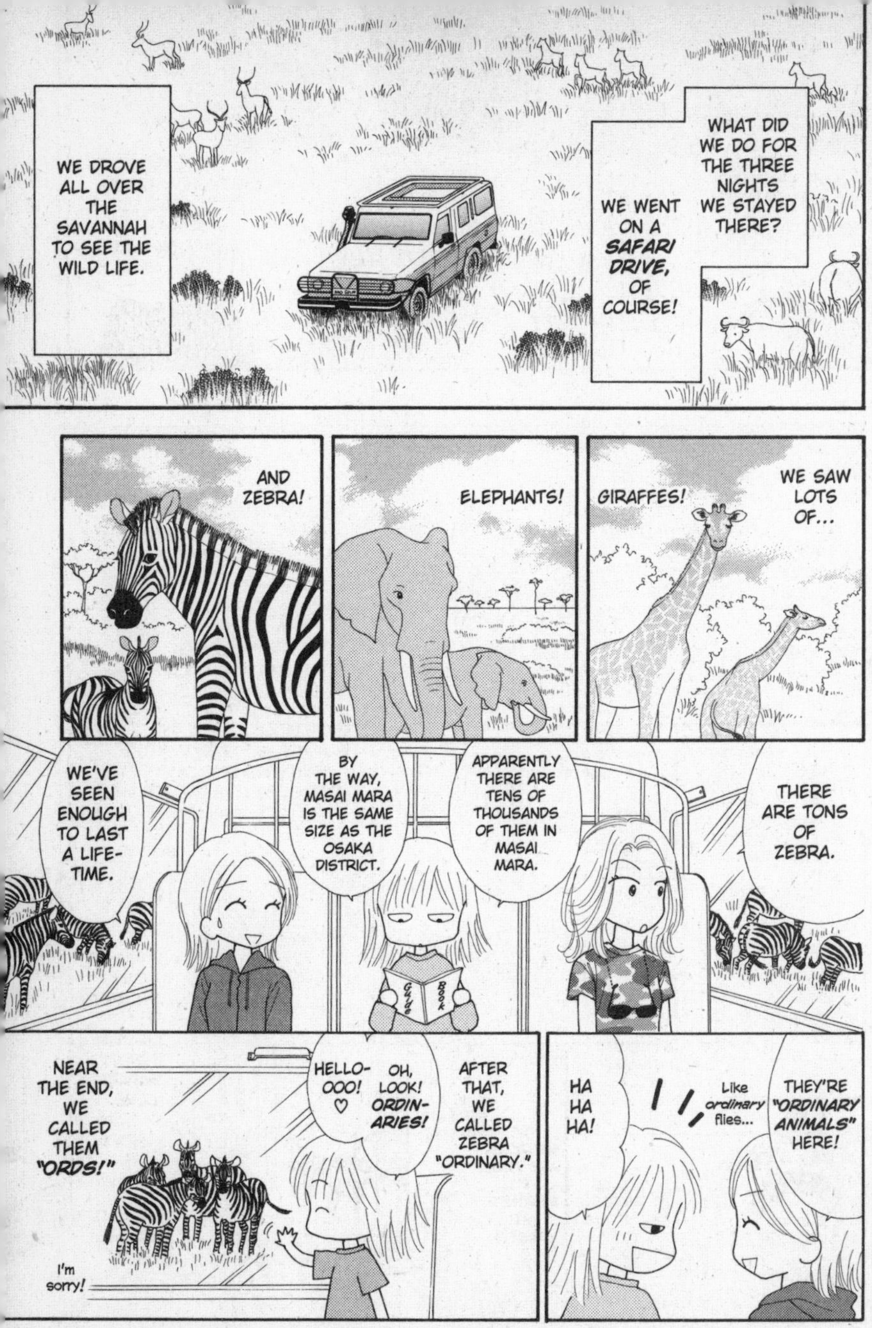
WHAT DID WE DO FOR THE THREE NIGHTS WE STAYED THERE?
WE WENT ON A SAFARI DRIVE, OF COURSE!
WE DROVE ALL OVER THE SAVANNAH TO SEE THE WILD LIFE.
WE SAW LOTS OF...
GIRAFFES!
ELEPHANTS!
AND ZEBRA!
THERE ARE TONS OF ZEBRA.
APPARENTLY THERE ARE TENS OF THOUSANDS OF THEM IN MASAI MARA.
BY THE WAY, MASAI MARA IS THE SAME SIZE AS THE OSAKA DISTRICT.
Guide Book
WE'VE SEEN ENOUGH TO LAST A LIFE-TIME.
THEY'RE "ORDINARY ANIMALS" HERE!
Like ordinary flies...
HA HA HA!
AFTER THAT, WE CALLED ZEBRA "ORDINARY."
OH, LOOK! ORDIN-ARIES!
HELLO-OOO! ♡
NEAR THE END, WE CALLED THEM "ORDS!"
I'm sorry!

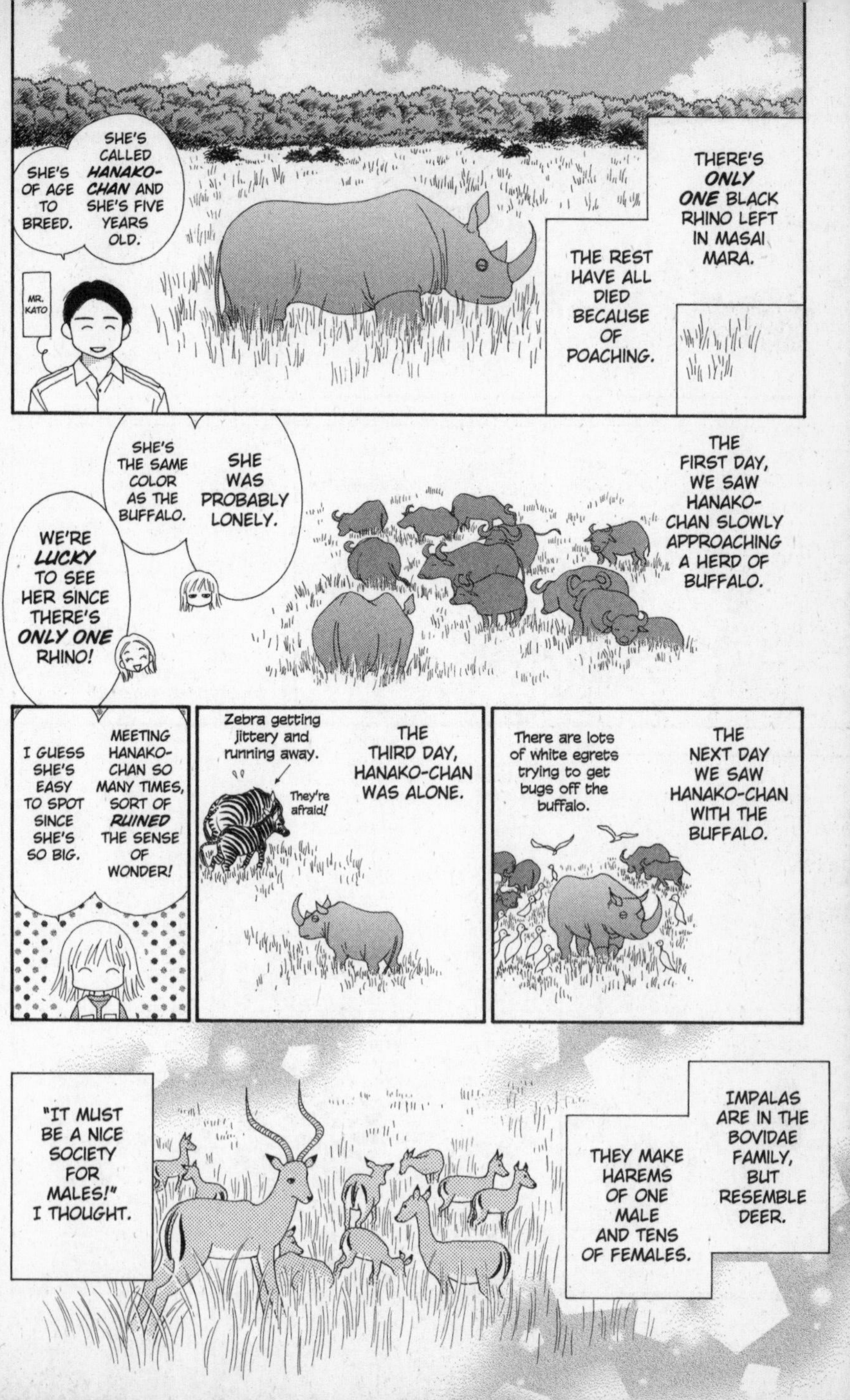
THERE'S ONLY ONE BLACK RHINO LEFT IN MASAI MARA.
THE REST HAVE ALL DIED BECAUSE OF POACHING.
SHE'S CALLED HANAKO-CHAN AND SHE'S FIVE YEARS OLD.
SHE'S OF AGE TO BREED.
MR. KATO
THE FIRST DAY, WE SAW HANAKO-CHAN SLOWLY APPROACHING A HERD OF BUFFALO.
SHE WAS PROBABLY LONELY.
SHE'S THE SAME COLOR AS THE BUFFALO.
WE'RE LUCKY TO SEE HER SINCE THERE'S ONLY ONE RHINO!
THE NEXT DAY WE SAW HANAKO-CHAN WITH THE BUFFALO.
There are lots of white egrets trying to get bugs off the buffalo.
THE THIRD DAY, HANAKO-CHAN WAS ALONE.
Zebra getting jittery and running away.
They're afraid!
MEETING HANAKO-CHAN SO MANY TIMES, SORT OF RUINED THE SENSE OF WONDER!
I GUESS SHE'S EASY TO SPOT SINCE SHE'S SO BIG.
IMPALAS ARE IN THE BOVIDAE FAMILY, BUT RESEMBLE DEER.
THEY MAKE HAREMS OF ONE MALE AND TENS OF FEMALES.
"IT MUST BE A NICE SOCIETY FOR MALES!" I THOUGHT.

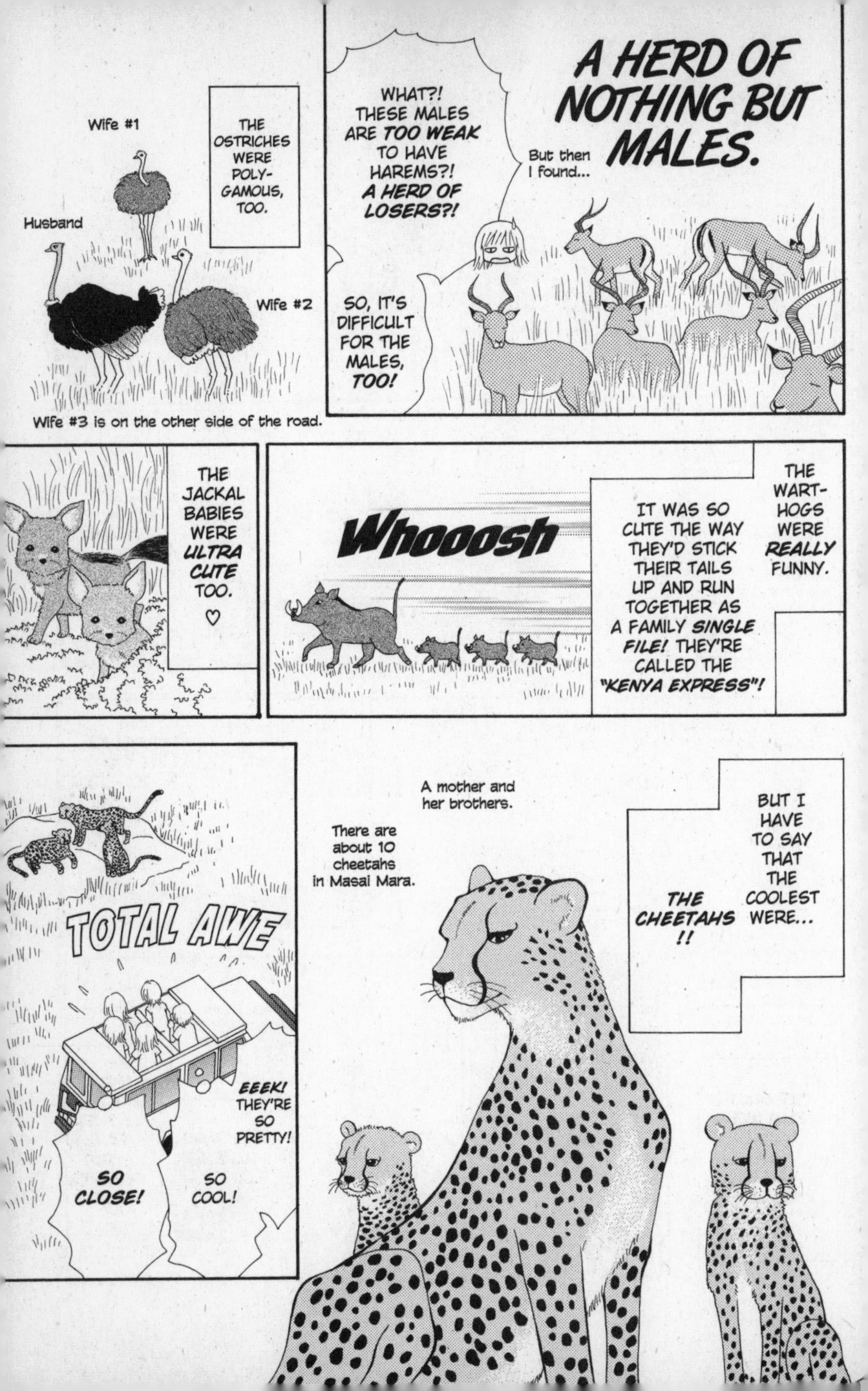

But then I found...
A HERD OF NOTHING BUT MALES.
WHAT?! THESE MALES ARE *TOO WEAK* TO HAVE HAREMS?! *A HERD OF LOSERS?!*
SO, IT'S DIFFICULT FOR THE MALES, *TOO!*
THE OSTRICHES WERE POLY-GAMOUS, TOO.
Wife #1
Husband
Wife #2
Wife #3 is on the other side of the road.
THE WART-HOGS WERE *REALLY* FUNNY.
IT WAS SO CUTE THE WAY THEY'D STICK THEIR TAILS UP AND RUN TOGETHER AS A FAMILY *SINGLE FILE!* THEY'RE CALLED THE *"KENYA EXPRESS"!*
Whoooosh
THE JACKAL BABIES WERE *ULTRA CUTE* TOO. ♡
BUT I HAVE TO SAY THAT THE COOLEST WERE...
THE CHEETAHS !!
A mother and her brothers.
There are about 10 cheetahs in Masai Mara.
TOTAL AWE
EEEK! THEY'RE SO PRETTY!
SO COOL!
SO CLOSE!

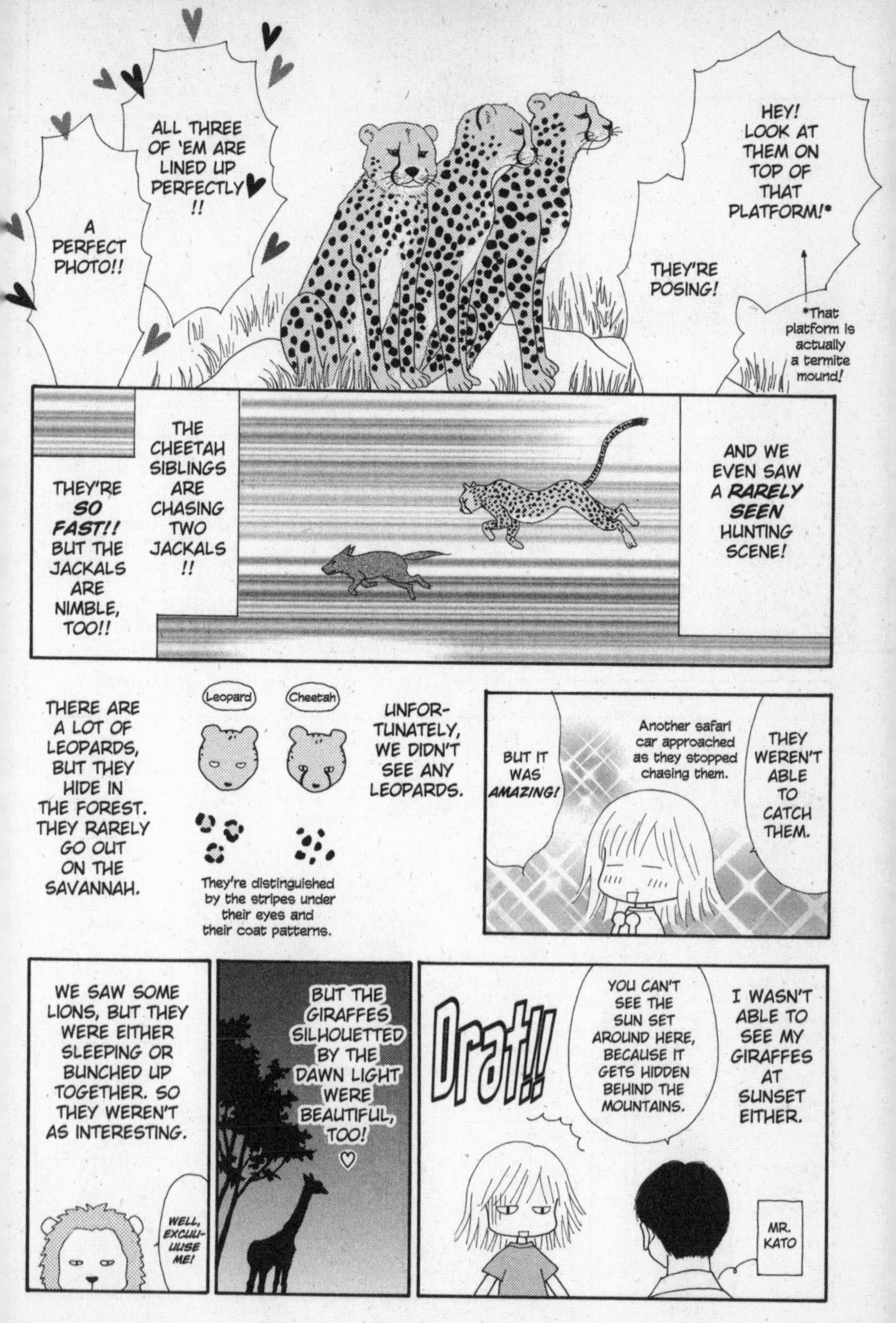
HEY! LOOK AT THEM ON TOP OF THAT PLATFORM!*
THEY'RE POSING!
*That platform is actually a termite mound!
ALL THREE OF 'EM ARE LINED UP PERFECTLY!!
A PERFECT PHOTO!!
AND WE EVEN SAW A RARELY SEEN HUNTING SCENE!
THE CHEETAH SIBLINGS ARE CHASING TWO JACKALS!!
THEY'RE SO FAST!! BUT THE JACKALS ARE NIMBLE, TOO!!
THEY WEREN'T ABLE TO CATCH THEM.
Another safari car approached as they stopped chasing them.
BUT IT WAS AMAZING!
UNFOR-TUNATELY, WE DIDN'T SEE ANY LEOPARDS.
Cheetah
Leopard
They're distinguished by the stripes under their eyes and their coat patterns.
THERE ARE A LOT OF LEOPARDS, BUT THEY HIDE IN THE FOREST. THEY RARELY GO OUT ON THE SAVANNAH.
I WASN'T ABLE TO SEE MY GIRAFFES AT SUNSET EITHER.
YOU CAN'T SEE THE SUN SET AROUND HERE, BECAUSE IT GETS HIDDEN BEHIND THE MOUNTAINS.
Drat!!
MR. KATO
BUT THE GIRAFFES SILHOUETTED BY THE DAWN LIGHT WERE BEAUTIFUL, TOO!
WE SAW SOME LIONS, BUT THEY WERE EITHER SLEEPING OR BUNCHED UP TOGETHER. SO THEY WEREN'T AS INTERESTING.
WELL, EXCULUUSE ME!

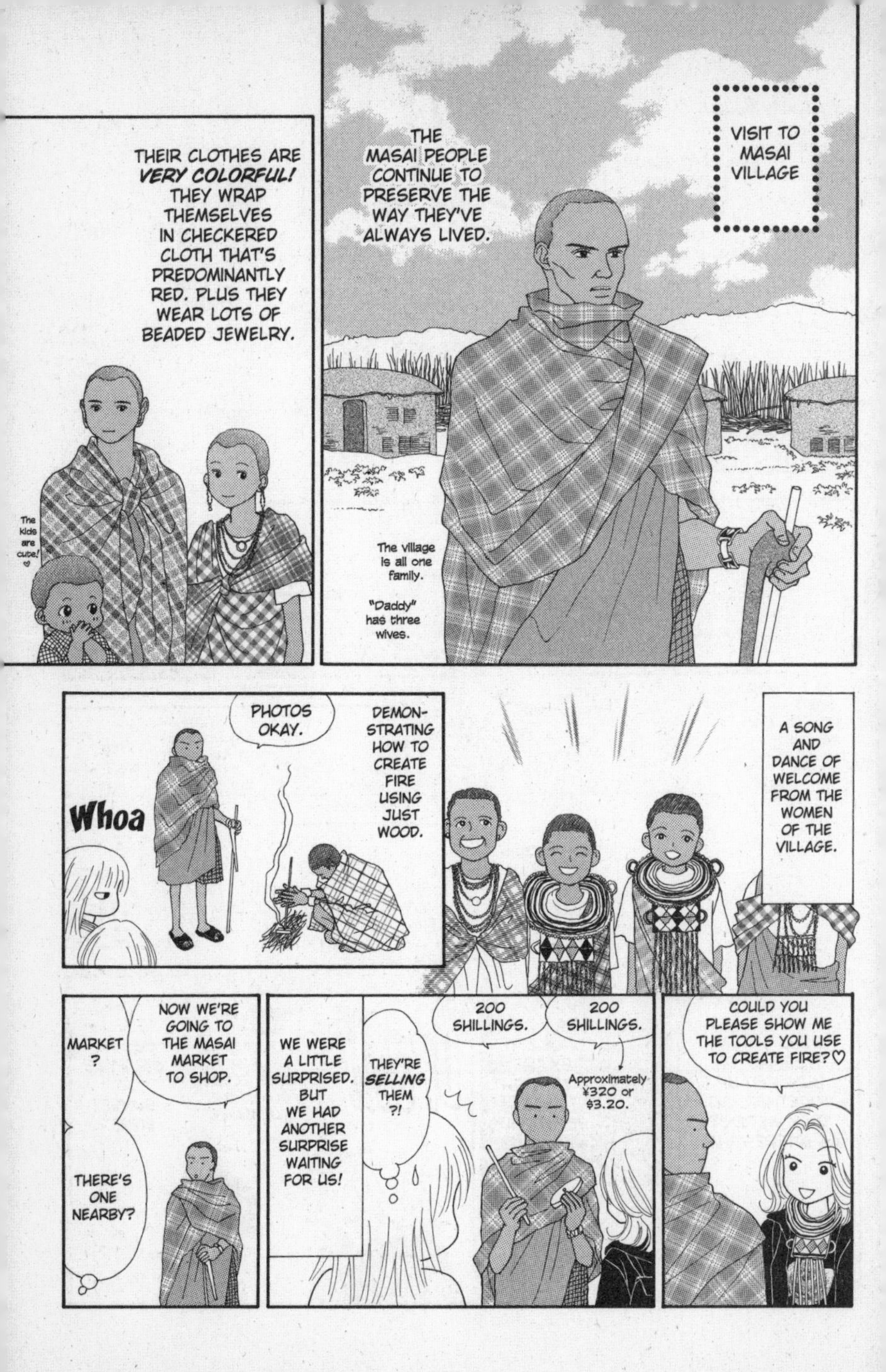
VISIT TO MASAI VILLAGE
THE MASAI PEOPLE CONTINUE TO PRESERVE THE WAY THEY'VE ALWAYS LIVED.
The village is all one family.
"Daddy" has three wives.
THEIR CLOTHES ARE *VERY COLORFUL!* THEY WRAP THEMSELVES IN CHECKERED CLOTH THAT'S PREDOMINANTLY RED. PLUS THEY WEAR LOTS OF BEADED JEWELRY.
The kids are cute! ♡
A SONG AND DANCE OF WELCOME FROM THE WOMEN OF THE VILLAGE.
DEMONSTRATING HOW TO CREATE FIRE USING JUST WOOD.
PHOTOS OKAY.
Whoa
COULD YOU PLEASE SHOW ME THE TOOLS YOU USE TO CREATE FIRE?♡
200 SHILLINGS.
200 SHILLINGS.
Approximately ¥320 or $3.20.
THEY'RE *SELLING* THEM?!
WE WERE A LITTLE SURPRISED. BUT WE HAD ANOTHER SURPRISE WAITING FOR US!
NOW WE'RE GOING TO THE MASAI MARKET TO SHOP.
MARKET?
THERE'S ONE NEARBY?

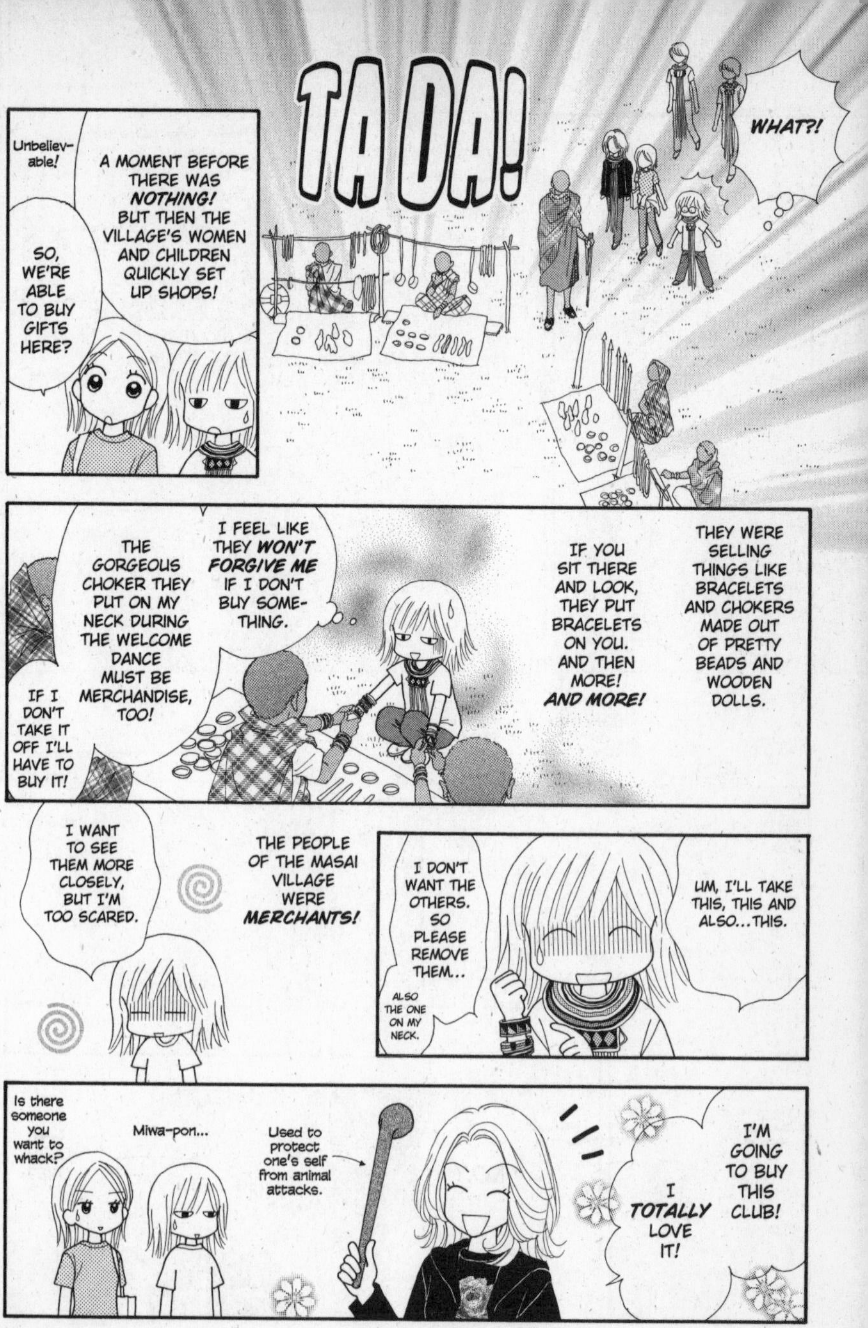
TA DA!
WHAT?!
A MOMENT BEFORE THERE WAS **NOTHING!** BUT THEN THE VILLAGE'S WOMEN AND CHILDREN QUICKLY SET UP SHOPS!
Unbelievable!
SO, WE'RE ABLE TO BUY GIFTS HERE?
THEY WERE SELLING THINGS LIKE BRACELETS AND CHOKERS MADE OUT OF PRETTY BEADS AND WOODEN DOLLS.
IF YOU SIT THERE AND LOOK, THEY PUT BRACELETS ON YOU. AND THEN MORE! **AND MORE!**
I FEEL LIKE THEY **WON'T FORGIVE ME** IF I DON'T BUY SOMETHING.
THE GORGEOUS CHOKER THEY PUT ON MY NECK DURING THE WELCOME DANCE MUST BE MERCHANDISE, TOO!
IF I DON'T TAKE IT OFF I'LL HAVE TO BUY IT!
UM, I'LL TAKE THIS, THIS AND ALSO...THIS.
I DON'T WANT THE OTHERS. SO PLEASE REMOVE THEM...
ALSO THE ONE ON MY NECK.
THE PEOPLE OF THE MASAI VILLAGE WERE **MERCHANTS!**
I WANT TO SEE THEM MORE CLOSELY, BUT I'M TOO SCARED.
I'M GOING TO BUY THIS CLUB!
I **TOTALLY** LOVE IT!
Used to protect one's self from animal attacks.
Miwa-pon...
Is there someone you want to whack?

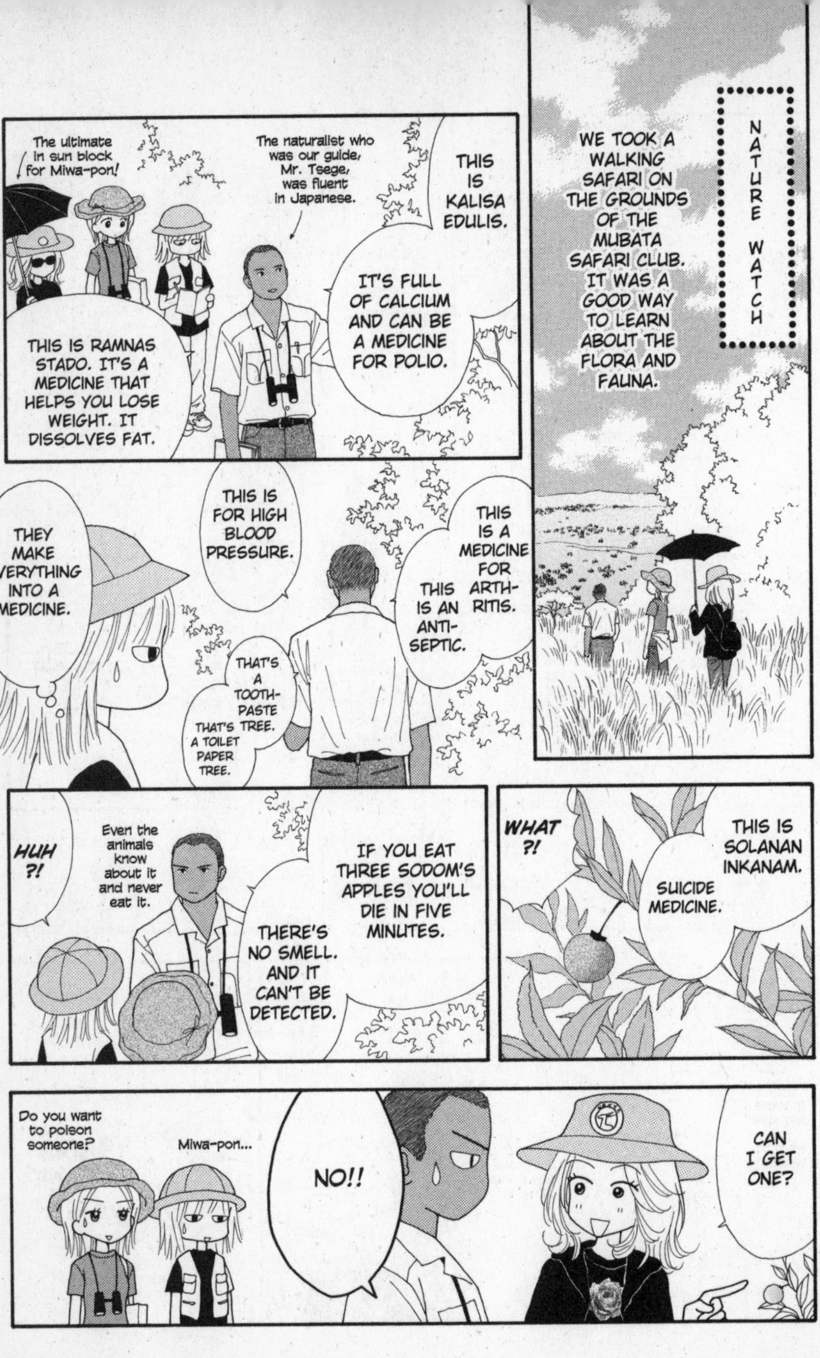
NATURE WATCH
WE TOOK A WALKING SAFARI ON THE GROUNDS OF THE MUBATA SAFARI CLUB. IT WAS A GOOD WAY TO LEARN ABOUT THE FLORA AND FAUNA.
THIS IS KALISA EDULIS.
IT'S FULL OF CALCIUM AND CAN BE A MEDICINE FOR POLIO.
The naturalist who was our guide, Mr. Tsege, was fluent in Japanese.
The ultimate in sun block for Miwa-pon!
THIS IS RAMNAS STADO. IT'S A MEDICINE THAT HELPS YOU LOSE WEIGHT. IT DISSOLVES FAT.
THIS IS A MEDICINE FOR ARTHRITIS.
THIS IS AN ANTISEPTIC.
THIS IS FOR HIGH BLOOD PRESSURE.
THAT'S A TOOTHPASTE TREE.
THAT'S A TOILET PAPER TREE.
THEY MAKE EVERYTHING INTO A MEDICINE.
THIS IS SOLANAN INKANAM.
SUICIDE MEDICINE.
WHAT?!
IF YOU EAT THREE SODOM'S APPLES YOU'LL DIE IN FIVE MINUTES.
THERE'S NO SMELL. AND IT CAN'T BE DETECTED.
Even the animals know about it and never eat it.
HUH?!
CAN I GET ONE?
NO!!
Miwa-pon...
Do you want to poison someone?

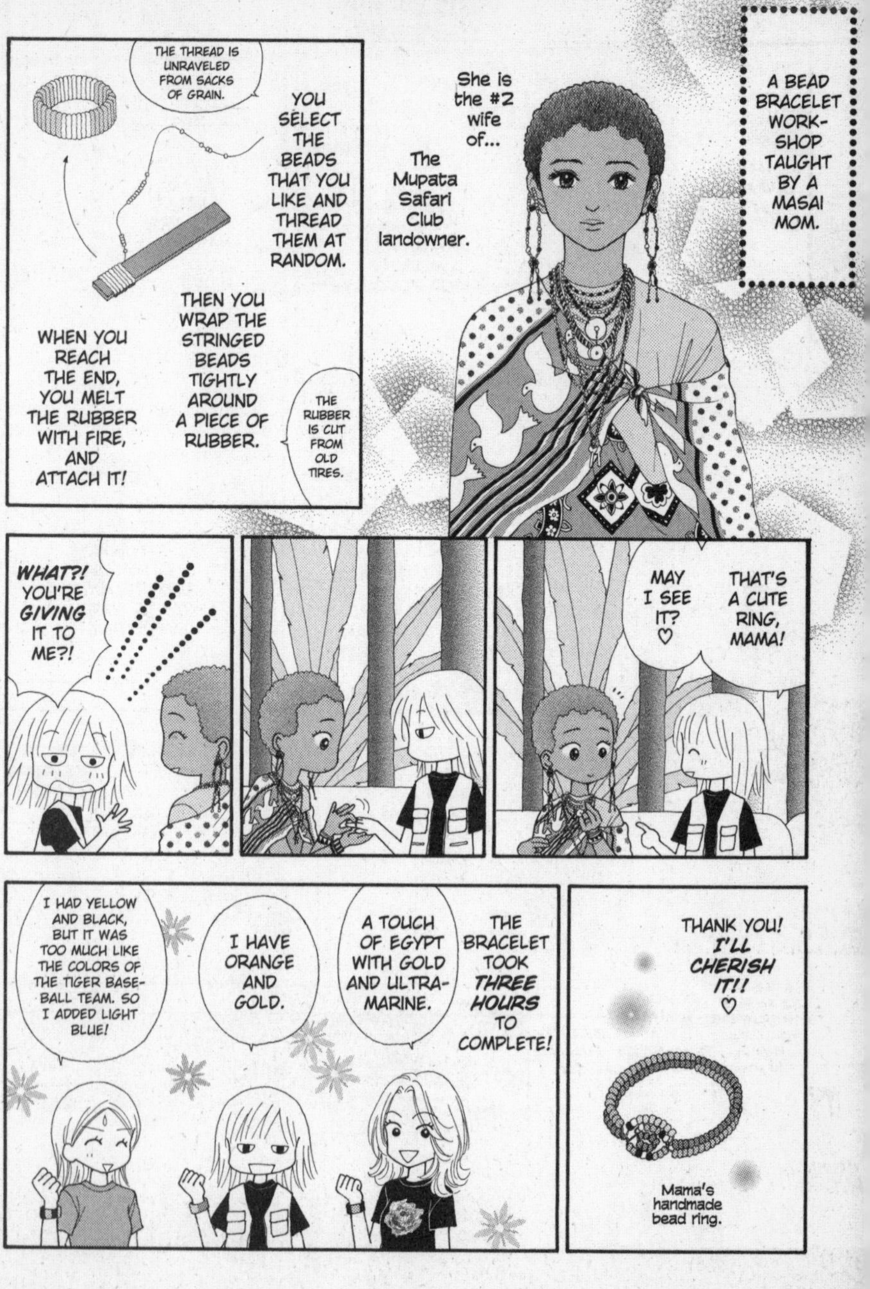
A BEAD BRACELET WORKSHOP TAUGHT BY A MASAI MOM.
She is the #2 wife of...
The Mupata Safari Club landowner.
THE THREAD IS UNRAVELED FROM SACKS OF GRAIN.
YOU SELECT THE BEADS THAT YOU LIKE AND THREAD THEM AT RANDOM.
THE RUBBER IS CUT FROM OLD TIRES.
THEN YOU WRAP THE STRINGED BEADS TIGHTLY AROUND A PIECE OF RUBBER.
WHEN YOU REACH THE END, YOU MELT THE RUBBER WITH FIRE, AND ATTACH IT!
THAT'S A CUTE RING, MAMA!
MAY I SEE IT? ♡
WHAT?! YOU'RE *GIVING* IT TO ME?!
THANK YOU! *I'LL CHERISH IT!!* ♡
Mama's handmade bead ring.
THE BRACELET TOOK *THREE HOURS* TO COMPLETE!
A TOUCH OF EGYPT WITH GOLD AND ULTRA-MARINE.
I HAVE ORANGE AND GOLD.
I HAD YELLOW AND BLACK, BUT IT WAS TOO MUCH LIKE THE COLORS OF THE TIGER BASE-BALL TEAM. SO I ADDED LIGHT BLUE!

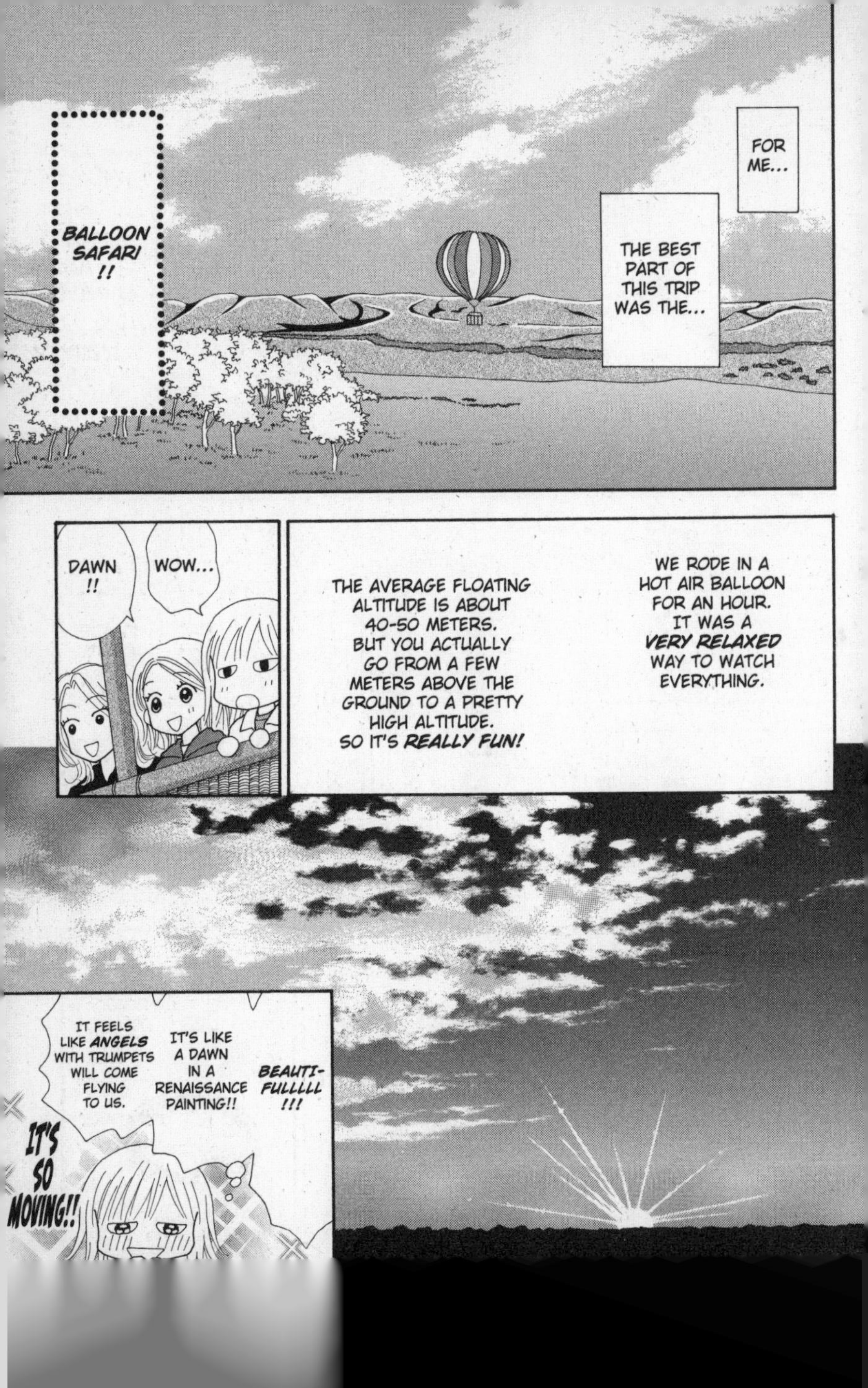
FOR ME...
THE BEST PART OF THIS TRIP WAS THE...
BALLOON SAFARI !!
WE RODE IN A HOT AIR BALLOON FOR AN HOUR. IT WAS A VERY RELAXED WAY TO WATCH EVERYTHING.
THE AVERAGE FLOATING ALTITUDE IS ABOUT 40-50 METERS. BUT YOU ACTUALLY GO FROM A FEW METERS ABOVE THE GROUND TO A PRETTY HIGH ALTITUDE. SO IT'S REALLY FUN!
WOW...
DAWN !!
BEAUTI-FULLLLL !!!
IT'S LIKE A DAWN IN A RENAISSANCE PAINTING!!
IT FEELS LIKE ANGELS WITH TRUMPETS WILL COME FLYING TO US.
IT'S SO MOVING!!

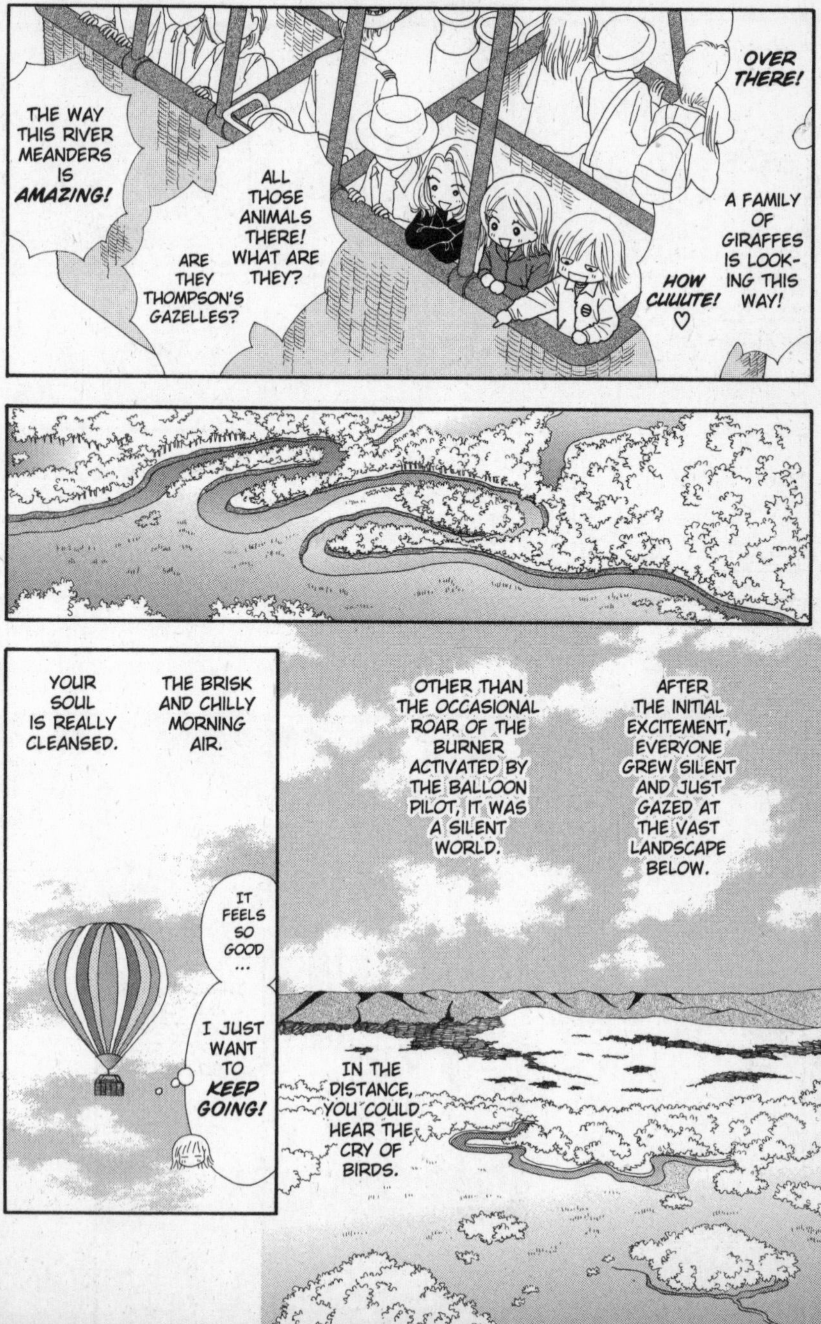
OVER THERE!
A FAMILY OF GIRAFFES IS LOOKING THIS WAY!
HOW CUUUTE! ♡
ALL THOSE ANIMALS THERE! WHAT ARE THEY?
ARE THEY THOMPSON'S GAZELLES?
THE WAY THIS RIVER MEANDERS IS AMAZING!
AFTER THE INITIAL EXCITEMENT, EVERYONE GREW SILENT AND JUST GAZED AT THE VAST LANDSCAPE BELOW.
OTHER THAN THE OCCASIONAL ROAR OF THE BURNER ACTIVATED BY THE BALLOON PILOT, IT WAS A SILENT WORLD.
THE BRISK AND CHILLY MORNING AIR.
YOUR SOUL IS REALLY CLEANSED.
IN THE DISTANCE, YOU COULD HEAR THE CRY OF BIRDS.
IT FEELS SO GOOD ...
I JUST WANT TO KEEP GOING!

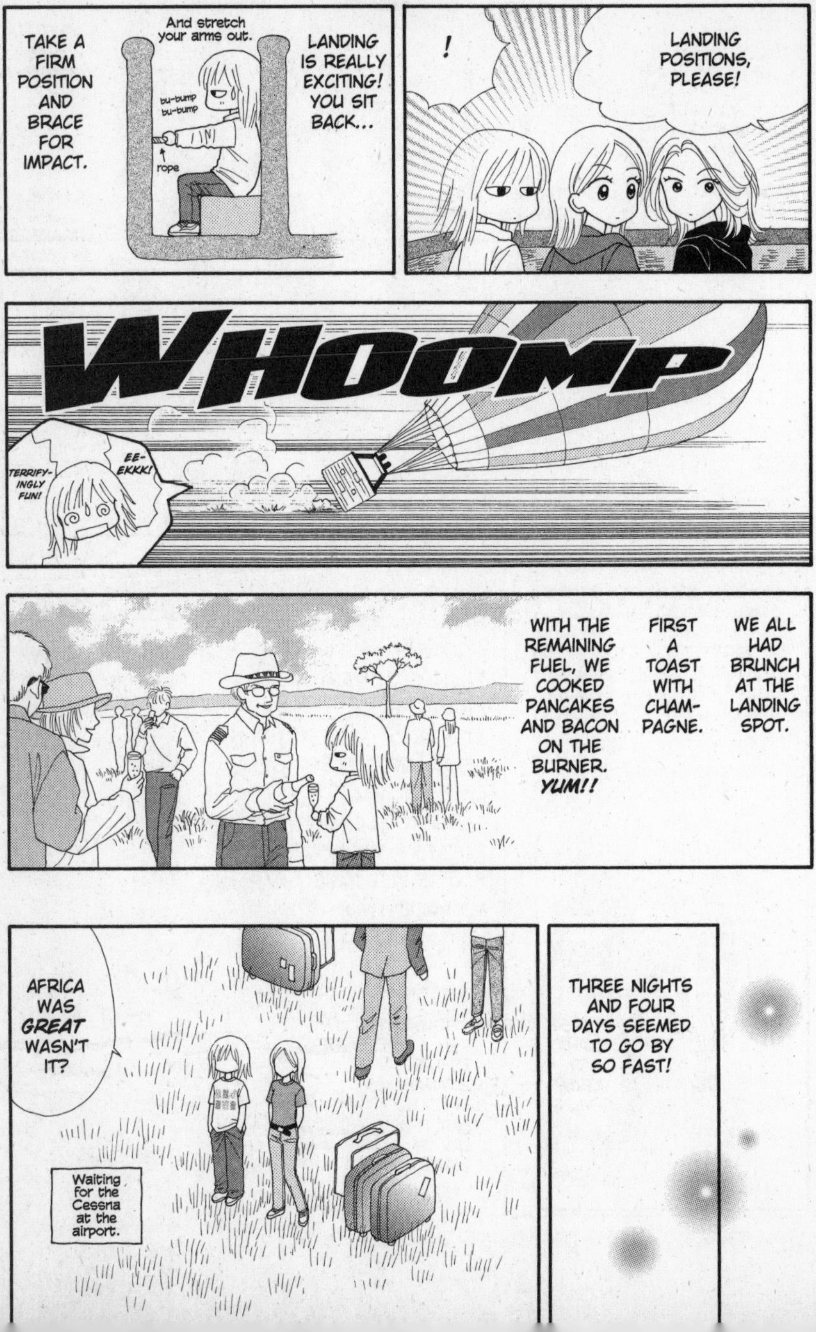
!
LANDING POSITIONS, PLEASE!
LANDING IS REALLY EXCITING! YOU SIT BACK...
And stretch your arms out.
bu-bump bu-bump
rope
TAKE A FIRM POSITION AND BRACE FOR IMPACT.
WHOOMP
EE-EKKK!
TERRIFY-INGLY FUN!
WE ALL HAD BRUNCH AT THE LANDING SPOT.
FIRST A TOAST WITH CHAM-PAGNE.
WITH THE REMAINING FUEL, WE COOKED PANCAKES AND BACON ON THE BURNER. YUM!!
THREE NIGHTS AND FOUR DAYS SEEMED TO GO BY SO FAST!
AFRICA WAS GREAT WASN'T IT?
Waiting for the Cessna at the airport.

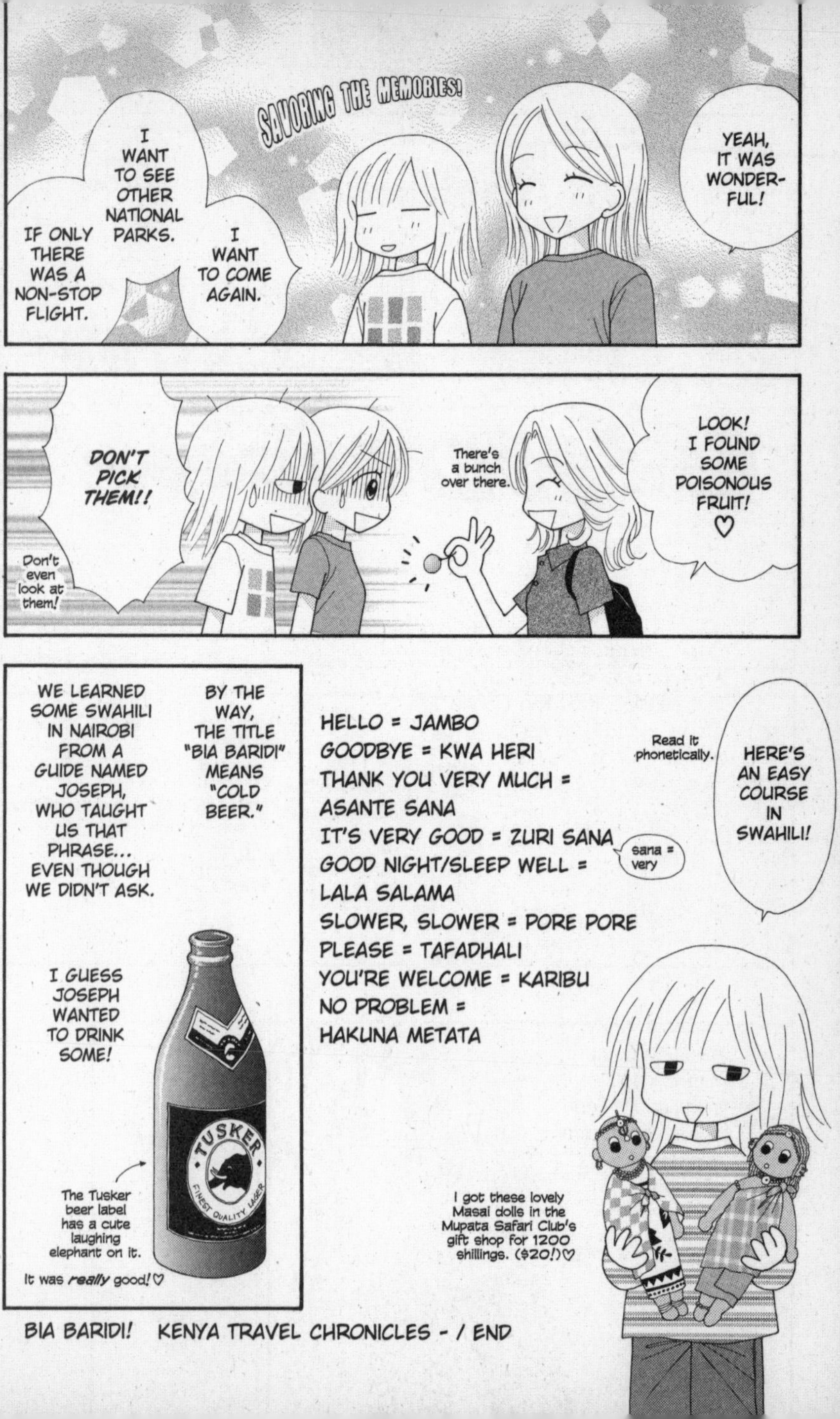
SAVORING THE MEMORIES!
YEAH, IT WAS WONDERFUL!
I WANT TO COME AGAIN.
I WANT TO SEE OTHER NATIONAL PARKS.
IF ONLY THERE WAS A NON-STOP FLIGHT.
LOOK! I FOUND SOME POISONOUS FRUIT! ♡
There's a bunch over there.
DON'T PICK THEM!!
Don't even look at them!
HERE'S AN EASY COURSE IN SWAHILI!
Read it phonetically.
HELLO = JAMBO
GOODBYE = KWA HERI
THANK YOU VERY MUCH = ASANTE SANA
IT'S VERY GOOD = ZURI SANA
sana = very
GOOD NIGHT/SLEEP WELL = LALA SALAMA
SLOWER, SLOWER = PORE PORE
PLEASE = TAFADHALI
YOU'RE WELCOME = KARIBU
NO PROBLEM = HAKUNA METATA
I got these lovely Masai dolls in the Mupata Safari Club's gift shop for 1200 shillings. ($20!)♡
BY THE WAY, THE TITLE "BIA BARIDI" MEANS "COLD BEER."
WE LEARNED SOME SWAHILI IN NAIROBI FROM A GUIDE NAMED JOSEPH, WHO TAUGHT US THAT PHRASE... EVEN THOUGH WE DIDN'T ASK.
I GUESS JOSEPH WANTED TO DRINK SOME!
TUSKER
FINEST QUALITY LAGER
The Tusker beer label has a cute laughing elephant on it.
It was really good!♡
BIA BARIDI! KENYA TRAVEL CHRONICLES - / END

Wataru Yoshizumi

Comments

Yoshizumi Wataru writes: "Since the Kenya trip, I've been busy with *Ultra Maniac*. It's been over two years since I've traveled overseas. I want to see the aurora borealis, the Machu Picchu ruins and the Nazca lines; a vacation on Bora Bora Island would be nice. It would be nice if I could make it a reality."

Bio

Wataru Yoshizumi hails from Tokyo and made her manga debut in 1984 with *Radical Romance* in *Ribon Original* magazine. The artist has since produced a string of fan-favorite titles, including *Quartet Game, Handsome na Kanojo* (Handsome Girl), *Marmalade Boy*, and *Random Walk. Ultra Maniac,* a magical screwball comedy, is only the second time her work has been available in the U.S. Many of her titles, however, are available throughout Asia and Europe. Yoshizumi loves to travel and is keen on making original accessories out of beads.

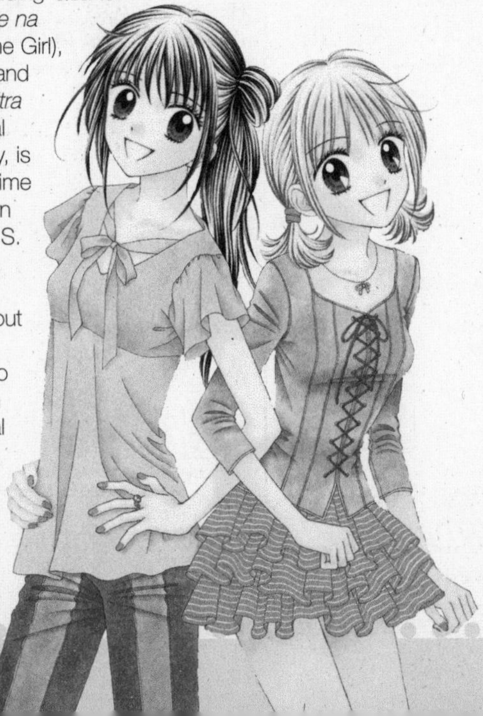

Shojo Beat

ULTRA MANIAC VOL. 4

Shojo Beat Edition

STORY AND ART BY
WATARU YOSHIZUMI

English Adaptation/John Lustig
Translation/Koji Goto
Touch-up Art & Lettering/Elizabeth Watasin
Cover & Graphic Design/Izumi Evers
Editor/Eric Searleman

Printed in Canada

Published by VIZ Media, LLC
P.O. Box 77010
San Francisco, CA 94107

10 9 8 7 6 5
First printing, December 2005
Fifth printing, September 2011

VIZ media
www.viz.com
www.shojobeat.com

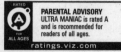

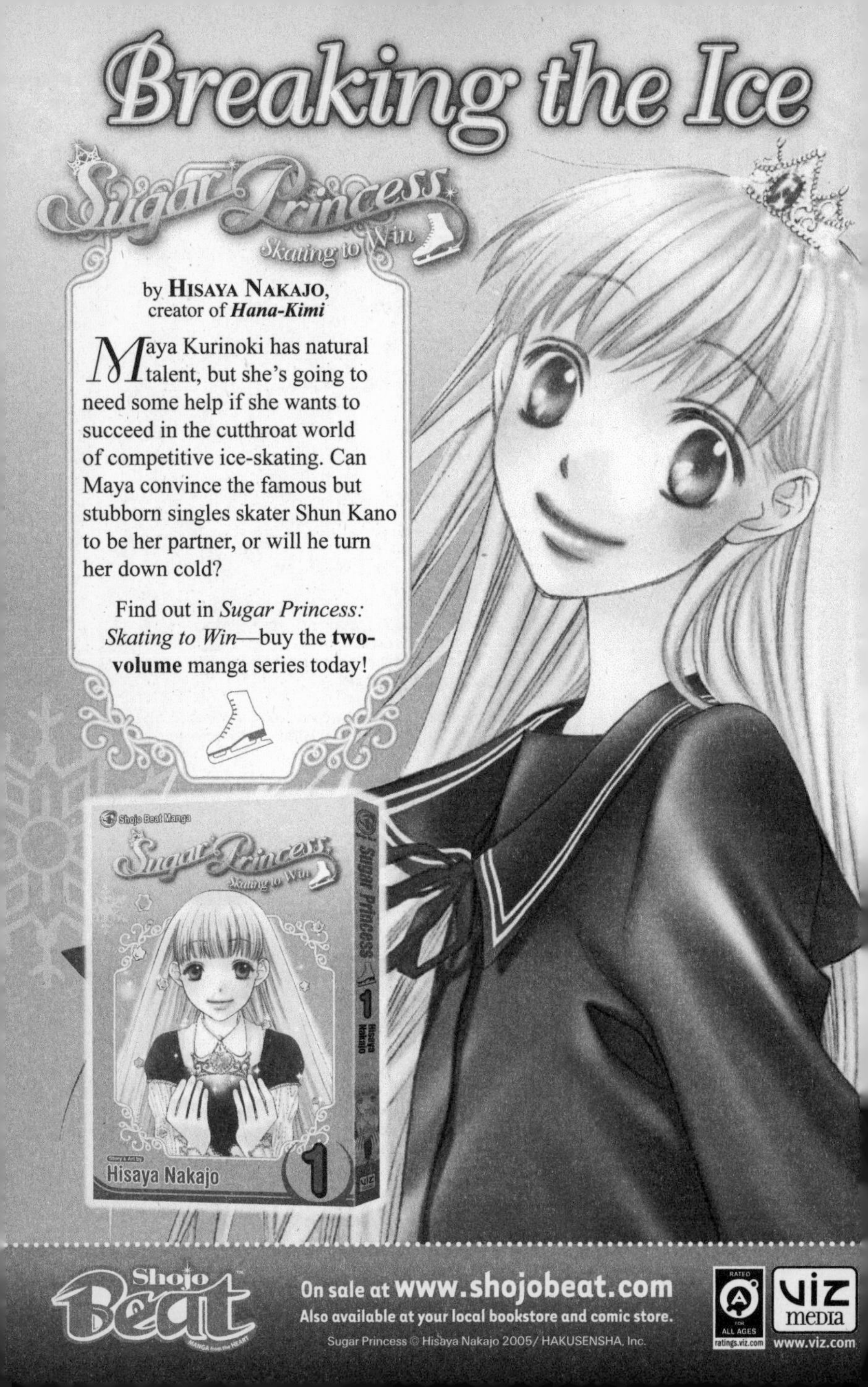
Breaking the Ice
Sugar Princess
Skating to Win
by HISAYA NAKAJO, creator of Hana-Kimi
Maya Kurinoki has natural talent, but she's going to need some help if she wants to succeed in the cutthroat world of competitive ice-skating. Can Maya convince the famous but stubborn singles skater Shun Kano to be her partner, or will he turn her down cold?
Find out in Sugar Princess: Skating to Win—buy the two-volume manga series today!
Shojo Beat Manga
Sugar Princess
Skating to Win
Story & Art by
Hisaya Nakajo
1
Sugar Princess
1
Hisaya Nakajo
Shojo Beat
MANGA from the HEART
On sale at www.shojobeat.com
Also available at your local bookstore and comic store.
Sugar Princess © Hisaya Nakajo 2005/ HAKUSENSHA, Inc.
RATED
A
FOR ALL AGES
ratings.viz.com
VIZ media
www.viz.com

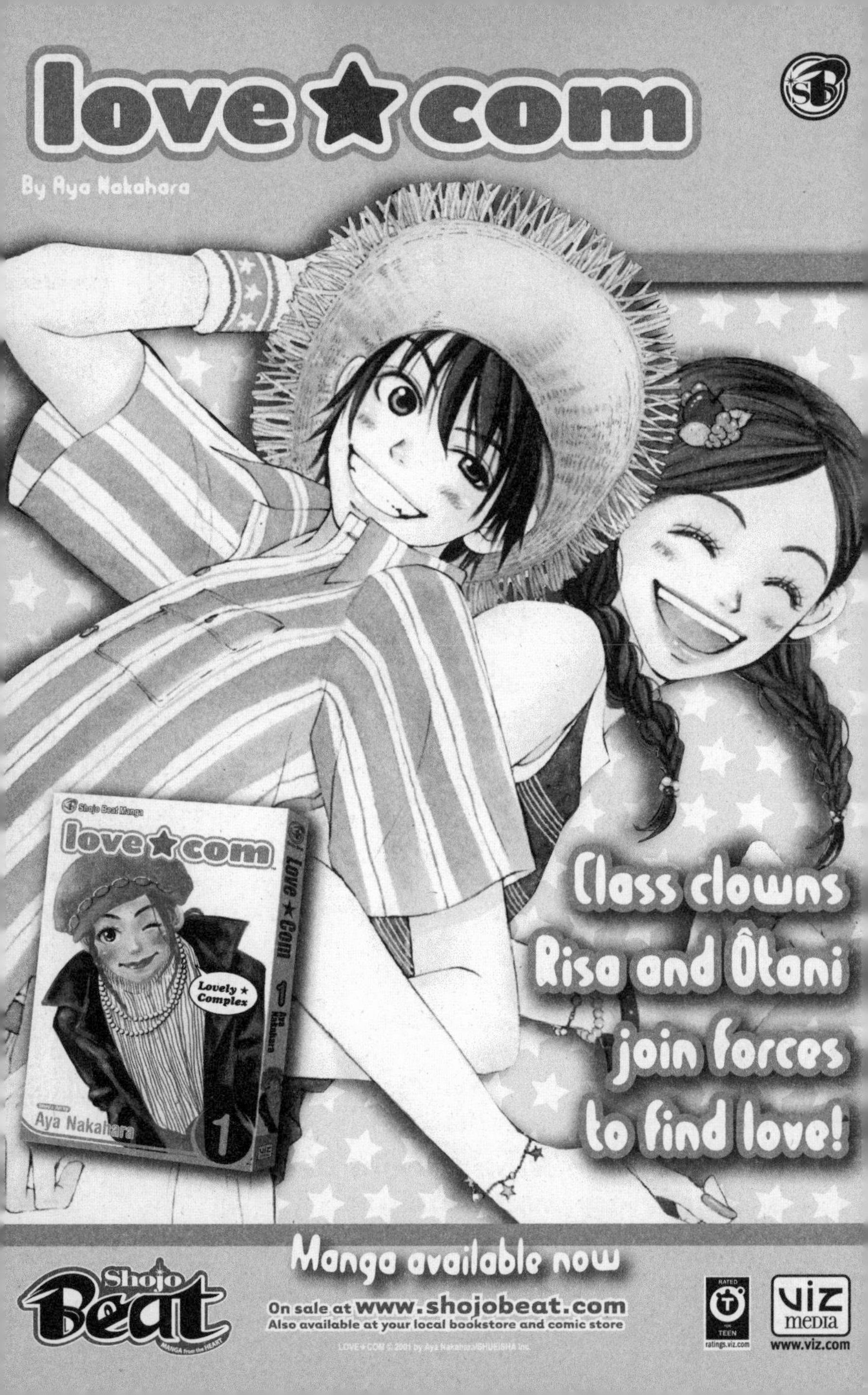
love★com
By Aya Nakahara
Shojo Beat Manga
love★com
Love★Com
1
Lovely ★ Complex
Aya Nakahara
1
Class clowns Risa and Ôtani join forces to find love!
Manga available now
Shojo Beat
MANGA from the HEART
On sale at www.shojobeat.com
Also available at your local bookstore and comic store
LOVE★COM © 2001 by Aya Nakahara/SHUEISHA Inc.
RATED T TEEN
ratings.viz.com
VIZ media
www.viz.com

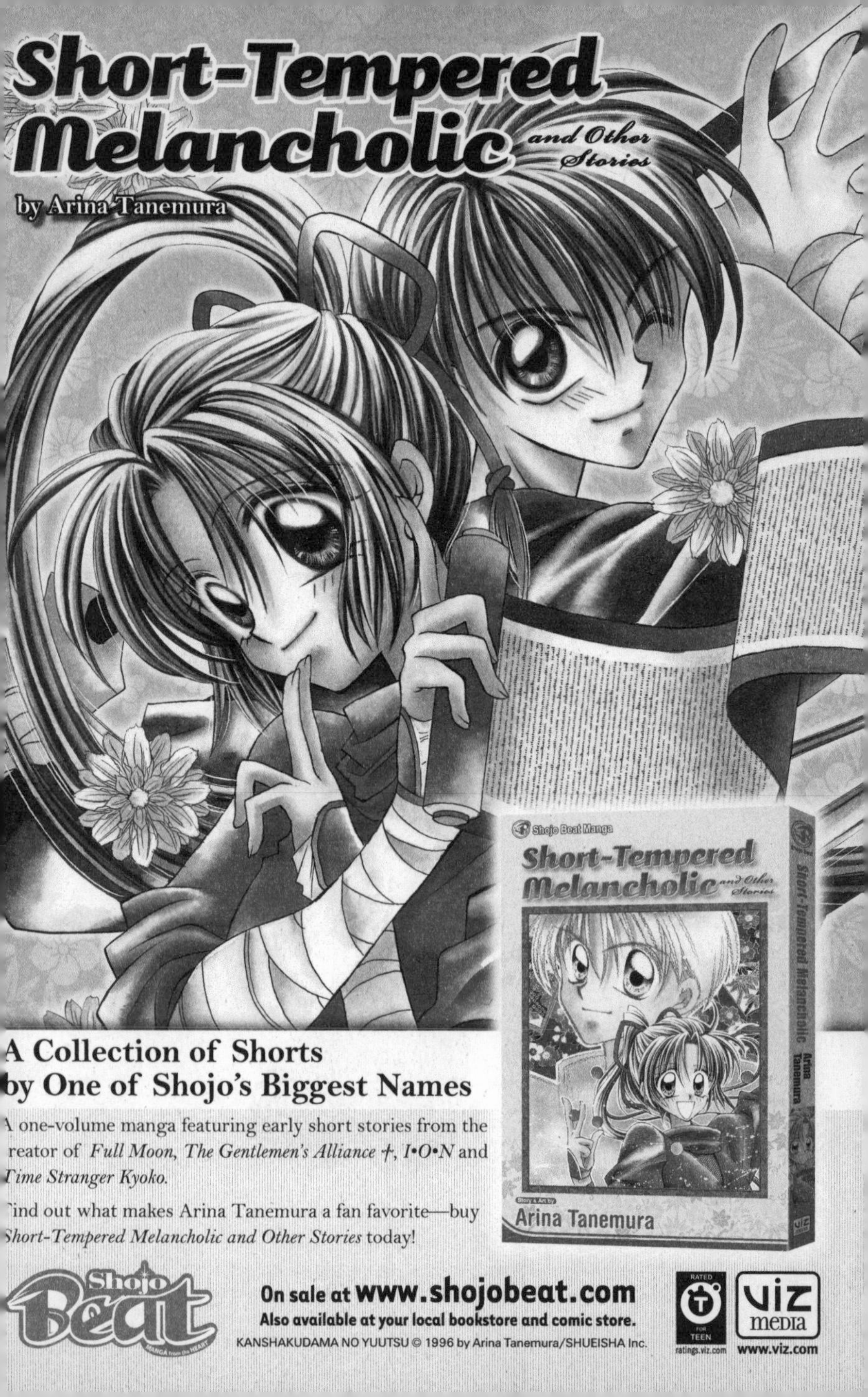
Short-Tempered Melancholic and Other Stories
by Arina Tanemura
Shojo Beat Manga
Short-Tempered Melancholic and Other Stories
Story & Art by
Arina Tanemura
A Collection of Shorts
by One of Shojo's Biggest Names
A one-volume manga featuring early short stories from the
reator of Full Moon, The Gentlemen's Alliance †, I•O•N and
Time Stranger Kyoko.
Find out what makes Arina Tanemura a fan favorite—buy
Short-Tempered Melancholic and Other Stories today!
Shojo Beat
MANGA from the HEART
On sale at www.shojobeat.com
Also available at your local bookstore and comic store.
KANSHAKUDAMA NO YUUTSU © 1996 by Arina Tanemura/SHUEISHA Inc.
RATED T FOR TEEN
ratings.viz.com
VIZ media
www.viz.com

Yume Kira Dream Shoppe

By Aqua Mizuto

Welcome to a bright and shiny magical place where people's dreams come true. But be careful what you wish for, dear reader. Sometimes the most passionate desires can bring about the biggest heartbreak!

Four short stories of fantasy and imagination recommended for everyone who's ever wished for a dream to come true.

Only $8.99

Tell us what you think about Shojo Beat Manga!

Our survey is now available online. Go to:

shojobeat.com/mangasurvey

Help us make our product offerings better!